W9-CTW-483

SOMETHING ABOUT THE AUTHOR

AUTOBIOGRAPHY SERIES

ISSN 0885-6842

SOMETHING ABOUT THE AUTHOR

AUTOBIOGRAPHY SERIES

Joyce Nakamura
Gerard J. Senick
Editors

VOLUME 20

Gale Research Inc.

An International Thomson Publishing Company

I(T)P

NEW YORK • LONDON • BONN • BOSTON • DETROIT • MADRID
MELBOURNE • MEXICO CITY • PARIS • SINGAPORE • TOKYO
TORONTO • WASHINGTON • ALBANY NY • BELMONT CA • CINCINNATI OH

STAFF

Joyce Nakamura and Gerard J. Senick, *Editors*
Linda R. Andres, Shelly Andrews, Sharon Gunton, and Motoko Fujishiro Huthwaite, *Associate Editors*
Marilyn O'Connell Allen and Paul Zyskowski, *Assistant Editors*
E. A. Des Chenes, Heidi J. Hagen, Laurie Collier Hillstrom, Carolyn C. March,
and Lori J. Sawicki, *Contributing Copyeditors*

Victoria B. Cariappa, *Research Manager*

Hal May, *Publisher*

Mary Beth Trimper, *Production Director*
Shanna Philpott Heilveil, *Production Assistant*

Cynthia Baldwin, *Art Director*
C. J. Jonik, *Keyliner*
Willie Mathis, *Camera Operator*

Theresa Rocklin, *Manager, Technical Support Services*

Contents

Preface   vii
A Brief Sampler   ix
Acknowledgments   xiii

Preface

A Unique Collection of Essays

Each volume in the *Something about the Author Autobiography Series* (*SAAS*) presents an original collection of autobiographical essays written especially for the series by prominent authors and illustrators of books for children and young adults.

The *SAAS* series is designed to be a place where young readers, students of children's and YA literature, teachers, librarians, and parents can meet their favorite authors and illustrators "in person" and make the first acquaintance of many others. In *SAAS*, readers can find the answers to an endless list of questions about these creative individuals: What people and events influenced their early lives? How did they begin their careers? What prompted them to write or illustrate particular books? What advice would they give to aspiring writers and illustrators? And so much more.

SAAS provides an opportunity for writers and artists who may never write a full-length autobiography to let their readers know how they see themselves and their work, what brought them to this time and place, and what they envision for the future. Individually, the essays in this series can enhance the reader's understanding of a writer's or artist's work; collectively, they are lessons in the creative process and in the discovery of its roots.

Even for those who have already published full-length autobiographies, *SAAS* allows these figures to bring their readers "up to date" or perhaps take a different approach in the essay format. In some instances, previously published material may be reprinted or expanded upon; this fact is always noted at the end of such an essay.

SAAS makes no attempt to give a comprehensive overview of authors or illustrators and their works. That outlook is already well represented in biographies, reviews, and critiques published in a wide variety of sources. Instead, *SAAS* complements that perspective and presents what no other ongoing reference source does: the view of writers and illustrators that is shaped by their own choice of materials and their own manner of storytelling.

Who Is Covered?

Like its parent series *Something about the Author*, the *Something about the Author Autobiography Series* sets out to meet the needs and interests of a wide range of readers from upper elementary school through junior and senior high school. Each volume includes essays by international writers and artists whose work has special appeal for young readers. We consider it extraordinary that so many busy authors and illustrators from throughout the world are able to interrupt their existing writing, drawing, teaching, speaking, traveling, and other schedules to converge on a given deadline for any one volume. So it is not always possible that all genres can be equally and uniformly represented from volume to volume, although we strive to include individuals working in a variety of categories, including fiction, nonfiction, picture books, and poetry. These categories, however, do not begin to suggest the diversity of the works of the authors and illustrators represented in the series. Many of the contributors to this volume have also written fiction and nonfiction for adults as well as worked in movies, television, radio as well as for newspapers and journals.

What Each Essay Includes

Authors who contribute to *SAAS* are invited to write a "mini-autobiography" of approximately 10,000 words. In order to give the writer's imagination free rein, we suggest no guidelines or pattern for the essay. We ask only that each writer tell his or her story in the manner and to the extent that feels most natural and appropriate. In addition, writers are asked to supply a selection of personal photographs showing themselves at various ages, as well as important people and special moments in their lives. Our contributors have responded generously, sharing with us some of their most treasured mementos. Illustrators also provide a small representative selection of their published work. The result is a special blend of text, photographs, and illustrations that provides a wealth of distinctive information in a format that will attract even the casual browser.

Other Features

- A **Bibliography** at the end of each essay lists book-length works in chronological order of publication. Each bibliography in this volume was compiled by members of the *SAAS* editorial staff and submitted to the author or illustrator for review.

- A **Cumulative Index** in each volume cites all the essayists in the series as well as the subjects presented in the essays: personal names, titles of works, geographical names, schools of writing, etc. To ensure ease of use for these cumulating references, the name of the essayist is given before the volume and page number(s) for every reference that appears *in more than one essay*. In the following example, the entry in the index allows the user to identify the essay writers by name:

> Andersen, Hans Christian
> Aiken **1**:24
> Beatty **4**:41
> Cavanna **4**:113
> etc.

For references that appear *in only one essay,* the volume and page number(s) are given but the name of the essayist is omitted. For example:

> Butterflies **4**:330

SAAS is something more than the sum of its individual essays. At many points the essays touch common ground, and from these intersections emerge new patterns of information and impressions. The index is an important guide to these interconnections.

For Additional Information

For detailed information on awards, adaptations of works, critical reviews, and more, readers are encouraged to consult Gale's *Contemporary Authors* cumulative index for listings in other Gale sources. These include, among others, *Something about the Author, Contemporary Authors, Contemporary Authors New Revision Series, Dictionary of Literary Biography,* and *Children's Literature Review.*

Special Thanks

We wish to acknowledge our special gratitude to each of the authors and illustrators in this volume. They all have been most kind and cooperative in contributing not only their talents but their enthusiasm and encouragement to this project.

A Brief Sampler

Each essay in the series has a special character and point of view that sets it apart from its companions. A small sampler of anecdotes and musings from the essays in this volume hints at the unique perspective of these life stories.

Stan and Jan Berenstain, describing their original "Berenstain Bears": " . . . those early Bears *were* wild and wacky. They were long, rangy, and very unbearlike. They were all elbows and knees. They had long upturned sausage-like muzzles with noses that looked like hockey pucks perched on the end of them. They wore pretty much the same clothes, though. Papa Bear wore bib overalls and a plaid shirt, though in the first book it was red plaid—we didn't go to a yellow plaid until the second book. Mama Bear wore a blue dress with white polka dots and a duster for a hat. Mama also had a yellow dress-up hat, and Small Bear had blue pants and a red shirt. We get a lot of mail from children, and the Bears' limited wardrobe is a source of some concern. Kids often suggest titles for new Bear books, and one of the most frequently suggested titles is *The Berenstain Bears Get New Clothes*."

Elisabeth Beresford, telling about an unusual book reading: "Twice I was asked to South Africa to talk to children. Once the organisers have got you on their schedules they really work you hard and quite often I had no idea where I was or, indeed, where I'd been. But one location did stick firmly in my mind. It was a Zulu Township and a thousand *adult* Zulus turned up at the hall. The place was crammed with just me and a librarian called Michael on the platform. It seemed like madness to be talking about the Wombles of Wimbledon to these tall, dignified people. But everybody likes to be told a story so I launched into recounting some of the scripts with the Wombles transformed into humans. There wasn't a sound. At the end of thirty minutes I was exhausted so I bowed, said thank-you and stepped back. We then discovered something which was quite new to us. If Zulus like you they give you a high-pitched call from the back of the throat and advance slowly, right arm up as if they are throwing a spear. One thousand of them. 'What do we do now?' I said desperately. 'Retreat,' said Michael, grabbing my skirt, 'step by step. . . .' We did too."

Ann Cameron, on an influential experience: "My second-grade teacher, Miss Nerlene, was my worst teacher. Miss Nerlene was very strict—but perhaps more flustered and inadequate than strict. One day I looked across the room and saw her shaking a small boy, Charles Gavin, by the shoulders. Then she slapped him hard across the face. I knew Charles Gavin was a poor boy, though I'm not sure how I knew. Perhaps by his pallor and skinniness. Perhaps because he said 'ain't.' That was a word poor people said. I thought he must be a very dangerous boy if Miss Nerlene had slapped him like that. He must deserve it. He walked the same long lonely way home that I did, and I became afraid of him. Soon one day after school I spotted him, trailing down the street behind me. I got scared. I picked up a stone and threw it at him. I was never a very good thrower, but this time I was more successful than I ever expected. The stone hit him hard, right in the middle of his forehead. I ran. The next day at school I could see the cut on his forehead. I wanted to say I was sorry, but I was terribly afraid to go near him, afraid he'd hit me. I didn't tell anyone what I had done. I waited for Charles Gavin to get even, to follow me home from school and beat me up. But he didn't. The cut on his forehead turned to a thin white scar. By the end of the school year I could tell that it would be with him for life . . . Forty-five years have passed since I threw the stone at Charles Gavin. I still can see his face. I would like to write books that could comfort the Charles Gavins of this world."

Beverly Cleary, remembering . . . "Thanksgiving. Relatives are coming to dinner. The oak pedestal table is stretched to its limit and covered with a silence cloth and white damask. The sight of that smooth, faintly patterned cloth fills me with longing. I find a bottle of blue ink, pour it out at one end of the table, and dip my hands into it. Pat-a-pat, pat-a-pat, all around the table I go, inking handprints on that smooth white cloth. I do not recall what happened when aunts, uncles, and cousins arrived. All I recall is my satisfaction in marking with ink on that white surface."

Helen Cresswell, writing of the time after her sciatica at the age of twelve, "For the latter part of my childhood I am two people. I am the popular class clown, one of the top clique. But my real, secret self is the one who sits up into the early hours to finish poems. When I am with other people I am wearing a mask, I am the spy in the camp. I do not really accept the daily round and am constantly aware of a mystery beyond the banalities of everyday life. I can mark the moment when this begins. I am around nine or ten and walking, on a very hot day, down Davis Road. It is straight and long, possibly half a mile or more, and lined with neat houses with small front gardens and dusty hedges. The tar on the road is melting, I can smell it. Suddenly I stop, overcome by a powerful sense of displacement. The world about me is suddenly foreign. I think 'This is not real,' I think it, and I know it. Then 'I don't belong here—what am I doing here?' I think it, and I know it, and am transfixed by the knowledge. It is at once terrifying and comforting. At that moment the boundaries of reality are irrevocably shifted. I have a new secret treasure and it is hidden, not under a mattress or in a hole in the wall, but within my own self. . . ."

Arthur Dorros, relating an incident that inspired his later interest in the tropics: "We stopped at an alligator farm and there in pens were dozens of alligators. Sleeping gators I thought, as my sister Ellen and I climbed over the low pen fence. Times were different then—it seemed like climbing in with the alligators was okay. Until we were among them, ten- to twelve-foot-long creatures with mouths big enough to swallow the odd dog, cat, or four-year-old that wandered by, I thought. Sleeping gators now appeared ferocious or hungry gators to me. Fortunately, they were not hungry, and both my sister and I walked among the gators and were able to tell about it later. I sat on the tail of one of the sleepy giants while my father took a picture. I tried to keep still so the gators wouldn't notice me and reached down discreetly just long enough to touch the tail of my alligator chair."

Charles Ferry, who before becoming a writer for young adults battled an alcohol addiction that led to a crime spree and, later, to prison: "In 1970, I bottomed out. For me, hitting bottom was a matter of totally running out of gas, so to speak. I was completely drained of energy. I didn't have the energy to pour a drink or hold a gun to my head, which is what I felt like doing, I didn't have the energy to think. I was in a black pit of despair. But once you hit bottom, I learned, once you decide that you're tired of the pain and anguish, tired of kicking yourself in the head, tired of the vomit and urine of drunk tanks, tired of seventeen different jails, three of them twice and one of them the largest walled jail in the world; once you decide you're tired of all that—there's no way to go but up. Somehow, I found the strength to start clawing my way out of the pit. I wasn't at all hopeful; I had tried to lick alcohol so many times before and had always failed. But inch by inch, with the help of my loving wife, the principles of AA, and William Shakespeare I made it. I am now in my twenty-third year of recovery. You're probably wondering how William Shakespeare figures into this story? Very importantly. From him, I learned a rule of life that I recommend to everyone, especially alcoholics: *Hamlet,* Act I, Scene 3. Polonius, the father of Ophelia, is speaking: 'This above all, to thine own self be true, / And it must follow, as the night the day, / Thou canst not then be false to any man.' I have revised those words and added an important proviso: 'This above all, be true to the best that is in you / And help other people.' We all need help. Everyone reading this needs help; the only difference is in the intensity of the need."

These brief examples only suggest what lies ahead in this volume. The essays will speak differently to different readers; but they are certain to speak best, and most eloquently, for themselves.

Acknowledgments

Grateful acknowledgment is made to those publishers, photographers, and artists whose works appear with the essays by the authors in this volume.

Photographs

Elisabeth Beresford: p. 25, © *Daily Star*/Robin Jones

Ann Cameron: p. 43, Photo by Das Anudas; p. 48, Lundgren Studios

Kevin Crossley-Holland: pp. 123, 126, 129, 130, Godfrey Cake/ p. 124, from *The Stones Remain: Megalithic Sites of Britain*. Century Hutchinson (Rider), 1989. Photographs copyright © 1989 by Andrew Rafferty./ p. 127, Madame Yevonde/ p. 132, © Nicolette Hallett

Arthur Dorros: p. 141, Sidney Dorros; p. 159, Ellen Crandall

Max Fatchen: p. 183, Marchants Studio; pp. 194, 197, courtesy of Port Victoria Museum; p. 198, courtesy of *The Advertiser;* p. 199, D. Sands/courtesy of *Messenger Press*

Charles Ferry: p. 201, Herral Long/*The (Toledo) Blade;* p. 217, Edward R. Noble

Paul Fleischman: p. 228, Becky Mojica Fleischman

Belinda Hurmence: p. 240, photo by U. S. Army Signal Corps; p. 243, Fabian Bachrach; p. 245, Freudy Photos

Illustrations/Art

Stan and Jan Berenstain: Cover illustration from *Collier's*, March 4, 1950, painted by Stan and Jan Berenstain./ "It's All in the Family," cartoon by Stan and Jan Berenstain. *Good Housekeeping*, August 1980. Reprinted with permission of *Good Housekeeping* magazine./ Illustration from *The Berenstain Bears Learn about Strangers*, written and illustrated by Stan and Jan Berenstain. Random House, 1985. Copyright © 1985 by Berenstains, Inc./ Illustration from *The Berenstain Bears and the Bully*, written and illustrated by Stan and Jan Berenstain. Random House, 1993. Copyright © 1993 by Berenstains, Inc./ Illustration from *The Berenstain Bears' New Neighbors*, written and illustrated by Stan and Jan Berenstain. Random House, 1994. Copyright © 1994 by Berenstains, Inc. All reprinted with permission of Random House, Inc.

Arthur Dorros: Illustration from *Alligator Shoes*, written and illustrated by Arthur Dorros. Copyright © 1982 by Arthur Dorros. Used by permission of Dutton Children's Books, a division of Penguin Books USA Inc. Reprinted in the British Commonwealth by permission of Arthur Dorros./Illustration from *Animal Tracks*, written and illustrated by Arthur Dorros. Scholastic Inc., 1991. Copyright © 1991 by Arthur Dorros. Reprinted with permission of Scholastic Inc./ Illustration from *Rain Forest Secrets*, written and illustrated by Arthur Dorros. Scholastic Inc., 1990. Copyright © 1990 by Arthur Dorros. Reprinted with permission of Scholastic Inc.

something
ABOUT the
AUThOR

AUTOBIOGRAPHY
SERIES

Stan and Jan Berenstain

1923-

Except for a three-year separation occasioned by Stan's military service during World War II, we have been drawing, painting, cartooning, writing, and illustrating together virtually every day of our lives since we met on our first day of art school in 1941. Together we have created dozens of magazine covers, hundreds of magazine features, thousands of cartoons, and well over one hundred books about our eponymous Berenstain Bears, a series that has sold about two hundred million books to date.

By the time Stan Berenstain and Jan Grant met on their first day at the Philadelphia College of Art (then called the Philadelphia Museum School of Art) in September 1941, each had evinced a compelling interest in drawing and painting. Both of us had been drawing on any surface we could find—wrapping paper, paper bags, shirt cardboards—since we were tots.

On one memorable occasion, five-year-old Stan found a particularly irresistible set of surfaces: the pristine walls of a newly papered upstairs room. It was during that period when, contrary to what newly elected President Hoover was promising, continued Depression was just around the corner. Stan was living with his parents in a flat behind and above a run-down clothing store hard by the "el" in the Frankford section of Philadelphia. His father, Harry, was on the road with a store-opening crew for the then-expanding—but shortly to cease being so—Sears, Roebuck chain. His mother, Rose, took care of the house and the store, which were owned by Stan's paternal grandmother, Sadie, a tough old matriarch who ruled the roost.

Stan would occasionally be taken to the upstairs room where his bedridden maternal grandmother lay ill and dying. Though he wasn't clear on what was happening—grown-ups didn't say much more than "go play" to children in those days—there came a time when Stan sensed that there was something different about the upstairs room—that somehow it was now empty. Left to his own devices—the device on this

Stan and Jan Berenstain, 1994

particular occasion being a thick, red marking crayon that he had taken from the store—he climbed the stair and found that the room was not only empty but offered the most inviting surfaces he had ever seen. With his trusty red crayon, he proceeded to execute a vast mural depicting embattled prizefighters. Next door to Grandmother Sadie's store was Vitacollona's shoe repair shop, and displayed in the shop window was an enormous shoe that Mr. Vitacollona had constructed in honor of Primo Carnera, an outsize prizefighter who had been imported from Italy. Also displayed was a collection of action photos celebrating Mr. Carnera's pugilistic prowess. It was these photos, along with the great

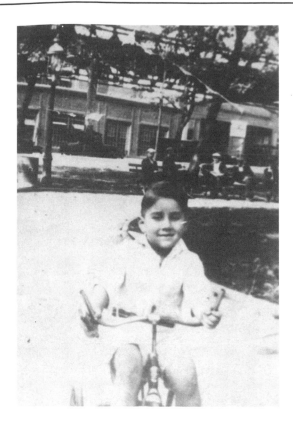

Stan Berenstain on his trike in a Frankford square, 1928

Jan Grant with her brothers, 1929

shoe, that inspired the mural. Family lore has it that the young artist's effort demonstrated a phenomenal talent. But Stan remembers the incident well—the punishment he got as a consequence of his effort was only slightly less severe than that which Carnera later received at the hands of Max Baer—and recalls that his prizefight mural in red marking crayon was an incomprehensible scrawl.

During the period when Stan grew from his tot years to his preteen years, he didn't see much of his father. Stan's dad worked long hours six days a week in the army-and-navy store business in Philadelphia and slept most of Sunday. Stan's mother belonged to a bridge club that played for modest prizes and placed modest bets. She was an excellent card player and gave him her winnings each Saturday to buy books at the secondhand bookstore. He became a precocious reader and a precocious artist as well, because among his selections were some fascinating how-to-paint-and-draw books. He soon mastered the drawing of his favorite comics, too—he can still draw Popeye on demand.

When the Depression hit, his family moved around a lot. For a short period, he lived only blocks away from Janice Grant, his future collaborator in cartooning, writing, and illustration, as well as in marriage and parenting, although he never met her until he entered the Philadelphia College of Art years later.

As far as Stan can remember, no one in his family had shown any artistic talent. Not so in Jan's case. Her father, a carpenter and builder by trade, was a serious amateur artist with considerable drawing and painting talent and some art school training. Jan recalls that even before Al Grant lost his building business in the Depression, his easel, with some work in progress on it, stood by one front bedroom window. His drafting table was positioned by the other. From the time she could perch on the high stool at the drafting table, she drew pictures on Daddy's scrap pastel paper and even strips of linen canvas. Besides her own crayons and paintbox, she had a collection of Al's "used up" drawing pencils and French pastels. When she was five he showed her his prized edition of *Alice in Wonderland* and *Through the Looking Glass.* In addition to the many Tenniel black-and-white illustrations, there were four color plates protected by tissue. They admired the drawings together, and he left the book out of his glass-doored bookcase for her to look at and for daily readings. Somewhere between Alice's playing croquet with the Queen of Hearts and talking to the live flowers, Al's little artist could resist the tempting tissues no longer and traced the White Knight onto one of them with a 2B drawing pencil (very black). She didn't get spanked—Al must have understood the urge—but she knew he didn't appreciate the desecration of a favorite book, because he sat her on the stool by the drafting table while he removed the tissue with his straight razor and painstakingly replaced it before reading on.

Al was always at work at his drawing board or workbench and extremely available to his three children. Jan's brothers followed their mechanical inclinations under his guidance and she her artistic ones. Both parents and a grandfather who lived with them were also very generous guides into the world of books. Besides her favorite illustrated editions of *A Child's Garden of Verses,* *The World Book of Nursery Tales,* and *Alice's Adventures in Wonderland,* she adored the daily and Sunday funnies—especially the ones she considered well drawn. Every day, some neat, new, facile penwork challenged her to reproduce it—and the materials she needed were right on her father's shelves. Later, as a parent, she knew how important it was to have books and supplies related to a child's special interests handy at the times those interests blossomed.

All in all, Jan got lots of encouragement through her school years as her artistic urges continued to assert themselves. And although she took a college-preparatory course load in high school, her graduating year found her applying to her dad's old alma mater, which had become affiliated with the Philadelphia Museum of Art.

At the Philadelphia College of Art, Miss Sweeny's approach to "first day" was to arrange the studio with chairs, low easels, and a selection of "casts" (plaster replicas of classic sculpture): Venus de Milo, Michelangelo's Lorenzo de' Medici, a Della Robbia madonna, etc. Her purpose: to get a line on that year's crop of aspiring artists. At first rest, the stu-

"Head of Alexander," charcoal drawing by Jan Grant, 1942

"Head of Pan," charcoal drawing by Stan Berenstain, 1942

dents extricated themselves from the tangle of chairs and easels, circulated, and surveyed the field. Art schools are notorious cockpits of competitiveness, so Miss Sweeny's first-day scheme afforded the kids an easy opportunity to check out the competition. Stan observed that a tanned,

Corporal Stan Berenstain, medical artist, with one of his pen and ink medical drawings (below), 1943

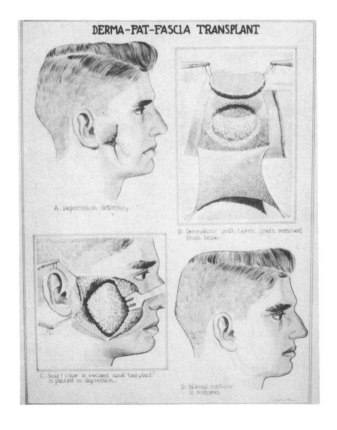

blue-eyed, blonde girl wearing a powder-blue sweater, gray skirt, and white moccasins had chosen to draw "The Flayed Man," a classic figure of a chap whose skin has been removed. Stan was tremendously impressed with Jan's drawing. Jan noted a skinny guy wearing strange glasses with smoke-colored plastic rims that sported a cactus needle in place of a missing wing screw, who had chosen to draw "Head of Zeus." Jan was impressed with Stan's Zeus. It was fully rendered, and every curl was in place. So it is fair and accurate to say that we, who have been drawing together for half a century, were originally drawn together by drawing.

We also shared an early enthusiasm for the work of the same comics artists as well as the same illustrators. With it all, we were both serious art students with the same current interest in the work of the old masters, French Impressionists, American realists, etc. We did, however, develop individual painting styles. We also shared an interest in classical music. Some of our early "dates" were in the peanut gallery at concerts of the Philadelphia Orchestra.

The sequence of events that brought Stan to his post as staff medical artist for the plastic surgery service of Wakeman General Army Hospital at Camp Atterbury, Indiana, in 1944 is rich in that random quality that typifies many, if not most, army stories. Having received his basic training at Fort Bragg, North Carolina, an artillery training center, Stan was posted to the artillery battalion of the Atterbury-based 106th Division after the abandonment of an engineering program at the University of Maine. While on maneuvers as a member of a 105-howitzer crew, he became acutely ill and was rushed to Wakeman General for emergency surgery. About ten days later, the 106th "Lionhead" Division shipped out and eventually became the green division that Von Rundstedt mauled and broke through in the Battle of the Bulge.

During an inspection tour of his new post, Major (soon to be Colonel) Truman Blocker, who had come to Wakeman to establish a plastic surgery service, noticed a patient sketching on the ward. Blocker asked the young sketcher (Stan was twenty-one at the time) if the sight of blood bothered him.

"Don't know, sir," Stan recalls answering. "I've never seen any."

"Well, son, you're going to see lots. Because as soon as I can get you off this ward you're going to be my medical artist."

During the seventeen months that Stan, who until that encounter didn't know there was such a thing as a medical artist, worked for Colonel Blocker, he watched and diagrammed more than three thousand plastic surgery procedures.

On August 5, 1945, Stan and his friend, Tech Sergeant Walter Waraksa, who ran a surgical dressing room at the hospital, were walking along the company street. As they walked past detachment headquarters, First Sergeant Brill, looking a bit dazed, poked his head out the door. He hardly knew Berenstain and Waraksa—there were more than four hundred GIs in the detachment—but he appeared to be looking for somebody—*anybody.*

"Did you hear?" he asked.

"Hear what, Sarge?"

"They set off some monster bomb in Japan and the damn war is going to be over in about twenty minutes."

Jan Grant (aka "Rosie the Riveter"), 1943

"Barbara," oil sketch by Jan Grant, 1944

Stan remembers what happened afterwards. That night he, Walter Waraksa, who had been a coal miner in civilian life, and Warren Reynolds, who had been an insurance executive and was the third member of their disparate "buddy" trio, celebrated with Southern Comfort and Coke in Walter's room in the NCO barracks. Of course, the war took longer than twenty minutes, but not much longer. For the first time in a long time there was some sense that there would be a future.

Though we didn't think in conventional terms like "being engaged," it was dead certain we were going to be married as soon after Stan's discharge as possible. (As it turned out, his discharge was dated April 1, 1946, and we were married on April 13, 1946.) So the idea of figuring out some way of making a living had begun to flicker in Stan's consciousness. Not that eating money was going to be an immediate problem. Shortly after Stan had gone into the army, Jan left art school for a year of war work, first as a skilled draftsperson for ITE, a circuit breaker company, then going for the

Stan and Jan in their new house in suburban Philadelphia, 1950

big bucks as a "Rosie the Riveter" in an aircraft factory. Later, back at the Philadelphia College of Art for a third year, she was asked to teach some drawing and painting classes. While the idea of an institution of higher learning asking a "dropout" to teach was precedent-breaking, to say the least, nobody thought twice about it.

Meanwhile, back in the army, Stan was weighing an offer from Colonel Blocker to come with him to the University of Texas Medical School, where he would resume his prewar post as chief of plastic surgery and Stan would found a medical art service. Stan appreciated the offer—Colonel Blocker was a good officer and a marvelous surgeon who went on to become president and chief of surgery at the University of Texas Plastic Surgery Hospital at Galveston and a world famous "plastic man"—but Stan figured he'd had enough of medical art, and it just didn't seem like a very civilian occupation.

During the period of his hospital service, Stan had become something of a cartoon fan—the kind of cartoons that appeared in magazines such as the *New Yorker,* the *Saturday Evening Post, Collier's,* and *Yank,* the army weekly where George Baker's "Sad Sack" did his weekly star turn. He had gotten into the habit of stopping by the hospital library to check out the back-of-the-book cartoons in the weekly magazines. During one of his visits, he discovered a magazine he'd never even heard of. It was called the *Saturday Review of Literature.* It consisted mainly of a review of literature and the arts but was salted with a half dozen or so cartoons about the broadly cultural kinds of subjects in which Stan was interested—art, music, history, and such. He had a vague knowledge that cartoons were customarily submitted to magazines by mail with an SASE. After work, over the next days, he created four cartoons. One was a parody of the familiar Tabu perfume ad in which a tuxedoed violinist and a gowned pianist engage in a passionate duet. Two were visual displacement gags imitative of Saul Steinberg, whose work he admired. The fourth depicted a fully armored knight with a battle-ax being confronted by a surly serf wielding a giant can opener. He sent the cartoons to a Mr. Norman Cousins, who was listed on the masthead as editor-in-chief. (He'd never heard of him, either.) About two weeks later, he received a note from Mr. Cousins. It said, "Dear Corporal Berenstain, Buying all four of your cartoons at $35 per. Terrific stuff. Send more. Check to follow. Yours truly, N. Cousins." "Wow!" thought Stan, with the arrant innocence of youth. "What a way to make a living!"

We were married by a magistrate on North Broad and almost immediately set up a rather ramshackle brand of housekeeping in a walk-up flat over an army-and-navy store owned by Stan's dad in southwest Philadelphia. With Stan studying painting at the Pennsylvania Academy of the Fine Arts on the GI Bill and Jan working two jobs—she was teaching drawing and painting at the Philadelphia College of Art and doing floral decorations on a piecework basis at a south Philadelphia giftware factory—we also found time to make a joint effort to expand on Stan's earlier success at the *Saturday Review of Literature.*

After more than three long years of separation, we were eager to find a career in which we could work together as a team. Free-lance cartooning seemed one of the few professions which both invited collaboration and accommodated our mutual interest in working with both words and pictures.

Looking back, it seems bold to the point of foolhardiness for us to have supposed we could actually make a living by combining funny words and pictures and sending them willy-nilly to magazines. But we had both been humor buffs even before we met. The fact of our shared enthusiasm for a broad range of both literary and graphic humorists just made being together that much more fun. We were both avid fans of Mark Twain, Edward Lear, Lewis Carroll, Ambrose Bierce, Oscar Wilde, Robert Benchley, James Thurber, and S. J. Perelman. In the area of cartooning, some of our favorites were Peter Arno, Whitney Darrow, Jr., Daniel Alain, Saul Steinberg, and Perry Barlow.

While we continued to submit and occasionally sell cartoons to the *Saturday Review,* we knew we would have to sell to the big general audience magazines like the *Saturday Evening Post* and *Collier's* before we could count on making even a semblance of a living. We created about twenty cartoons a week and submitted them in batches to a hierarchy of magazines which included the *Saturday Evening Post,*

Collier's, This Week (a Sunday supplement), *Ladies' Home Journal, Woman's Home Companion, Better Homes and Gardens,* and many others. It took about a year and a mountain of submissions before we broke into the "majors." After that long, desert-dry year of rejections, the first "OK" from *Collier's* was a relief almost beyond description. We don't remember how we celebrated, but we must have done something. Perhaps we had dinner at Linton's, the restaurant next door. Or maybe we went up the street and bought half a whipped cream cake at Horn and Hardart's day-old shop.

The cartoon that broke the dry spell was a domestic gag on what was then a very new phenomenon: frozen food. It showed a husband and wife at dinner. The wife was sporting a very conspicuous bandage on her index finger. The caption was her response to her husband's quizzical look: "I cut it on some frozen broccoli," she said.

Some of our favorite cartoons were the result of a team technique we invented. One of us would draw a picture that we hoped was pregnant with possibilities for humor. The other of us would then look at it and add the caption. The broccoli cartoon was the result of such a collaborative effort, as was a cartoon which appeared in the *Saturday Evening Post.* It showed a high perspective looking down a stair at a little girl with her mouth wide open. The caption read, "Ma! The coffee perked over into the gravy! Should I stir it?" In that example, picture courtesy of Stan, caption courtesy of Jan.

Once we broke the ice at *Collier's,* the other majors began to buy our cartoons. We quickly came to be among the most prolific contributors of cartoons to national magazines.

Without any conscious plan or design we gradually came to be recognized as specialists in humor about children and families. Our work was now sufficiently prominent to catch the attention of art directors in New York and Chicago. This interest in our work, especially in our work dealing with children, led to a number of advertising commissions from major companies. One such account from Abbott Laboratories went on for many years and was a major factor in our having the wherewithal to leave our walk-up over the army-and-navy store and move to a small house we built in a suburb of Philadelphia.

Shortly after the birth of Leo, in 1948, we received a letter from Al Hart, Jr. Al had come out of the marines at about the same time Stan had been separated from the army. The letter was short and to the point—and something of a bolt from the blue. Mr. Hart identified himself as an editor at Macmillan in New York. He further identified himself as a fan of our cartoons in the *Saturday Evening Post* and *Collier's.* The particular cartoon that prompted him to write was another domestic husband-and-wife exchange. In this one, a rather troglodytish male with a substantial stubble on his fat face is saying to his equally primitive, disapproving wife, "The day before yesterday. Why?" This cartoon also happened to be the product of our split picture/caption technique, though we can't recall which was whose. Why this particular cartoon prompted Mr. Hart to write and ask us to think about a book we might wish to do for Macmillan escaped us then and escapes us now. We corresponded with Mr. Hart and found out, to our further surprise, that what he had in mind was not, as we had supposed, a book of our cartoons. What he had in mind was a "written" book—a book of words, to be illustrated with cartoons.

After some thought, we overcame our trepidation (at that point we hadn't written anything longer than a cartoon caption and didn't even own a typewriter) and proposed a book about the subject we were then immersed in: bringing up baby. Some kindly relative had given us a work called *Better Homes Baby Book.* The advice it offered seemed to us to have little relationship to the exhausting, enervating, round-the-clock experience of tending to the not inconsiderable needs of a baby. Not that it wasn't fun. Because it was. Marvelous, wonderful fun. But, as Jan once told a child who asked her whether it was hard to do the Berenstain Bears books or was it fun, it was hard fun. Part of the fun was writing what came to be called *The Berenstains' Baby Book.* It turned out to be a book of about twenty thousand words with cartoon illustrations.

Macmillan was a very august sort of publisher. It was still owned by Macmillan of England and was the publisher of Rudyard Kipling, Sean O'Casey, Rabindranath Tagore (the Bengali poet), Arthur Koestler, and many others of the world's leading authors. Almost as memorable as having our first book published was our celebratory luncheon at Macmillan. It was the occasion of our first visit to Macmillan (all the work on the book had been done by mail), which at the time occupied an elegant and imposing building at 60 Fifth Avenue, just north of the Village. Its foyer opened onto a grand hall that was even more intimidating than the building itself. It had a marble floor. At each side of the room was a balustraded staircase which curved up to a second-floor gallery. Climbing the stairs on each side of the room were enormous photographic portraits of Kipling, O'Casey, Tagore, et al. What did Macmillan think it was doing publishing a funny little book about toilet training, grandparent management, and the like by a couple of cartoonists who had never written anything longer than a cartoon caption? Luncheon was formal, butler-served in a clubby, panelled room and preceded by a single glass of sherry. It was presided over by George Brett, chairman of Macmillan. Also present was Harold Latham, editor-in-chief, who was famous for having brought the manuscript of *Gone with the Wind* back from Atlanta in a suitcase.

But darned if our funny little book didn't do well. It went through a number of printings and was widely and favorably reviewed. A number of its sections were reprinted in various publications, most notably a section titled "First Books," which was included in Whit Burnett's anthology *This Is My Best Humor.* Other humorists represented were James Thurber, H. L. Mencken, Edward Streeter, and Fred Allen. We were in our early twenties at the time, and it was a real kick to be anthologized in the company of writers we had grown up on. To this day, at various Berenstain Bears book signings we are asked if we have anything to do with "those Berenstains who wrote the book that somebody gave my mom as a baby gift when I was born?" Our answer that we are two and the same Berenstains is usually met with a look of wonder that anybody could possibly be so old. Also published by Macmillan was *Baby Makes Four,* a book about the complexities and confusions which arise from the arrival of a second child.

Though we were doing well as contributors of "gag" cartoons to the *Saturday Evening Post, Collier's,* et al, we were beginning to feel confined by the small three-by-four-inch compass of back-of-the-book cartoons. We conceived the idea of creating panoramic, full-color cartoon "paintings" depicting large numbers of children being themselves in various settings. By 1948, the year our first child was born, the childhood theme had come to dominate our work. We taught a Saturday children's art class at Philadelphia Settlement School of Music and Art and had a vivid idea of the kind of comedic chaos forty to fifty hell-bent kids could create. Drawing upon our weekly descent into the moppet maelstrom and upon recollections of our own childhoods, we set about developing a work titled "Recess." It was a large, highly detailed work that depicted about 150 kids doing the simple ordinary things that kids have been doing in schoolyards since time immemorial: little boys filling their mouths with water at the drinking fountain and spritzing little girls; little girls playing "free show" on the monkey bars; kids playing hopscotch, crack-the-whip, mumblety-peg; kids buying mustard-slathered soft pretzels through the fence; etc., etc., etc.

We were excited about "Recess," and though we were not creating something new under the sun—artists have been depicting children at play since genre painting was invented—*Recess* was

a new and liberating experience for us. We sent if off to *Saturday Evening Post* humor editor John Bailey with a great sense of excitement and anticipation. John was enthusiastic about our work and had bought quite a lot of it. He had also signed us to a "first look" contract, which meant we were required to give the *Post* first look at all our work. While this didn't guarantee any sales, it did provide a higher than normal rate of payment for work they did buy.

The *Post* didn't buy "Recess." John Bailey very much wanted to, but he was overruled by managing editor Robert Fuoss. What we didn't know and didn't find out until much later was that John had been fighting a running battle with Fuoss, who found our work irritating and was, in fact, getting quite fed up with it. "Recess" was presented to him shortly after Bailey had run a record six of our cartoons in a single issue of the *Post*.

Looking back, we can understand Fuoss's objections to our work—better, perhaps, than Bailey's great enthusiasm for it. As nearly as

"Dancing School," Collier's *cover, March 4, 1950, painted by Stan and Jan Berenstain*

Jan, Leo, Michael, and Stan and a new Berenstain cartoon book, 1958

we can determine, Fuoss didn't like the way we drew people back then—our women in particular. They were ominous-looking, top-heavy creatures with enormous, blunt, projectile-like noses. What really annoyed him, though, was that they had no feet—just little points. We're not sure why we drew them that way; perhaps it was an unconscious comment on the inanity of high heels. Our men had feet, but they were equally unpleasant and more than a match for our women. Our children, though pesky and occasionally impertinent, were drawn with affection and sympathy.

So we were hoist by the petard of our excessive success at the *Post.* When the *Post* turned down "Recess," we sent it to Gurney Williams, humor editor of *Collier's,* the *Post*'s major competition. Gurney was the dean of U.S. humor editors; he had been humor editor of the old *Life* magazine. (Given the relatively recent reincarnation of the photographic *Life* after its demise in the seventies, we should say the old *old Life* magazine.) Gurney later went on to become humor editor of *Look* when *Collier's* began to seem shaky. Television was a young nine-

hundred-pound gorilla back then, and general audience magazines were demising all over the place.

Shortly after we sent "Recess" to *Collier's,* our doorbell rang. We were still living in that ramshackle railroad flat over the army-and-navy store owned by Stan's dad, across from an abandoned trolley factory. During the war the factory had been converted to manufacture center wing sections of PB-Y flying boats, and it happened to be where Jan worked as a riveter. Actually, Jan was the bucker-upper of a team. She crouched inside the gas tank between the spars and bucked up her partner's rivets.

Stan ran down the rickety stairs and answered the doorbell. It was Western Union with a telegram from *Collier's.* It said, "Dear Berenstains, Buying 'Recess.' Will publish as full-page feature. Will pay $500. Signed: Gurney Williams, Humor Editor, Collier's."

Five hundred dollars struck us as a prodigious amount of money, which indeed it was, viewed in the context of what we were being paid for our work at the time—as little as three dollars apiece for spot drawings that we were selling to the *Philadelphia Inquirer* and as much as seventy-five dollars each for cartoons sold to the *Saturday Evening Post,* our highest-paying market. It should be remembered that we created a batch of at least twenty cartoon "roughs" a week. Any week that yielded two or three OK's out of the eight or nine batches that the postal service was circulating to a list of magazines was considered a good week.

At about that time we were contacted by Knox Burger. Knox had been a combat correspondent for *Yank,* during World War II. He became fiction editor of *Collier's* and knew our work through our mutual connection with that magazine. He had become editor for a new line of original mass market paperbacks at Dell. We wrote and illustrated a number of original paperbacks for Knox and later for Don Fine, Marc Jaffe, and Arlene Donovan, subsequent editors of the line. These books bore titles like *Marital Blitz, Education Impossible, How to Teach Your Children about Sex without Making a Complete Fool of Yourself, How to Teach Your Children about God without Actually Scaring Them out of Their Wits,* and *Have a Baby, My Wife Just Had a Cigar.* Original paperbacks became an increasingly important part of our work as the magazine cartoon business began to diminish.

In 1955 another invitation, as unexpected as the letter from Al Hart, came in the form of a phone call from Peggy Bell, features editor of *McCall's.* Her magazine, she told us, was interested in developing a cartoon feature but wanted to avoid becoming part of the Wednesday "look day" circuit. Wednesday "look day" had evolved as the mechanism through which gag cartoonists from New York City and environs personally showed their gags to the cartoon editors of the magazines that were located in Manhattan—which were virtually all the magazines in the country that paid a living rate. The one exception was the *Saturday Evening Post,* which was a Philadelphia institution—and what an institution it was! The lobby of the Curtis Publishing Company was positively papal in its richness. Its decorative centerpiece was a vast and stunning mosaic mural, designed by Maxfield Parrish and executed by Tiffany. As the Curtis empire first slowly then rapidly self-destructed (Canute-like, the Curtis management took the position that they could beat television rather than join it), the magnificent Curtis Publishing Building was sold off and became simply the Curtis Building, a general

office building. It is perhaps a quirky shard in the mosaic of time that Al Hart, Jr., our mentor at Macmillan, is presently a literary agent with offices next door to that building.

Since we had conducted all our cartoon business by mail we had never enjoyed the efficiencies of Wednesday look days. We don't know how we would have handled the tumbril and guillotine efficiency of having a cartoon editor riffle through twenty of our best efforts to be funny in about a minute and dismiss them without so much as a smirk. Probably not very well.

But as it turned out, *McCall's* reluctance to have its posh halls cluttered with a lot of unsightly cartoonists led to "It's All in the Family" (yes, we used that title a decade before it was adopted by a similarly named television show), a monthly cartoon feature which ran in *McCall's* from 1956 to 1970, when Shana Alexander took over the editorship of the magazine. One of Ms. Alexander's first editorial decisions was to drop our feature on the grounds that cartoons weren't appropriate for a serious

Stan and Jan at work on "It's All in the Family" cartoons, 1964

magazine. Thousands of letters of complaint and hundreds of cancellations from subscribers prompted Ms. Alexander to publish her regrets in *McCall's* and ask us back. But we had jumped to *Good Housekeeping,* from whom we had a standing invitation. Our feature continued in *Good Housekeeping* until the Bears took over all our time in 1990, becoming one of the longest-running byline features in U.S. magazine history.

As our work expanded, the business side of our activities became more and more complicated. In addition to our continuing though diminished free-lance cartoon business, we had working relationships with a number of book publishers; there was our monthly feature in *McCall's,* as well as occasional advertising accounts. At about that time, Joyce C. Hall, the chairman and founder of Hallmark, noted our work in *McCall's* and invited us to come to Kansas City, the home of Hallmark, and learn something about the greetings industry. This visit led to a series of Berenstain greeting prod-

ucts—cards, booklets, etc. Each of these business relationships was covered by a contract. We had been unagented since the beginning of our joint career, but we were being overwhelmed by the business affairs that had to be dealt with. A number of our editors advised us to get an agent. In response to our request for recommendations (we knew nothing about the world of agentry), a number of our editors gave us lists of agents they thought would be suitable. The name "Sterling Lord" was included on all of the independently arrived at lists. When, intrigued by this anomaly, we asked why this particular agent was recommended by all the list providers, the consensus answer was something like, "You two are a kind of odd creative entity. Are you cartoonists who write, or are you writers who cartoon? And Sterling . . . well, he's flexible."

"Flexible, how?" we asked.

"Well," said one respondent, "right now he's booking Jack Kerouac into coffeehouses for poetry readings."

"Oh, boy! Just like the Wilderness Family!"
"It's All in the Family: Cabin in the Pines," Good Housekeeping, *August 1980*

Sterling Lord has been our agent, friend, and confidant for thirty-three years. The first deal Sterling negotiated for us was for the book that was to be the forerunner of our Berenstain Bears children's book series. The series featuring the funny, furry Bear family that "lives in the big tree house down a sunny dirt road deep in Bear Country" and which we frequently describe as consisting of "overbearing Papa, forbearing Mama, and two bright little cubs who bear with both of them," quickly came to dominate our professional lives.

The Berenstain Bears children's book series began in the early sixties with rides on two rickety elevators and a climb up a twisty stair to see a fellow named Theodor Seuss Geisel, better known as Dr. Seuss. Ted had started a line called Beginner Books, which grew out of his remarkably successful book *The Cat in the Hat,* which had earlier grown out of a wave of anxiety about children and reading triggered by a book called *Why Johnny Can't Read.*

We had submitted a book called *Freddy Bear's Spanking* to the good doctor and his editorial board, which consisted of his wife, Helen Palmer, and the Random House publisher's wife, Phyllis Cerf. Our purpose in visiting Dr. Seuss and his associates was to receive their advice and counsel on the book we had submitted. After introductions all around, we were startled to see our book staring at us from the walls. All the illustrated pages of our book were pinned in sequence to the walls of the tiny office. This, Ted explained, was a technique known as storyboarding. It came out of the movie business, and he had learned it during World War II while working for the Office of War Information under Major Frank Capra, the famous movie director. Ted then proceeded in a firm but kindly manner to walk us through our picture story and point out to us that there were about six things wrong with every page.

There were discontinuities in the story; it lacked the simplicity needed in an easy-to-read book; there were too few picture clues to the text; the language was too complicated; the pictures were too complicated; there were too many convenience rhymes—we had had the temerity to submit a rhymed story to the century's leading creator of rhymed children's books—and so on and so forth.

Well, we were a little confused. We didn't know quite what to make of the experience. If they thought our book was so awful, why had

they invited us up to New York to discuss our working with them on a book?

"That's simple," said Ted. "We think these wild, wacky bears of yours are sensational, and we're absolutely confident we're going to get a terrific book out of you."

A problem was that we didn't see our three-member Bear family as wild and wacky at all. We saw them as a comfortable, fairly normal family like our own family. But looking back at the book which eventually grew out of that first submission—and we do mean eventually; it took almost two years and about five complete versions before arriving at a work called *The Big Honey Hunt,* which, incidentally, is still in print and has sold about two-and-a-half million copies to date—those early Bears *were* wild and wacky. They were long, rangy, and very unbearlike. They were all elbows and knees. They had long upturned sausage-like muzzles with noses that looked like hockey pucks perched on the end of them.

They wore pretty much the same clothes, though. Papa Bear wore bib overalls and a plaid shirt, though in the first book it was red plaid—we didn't go to a yellow plaid until the second book. Mama Bear wore a blue dress with white polka dots and a duster for a hat. Mama also had a yellow dress-up hat, and Small Bear had blue pants and a red shirt.

We get a lot of mail from children, and the Bears' limited wardrobe is a source of some concern. Kids often suggest titles for new Bear books, and one of the most frequently suggested titles is *The Berenstain Bears Get New Clothes.*

Meanwhile, back at that meeting with Dr. Seuss and his editorial board, in our magazine and book work, which consisted of cartoons, magazine covers, and word-and-picture essays in book form, we had never had to deal with that classical entity known as "story." Now here we were being introduced to such concepts as "advancing the story," "motivation," "character," and the requirement that a story should have "a beginning, a middle, and an end."

Where we had gone wrong in creating our story was to do what many people who are trained as artists do when they infiltrate the children's literature field. We had dreamed up a story line that was really a series of picture opportunities—that is, a group of pictures that would be interesting and fun to draw. This sometimes leads to a successful book, but it never leads to a story. Just as the play's the

In their Bucks County studio, 1985

thing in a dramatic work, we believe the story's the thing in a work of fiction.

We were now being asked questions about our Bears that we'd never thought to ask ourselves. "Just who *are* these bears?" Ted wanted to know. Well, it turned out that *we* were the Bears. Stan was foolish, accident-prone Papa; Jan was warm, wise Mama; and our son, Leo, was bright, lively Small Bear. Small Bear didn't become Brother Bear until much later when Sister Bear was born in *The Berenstain Bears' New Baby* (which was really the story of the birth of Leo's brother, Michael).

In other words, we had met the Bears and they were us. Of course, Stan wasn't quite as foolish and accident-prone as Papa Bear, and Jan wasn't quite as calm and even-tempered as Mama Bear. But there was clearly something of a connection. To this day, when we are asked if Papa and Mama are based on ourselves, we decline to answer on the grounds that it may tend to incriminate us.

The analysis got hot and heavy. The Beginner Books editorial board was asking tough questions. What was the precise motivation of Papa Bear on page seventeen? What was the precise relationship of principal characters Papa and Small Bear? (Mama simply precipitated the stories in the first couple of books.) Our explanation that they were father and son wasn't enough. Not nearly. What *sort* of father and son? There were as many kinds of father-son relationships as there were fathers and sons.

We were sort of overwhelmed. All we wanted to do was a funny little book for kids, and here we were discussing our little book in terms befitting a graduate seminar on *War and Peace*. What we came to understand and appreciate was that as far as Ted was concerned, candidates for his list, if not *War and Peace*, deserved to be subjected to at least as rigorous an analysis as candidates for any adult publishing list.

By the time the nearly two-year editorial process was over, all that was left of *Freddy Bear's Spanking* was a brief, subsidiary episode depicting Papa and Small Bear searching for honey. It was decided in the interim that their relationship was akin to that of Wallace Beery and Jackie Cooper in *The Champ*. The honey-hunting episode was expanded into the book called *The Big Honey Hunt,* which was finally published in the fall of 1962.

Upon completion of *The Big Honey Hunt,* Ted and Helen took us out for a celebratory lunch at a fancy restaurant. Ted asked what we had in mind for a next book. We had a ready answer. "We sort of had in mind," Stan said, "to do a series about the Bears. So our next book . . ."

"Bad idea," said Ted. "You don't want to get stuck with a series. Worst possible thing you could do. Besides, there are too many bears on the market—there's Yogi Bear, Sendak's got some kind of bear, the Chicago Bears, all kinds of teddy bears. No, for your next book you want to do something as different from bears as possible."

We were disappointed. A Bear series seemed like a good idea to us. But we had learned a lot from Ted and had a high regard for him both professionally and personally, so we took his advice to heart. We discussed the situation on the train back to Philadelphia. Stan pointed to a poster on the front wall of the car. It was an ad for Kools mentholated cigarettes. It

showed the Kools penguin in a polar setting urging passengers to "smoke Kools!" "How about a book about a penguin?" Stan asked.

"A penguin," said Jan, "sure would be as different from bears as possible."

We went to work and did a very ambitious book called *Nothing Ever Happens at the South Pole*. It told the story of a penguin who lived in an igloo. It began with a mysterious package being tossed into the entrance. The package contained a diary, the kind with a pencil attached on a string and an instruction: "Write What Happens Every Day." The penguin is game and, carrying the diary, pencil at the ready, undertakes a polar walkabout. He is a rather forward-looking penguin, and he marches resolutely onward, looking straight ahead. But nothing seems to be happening. Nothing at all. Being literally forward-looking, he is entirely oblivious to all sorts of disasters which are occurring behind him: snowslides, polar bear attacks, walrus fights, etc. Discouraged, he returns to his igloo and writes in the diary, "Nothing ever happens at the South Pole!"

Back to New York, back up the two rickety elevators, back up the twisty stair to present our penguin book to Ted. He studied the book

From The Berenstain Bears Learn about Strangers, *1985*

very carefully. "Hmm," he said. "A penguin. Very interesting. This could be a helluva book . . . but, you know something—the salesmen are out on the road selling *The Big Honey Hunt* and it's going very well. Why don't you put this on the back burner and think about doing another Bear book? Maybe it could be a series."

The second book about our Bear family was called *The Bike Lesson.* It told the story of Papa Bear teaching Small Bear to ride a two-wheeler. When we received the first copy, we were surprised and pleased to see that Ted had incorporated a prominent blurb into our jacket design. It said, "Another Adventure of the Berenstain Bears."

A query we receive from children is the rather bemusing question, "How did you ever think of the name 'The Berenstain Bears'?" The answer is that we didn't. Dr. Seuss did. We wouldn't have had the nerve to do anything so egocentric.

There are now well over one hundred Berenstain Bears titles in print, with more on the way.

The bulk of our total sales and most of our work in recent years has been accounted for by a subseries called First Time Books. This line began in 1981 and was originally conceived of as a read-aloud series for preschoolers. It was designed to deal in an entertaining and helpful way with such problematic and potentially traumatic experiences as going to the doctor, visiting the dentist, having a sitter, and moving. Those subjects, in fact, provided the first four titles in the series. We and Random House thought that perhaps the series had the potential of generating eight to ten titles. And while we and our present editor and publisher, Janet Schulman, hoped First Time Books would be a success, neither of us anticipated how well accepted the line would be. There are now forty-one First Time titles. We are planning many more. We are also developing a spin-off series which will combine the "first time" concept with activities in what we believe will be a novel and interesting way.

Through the years we have received many thousands of letters from children, parents, teachers, and librarians. The range of children's letters is, as one might suppose, wide and varied. We found the question "What do you do

From The Berenstain Bears and the Bully, *1993*

From The Berenstain Bears' New Neighbors, *1994*

for a living?" (asked more than once) puzzling at first. But on further consideration, we found it rather sweetly innocent. It seemed to suggest that what we do looks like so much fun that we could hardly expect to be paid for it. At the other end of the innocence-reality axis was a boy from Texas who asked, "How much money do you make?" Other memorable questions have been, "How do you draw water?" "How are you two getting along?" and (from a three-year-old, as dictated to Mom) "Are you bears or people?"

The three most frequently asked questions are

1. Which one of you draws and which one of you writes?

2. Why do you draw just bears?

3. How can you possibly stand being together all the time?

The answer to the first question is that we both do both. That is, each of us draws and

each of us writes. We have compared notes, and we each have had a long-standing interest in drawing, going back to very early childhood. We were avid readers from an early age as well, but we did not begin to write professionally until a few years after we were established as professional artists.

The answer to the second question, which is usually asked by children, is that we don't draw just bears. We also draw trees, houses, birds, rocks, squirrels, lakes, streams, and just about anything else that is required to depict a place we've invented, called Bear Country.

Admittedly, that answer begs the question a bit: the answer to the question as to why we chose bears as subjects is probably at least twofold. Bears are traditionally prime subjects of children's books—the classic story "The Three Bears" is probably the most universally popular of all children's stories. There is also the fact that we had a weekly nature drawing class at the Philadelphia Zoo as part of our first year of art school training. We sort of gravitated to

Stan, Jan, Leo, and Michael with the first "Big Chapter Book," 1993

the bear pit area because the bears were not so popular with our fellow students, and I guess we wanted to be alone.

The answer to the third question—the one about how we can stand being together so much is usually asked by reporters, interviewers, and TV hosts, more than a few of whom, it turns out, are ex-husbands and ex-wives. The answer is that we get along extraordinarily well and always have. We rarely argue about anything and we never argue about our work.

Quite the contrary: it's an extraordinary help to have a partner to turn to when you can't quite figure something out. There's an enormous range of things you can get stuck on in the kind of work we do. Even tasks you've handled scores of times can stop you dead in your tracks when you least expect it: story problems, design problems, drawing problems, etc., etc.

Over the years and decades we have evolved a fairly systematic division of labor. Let us briefly tell you how it typically applies to one of our First Time Books. . . . First, there's the basic

question of subject matter and the closely related issue of title. Sometimes we have a strong subject but can't come up with just the right title. Sometimes the reverse is true. With two heads stewing, we usually recognize the best solution. Next, we call our editor to see if there's any objection, and there rarely is. Then, one or the other of us writes a two- to three-page story treatment. This is written in discursive rather than outline form. Next comes the writing of the manuscript. One or the other of us takes the first shot, usually ending with a story at least twice the necessary length of about 1100 words. Then the partner takes on the difficult job of compressing it down to a manageable length. It takes us from two to three weeks to go from idea to submittable manuscript.

Creating the illustrations is a similarly layered hand-it-back-and-forth process—Stan does the initial rough layout, Jan takes over, and based on Stan's very rough version, creates an absolutely perfect pencil drawing on kid-finish bristol board. Then Stan inks the pencil. We split the painting with transparent watercolors pretty much down the middle, then—Federal Express delivery of the finished book to Random House. Of course, it takes a lot longer to do than to tell about.

Starting in the mid-eighties, we began to get letters from children requesting that we do "chapter books" about the Berenstain Bears. They had enjoyed our books when they were "little" and wanted some "harder" longer books now that they were second, third, and fourth graders. We were not familiar with the term "chapter books," though when it was explained to us it seemed obvious enough: it simply meant books with chapters—i.e., longer books which not only had chapters but in which text rather than pictures dominated.

We thought it was an intriguing idea and so did our publisher. The difficulty was that we were doing just about all that we could reasonably do. Our sons, Leo and Mike, came to the rescue. Leo, who was trained as a scientist and had published research papers in scientific journals, had always written and had recently shifted to being a full-time writer. His first book, a collection of short stories titled *The Wind Monkey* had just been published to excellent reviews.

Son Michael had established himself as a successful author-illustrator of children's books, with more than twenty books to his credit. One of his books, *The Sorcerer's Scrapbook,* was named as one of the ten best children's books of the year by *Time* magazine.

Happily, Leo and Michael volunteered to make our twosome a foursome. After a period of adjustment during which we did much of the developmental work—Leo had never written for children, and Michael had to learn to draw our Bears—the foursome worked. Presently Leo is doing all writing of Berenstain Bearsy Big Chapter Books, based on outlines supplied by Stan, and Michael is doing all the illustrations with a bit of help here and there from Jan. Big Chapter Books have been well launched. There are now fifteen Big Chapter titles in print, with more on the way. We are encouraged by very enthusiastic mail we are receiving from Big Chapter Books readers.

Jan and Stan are both seventy-one at this writing. We are often asked if we are going to retire. Why would we want to retire from the best job anybody ever had? We thoroughly enjoy what we're doing. Our plan for the future is simplicity itself: we're going to keep on doing it until we get it wrong.

BIBLIOGRAPHY

FOR CHILDREN

Berenstain Bears books jointly written and illustrated and published by Random House unless otherwise indicated:

The Big Honey Hunt, Beginner Books, 1962.

The Bike Lesson, Beginner Books, 1964, reissued with cassette, 1987.

The Bears' Picnic, Beginner Books, 1966.

The Bear Scouts, Beginner Books, 1967.

The Bears' Vacation, Beginner Books, 1968, published in England as *The Bears' Holiday,* Harvill, 1969, reissued with cassette, Random House, 1987.

Inside, Outside, Upside Down, 1968.

Bears on Wheels, 1969.

The Bears' Christmas, Beginner Books, 1970, reissued with cassette, Random House, 1988.

Old Hat, New Hat, 1970.

The B Book, 1971.

Bears in the Night, 1971.

C Is for Clown, 1972.

The Bears' Almanac: A Year in Bear Country—Holidays, Seasons, Weather, Actual Facts about Snow, Wind, Rain, Thunder, Lightning, the Sun, the Moon, and Lots More, 1973, published as *The Berenstain Bears' Almanac: . . . ,* 1984.

The Berenstain Bears' Nursery Tales, 1973.

The Berenstain Bears' New Baby, 1974, reissued with cassette, 1985.

He Bear, She Bear, 1974.

The Bear Detectives: The Case of the Missing Pumpkin, 1975, reissued with cassette, 1988.

The Bears' Nature Guide, 1975, published as *The Berenstain Bears' Nature Guide,* 1984.

The Berenstain Bears' Counting Book, 1976.

The Berenstain Bears' Science Fair, 1977.

The Berenstain Bears and the Spooky Old Tree, 1978.

The Berenstain Bears Go to School, 1978, reissued with cassette, 1985.

Papa's Pizza: A Berenstain Bear Sniffy Book, 1978.

The Bears' Activity Book, 1979.

The Berenstain Bears and the Missing Dinosaur Bone, 1980.

The Berenstain Bears' Christmas Tree, 1980.

The Berenstain Bears and the Sitter, 1981, reissued with cassette, 1985, reissued with puppet package, 1987.

The Berenstain Bears Go to the Doctor, 1981, reissued with cassette, 1985, reissued with puppet package, 1987.

The Berenstain Bears' Moving Day, 1981.

The Berenstain Bears Visit the Dentist, 1981, reissued with cassette, 1985, reissued with puppet package, 1987.

The Berenstain Bears Get in a Fight, 1982, reissued with puppet package, 1987, reissued with cassette, 1988.

The Berenstain Bears Go to Camp, 1982, reissued with cassette, 1989.

The Berenstain Bears in the Dark, 1982.

The Berenstain Bears' Storybook Treehouse, 1982.

The Berenstain Bears and the Messy Room, 1983, reissued with puppet package, 1987.

The Berenstain Bears and the Truth, 1983, reissued with puppet package, 1988.

The Berenstain Bears and the Wild, Wild Honey, 1983.

The Berenstain Bears Go Fly a Kite, 1983.

The Berenstain Bears' Soccer Star, 1983.

The Berenstain Bears to the Rescue, 1983.

The Berenstain Bears' Trouble with Money, 1983.

The Berenstain Bears and Mama's New Job, 1984.

The Berenstain Bears and the Big Election, 1984.

The Berenstain Bears and the Dinosaurs, 1984.

The Berenstain Bears and the Neighborly Skunk, 1984.

The Berenstain Bears and Too Much TV, 1984, reissued with cassette, 1989.

The Berenstain Bears' Make and Do Book, 1984.

The Berenstain Bears Meet Santa Bear, 1984, reissued with puppet package, 1988, reissued with cassette, 1989.

The Berenstain Bears Shoot the Rapids, 1984.

The Berenstain Bears and Too Much Junk Food, 1985.

The Berenstain Bears Forget Their Manners, 1985, reissued with cassette, 1986, reissued with puppet package, 1988.

The Berenstain Bears Learn about Strangers, 1985, reissued with cassette, 1986.

The Berenstain Bears on the Moon, 1985.

The Berenstain Bears' Take-Along Library (includes *The Berenstain Bears Visit the Dentist, The Berenstain Bears and Too Much TV, The Berenstain Bears and the Sitter, The Berenstain Bears in the Dark,* and *The Berenstain Bears and the Messy Room*), 1985.

The Berenstain Bears' Toy Time, 1985.

The Berenstain Bears and the Week at Grandma's, 1986, reissued with puppet package, 1990.

The Berenstain Bears and Too Much Birthday, 1986.

The Berenstain Bears' Bath Book, 1986.

The Berenstain Bears Get Stage Fright, 1986.

The Berenstain Bears: No Girls Allowed, 1986.

The Berenstain Bears and the Bad Habit, 1987.

The Berenstain Bears and the Big Road Race, 1987.

The Berenstain Bears and the Missing Honey, 1987.

The Berenstain Bears and the Trouble with Friends, 1987.

The Berenstain Bears Blaze a Trail, 1987.

Berenstain Bears: Coughing Catfish, 1987.

The Berenstain Bears Go Out for the Team, 1987, reissued with cassette, 1991.

The Berenstain Bears on the Job, 1987.

The Berenstain Bears' Trouble at School, 1987, reissued with puppet package, 1990.

The Berenstain Kids: I Love Colors, 1987.

The Day of the Dinosaur (illustrated by Michael Berenstain), 1987.

After the Dinosaurs, 1988.

The Berenstain Bears and the Bad Dream, 1988.

The Berenstain Bears and the Double Dare, 1988.

The Berenstain Bears and the Ghost of the Forest, 1988.

The Berenstain Bears Get the Gimmies, 1988, reissued with cassette, 1990.

The Berenstain Bears Ready, Get Set, Go!, 1988.

The Berenstain Bears and the In-Crowd, 1989.

The Berenstain Bears and Too Much Vacation, 1989, reissued with cassette, 1990.

The Berenstain Bears' Trick or Treat, 1989.

The Berenstain Bears and the Prize Pumpkin, 1990.

The Berenstain Bears and the Slumber Party, 1990.

The Berenstain Bears' Trouble with Pets, 1990.

The Berenstain Bears Are a Family, 1991.

The Berenstain Bears at the Super-Duper Market, 1991.

The Berenstain Bears Don't Pollute (Anymore), 1991.

The Berenstain Bears' Four Seasons, 1991.

The Berenstain Bears Say Good Night, 1991.

The Berenstain Bears and the Big Red Kite, Western, 1992.

The Berenstain Bears and the Broken Piggy Bank, Western, 1992.

The Berenstain Bears and the Hiccup Cure, Western, 1992.

The Berenstain Bears and the Spooky Shadows, Western, 1992.

The Berenstain Bears and the Trouble with Grownups, 1992.

The Berenstain Bears at Fun Park, Western, 1992.

The Berenstain Bears Get Jealous, Western, 1992.

The Berenstain Bears' Home Sweet Tree, Western, 1992.

The Berenstain Bears Hug and Make Up, Western, 1992.

The Berenstain Bears Learn to Share, Western, 1992.

The Berenstain Bears on Time, Western, 1992.

The Berenstain Bears' Perfect Fishing Spot, Western, 1992.

The Berenstain Bears All Year 'Round, Western, 1993.

The Berenstain Bears and the Baby Chipmunk, Western, 1993.

The Berenstain Bears and the Excuse Note, Western, 1993.

The Berenstain Bears and the Good Deed, Western, 1993.

The Berenstain Bears and the Jump Rope Contest, Western, 1993.

The Berenstain Bears and the Spooky Old House, Western, 1993.

The Berenstain Bears and the Wishing Star, Western, 1993.

The Berenstain Bears and Too Much Pressure, 1993.

The Berenstain Bears at the Giant Mall, Western, 1993.

The Berenstain Bears' Bedtime Battle, Western, 1993.

The Berenstain Bears' Birthday Boy, Western, 1993.

The Berenstain Bears' Family Get-Together, Western, 1993.

The Berenstain Bears Get a Checkup, Western, 1993.

The Berenstain Bears Learn about Colors, Western, 1993.

The Berenstain Bears' Pet Show, Western, 1993.

The Berenstain Bears Visit Farmer Ben, Western, 1993.

The Berenstain Bears with Nothing to Do, Western, 1993.

The Berenstain Bears and the Big Picture, Reader's Digest, 1994.

The Berenstain Bears and the Big Yard Sale, Reader's Digest, 1994.

The Berenstain Bears and the Bully, 1994.

The Berenstain Bears and the Really Big Snow, Reader's Digest, 1994.

The Berenstain Bears and the Soccer Tryouts, Reader's Digest, 1994.

The Berenstain Bears and the Summer Job, Reader's Digest, 1994.

The Berenstain Bears at Big Bear Fair, Reader's Digest, 1994.

The Berenstain Bears by the Sea, Reader's Digest, 1994.

The Berenstain Bears' Deep Dark Secret, Reader's Digest, 1994.

The Berenstain Bears in Big Bear City, Reader's Digest, 1994.

The Berenstain Bears Lost in a Cave, Reader's Digest, 1994.

The Berenstain Bears' New Neighbors, 1994.

The Berenstain Bears on Rapid River, Reader's Digest, 1994.

The Berenstain Bears' Talent Show, Reader's Digest, 1994.

The Berenstain Bears Visit Uncle Tex, Reader's Digest, 1994.

The Berenstain Bears and the Green-Eyed Monster, 1995.

The Berenstain Bears and Too Much Teasing, forthcoming.

The Berenstain Bears Count Their Blessings, forthcoming.

Television scripts, jointly written:

The Berenstain Bears' Christmas Tree, National Broadcasting Company, Inc. (NBC-TV), 1979.

The Berenstain Bears Meet Bigpaw, NBC-TV, 1980.

The Berenstain Bears' Easter Surprise, NBC-TV, 1981.

The Berenstain Bears' Comic Valentine, NBC-TV, 1982.

The Berenstain Bears Play Ball, NBC-TV, 1983.

The Berenstain Bears' CBS Show, Columbia Broadcasting System, Inc. (CBS-TV), 1986–87.

FOR ADULTS

Fiction, jointly written and illustrated:

The Berenstain's Baby Book, Macmillan, 1951.

Sister (cartoons), Schuman, 1952.

Tax-Wise, Schuman, 1952.

Marital Blitz, Dutton, 1954.

Baby Makes Four, Macmillan, 1956.

It's All in the Family, Dutton, 1958.

Lover Boy, Macmillan, 1958.

And Beat Him When He Sneezes, McGraw, 1960, published as *Have a Baby, My Wife Just Had a Cigar,* Dell, 1960.

Bedside Lover Boy, Dell, 1960.

Call Me Mrs., Macmillan, 1961.

It's Still in the Family, Dutton, 1961.

Office Lover Boy, Dell, 1962.

The Facts of Life for Grown-ups, Dell, 1963.

Flipsville-Squaresville, Dial, 1965.

Mr. Dirty vs. Mr. Clean, Dell, 1967.

You Could Diet Laughing, Dell, 1969.

Be Good or I'll Belt You, Dell, 1970.

Education Impossible, Dell, 1970.

How to Teach Your Children about Sex without Making a Complete Fool of Yourself, Dutton, 1970.

Never Trust Anyone over 13, Bantam, 1970.

How to Teach Your Children about God without Actually Scaring Them out of Their Wits, Dutton, 1971.

Are Parents for Real?, Bantam, 1972.

What Your Parents Never Told You about Being a Mom or Dad, Crown, 1995.

Also creators of coloring books published by Random House, including *Berenstain Bears' around the Clock Coloring Book; Berenstain Bears' Bear Scout Coloring Book; Berenstain Bears' Count on Numbers Coloring Book; Berenstain Bears' on the Farm Coloring Book; Berenstain Bears' Safety First Coloring Book*, all 1987, and *Berenstain Bears' Storytime Coloring Book*, 1989.

In addition, Stan and Jan Berenstain are collaborators on the following Big Chapter Books, written by son Leo Berenstain and illustrated by son Michael Berenstain: *The Berenstain Bears Accept No Substitutes; The Berenstain Bears and the Drug Free Zone; The Berenstain Bears and the Female Fullback; The Berenstain Bears and the Nerdy Nephew; The Berenstain Bears and the New Girl in Town; The Berenstain Bears and the Wheelchair Commando; The Berenstain Bears Gotta Dance!*, all 1993; *The Berenstain Bears and the Galloping Ghost; The Berenstain Bears and the Giddy Grandma; The Berenstain Bears and the Dress Code; The Berenstain Bears and the School Scandal Sheet; The Berenstain Bears at Camp Crush*, all 1994; *The Berenstain Bears in the Freaky Funhouse* and *The Berenstain Bears' Media Madness*, both 1995, *The Berenstain Bears and the Showdown at Chain Saw Gap*, forthcoming.

Books which have also been recorded onto audiocassette include *The Berenstain Bears' Read Along Library* (includes *He Bear, She Bear; The Bear Scouts; The Bear Detectives; The Big Honey Hunt; Old Hat, New Hat;* and *The Bears' Christmas*), Random House, 1977; *The Bears' Picnic and Other Stories* (includes *The Bears' Picnic; The Bear Scouts; Bears in the Night; The Bears' New Baby; The Bears' Vacation;* and *The Big Honey Hunt*), Caedmon, 1977; *The Bears' Christmas and Other Stories* (includes *The Bears' Christmas; He Bear, She Bear; The Bear Detectives; The Bears' Almanac;* and *The Bike Lesson*), Random House, 1982; and *He Bear, She Bear* and *Bears on Wheels*, Random House, 1989.

Books adapted for filmstrips and released by Random House include *The Bears' Nature Guide*, 1976; *The Berenstain Bears' Science Fair*, 1978; *The Bear Detectives; The Bears' Almanac; The Bears' Vacation; Bears in the Night; The Bear Scouts; The Bike Lesson; The Bears' Picnic; Inside, Outside, Upside Down; Old Hat, New Hat; The Berenstain Bears and the Spooky Old Tree; He Bear, She Bear; C Is for Clown; The Berenstain Bears' B Book* (book titled *The B Book*); *The Big Honey Hunt;* and *The Bears' Christmas*, all 1986.

Books adapted for videocassette and released by Random House Home Video include *The Berenstain Bears Learn about Strangers; The Berenstain Bears Get in a Fight; The Berenstain Bears and the Truth; The Berenstain Bears and the Messy Room*, all 1988; *The Berenstain Bears in the Dark; The Berenstain Bears and Too Much Birthday; The Berenstain Bears and the Trouble with Friends; The Berenstain Bears: No Girls Allowed; The Berenstain Bears Get Stage Fright; The Berenstain Bears Forget Their Manners*, all 1989; *The Berenstain Bears and The Missing Dinosaur Bone* and *The Berenstain Bears' Christmas*, both 1990.

The Berenstain Bears Get in a Fight was adapted for CD-ROM by Living Books, 1995.

A Stanley and Janice Berenstain manuscript collection is housed at Syracuse University.

Elisabeth Beresford

Elisabeth Beresford and Wombles

It's very strange writing about myself when as a journalist and author I'm more used to writing about other people. Writing has taken me all round the world—up mountains, down silver mines, into jungles. And in a way this very interesting if topsy-turvy life began the day I was born. My mother, father and three elder brothers were living in Paris although our home was England. Father was quite a well-known novelist, and Paris was a great gathering place for writers and artists worldwide. What father did not know was that the law in France states that a baby *must* be registered at birth. So he was arrested and escorted to the local police station, where, he always said, he had a very pleasant afternoon playing cards and drinking wine. Honour satisfied, he was then escorted home again. Fortunately, my mother, a farsighted

woman, got the mayor of the local district to write a letter saying I had indeed arrived in the world and I had no birth certificate, this having got overlooked somewhere along the line during the "arrest." There were two consequences. The next day the English papers all carried the item "Baby daughter gaols author father," and the only proof I have that I do indeed exist is that now very creased letter from the mayor. Perhaps I could commit the perfect crime because who can judge and convict an "invisible" person?

Back in England our house was always full of books as Father also worked as a book reviewer for several newspapers. One room was set aside just for books, a kind of squirrel library, and as soon as I could read I was in there. And read everything. Some of the books

I now realise were *highly* unsuitable, but a child's mind can censor and discard what it is too young to absorb. And ever since, I've been a compulsive reader and cannot manage without a daily fix of print. Not long ago, staying in a friend's house in London, I discovered there wasn't a book, a magazine or a newspaper in the place. They were all out at work and I couldn't get round to the shops because a TV crew was due to arrive. There was TV and radio, but I wanted *print.* In desperation I rolled back some of the rugs in the conservatory and on my knees read the faded, dusty old newspapers underneath. The TV crew thought it was hilarious.

I started work as a shorthand typist in a big firm. My boss was Mr. H. S. Woodham, a wonderful elderly man who had been a war correspondent. My shorthand was wobbly, my typing worse. Father was dead by now and, alas, his fame with him, and Mother was taking in lodgers to earn a living. Money was very tight indeed, and we could only afford a six-month course at a secretarial college. It wasn't long enough! But one thing I could write perfectly in shorthand was "Dear Sir." Pencil poised over my new notebook I waited. Mr. Woodham began to dictate.

"George, you old devil you . . ."

Of course it was a disaster from the start. The other girls in the office would gather round, and I'd make the sounds of what appeared to be written down. Mr. Woodham, or Woody as he soon became known, was large, amazingly untidy and very overworked. He was a ghostwriter, specialising in writing speeches for the rich and famous. This great bear of a man in his rumpled suit could transform himself instantly into the celebrity for whom he was ghosting, such as a glamorous *woman* film star.

"As I was saying to my husband only the other evening . . . ," he would growl. I did my best, but it wasn't nearly good enough and it drove poor Woody to madness. Under his gruffness was a heart of pure marshmallow, and as my tears dripped onto the notebook he too got more and more upset. He'd been an admirer of my father and he knew our circumstances. Mother and I really needed my meagre salary. We'd already had the bailiffs in once. And then in stepped fate.

"Sweetheart," said Woody, "you'll never make a sec-er-tery. Let's see if we can teach you to be a journalist."

With her father, J. D. Beresford

And he began to train me. I was pretty bad at journalism to start with. Woody used to throw my work across the office roaring, "No no NO, you piecan!" (Whatever that is.) "Do it again. I want everything in the first line. You've got to make people want to read on. This is rubbish." And gradually I started to get a little better, although Woody still had to rewrite nearly everything. He gave me my own column, "Fashion, Food and the Family." It was circulated and sold to the provincial press, who fortunately didn't know me. Take fashion. I normally wore a very old raincoat. Now, you cannot go to an upmarket fashion show dressed like that. The fashion press were in competition with the models, believe me, so I had to smarten up a bit. Food? I could make toast and that was about it. But fortunately there were cookery experts out there who were only too keen to give you their exclusive recipes as long as you slid in the name of their margarine or flour or whatever. So I did. Family . . . total ignorance about children although I *had* been one myself. But I soon discovered there are toy manufacturers who will give you a very good lunch if you mention their latest doll.

A whole new world began to open up thanks to Woody, who then got me a film column—which I loved. Going to the press shows at ten-thirty in the morning was magic, although you don't feel too much like absorbing violence or romance at that hour. But I met a great many film stars—most of whom seemed to be a lot smaller than one had imagined. Then to top it all I was given a radio and TV column. Written, I have to admit, largely from press handouts, although I was sent to the apartment of one mega TV star of the time. "Come in darling," he called, "we'll do the interview in here. . . ." And we did too, although he happened to be in the bath at the time. Fortunately he stayed there.

My salary had doubled so it was now only semi-meagre, but thanks to Woody I was learning the trade of writing. If he didn't like what I'd written, he quite literally used to throw it at me, shout and then bang out of the office. Later he'd stump back in, glare at my rewrite and then take me out for a drink. He treated everybody the same, no matter who they were, and he had simplified his social code by calling everybody—regardless of background or gender—George.

One day as I thumped away at the ancient typewriter a very grand duchess arrived to have lunch with him. Woody, as usual surrounded by a sea of papers, newspapers and files, looked over the top of his spectacles at her and growled, "George—I'd like you to meet George."

Which was me. She didn't seem to mind.

All this was quite gentle domestic journalism, but Woody decided that it was time I went into deeper water and I was sent off to interview a group of politicians. They were all charming. Professionally charming, but when you read back what they had actually said, there was very little substance. A journalist friend of mine was covering a big political rally and beside him was an expert in sign language for those with hearing difficulties who could watch him on a special TV channel. The leader of the party was in full flow, but the expert slowed down and then stopped.

"Why?" my friend whispered.

"Because he's not saying anything," the expert replied.

Like Woody I became a ghostwriter, and it rather put me off politics even further when I read "my" speeches in print with hardly a word changed. If I could write them—anybody could. It wasn't my scene, and the only excitement was when I was sent to interview a very famous politician at home. Unfortunately, his secretary had forgotten to inform the man's wife. She obviously thought I was a dangerous character and called for help. The next second two very large policemen came out of the woodwork, and I was marched off with my feet literally not touching the ground.

It was about this time that I got married to a sports commentator. It was the classic situation—I'd been sent to interview him. "Let's get one thing straight from the start," he said, "you're not stopping work." And I didn't.

I left the firm (where they still had me on the books as a shorthand typist) but Woody retained me as a freelance and slowly other work began to come in. Journalism is a fascinating career because it plunges you straight into the centre of things, and if you keep your mouth shut and your ears open you can learn a lot. It also lands you in some funny situations. I was sent to interview a successful businessman who was a relation by marriage of the royal family. The exhibition where he was presenting his products was noisy so we finally did the interview in a small cupboard under the stairs. He didn't mind in the least.

A famous actor, a notorious womaniser, was appearing at the Oxford Playhouse, and we met in a small local radio studio. He was a dish (although smaller than I'd imagined . . .). We sat down on opposite sides of the table, the mike between us. The engineer gave us the "Go" signal from the outer studio. The actor leant round the side of the mike, fixed his very blue eyes on mine and smiled very, very gently. Everything went out of my head. I was like a transfixed rabbit. We did the interview eventually, but I was deeply unconscious for most of it.

By now I was also working as a freelance for the BBC, mostly for the radio side, starting with a fortnightly programme "Calling Newfoundland." It always began with the sound of seagulls and it wasn't easy living in the middle of London to find stories of interest for that faraway land. But if you need the money . . . you'll find the stories. The training as a radio reporter was curiously haphazard, and I'd been working for a top news programme for a couple of years—covering everything from strikes to

As a young reporter

sporting events—when some overworked news editor realised I hadn't been trained. It seemed a bit late in the day, but as a token gesture I was sent down to the sound engineers' section where they showed me exactly how to use the recording gear I'd been heaving round on assignments for some time. They also instructed me never, never to take it on public transport. It was something to do with insurance—so from then on I was hailing cabs all the way.

Then I became pregnant and nobody wants pale green women reporters at Lord Mayor's banquets, so for a while I stayed at home and wrote very romantic short stories for women's magazines—which I really enjoyed—and my first children's book, *The Television Mystery,* set in the studios I now knew so well. The publisher paid me fifty pounds outright, the agent took 10 percent and all the rest was mine. Well, the household's.

By this time we were living in a large old house in the London suburb of Wandsworth. Mother had moved in with us, and this worked very well as she was a superb cook and organiser,

although she was into her seventies. We also took in boarders so, when Kate was born, we were never short of baby-sitters, and there was always somebody to tell her good-night stories. One of our lodgers was a shy young advisor at the Foreign Office who became an ambassador years later, another was a young American actor who decamped without paying his rent but who left me a whole folder of photographs of himself, while a third was a Spanish airline pilot who met a beautiful girl on Victoria Railway Station and was never seen again. . . .

It was all great stuff for a writer and I absorbed it like a sponge. Some of our lodgers have remained friends to this day and are now highly respectable chairmen of companies and in one case a high court judge. But as young men—and young women—they got up to some real high jinks. Mother had a small bed-sitting-room at the back of the house and watched TV avidly every night, so she never heard a thing, and my husband was away a lot, so the lodgers hid from their creditors, slid girls up to their rooms, climbed out of bedroom windows and generally got away with murder. And at Sunday lunch, which we all had together in the big front dining room, they looked as if they were all Too Good to Be True.

Then Kate was joined by her brother, Marcus. Fortunately they got on very well together and whenever I could I took them with me on reporting jobs. They met all kinds of people and seemed to enjoy it all, and as Kate is now an editorial advisor and Marcus has his own very successful public relations company, obviously some of those early days of learning to meet people and adjust to all kinds of situations was good background. Then they used to refer to it as "Mum's workings. . . ."

My husband, who had once worked in Australia as a very young man, decided that he wanted to go back there for the Melbourne Olympics. He got himself a job as a commentator, I picked up a few commissions, we somehow got free seats on an airline and we were off. The flight seemed to take forever—it still does—and straightaway we were plunged into Olympic life in Melbourne. It was confusing but wonderful—and after winter in England beautifully warm. Somebody lent us an ancient Landrover and my husband was whisked away at once to start work and so was I . . . by one of my bosses in London who cabled from his magazine, *Cover Boxing*. I'd never been to a boxing match in my life, but fortunately a young photographer came to my rescue.

"You sit outside the arena," he said in his Australian drawl, "and I'll take the pickies. . . ."

He rushed out between rounds, dictated what he'd seen, I added a few bits of purple prose and it was all dispatched with the "pickies" and duly appeared under my byline. Which may make me the only invisible woman boxing commentator in the world.

No sooner was I back from that job than I was offered a trip to Broken Hill. In Australia the strange and magical "Outback" is always another one hundred miles away, so let's just say that Broken Hill is quite close to it. We certainly seemed to fly over quite a lot of empty space before we arrived and I was met and driven off to the famous silver mines. Having just about recovered from travelling a considerable distance at several thousand feet above ground, I was now plunged deep underground. Me and my trusty BBC recorder. The miners were friendly but not very talkative until I had the temerity to ask if mining was a well-paid job. To a man they banded together. Never mind that this tape was intended for BBC ears in Britain only. The foreman took me aside.

"We never say what we earn," he said in a low voice, just in case the mining shafts had ears, "because we don't tell the missus back at home. See?" I saw. He did whisper to me what he earned—about twenty-five times what I did.

Back in the sunny outside world again I was bundled off to the local radio station, which appeared to be run by one man. He met me, raced us up the studio where a record was playing, sat me down at the mike, did an interview, put on another record and saw me out.

A large, laconic man was waiting for me.

"The flying doctor says would you like to come out on a call. Now?"

Off down the dusty road, this time to a very small airstrip with a couple of hangers. I was decanted and he drove off. There didn't seem to be anybody about so I knocked on a hanger wall. A small man in white overalls looked at me without much enthusiasm.

"Ever pushed an aircraft?" he said.

I shook my head.

"Well, now's your chance to learn."

It's surprisingly easy once you're shown which bit to push. Out the small plane trundled just as the doctor arrived with his pilot. The pilot obviously didn't think much of taking an unknown female passenger on an emergency flight, so he ignored me. The doctor was elderly and very kind and gentle. As we settled in and fastened our seat belts, he told me he was going to pick up a jackeroo—a young farmhand—from a sheep station "only about a hundred miles from the outback . . ." It looked as if we were slap in the *middle* of the outback to me. We weren't flying very high and there was nothing . . . Once we saw a truck sending up a cloud of red dust. Later some kangaroos apparently playing some mysterious game of their own as they leapt round and round in a circle. A few dingoes. One house. Nothing. And then a shadowy mountain range began to take shape and we started to circle and for the first time it occurred to me that we were going to land on ordinary open ground. There was a farm vehicle, with a wind sock flying from its aerial, driving backwards and forwards to show the pilot the flattest piece of ground. Then it moved over to one side and stopped. I shut my eyes and the pilot made a perfect landing. We were driven to the sheep station, right by the foot of the mountains, and given a very warm, if laconic welcome.

The nineteen-year-old jackeroo was carried out on a stretcher by two of his mates. He had appendix trouble and had been told to pack for a stay in hospital at Broken Hill, but all he had with him was his most prized possession, a pair of brand-new, highly polished boots which he wasn't letting out of his sight. Once on board again the doctor asked me to talk to the boy, who was very worried indeed— not about the operation, but about going to a town for the first time in his life. I knelt beside him on the plane, holding his hand while he talked.

"Supposing after I've had the op and they let me out and I go walk about and get lost!" he said.

"You just stop and ask somebody in the street the way back."

His face cleared. The pilot had decided that I wasn't going to jinx the flight after all and he began to talk too, so it was quite a noisy flight back. About a week later, after a successful operation, the jackeroo sent me a photograph of himself, smiling away in his hospital bed with the matron, doctor and staff grouped round him. And perched on his stomach were—the boots.

Flying back to Melbourne on an ordinary humdrum domestic flight, the pilot came and sat with me. I lied and told him how sorry I was to be missing the closing ceremony of the Games—of which I had seen precious little—and he immediately said he'd do something about it. He did too. That big commercial plane, full of passengers, was diverted to fly twice over the stadium. I was exhausted, airsick and quite dirty as I waved, cheered and said thank-you over and over again.

Meanwhile, unknown to me, my enterprising husband had found a freelance cameraman with sound camera and a map. We were going to drive from Melbourne to Sydney, not by the usual coastal route but via the outback. It took us six days and into some most unusual places. We just drove, stopped when we saw something interesting, filmed and talked to anybody who happened to be passing by.

One of the most unusual places we stopped at was a town with a population of 128, twenty-four of whom were children plus *one* very lonely teenager. The big excitement was when a train came through every Thursday and everybody downed tools to go and see it. There was also an emu, a very large, rather truculent bird which had just wandered into town one day and decided to stay. There was only one dusty street and George, as the children christened the emu, used to wander moodily up and down. Sometimes he visited the local hotel where we were staying (it had two bedrooms and a very long bar). Then one day George laid an egg. The children gave it to me and a very old Aboriginal blew it and carved it. I have it still. The emu's name was changed to Georgina.

Wherever we went people made us welcome. One night we stayed with a millionaire land-owner who had two private planes, his own landing strip and silver taps on every bath and basin. Another night we were in a four-roomed "guest house." The owner looked at me and then took me aside.

"I can see you've got taste," she whispered. "You can use the special place."

She took me outside and led the way to a very small wooden hut, rather like a sentry box. It faced out across the great emptiness and it had three walls and a chain across the fourth open space.

"I don't let the fellas use it," she said, politely lifting the chain for me.

We saw the start of one of those terrifying bush fires when the wind just lifts a burning bush and carries it like a flaming torch. We'd been told always to carry wet sacks to douse anything that showed even a glowing ember and to never throw away cigarette ends. We chased after kangaroos who would leap alongside us in a friendly way and then suddenly get bored and accelerate effortlessly away. We saw koala bears nodding backwards and forwards high up in their gum trees, babies on their backs, flights of the most beautiful tropical birds, and sheep. The outback is a very large and empty place. And beautiful.

Sydney seemed overwhelming after that. My husband was working for Australian radio and television and I was sent off to do interviews, including at one point Surfers Paradise where the cameraman tried to teach me to surf. At first I seemed to spend a lot of time upside down deeply buried in a wave, but I've always loved swimming and the sea and at last managed to actually come in on a board, and then to come in on a board on a wave. Flat on the board, although I did manage to do a kind of crouch occasionally. It was fabulous. The real surfers were amazing to watch as they rode the enormous waves.

We spent Christmas with some kind strangers on a small farm on the edge of nowhere. It was very, very hot and dry, but we had turkey and Christmas pudding and mosquitoes with everything. I also couldn't quite get used to the fact that the abattoir was just across the yard from the kitchen. . . .

I loved Australia, but it was great to be back in England. Kate was a bit solemn, but we raced upstairs to where Marcus was standing up in his cot. He gave me a suspicious look.

"Who are you?" he said.

"I'm your mother, you fool," I said and burst into tears.

The Australian adventure was, of course, turned into a children's book, *The Flying Doctor Mystery,* and into a TV series *Seven Days to Sydney.* It had been made on a tiny budget and we linked the film live in the TV studios. There were six half-hour weekly shows and, much to the BBC's surprise, I think, they were a great success.

There was a lot of fan mail which all had to be answered, but it did lead to me being

Assorted Wombles

asked to go and talk to children in schools and libraries. It was about then that I realised that the atmosphere in a school depends largely on the head teacher. You can go into some really run-down and poor neighbourhoods where the school buildings are a hundred years old and show it. But if the head teacher has enthusiasm and discipline, the children will be happy, bright and well-behaved.

If there was an incipient troublemaker at the back I'd say, "I wonder if you would come and help me?" and get that child to the front to hold up the famous emu egg or the stills. Once the child had a legitimate reason for being in the spotlight, he or she would behave perfectly. At one school in a really rough neighbourhood where a large percentage of the population was black and unemployed, one small ten-year-old said, "'Ere, Miss. How old you then?"

"As old as my tongue and a little older than my teeth."

He dug his friend in the ribs with one sharp elbow and said in a loud aside, "That makes her pretty ancient then."

Afterwards, when they were all crowding round asking for autographs on those crumpled bits of paper children produce by magic, the boy put his wrist against mine and gazed up with liquid eyes.

"'Ere, Miss. Aren't you a lovely colour then?"

He's a minicab driver now and if he hears me on the radio he calls up the studio at once to say "Hallo."

The year after Australia we were off again, this time to South America and the West Indies, with a new cameraman, Dave. We had a few introductions, maps, a sound camera and this time the good wishes of the BBC. My job was sound recordist (ten minutes' training), clapper *boy*, continuity *girl*, interviewer and general gofer. That is, Go for this, Go for that. It was also my job to label all the cans of films and to get them through customs. Not an easy job on some of the smaller islands where the customs men could be highly suspicious of us. When this happened Dave and my husband faded into the woodwork and left me to it. I employed the "helpless" bit quite a lot, gazing at the customs officials and saying with a deep sigh, "I wonder if you could help me?"

And they often did.

As usual we interviewed everybody in sight. Children sang for us. Steel bands played for us on the streets, on the endless palm-fringed beaches, on the sweet corn plantations. And politicians made speeches. I had to interview one on my own. Dave got him sitting on a bench with a beautiful, tropical floral background, I snapped the clapperboard in front of the camera, raced to the bench with the mike, identified the shot for the sound tape, started the stopwatch and turned, a little breathlessly, to do the interview. The politician, who had been watching all this with his mouth open, just started to laugh. It was hopeless, we all three cracked up into hysterical laughter. Eventually we had to wait for my husband to get back to do the interview, because every time I snapped the board, started to run . . . one of us would go off into hysterics.

We were all three totally overworked, but it was worth it for the experience, and we got some wonderful material because we weren't intimidating. Ridiculous perhaps . . . but we had our priorities right. One night in a hotel bedroom, typing desperately at my continuity notes, I was dimly aware of a distant rumble and then the dressing table tilted and the type-writer slid away. I caught it just before it fell.

"Earthquake!" said my husband.

"Don't be silly, I haven't got time," I said and resumed typing.

At one point we travelled on a very old, very dirty cargo boat. I stayed firmly on deck. The captain came aboard. He was wearing a straw hat, a blinding floral shirt, grey trousers and no shoes. He slapped up the greasy deck, a large cigar in one corner of his mouth, waved and smiled at me and called for a tea for both of us. Just before he reached the wheel-house a whole family of rats came running out of it and vanished below decks. A stoker brought the mugs of tea.

"No spoon," he said with a dazzling smile, "so never mind," and stirred my tea for me with one oily finger.

There was no harbour on this particular island, so we moored off it. Small boats rowed out and for the last few yards we were carried ashore on the shoulders of large, smiling island ladies. There was no electricity and the

With Womble Marble Arch, at the great Womble reunion, London, 1994

one guest house was lit by gas. There were two permanent lodgers and one of them turned out to be the cousin of the BBC producer to whom I was sending back tapes. There were no roads either, just tracks, but it didn't matter because there was only one vehicle. Known as a "v-hickle," it was a kind of open truck.

There was an election in progress on this very small island with its very, very small population. Our driver had an enormous loudspeaker strapped to the bonnet of the truck and he was longing to use it. Up the mountain track we bounced, not a soul in sight, and then as we rounded the top a very large, yellow-eyed goat appeared out of the dust. The driver slammed on the brakes, picked up his mike and addressed the goat in a voice which rico-cheted round the mountain pass.

"Vote!" he roared. "Come out in your numbers and VOTE!"

I often wondered if it did.

Filming in South America was quite different because of the enormous distances we had to cover. Quite often there was thick jungle and no roads, so it was either by river launch or seaplane. We chugged down the vast, slow Orinoco River and it made such an impression on me that, years later, when I wrote the Wombles, one of the favourite characters was called Orinoco because he's fat and lethargic. We took off in a small seaplane to fly to the Kaieteur Falls. Never very good at air travel at the best of times, I had my eyes shut as we approached the enormous waterfall—twice as high as Niagara, with a complete circular rainbow dancing in the spray which flew up hundreds of feet into the air. There was a tremendous updraft and our small plane shot upwards.

"Didn't get that right," Dave shouted to the pilot. He was filming out of a side window. "Go round again, will you?"

So we did, buffeted round the sky as though we weighed nothing. The pilot made a perfect landing just over the lip of the falls, and from a clearing in the jungle two Amerindians rowed out to us in a very basic canoe. It was nice to be back on firm ground, but we had to hurry to get the filming done before the light went. We left most of the gear at the hut in the clearing and then set out in single file with an Amerindian guide leading the way. He was carrying a very large and ancient gun. Dave reckoned it was well over a hundred years old and was probably quite incapable of being fired, but it had a comforting feel, especially as "something" was obviously keeping in step with us in the jungle.

It was about a mile to the open space at the top of the falls and the view was spectacular. The water was the colour of Coca-Cola and it moved surprisingly slow until it reached the lip and then roared into space. I was aware that the three men were huddled together looking worried. My husband came over to where I was lying on a slab of rock taking photographs.

"We've got to go back for some gear," he shouted, "so we'll leave you here to look after the rest of the stuff. Shan't be long . . ." And off they went towards that dark, cavernous hole in the jungle. The guide suddenly came loping back to me. He sounded concerned.

"Me see alligator in the river," he said pointing to the placid brown water. "But you no bother alligator and he no bother you. . . ."

And he was gone. I am probably the best non-alligator botherer in the entire world. I sat very, very still and wrote picture postcards to all my family. . . .

"Come to the Caribbean" was another six-week BBC-TV series for children. Again we linked it live in the studio, which is quite an alarming experience, but we were in with the bosses because we were popular and we didn't cost a lot. I wrote another children's book based on some of our adventures, *Gappy Goes West,* and my husband began to plan ahead for another TV series. We were really getting into the swing of things. Life was on the up.

Never believe that, as fate is always hanging round in the wings and on this occasion took on the shape of the union who had, apparently, been watching us for some time. The union put its foot down. Take me for instance. I was doing at least six people out of their jobs: clapper boy, scriptwriter, continuity girl, sound recordist, gofer, interviewer . . . let alone tea maker, wardrobe mistress, makeup girl, etc., etc. We were lucky to have got away with it for so long.

These days I think the pendulum has swung too far. Not long ago I was working with a TV unit on the small English Channel Island of Alderney. There were nineteen people in the unit, most of whom had never worked together before. They were lovely people—they seemed to spend a lot of time drinking coffee in my kitchen—but the unit was so cumbersome. They had three buses for a start, not for them the back of one old van. I'd set up interviews with fishermen, the lighthouse keeper on a small island inhabited only by puffins, the amateur railway and some of the local government members . . . it was a disaster. Getting everybody together and then setting up all the gear took forever. They were four hours at the lighthouse to get two minutes of film. The principal lighthouse keeper, a charming, even-tempered man, wouldn't speak to me for a month.

So for my husband it was back to sports commentating and for me books and journalism. I was writing up to three children's books a year and even ventured into the romantic novels market. The money was miserable, but I enjoyed writing them and I sometimes wondered if the editors even bothered to read them—they just sold them like jars of coffee. Never mind the novels paid the school bills and we gradually eased out of taking in lodgers.

By sheer luck I got offered a job by an independent company to make two radio "magazine" programmes a month. The producer was a very professional, very pretty girl called Chrissy, and it didn't take us long to get everything wrapped up just the way we wanted it. A charity show at the Savoy? *Just* what the programme wanted. An open day at a ducal palace? We were off. A press reception for an American TV star? There we were. The *Queen Elizabeth II* was in for a refit—Chrissy and I were on the boat train. Some of our male colleagues who were trudging round interviewing industrialists in offices in Birmingham and Manchester used to get a bit upset, but as most of them had a very soft spot for Chrissy she only had to shake her blonde curls at them and the grumbling stopped.

Chrissy and I interviewed all kinds of people, including Mrs. Thatcher as she then was—twice. And the strange thing is I have no memory of it at all. But I do remember the militant fishermen's wives who were determined to get a better business deal for their husbands. With placards held over their heads they invaded a government department. The pressmen were after them and we stood no chance of getting a reasonable interview until we got the girls into the ladies' cloakroom. We were getting some good stuff when the men worked out where we were and tried to break the door down. We got it all on tape.

I was on my own on the day when permission finally came through to record some background noises at the one-thousand-year-old Tower of London. One of the sounds we really wanted was the "cawing" of the famous Ravens of the Tower. There were five or six of these large, coal-black birds strutting up and down under the shadow of the house where Anne Boleyn, wife of Henry VIII, had once been held prisoner. Between the birds and me was a small lawn and a chain-link fence. A yeoman warder gallantly lifted the fence and I crawled underneath it with my recorder. Very cautiously on hands and knees I approached the birds, which eyed me sideways and hopped about a bit but wouldn't make a sound. I got the mike right up to them and as an encouragement began to "caw" myself. They hopped even more but remained mute. I cawed even louder. No response. So in the end I switched off, turned round and saw at least a hundred American tourists pressed against the fence and furiously clicking their cameras. They even gave me a round of applause as, scarlet in the face, I crawled back across the perfect turf.

About a month later Alan, one of the senior sound engineers, stopped me in the canteen.

"Thought you'd like to know," he said. "That Raven recording you got in the Tower. It's so good it's gone into archives."

I opened my mouth to explain, but not a single sound came out. Not even a "caw." I heard "the ravens" only recently on a radio programme. It's not bad.

By the time Kate was in her teens I'd written about fifty or sixty books, including a whole series with a modern magic background. I really enjoyed writing these as you could make anything happen in a perfectly ordinary setting. Some of them were published in America, Germany, France, Spain, Sweden, Finland and so on. Publishers, as they always do, kept asking for something "new." As the school fees were still coming in, I kept promising that I would . . .

That particular Christmas, apart from having my now quite elderly mother in the house, we also had my husband's parents, so I seemed to spend a lot of time getting Kate and Marcus to keep the noise down. They were very good, but by 26 December they had steam coming out of their ears. We got into my Mini and drove to Wimbledon Common a few miles away.

"Let it all go . . ." I said.

There was nobody else in sight. We parked near the famous old windmill and before us stretched the beautiful, undulating, deserted Common. The three of us ran up and down screaming at the top pitch of our lungs. All that keeping quiet for three days was let free and one of the children came panting up to me and said, "Oh Ma, isn't it great on Wimbledon Common. . . ?"

And I said, "That's where the Wombles live . . ."

As soon as we got home I typed out a list of Womble characters, taking their names out of the old atlas that belonged to my grandfather a hundred years ago. There was the patriarch of the Wombles, Great-Uncle Bulgaria (who later in the books and films bore a very strong resemblance to my father-in-law and was not unlike him in character), full name Bulgaria Coburg Womble, because my mother loved European royalty. Madame Cholet, the world-famous Womble cook, was based on my mother. Her family came originally from France and she was the best cook I've ever known, and Kate had been on a school exchange to the small French town of Cholet. The greedy, lazy Orinoco was named after a certain river (and based on another member of my family). Tobermory is the spitting image of my brother Aden—a very clever and inventive scientist who worked for a time as an attaché to the British ambassador in Washington, and who, the week after he retired and long after the Womble books and films had been made, left England with his wife and family and went to live on the Isle of Mull—just a few miles from Tobermory. . . .

The short, fat, furry Wombles in their comfortable burrow underneath Wimbledon Common were rather ahead of the times. Their motto is Make Good Use of Bad Rubbish because they can't bear waste of any kind. They were recycling long before human beings had got round to it—in fact, their opinion of people is pretty low altogether. It was an idea that caught on with children who began organising "Womble Clearing Up Groups" and when the first five-minute films appeared on BBC-TV the Wombles' popularity grew and grew. It was a combination of many things. Bernard Cribbins, the actor, did the voices beautifully. Ivor Wood, a master puppetmaker, produced little works of art, and Mike Batt wrote the popular music, which was played all over the world. The producer/director Graham Clutterbuck masterminded everything. Including me. I sold my scripts outright forever and ever at fifty pounds each. It sounds as if I needed my head examined but at the start none of us quite realised what was happening and by the time we did— it was too late. Some people laughed all the way to the bank. I just kept on working.

The press parked themselves outside our house. There were threatening phone calls from people actually called "Wombell," the fan mail came in by the sack, I got a couple of death threats from loonies, and there were moments when I felt as if I too was going quite mad.

As a station master of the local Alderney railway

A Japanese professor of English came to see me. He had a sheaf of papers all about the Wombles. He was very polite. After several bows he said, "Character of Great-Uncle Bulgaria is based on that of great philosopher Doctor Johnson. Yes?"

"Well, not really . . . ," I began feebly. The professor wasn't having any. He'd written a *paper* on the subject and was about to deliver it at a university conference.

One of the aides of a certain United States president came knocking on the door.

"Mr. President would like you to know that he himself is very fond of Madame Cholet. . . ."

There were live phone-ins with children in Australia and I seemed to be forever travelling, quite often with a walking, talking Womble. These were known as Rent-a-Wombles and were usually very small schoolteachers who were used to controlling crowds, because a lot of people used to turn up at public appearances. Ten thousand turned up when four Wombles and I together with some rangers were supposed to be starting a "clean up" campaign in the New Forest in Hampshire. The crowd went mad and we took to our heels and ended up in a ranger's hut, and I had four really scared (small) schoolteachers attached to me like burrs. We were glad to get out of that one.

Twice I was asked to South Africa to talk to children. Once the organisers have got you on their schedules they really work you hard, and quite often I had no idea where I was or, indeed, where I'd been. But one location did stick firmly in my mind. It was a Zulu Township and a thousand *adult* Zulus turned up at the hall. The place was crammed with just me and a librarian called Michael on the platform. It seemed like madness to be talking about the Wombles of Wimbledon to these tall, dignified people. But everybody likes to be told a story so I launched into recounting some of the scripts with the Wombles transformed into humans. There wasn't a sound. At the end of thirty minutes I was exhausted so I bowed, said thank-you and stepped back. We then discovered something which was quite new to us. If Zulus like you they give you a high-pitched call from the back of the throat and advance slowly, right arm up as if they are throwing a spear. One thousand of them.

"What do we do now?" I said desperately.

"Retreat," said Michael, grabbing my skirt, "step by step. . . ."

We did too.

Another quite different occasion was when the pride of the Royal Navy, HMS *Ark Royal*, aircraft carrier, was having a refit in a west country port and I was asked on board as a guest of the captain, officers and crew. It was an evening party and they politely informed me that as they would all be wearing their number one uniforms perhaps I too could be formally dressed? At exactly half-past seven a very smart lieutenant commander arrived at my hotel. I swished out in a long skirt and evening jacket, evening bag under my arm, and we drove through the dark to the docks. The enormous bulk of the *Ark Royal* was framed against the night sky and for the first time it dawned on me that I wasn't going on board a luxury liner but a fighting ship, up quite a flimsy looking ladder thing. In an evening skirt? I turned to my escort.

"How do you feel about carrying a ladies' handbag?" I said huskily.

"No trouble at all, Ma'am," he said and took off his gold braided cap, put my handbag inside it and folded it neatly under his arm. I fell in love with the entire Royal Navy at that moment.

We were piped on board and led down echoing, half-repaired companion ways to the captain's quarters. He was waiting for me with some of his officers and a couple of stewards in his dayroom. I knew that I was working with a Rent-a-Womble, but there was no sign of him. Drinks were handed round and we all made very polite but rather awkward conversation until a somewhat strangulated voice from outside said, "Someone to see you, Sir."

"Show him in," ordered the captain.

And into the dayroom stepped Great-Uncle Bulgaria. Everything stopped—the captain half out of his chair, the steward with a bottle raised, an officer about to have a drink. We were like waxworks. GUB shuffled forward, got me in his sights and held out his furry white arms. He said one word, "Mother!"

We fell into each others' arms, both of us trembling, and everything came back to life. All of them, officers and men, collapsed with laughter. It turned into a great party.

But the real point of the evening were hundreds and hundreds of sailors gathered on the flight deck with a very large Marine band. And a recording unit. The crew were going to make a disc with "We Are Sailing" on one side

The author with some of her books and manuscripts

and the Wombles theme song, "Underground, Overground Wombling Free," on the other. And what *I* didn't know was that this particular Rent-a-Womble was a (small) music teacher. Still holding my arm for support and with the captain leading us, we came out onto the floodlit flight deck. It was quite a sight. The sailors clapped, shouted, waved their sheet music and drummed their heels. Great-Uncle Bulgaria eyed them solemnly, let go of my arm and shuffled over to the conductor of the Royal Marine Band, who was standing there with his mouth open. With great politeness the Womble took away his baton and moved up onto the conductor's platform. He tapped the music stand and looked round slowly. There was complete silence on the flight deck. Very slowly the old Womble raised both paws and then down came the baton. He conducted beautifully. The band played, the crew sang their hearts out. I think I cried.

In the ten years that the Wombles were at their peak I wrote over twenty Womble books, another thirty TV shows (I got paid seventy-five pounds outright this time) and a Womble stage show, one version of which ran in the West End of London. You could buy anything from Womble soap to T-shirts to mugs to washing-up cloths. A company was formed to deal with all this and the strange thing was that the other directors were going to conferences in the South of France and I was either talking to children or glued to my typewriter. And there were Womble pirates everywhere. A factory would start up one week making soft toys and by the time our lawyer got there it would have shut down and reopened somewhere else. The pirate toys were so badly made that furious parents would write to me and threaten to sue because their child had swallowed a Womble nose.

I was asked for a quote for a very famous book of quotations and with some feeling I wrote back:

Build a better mousetrap and every rat in
the world will beat a pathway to your door.

At this time I had in a way crossed a kind of divide because now the journalists were interviewing me. And I saw them all because you remember what it's like when you're scrambling after a story and you really need that job. Not a great many of them would have passed Woody's accuracy test! And oddly enough it was often the most prestigous publications that made the most mistakes. Maybe deliberately to get a "good" story. The really good journalists were the ones who rang back and checked their copy with me. It makes you very suspicious of what you read in the press. Take at least a dessert spoon of salt with it.

Slowly the excitement and the interest began to die down and I went on to write other books for children, many of them based on the small island of Alderney in the English Channel, my new home. Alderney is only 3½ miles long by 1½ miles across at its widest. The streets are cobbled, my house is nearly three hundred years old and none of the walls are straight, which drives very tidy people wild. The population is about 2,400, of whom 400 are children. I believe we have one of the highest birth rates in the United Kingdom. A national newspaper rang recently and asked me to comment on it.

"It's our pleasant climate and all those beautiful girls. . . ." I said. The journalist snorted and rang off.

There's a harbour, beautiful (very cold) unpolluted sea, lovely beaches, a tiny airport with tiny planes called Trilanders. And if you're very lucky you may get to sit beside the pilot (there's a crew of one and he's it) and wear the headphones. England is forty minutes' flying time and France twenty if you're going direct. The island's history is "interesting." Smuggling was the best way to earn a living for hundreds of years. And old customs die hard. But the other side of the coin is that we have very little crime. A child can talk to strangers or go out exploring. People don't bother to lock their doors—how could a neighbour leave you some still warm, newly laid eggs if unable to get to your kitchen table? And if the weather suddenly closes in, a car tours round with loudspeakers appealing for beds for the night for stranded travellers.

There is always something going on. Writing an article for a magazine I discovered that there are forty-three clubs and societies. You can learn anything—from art to yoga, boxing to deep-sea diving. It is in fact a great place for a writer to live.

Altogether I've written between 130 and 140 books and I don't know how many TV scripts and articles. Children often tell me about my books—they know more about them than I do and they can be pretty blunt about what they don't like. It's a great way to earn a living. One of my island friends is over eighty and she's a reporter and a very good one too, because she's accurate. She asked me recently what my favourite book was out of the 130 plus. And I think it has to be *Lizzy's War* (1992), sequel forthcoming. It is based absolutely on my own experiences as an evacuee during the war. Perhaps writers don't invent, they just adapt.

But that's another story.

BIBLIOGRAPHY

FOR CHILDREN

Fiction:

The Television Mystery, Parrish, 1957.

The Flying Doctor Mystery, Parrish, 1958.

Trouble at Tullington Castle, Parrish, 1958.

Cocky and the Missing Castle, illustrated by Jennifer Miles, Constable, 1959.

Gappy Goes West, Parrish, 1959.

The Tullington Film-Makers, Parrish, 1960.

Two Gold Dolphins, illustrated by Peggy Fortnum, Constable (London), 1961, Bobbs Merrill (Indianapolis), 1964.

Danger on the Old Pull 'n Push, Parrish, 1962.

Strange Hiding Place, Parrish, 1962.

Diana in Television, Collins, 1963.

The Missing Formula Mystery, Parrish, 1963.

The Mulberry Street Team, illustrated by Juliet Pannett, Friday Press, 1963.

Awkward Magic, illustrated by Judith Valpy, Hart Davis (London), 1964, as *The Magic World,* Bobbs Merrill, 1965.

The Flying Doctor to the Rescue, Parrish, 1964.

Holiday for Slippy, illustrated by Pat Williams, Friday Press, 1964.

Game, Set, and Match, Parrish, 1965.

The Hidden Mill, illustrated by Margery Gill, Benn (London), 1965, Meredith Press (New York), 1967.

Knights of the Cardboard Castle, illustrated by C. R. Evans, Methuen, 1965.

Travelling Magic, illustrated by Judith Valpy, Hart Davis, 1965, as *The Vanishing Garden,* Funk and Wagnalls (New York), 1967.

Peter Climbs a Tree, illustrated by Margery Gill, Benn, 1966.

The Black Mountain Mystery, Parrish, 1967.

Fashion Girl, Collins, 1967.

Looking for a Friend, illustrated by Margery Gill, Benn, 1967.

The Island Bus, illustrated by Robert Hodgson, Methuen, 1968.

Sea-Green Magic, illustrated by Ann Tout, Hart Davis, 1968.

The Wombles, illustrated by Margaret Gordon, Benn, 1968, Meredith Press, 1969.

David Goes Fishing, illustrated by Imre Hofbauer, Benn, 1969.

Gordon's Go-Kart, illustrated by Margery Gill, Benn, 1970.

Stephen and the Shaggy Dog, illustrated by Robert Hales, Methuen, 1970.

Vanishing Magic, illustrated by Ann Tout, Hart Davis, 1970.

The Wandering Wombles, illustrated by Oliver Chadwick, Benn, 1970.

Dangerous Magic, illustrated by Oliver Chadwick, Hart Davis, 1972.

The Invisible Womble and Other Stories, illustrated by Ivor Wood, Benn, 1973.

The Secret Railway, illustrated by James Hunt, Methuen, 1973.

The Wombles in Danger, Benn, 1973.

The Wombles at Work, illustrated by Margaret Gordon, Benn, 1973.

Invisible Magic, illustrated by Reg Gray, Hart Davis, 1974.

The Wombles Go to the Seaside, World Distributors, 1974.

Orinoco Runs Away, illustrated by Margaret Gordon, Benn, 1975.

The Snow Womble, illustrated by Margaret Gordon, Benn, 1975.

Snuffle to the Rescue, illustrated by Gunvor Edwards, Kestrel, 1975.

Tomsk and the Tired Tree, illustrated by Margaret Gordon, Benn, 1975.

Wellington and the Blue Balloon, illustrated by Margaret Gordon, Benn, 1975.

The Wombles Gift Book, illustrated by Margaret Gordon, Benn, 1975.

The Wombles Make a Clean Sweep, illustrated by Ivor Wood, Benn, 1975.

The Wombles to the Rescue, illustrated by Margaret Gordon, Benn, 1975.

Bungo Knows Best, illustrated by Margaret Gordon, Benn, 1976.

The MacWomble's Pipe Band, illustrated by Margaret Gordon, Benn, 1976.

Madame Cholet's Picnic Party, illustrated by Margaret Gordon, Benn, 1976.

Tobermory's Big Surprise, illustrated by Margaret Gordon, Benn, 1976.

The Wombles Go round the World, illustrated by Margaret Gordon, Benn, 1976.

The World of the Wombles, illustrated by Edgar Hodges, World Distributors, 1976.

Secret Magic, illustrated by Caroline Sharpe, Hart Davis, 1978.

Toby's Luck, illustrated by Doreen Caldwell, Methuen, 1978.

Wombling Free, illustrated by Edgar Hodges, Benn, 1978.

The Happy Ghost, illustrated by Joanna Carey, Methuen, 1979.

Curious Magic, illustrated by Claire Upsdale-Jones. Granada (London), 1980, Elsevier Nelson, 1980.

The Treasure Hunters, illustrated by Joanna Carey, Methuen (London), 1980, Elsevier Nelson (New York), 1980.

The Four of Us, illustrated by Trevor Stubley, Hutchinson, 1981.

The Animals Nobody Wanted, illustrated by Joanna Carey, Methuen, 1982.

The Tovers, illustrated by Geoffrey Beitz, Methuen, 1982.

The Adventures of Poon, illustrated by Dinah Shedden, Hutchinson, 1984.

The Mysterious Island, illustrated by Joanna Carey, Methuen, 1984.

One of the Family, illustrated by Barrie Thorpe, Hutchinson, 1985.

The Ghosts of Lupus Street School, Methuen, 1986.

Strange Magic, illustrated by Cathy Wood, Methuen, 1986.

Emily and the Haunted Castle, illustrated by Kate Rogers, Hutchinson, 1987.

Once upon a Time Stories, illustrated by Alice Englander, Methuen, 1987.

The Secret Room, illustrated by Michael Bragg, Methuen, 1987.

The Armada Adventure, Methuen, 1988.

The Island Railway, illustrated by Maggie Harrison, Hamish Hamilton, 1988.

Charlie's Ark, Methuen, 1989.

Rose, Hutchinson, 1989.

The Wooden Gun, Hippo, 1989.

Tim the Trumpet, Blackie, 1992.

Jamie and the Rola Polar Bear, illustrated by Janet Robertson, Blackie, 1993.

Lizzy's War, illustrated by James Mayhew, Simon & Schuster, 1993.

Lizzy's War, Part 2, illustrated by James Mayhew, Macdonald Young Books, 1995.

Rola Polar Bear and the Heatwave, illustrated by Janet Robertson, Blackie, 1995.

The Smallest Whale, illustrated by Susan Field, Orchard Books, 1996.

Other:

The Wombles (screenplay), 1971.

The Wombles (play), adaptation of her own stories (produced London, 1974).

The Wombles Annual 1975–1978, World Distributors, 4 vols., 1974–77.

Jack and the Magic Stove (folktale), illustrated by Rita van Bilsen, Hutchinson, 1982.

Also author of sixty television scripts for *The Wombles* series, from 1973.

FOR ADULTS

Fiction:

Paradise Island, Hale, 1963.

Escape to Happiness, Hale (London), 1964, Nordon (New York), 1980.

Roses round the Door, Hale, 1965, Paperback Library (New York), 1965.

Island of Shadows, Hale, 1966, Dale (New York), 1980.

A Tropical Affair, Hale, 1967, as *Tropical Affairs,* Dell (New York), 1978.

Veronica, Hale, 1967, Nordon, 1980.

Saturday's Child, Hale, 1968, as *Echoes of Love,* Dell, 1979.

Love Remembered, Hale, 1970, Dale, 1978.

Love and the S.S. Beatrice, Hale, 1972, as *Thunder of Her Heart,* Dale, 1978.

Pandora, Hale, 1974.

The Silver Chain, Hale, 1980.

The Steadfast Lover, Hale, 1980.

The Restless Heart, Valueback, 1982.

Flight to Happiness, Hale, 1983.

A Passionate Adventure, Hale, 1983.

Other:

With Nick Renton, *Road to Albutal* (play, produced Edinburgh, 1976).

With Peter Spence, *Move On,* BBC Publications, 1978.

The Best of Friends (play, produced in the Channel Islands, 1982).

Ann Cameron

1943-

Ann Cameron, in her backyard with her cat, Jane, Panajachel, Guatemala, 1989

I was a child who loved books. In children's fiction, characters talked about things we never talked about at home—why people did evil, how they felt inside, what their dreams were. Authors were so wise! How could they know so much? They seemed to know everything. They got their names on their books and they were famous. Through their books they were everywhere; but at the same time, I had never actually seen one: authors were magnificent, unseen, unknown, floating somewhere above life, almost like God . . . just the way I wanted to be, one day.

As I grew up I discovered that everybody—author or not—learns his wisdom bit by bit,

right here on earth—and sometimes painfully. For most people, including authors, being a happy person isn't always easy. As the poet Wallace Stevens said, "Happiness is an achievement."

By learning, working, thinking, we can reach a point where we have something valuable to share with others—even if we had to walk a painful road to get there. Having wisdom and learning we can share is a great source of happiness.

Each person's life is really his own experimental work of art. Since the "life artist" begins with absolutely no training and doesn't even know that he's an artist, the work can look pretty messy. Sometimes, you wonder if it's going anywhere at all. My stories are about "life artists"—their mistakes and turning points and successes on the road to being who they want to be. I try to take what I've learned and am learning to shape the story. My characters aren't perfect, but they are generally hopeful and courageous. I try to fill my stories with their energy—so it can pour out to my readers and help them to maintain their own courage, pride, and hope. I want my characters to overcome, to make their lives as good as they can possibly be. I want the same for my readers, and for me.

I was born in Rice Lake, Wisconsin, in the middle of a blizzard at 3:30 P.M. on the 21st of October, 1943.

My family—my father and mother and sister, my grandfather and I—lived west of town in an old farmhouse on a hill. We owned forty acres of land around the farmhouse. Almost as soon as I could walk I wandered all over those forty acres—inspecting cows and horses, crouching in the grass and watching it close like a roof above me. To the west, beyond our land, fields rolled away to the horizon, the shadows of clouds marching swiftly across them like invisible armies.

Except for my sister, Jennifer, who was six years older than I and usually didn't want to play with me, I didn't have any playmates. For entertainment, I used to go out to the edge of the road at sunset, sit on the rough sawhorse that supported the mailbox, and count the cars that passed by. When no cars came, I would stare west at the darkening horizon, wondering what lay beyond it. How far did the world stretch? Would I ever see the unknown lands to which the sun was traveling?

The excitement I felt about the land beyond the horizon as a young child is very much like the exhilaration and expectancy I feel now when I write stories. Inside my head I sense a world magnificent and free, not yet defined. It is mine alone. Only I will be able to discover its people and its glories. Perhaps my early childhood roaming in the fields made me love solitude, freedom, and creation.

My Swedish grandfather, Oscar Lofgren, was the dearest companion of my childhood. When I was six months old, he saved my life. My parents were out. It was evening, a time when he usually left me sleeping in my crib. But that night for some reason he chose to wake me up, take me downstairs, and play with me.

A half hour later, the heavy plaster ceiling in my bedroom fell, huge chunks of it smashing down onto my crib. Thanks to my grandpa, I was not in it. Why did he move me that night, when he never had before? Perhaps he had a premonition—a feeling there was something he must do even if he didn't know why. Sometimes heeding a premonition may be essential to our survival. But where does the premonition come from? Does our environment send us messages? Or do our own minds have capacities we don't really understand?

My grandfather had trained to be a blacksmith in Sweden. At age sixteen, he had emigrated to the United States and set up a blacksmith shop in Cameron, Wisconsin, a town of three hundred people seven miles south of Rice Lake. When he retired and came to live with my parents, he set up his shop again on our land in a building we called "the monkey house." Every day I went to see him there I hoped to see monkeys; but I was always disappointed. Only when I was much older did I realize the monkey house was my grandpa's workshop for monkeying around making things.

I spent hours watching him at the forge. Over its coals, the iron turned red and then white-hot. Sparks flew as he shaped it on the anvil. My grandfather was a carpenter, too; he made a playhouse for my sister and me, with handmade wrought-iron hinges and latches, a cedar-shingled roof, and a screened porch with canvas shades that could close tight against the rain. When I was older and other kids had moved near us, the best thing about the playhouse was daring ourselves to jump off its roof, flying free for an instant before we crashed to earth.

In the forties, nobody in our world had TV (we got a TV when I was nine). At age three and four I liked to lie for hours on the living-room rug listening to soap operas on the radio. The radio was enormous, a huge stand-up Stromberg-Carlson much taller than I. My favorite soap operas were "Our Gal Sunday," whose eternal question was: "Can a girl from a little mining town in the West find happiness as the wife of England's richest, most handsome lord, Lord Henry Brinthrop?" and "The Romance of Helen Trent." More exciting and affirmative, "The Romance of Helen Trent" was heralded by a deep-voiced announcer who explained that romance in life was never over and that Helen's story proved "life begins at forty." The announcer convinced me. Listening intently to the adventures of Helen and her boyfriend, Gil, I could hardly wait to be forty. In fact, in first grade I decided not to wait, to just go ahead right then and marry a wonderful boy named Wayne Emerson. Unfortunately the wedding we planned was delayed, and Wayne moved away.

More puzzling than matrimony was the ultimate secret of Helen and Gil's life. I could see how they and all their friends and enemies could be living inside the enormous radio, but I never could figure out how and when they got their food in.

From my grandpa I learned that disobedience was possible—as vital a thing to learn in life as the virtue of obedience. I can still hear him protesting, "Nay, child, nay!" as I climbed from a chair to a high counter to stand and reach the jar that held my mother's homemade cookies. When I kept climbing, I was amazed that he didn't stop me or punish me.

My grandpa's indoor territory was the end room in the house, the laundry room next to the garage. There he brought in firewood for the wood stove and ironed sheets for my mother in a press called a mangle. I hardly remember his ever being in the rest of the house. Many times I ran to his chair when I was in trouble with my parents, rushing into his arms. Where my grandpa was, was goodness, love, sanctuary.

He died when I was six. I saw him in the hospital once before his death. I hugged him very hard to show him how much I loved him, and my mother told me not to. He was frail, and my hug could hurt him. I didn't go to his funeral, but I knew what death meant. I would never see him again. He would never come back, never. I pictured him alone in a tiny boat, rowing toward Heaven. He could not turn back to look at us. He had to keep going. How long would it take him to get there? Out of my sight, gone beyond my power to comprehend, he kept moving away into a distance that never stopped growing.

But I had to show him, or at least myself, how much I loved him, to recapture some part of him. I moved into his old room, a small, cold room between the laundry and the garage. It wasn't fixed up like the rest of the house. It had one old dresser and a bed with a shadeless light bulb over it, hanging from a cord. Also, the room wasn't connected to the central heating of the rest of the house, so it was shivery cold in the mornings. But it was his room, and I loved it. In the open closet at the end of the room, some of his clothes still hung. The fragrance of the cigars he always smoked was in them. Being in the room that had been his was like being with him. It must be from this time that I developed a love for simple furnishings and a touch of cold.

I don't remember how long I lived in his room. Probably months. Every day when I woke, I tiptoed across the cold floor into the laundry room to the old wooden chair where I used to sit in his arms. The chair was empty, but through the window behind it the light of the sunrise poured in, glorious, a flood, telling me over and over again that the world was still good until, at last, I believed it.

From my earliest childhood my parents were strict and I was a little afraid of them. They were pre–Dr. Spock parents and insisted on immediate obedience. "Children should be seen but not heard," they often said. If I questioned them they'd growl, "No back talk!" Persisting

"My grandfather, Oscar Lofgren"

could bring a spanking from my father. I didn't get many spankings because I learned that even if I didn't understand something I had better keep quiet and obey. To this day I find it hard to disagree: I can sometimes be railroaded into going along with someone when I should be saying, "Give me time to think about that."

My relationship with my father was very strong—at times strongly negative, at times strongly positive, but always strong. When I was three, he suggested that we observe "lumberjack rules" at the dinner table. In the old days in the Wisconsin logging camps, he said, lumberjacks didn't talk while they ate. That way they didn't get in fights.

For awhile I thought this was an exciting way to have dinner; but then I realized the rule didn't have much to do with logging camps. It just saved my father from the bother of listening to me. The moment I realized I had been tricked into silence, my resentment of him was born. It never ever fully left me.

But perhaps "lumberjack rules" weren't entirely a trick invented just to silence me. My father, who could be jovial and tell wonderful stories, could also be taciturn and dour, fond of declaring that suffering was good for the soul.

From the time I was small he used to advise me "to keep a poker face." It was only when I was an adult that I realized he was referring to poker, the card game. I thought he was talking about the fireplace poker, telling me that I should always keep my face stiff and hard, like iron. I didn't want to do it.

I think he was trying to tell me: hide your ignorance, lest you be ridiculed; hide your deepest feelings, for the same reason; hide your resentments, lest in bringing them out they cause trouble. There were many silences in our house and sometimes they were angry ones. They were inexplicable to me. I didn't know what they were about, and I was afraid to ask. Several times a year they ended in fights between my parents that terrified and shamed me. One, when I was about six, was especially scary because in the middle of it my mother came to me and told me my dad was going to shoot me. I remember feeling strangely calm about this, as if I'd been told a pot on the stove might boil over. I knew it was possible, since he was a hunter and there were several guns in the house. A half hour passed. My dad didn't shoot me. It looked like he wasn't going to

do it, after all. But would he? Could he? Some day? Thus I became a hostage for my mother in her war against my father.

Heavy drinking made my parents' fights wild and incoherent. The fighting and the drinking both were family secrets, the deepest blight upon my life. The things that happen at home, my mother said, you must never tell to anybody. According to her, we were a very fine proud family, a pillar of the community. Then why was there so much that I should never tell? The things never to be told were not things to be proud of. As I grew up, I never mentioned any of them to anyone, but I felt deeply ashamed and cut off from the world. Other people, no matter how interesting, no matter how much I liked them, were ultimately people from whom I had much to hide. I carried this burden of secrecy for many years.

My father had grown up on a farm fifty miles south of Rice Lake, outside Chippewa Falls, Wisconsin. He knew lots of things. He knew how to use a scythe to cut hay by hand, the way it had been done when he was a boy, and sometimes he'd cut hay that way around our place. He'd worked his way through college and law school—he'd been a waiter, a telephone lineman, a shoe salesman, and an undertaker's assistant before he got his law degree. He told funny stories about all his old jobs and he seemed to have enjoyed them all. By the time I was born, he was forty-two years old and had become very successful as a small-town lawyer. He also liked to hunt and fish; he was a good photographer and had a darkroom; he had an airplane pilot's license and owned a small, open cockpit airplane in which he gave me rides. Later, he founded a bank and a steam corporation that used excess steam from a creamery to heat all the downtown office buildings.

According to my mother, my dad had planned to move to Washington, D.C., when he finished law school in the late twenties. But without consulting him, his father had bought him the practice of a lawyer who had just died in Rice Lake; and that brought his plan to go east to an end. My mother told this as a kind of tragic story, but my dad never mentioned it himself. Wherever his bad moods came from, they didn't seem to be caused by living in the wrong place.

My mother herself had big plans for her adult life that got derailed.

She was the oldest child in a poor family, with four younger brothers and sisters. When she was sixteen, she took one of the first IQ tests ever given in the United States—the first given in her town. After scoring it, the high-school principal came looking for her, very excited, and called her into his office. "Lolita," he said, "you're a genius!" I am sure the principal never thought that what he told my mother could damage her. To be a genius is a great thing. However, what an IQ tester means by genius is a high score on a test—a test made up by people who are not geniuses in the traditional sense. That is, not Leonardo da Vinci, not Martin Luther King, not Einstein, not Beethoven, not Virginia Woolf or Madame Curie. Genius in the traditional sense of the word refers to those few hundreds of people per century who form our culture, whose words and works we treasure and pass on to the next generation. When my mother listened to her principal, she must have thought she was destined to be one of those people. Maybe she was. Maybe she could have been. But she took a different road. Probably she felt her whole life that she had taken the wrong road—that she was a failure.

Like my dad, my mother worked her way through college. Afterward, she planned to go to New York City—to live in Greenwich Village and be a writer. But her mother died suddenly. So, to help care for her younger brothers and sisters, she took a job teaching high-school English close by in Rice Lake. I imagine that she was an excellent teacher—the kind who pushes students to think and learn, and who makes literature exciting. She taught only three years. In the following summer, she married my dad. The Rice Lake superintendent of schools immediately fired her. The Depression was on, and jobs were scarce. All over the United States the men who ran things fired young women teachers who married. Once a young woman married, they thought, she was taken care of. Her job should go to a man, no matter how well she performed it, how great the loss to students, or how much damage not using her talents might do her.

Some people take a derailment of their life's dreams better than others. My mother, I think, always felt she should really be somewhere else, doing something greater and better than what she was doing raising two daughters and being active in small-town civic affairs. I had the feeling,

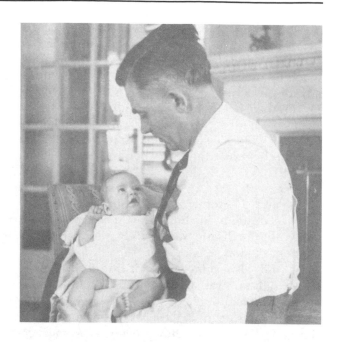

Ann, as an infant, with her father, William Angus Cameron

growing up, that our family, our town, and I had really not been worth her sacrifice—that we could never measure up to the life she should have had. I think she was also angry at society in general, which in the United States in the forties and the fifties insisted that fulfillment for every woman should and would come from being a mother and serving a family. It was considered to be "masculine" to want a job outside the home. It was "masculine" to want to use all your abilities to the fullest. (Lots of women worked all kinds of "male" jobs during World War II; the heaviest propaganda in favor of women staying home was intended to make sure that all those jobs were once again available for men after the war.) Anyhow, society—or the people who were shaping its propaganda—sold my mother a bill of goods, and our whole family paid the price. Nevertheless, she always insisted to my sister and me that women who had careers and earned their own money got treated with more respect in their marriages and had happier lives. She was saying, really, that any person or group that wants social equality needs economic power.

She hoped that my sister and I would have careers when we grew up. And yet I think she idealized a kind of domestic life that was never a reality for her.

When I was a child, her favorite picture hung in the living room, a Dutch engraving of a mother and her two daughters—the mother teaching her daughters to sew, while a kitten dozed on a rug. This was a bit odd because my mother hated both cats and sewing. It was as if she had a yearning for something impossible . . . far away, under glass, unreachable; and in her yearning she became untouchable herself.

When I was three, she decided that my sister and I should collect china. So on my sister Jennifer's birthday, my mother's friends came to the house with nicely wrapped china slippers. I was envious of the slipper collection, and also somewhat critical of it: for instance, there was only one of each kind of slipper, even though everybody I knew had two feet. Besides, the biggest of the slippers was tiny, so I didn't see how anyone was ever going to use them anyway. Not even Cinderella could have fit.

My own collection—as dictated by my mother—was of china cups and saucers. They were not too interesting to me, perhaps because I never saw them up close for long. As soon as I unwrapped a cup and saucer set, my mother took it and put it with the others, high up in the glass cabinet that hung on the wall in the living room.

Things that were mine that my mother liked tended to become hers. At age three I got a doll I named Mimi, a present from my godparents. Mimi's blue eyes opened and closed. She had real hair and a beautiful embroidered white dress and bonnet. Mimi sat on top of my bookshelf in my sister's and my bedroom, and I wasn't allowed to touch her. I could have and I wanted to: her legs were just within my reach; but I wasn't supposed to and I didn't. I stared at her for months, though, until I became thoroughly disgusted with her cleanliness and untouchability—even her beauty. Soon my disgust extended to all dolls. I began to play with toy cars and trucks and embarked on a program of road building out-of-doors that took my attention for years. I forgot Mimi. Then one day, when I was thirty-eight years old and my mother was seventy-six, I visited her apartment in Connecticut and happened to glance into her bedroom. On her bed, still immaculate in white dress and bonnet, lay Mimi.

I think every person has a "happiness level"— a level of happiness that they are used to and

Age four, with sister, Jennifer, and mother, Lolita Lofgren Cameron

feel safe with. To change that level is difficult. Unfortunately, my mother's happiness level must have gotten stuck on Low or Off at a very early age. To see her children feeling an intensity of happiness that she could not share must have been almost unbearable to her. To show too much happiness was dangerous at our house. My mother seemed to tolerate our happiness only when she had the power to create it and take it away: for example, to give a compliment that would suddenly twist into a putdown. By the time I was an adult, compliments from anybody made me very tense. I was always waiting for the second part, the part that was going to hurt.

As a child I had another favorite person besides my grandfather—the lady who cleaned for us once a week, Mrs. Harback. Mrs. Harback liked me, and I often stayed at her house. She and her husband had a farm where ripe raspberries fell off the stalk into your hand, and newborn baby pigs, shining clean and beautiful, were warmed in the kitchen by the coal-burning stove. She had a collection of beautiful ceramic horses—nearly a hundred of them on shelves in front of her porch windows. And I could take them down, one at a time, and hold them. In fact, at Mrs. Harback's house, I could pet or touch everything. My mother said we were rich, but I thought Mrs. Harback was the rich one. Once, in my own bed at home, I dreamed I was at Mrs. Harback's house. When

I woke up and found I wasn't, my bitterness and incredulity were almost more than I could bear.

Luckily for me, Mrs. Harback reached out to me. As I grew and moved from a love of cars and trucks to a love of horses, Mrs. Harback gave me presents that were really mine—a lamp with a cowgirl doll to sit beside my bed and two flannel shirts patterned just like a pinto pony. Putting them on was almost as good as having a horse. Mrs. Harback had black hair, round cheeks, and warm brown skin. I suppose, though no one ever said so, that she was part American Indian. From somewhere—perhaps starting from my grandfather's Swedish accent and Mrs. Harback's warm brownness, I got a feeling that people with warm brown skin or accents were the people who would love me most.

After all my wanderings on our land, the regimentation of school was a most unpleasant shock to me. I didn't like waiting in line to use the kindergarten's fascinating toy stove and its toy pots and pans. I didn't like lying down to take a nap when I didn't want one. I also disliked the teacher immensely. I became a kindergarten dropout.

The following year my parents put me in the first grade at the parochial school. This was worse than kindergarten, partly because on the long walk home from school bigger boys would trap first graders on a bridge and extort money from us, and partly because the nun who taught us terrified me. We children sat two to a seat with instructions not to talk to each other. I was afraid to ask to borrow an eraser from the little girl next to me, lest I be punished. When the nun asked me to come up to the front of the class to say which color was red and which was blue, I couldn't remember. When we learned to write numbers, perhaps because I was left-handed, I wrote mine in reverse.

One day, not long after school started, my mother found me alone in the first-grade classroom, kept after school writing numbers. She looked for the nun, who explained that I was very stupid. In fact, the nun said, she was about to give an IQ test the following week that would prove that I was the stupidest child in her class. Fortunately, my mother had enough confidence in me and in herself to take me out of that nun's tender care. I am sure if I had

stayed on to take the IQ test, I would indeed have been proved the stupidest child in the class, and would have progressed quickly to even greater and more extraordinary stupidity.

After a few days at home, blissful for me, worried for my parents, my mother brought me a workbook from the public school, and I filled some of it in, correctly. I was admitted to first grade there. From then on, all my studies went fairly well.

My best primary-school teacher was my third-grade teacher, Vivian Anderson. She made us feel that we were discovering what we learned, that we were a big family working together. She was a very intelligent teacher, and also she loved her students. When I grew up, I learned that she had spent her own money taking poor kids in my class to the doctor and the dentist.

My second-grade teacher, Miss Nerlene, was my worst teacher. Miss Nerlene was very strict—but perhaps more flustered and inadequate than strict. One day I looked across the room and saw her shaking a small boy, Charles Gavin, by the shoulders. Then she slapped him hard across the face. I knew Charles Gavin was a poor boy, though I'm not sure how I knew. Perhaps by his pallor and skinniness. Perhaps because he said "ain't." That was a word poor people said. I thought he must be a very dangerous boy if Miss Nerlene had slapped him like that. He must deserve it. He walked the same long lonely way home that I did, and I became afraid of him.

Soon one day after school I spotted him, trailing down the street behind me. I got scared. I picked up a stone and threw it at him. I was never a very good thrower, but this time I was more successful than I ever expected. The stone hit him hard, right in the middle of his forehead. I ran.

The next day at school I could see the cut on his forehead. I wanted to say I was sorry, but I was terribly afraid to go near him, afraid he'd hit me. I didn't tell anyone what I had done. I waited for Charles Gavin to get even, to follow me home from school and beat me up. But he didn't. The cut on his forehead turned to a thin white scar. By the end of the school year I could tell that it would be with him for life. When third grade started, Charles Gavin wasn't in my school anymore. Meantime, I had found out that my mother used to bring old clothes and other help to his family. Perhaps that's why he wanted to talk to me in the first place, or why he didn't take revenge on me. Forty-five years have passed since I threw the stone at Charles Gavin. I still can see his face. I would like to write books that could comfort the Charles Gavins of this world.

My own favorite books when I began to read well were the Joseph Altsheler "Young Trailers" series. There were twenty-two books in this series, in which I can't remember a single female character. The heroes were Henry and Paul—two adolescent white boys on the Kentucky frontier in the 1700s who were scouts and ex officio diplomats—so important in preventing conflicts that they were exempted from going to school. They spent their time moving through the trackless forest preventing wars, working out peace plans with Indians as strong and wise and brilliant as they were. Despite their short time in school, Henry and Paul philosophized a lot. Paul, though not quite so strong as Henry, was an intellectual and could quote Shakespeare.

By this time we had a cottage on a lake where we spent the summers. Sometimes I would play with three older boys who lived in the cottage down the road, but often I played alone. I would read the Altsheler books and go off into the woods in my flannel pinto-pony shirts, pretending to be Henry and Paul both, "gliding powerfully and soundless as a phantom through the forest," which was the kind of thing Henry and Paul did.

I had never met an American Indian, but there was an Indian reservation about fifty miles north of us. The summer I was eight an Indian man came to our cottage, asking if we had knives to sharpen. He was old, and he looked poor. I was thrilled to see him. From reading Joseph Altsheler I knew that his ancestors and not George Washington were the fathers of our country. Everything, even our cottage and the land we were standing on, really belonged to him.

My parents were not at home. I thought that Jennifer, who was fourteen, would at once invite the Indian man in and give him all our knives to sharpen and maybe something to eat and drink besides. But she didn't. She told him we didn't have any knives to sharpen and sent him away.

I asked her why. He was a stranger, she said, and our parents weren't home. I said, "But you could have brought the knives outside to him." She said she didn't think of that.

A few minutes later, the neighbor boys—the Danielson boys, whom I associated with Daniel Boone—came running over. They'd seen an Injun coming down their driveway! They'd shot at him with their air rifles and driven him off. And they laughed with delight and triumph.

After that I wouldn't play with the Danielson boys. But I was afraid to tell them what they had done was wrong, in case they would hit me. My sister and I told our parents what had happened and they agreed it was wrong and said they'd speak to the boys' parents about it. But I don't know if they ever did or if they thought what we told them was important. To me what had happened was more than wrong. It was cataclysmic. It was an attack on a poor old man, but also on my idea of how the world should be and was. From that day on I knew the real world was not the world of the Altsheler books. It never occurred to me that what the Danielson boys had done in ignorance and fear was very similar to what I had done to Charles Gavin.

Every summer I waited for the old Indian man's return. I dreamed of the chance to tell him how sorry I was for what had happened, and to bring him, one by one, our knives to sharpen.

Rice Lake was surrounded by dairy farms, woods, and dozens of beautiful lakes. It has what I would now call an inhospitable climate. Sometimes it snowed in September, and sometimes in June. From November to March it was very cold. Every winter for a few days temperatures dropped to between minus twenty and minus thirty degrees Fahrenheit. I would always wait for these days with the highest expectation, because they gave me a chance to prove how strong I was: I could walk to school and back and not die. Other families moved up near us, and then every day in wintertime I would play outside with neighbor children, skiing or sledding down icy slopes for hours. My fingers and toes would turn numb and thaw only painfully, slowly, in front of the radiator. "Come in before you get too cold," my mother would warn. But I never got cold. I just froze.

Still, summer was the season I loved most. After we got our lakeside cottage, my father began to be a close part of my life. He taught me to swim, to drive a motorboat, and to water ski; to use a gun and go hunting, to go fishing and clean the fish once I caught them. I already had a dog, Nickie. When I was nine, after years of my pleading, my dad bought me a horse. Before he bought it, he went with me to look at about a dozen horses advertised for sale. He handled each of them and rejected every one until he found a horse gentle enough for me—a pinto pony that I named Paint. Paint became my best friend. Together, Paint and I would lick the frosting bowl after my mother made a cake. Paint loved people. My little cousin could toddle under his legs and pull his tail, and Paint would never move. Every day I'd saddle Paint and explore old logging trails on his back, feeling like the happiest and proudest kid in the world.

Sometimes at night in the cottage, we all played cards, my mother, too, and everybody was really happy, just the way a family should be. My dad taught me chess, and we started playing every single night. I played the white pieces because they went first and were prettier—soft blonde varnished wood. My father almost always chose the black ones. I tried as hard as I could to beat him. He never just let me win. I got a feeling that the black pieces were like my father, devilish and tough, and the white pieces of blonde wood were sunny, innocent, and sweet—born losers, like little blonde-haired me. I started playing the black pieces whenever I could, and finally I won a game. To do it had taken me three years.

I learned daring, persistence, and a great deal of physical confidence from my father. At times his sense of drama completely transformed my everyday world.

When I turned nine, warts sprouted on my fingers, more and more of them crowding around my cuticles. I was ashamed of them and wanted them gone. My dad promised magic would take them away. He had me soak a white bean in water. In a day, when it was all shriveled and warty looking, he had me rub it on my warts. Then I buried it under a rock. This, he said, would make my warts disappear.

But it didn't work.

We went to the family doctor. He said since I had a pony, currying the pony a lot would make the warts come off my hands. My dad said this might be true, but he had a more powerful solution.

Five miles from our cottage was the small Czech town of Haugen. Haugen was where we went to church in the summertime, and the kind old priest, Father Bauer, always broke down and cried in the middle of the sermon when he told us how much Jesus loved us. A year earlier, I had made my First Communion in Haugen. When Father Bauer had asked us children, "Do you renounce the Devil and all his pomps?" I had answered with the rest, "We do renounce him." I hadn't been sure what the Devil was doing with the pumps. What with all the fire down in hell, I figured they were water pumps, for safety.

My dad explained to me that besides its Catholics, Haugen had a whole other community: Bohemian Communists who didn't believe

The Cameron family farmhouse in the 1940s

in God. And in Haugen, my father said, the Communists and the Catholics had their cemeteries next to each other. He took me down a dirt road on the outskirts of Haugen to show me. Sure enough, right where I had ridden Paint a dozen times and never noticed, there were the two cemeteries side by side, each with mysterious writing in Czech above its entrance.

To get rid of my warts, my dad said, I needed to go into the Communist cemetery at night when the moon was full and throw a dish towel over my left shoulder, and ask the Devil to take them away. I was dubious. I wasn't sure that this was the right thing for a Catholic girl to do. What would Jesus think about it? But, on the other hand, Jesus loved us more than we would ever know, and anything my dad said to do must be right. The big night of nights arrived. Past darkened woods and ripening cornfields, my dad and I drove to Haugen. Together, we walked into the Communist cemetery. Among the looming atheist gravestones, I turned my back on the moon and threw the dish towel over my left shoulder, asking for the Devil's help. Then I looked up at the sky, waiting to see if God would send lightning out of it to strike me down. He didn't. Not many weeks later, the warts went away. But maybe it's because I curried my pony.

My closeness to my dad ended when I became an adolescent. Partly because of my parents' fights; partly because he never had learned to listen to me; partly because I wanted him to notice I was changing and to say I was pretty. I couldn't admit I wanted that, and he couldn't say it. Probably he didn't compliment me because he was mean, I thought. Or else, worse—because I was not pretty. Or, worst case of all: he was mean and I was not pretty.

Mean or not, what he did do faithfully was to wake me up each morning so that I would get to school on time. Every morning he knocked on my door. "Daylight in the swamp," he'd say—that was what they had said in the old days in the logging camps to wake the loggers.

But I wasn't a logger! I was a fourteen-year-old girl becoming a woman. If I had known of it, I would have loved a wake-up like the traditional Mexican birthday song, "Las Mañanitas": "Wake my dear, awaken . . . dawn is here, the moon has set, and the little birds are singing. . . . On the day of your birth all the flowers were born . . . you were baptized to songs of nightingales." Nothing excessive. Just some simple compliment. Not "daylight in the swamp."

My dad had showed me how to do things, but he didn't talk much. My mother, on the other hand, had a pretty complete, if contradictory, world view, which she passed on freely. As I understood it, there were only three reasons for leaving Rice Lake. One was because you were young and got married. You had a big party with hundreds of wellwishers. Then you left. The second reason for leaving Rice Lake was because of death, in which case you left and then had a party with hundreds of wellwishers. The third possibility was that you left because your business had gone bankrupt. (If it was a client of my father's who had gone bankrupt, it was inevitably because he had made

"My class picture from St. Joseph's School,"
1956–57

the fatal mistake of not following my father's advice.) Leaving because of bankruptcy was as mysterious as death, but worse: people left very quietly, there was no party, and they didn't come back. My mother generally discerned a wife's role in the bankruptcy catastrophe: the husband's operation had capsized partly because his wife slept until ten in the morning and cleaned her house irregularly. My complete faith in this theory had a shadow side: an almost suicidal urge to grow up, sleep until ten, let the dust balls roll, and see what happened.

My mother had a hierarchical view of the world's jobs and could have placed anybody on her scale, starting from Rice Lake's dog catcher, who was the absolute bottom rung of the social universe, and going up to teachers, whom she esteemed highly but pitied for their folly in not becoming doctors and lawyers. Somewhere above doctors and lawyers were major political figures like Adlai Stevenson, Ralph Bunche, Eleanor Roosevelt, and Dag Hammarskjöld. Being president of the United States was the second most important job in the world.

The most important job of all was to be an author—"the most difficult job in the world." I never questioned this hierarchy: first because my mother was my mother, but also because I loved books myself, especially fiction.

Partly to please her, and partly because I too loved books, when I was eight I declared that when I grew up I would be a writer. A few years later, when I was nine or ten, I watched my mother sitting slumped on her bed with sheets of writing paper in her hand. "I was going to write a story," she said helplessly, "but I can't do it." I felt bad for her, and a little scared. If my mother couldn't do it, how could I?

As we got older, it was embarrassing to me and my sister to grow up in a town no one had ever heard of. When our family traveled, nobody ever recognized the name "Rice Lake." "Rice Lake. Oh. What big city is that near?" they would ask. At times we would mention five towns nobody recognized before settling on Chicago, nearly four hundred miles away, to anchor us to the continent. Being nobody from nowhere was scary. It made me feel I would somehow have to prove the significance of my existence to somebody, when I grew up.

My mother's dream for me and my sister was that we would go East to college. She kept reading articles about which colleges were considered best and would inform us as their ratings changed. My sister fulfilled my mother's dream by being editor of the high-school newspaper, valedictorian of her class, and going off to Swarthmore College in Pennsylvania, where for awhile she was unhappy. Easterners mocked her accent and made her practice saying, "Harry has a hairy chest," which was supposed to help her say her "r's" in the appropriate Eastern way. There was supposed to be a difference in the pronunciation of "Harry" and "hairy," they told her. We, or at least I, couldn't figure out what it was.

One day when I was in seventh grade, a lady I hardly knew and afterward despised asked me sweetly, "Are you as smart as your sister?" I was furious—why should I have to be compared to my sister? I didn't even answer the woman, but poisonous doubts bit at my brain. Although I read much more than my sister—with the encouragement of my mother and the local librarian, I had already read most of the novels of Dickens and some of the dialogues of Plato by the time I was twelve—I didn't do well in school. I scraped by, reading library books hidden under my textbooks, and did just enough work to keep out of trouble. I decided to prove I was as smart as my sister—most of all, to prove it to myself. I began to work harder. My mother had always told me "if you get 100s one day, you can get them every day," and "if you can excel at one subject, you can excel at every subject." This probably isn't true for everyone, but it was helpful for me that I believed her. I also benefited by a return to parochial school where a young nun who was an excellent teacher pushed me to excel. I got A's in all my subjects. In public high school, I became first a reporter and then editor of the high-school newspaper, and, like my sister, I ended up valedictorian of my high-school class. Now I'm grateful to my sister and even slightly grateful to that hateful woman I disliked so intensely. If it hadn't been for trying to compete with my sister, I might never have learned to work hard at my studies or have won the self-confidence that comes from doing well.

My parents both passionately believed in participating in politics. They said that people who didn't pay attention to politics were not paying attention to their own lives—because in the end what happened in politics affected everybody's life. When I was a freshman in high school my uncle declared himself a candidate for the Wisconsin State Senate and asked me to help him with his campaign. I helped him write press releases and send them around the district. Watching the TV as the vote came in and he won the election was very exciting. Thanks to my uncle, when I was sixteen I met John Kennedy and his wife, Jacqueline, during their 1960 presidential primary campaign. I was chosen by my uncle to pin a corsage on Mrs. Kennedy when she came in the door of the fanciest hotel in town. (This was an aborted ceremony, since it turned out that Mrs. Kennedy didn't wear corsages.) The most exciting part of meeting the Kennedys was that there were two *New York Times* reporters along on the campaign trip. I was shy with the Kennedys but talked to the reporters a mile a minute. They were great! They were *writers!*

By the time I was a junior in high school, we had a textbook that claimed to explain short stories. All short stories, it said, were about one of three kinds of conflict: *a)* Man vs. Society; *b*) Man vs. Nature; *c*) Man vs. Man. (Women, girls, boys, children, babies, and animals had no place in this model, which made stories sound like court battles where the plaintiffs and the defendants could only be male.) I found this scheme about as interesting and exciting as a cement wall. "If this is the way writing really is," I thought, "then I can't do it, so it better not be that way." I suspect the textbook description of short-story writing was written by someone who had never written one. I've never met a writer who organized his story around such abstractions. Every writer gropes his own way to particular meanings latent in his material. General "rules of the short story" are more a hindrance than a help.

While I was finishing high school, the magazines with the power to assess which were the four or five best colleges had changed their minds. Now, my mother said, Radcliffe was the best. Radcliffe, however, was actually the same as Harvard College. At the turn of the century, Radcliffe had been created as "the back door to Harvard"—the way for a few women to have the benefit of an education previously prohibited to women. Radcliffe had no separate faculty, no courses and classes of its own. It was harder for a girl to get into Radcliffe than for a boy to get into Harvard. Only one girl out of ten who applied was admitted. I applied, feeling confident that I would be accepted, and I was right. I owed a lot to Rice Lake's very good school system and excellent teachers.

Once I was admitted, though, my confidence failed me. I was very excited about going to Radcliffe—to Harvard, that is—but also I was scared. Was I really good enough? Had they maybe just admitted me out of pity because I was from a little town nobody had ever heard of? Would I just fail out? To get along, would I have to practice saying "Harry has a hairy chest"? Or would I meet the most exciting and interesting people in the world?

I pondered all this over the summer while I worked in my dad's law office, doing a very bad job at being an extra secretary and writing a short story in my spare time. My dad scolded me for typing badly and wasting paper, for not timing phone calls so they could be billed out to clients. I didn't care. The whole world of money didn't matter to me. It was just what my parents used to paper over their fights. And there was my dad, in his fine tailor-made three-piece suits, and his office almost bare except for the little wooden plaque on the wall reading, in fake Swedish: "Ve git too soon old and too late smart." He couldn't possibly mean that, he was so successful. What a fraud! But once in my summer of disdain, I saw my dad welcome two worried-looking strangers into his office with great energy and gentleness. Against my will, I thought, "If I were that couple, I would trust him."

My mother, my father, and I went out for dinner in Madison, Wisconsin, the night before I left for college. "When you're out there in the East," my dad said to me, "just remember: silence is golden." He made a strange sound, picked up his napkin and dabbed at his face. "What's the matter?" I asked, and he got very angry. Suddenly I realized he was crying—crying because I was leaving, and that must mean he loved me. Nobody in our family but my mother ever said "I love you," and when she said it, she was not to be believed.

I got to Harvard and was awed. Its main library was as big as downtown Rice Lake. There were thousands upon thousands of books in it. You could learn everything at Harvard, I thought. Just go into Widener Library and come out fifty years later: you would know ALL. But since what I wanted most was to be a writer, I set out to compete for a place in a freshman writing seminar. The young instructor took the story I'd written over the summer while I worked in my dad's law office and read it. He interviewed me briefly and asked if I had ever read Faulkner. I hadn't. The names of the people admitted to his class were posted the next week. My name was not on the list. I had been rejected—not, to my mind, by a mere human being. To me the young man who had rejected me was three-hundred-year-old Harvard University, infallible judge of wisdom, art, and scholarship. Harvard University did not say, "Good try. Try again later." It just posted lists. The moving finger of Harvard had written the ten names of those who were destined to succeed and had moved on. I thought of asking the instructor why he hadn't admitted me to his class, but the pain of finding out why I had failed from the person who had rejected me would have been too great. Harvard had spoken. I was not good enough to be a writer. And my dad was right: silence *was* golden. I didn't tell anyone about my failure or how I felt. I had to go on living. Maybe, I thought, I could become a historian; and I enrolled in history classes. I felt like a bird whose wings had been cut off, who would go about for the rest of its life on foot, staring from a sidewalk at the sky.

Except for my feeling that I had died, college was fine—exciting even. I liked my classes and mostly got A's. I heard W. H. Auden, his face a map of wrinkles, and Marianne Moore, in an enormous black hat, read poetry. I heard Martin Luther King speak, and I went on two civil rights sit-ins. Nobody mocked my accent, though one girl from California told other girls that she felt sorry for me and the one other girl from the Midwest, who had grown up "culturally deprived." I thought she was cerebrally deprived—and promptly started looking down on girls from Texas for their accents and the extraordinary length of time they spent doing their hair. After awhile I realized the Texas girls were smart and warm and much more relaxed than many girls at Radcliffe. I had to respect them, and I stopped using prejudice as a weapon to make me comfortable. Unfortunately it took me many years to realize that people who looked down on me without knowing me were not worth thinking about.

When I was a junior, I was asked to do research for some professors of American history. This was an honor and a great pleasure, even though it wasn't what I really had wanted to do with my life. One day one of the professors said to me that I didn't seem to be committed to anything. "If I were to be committed to anything," I said very shyly, very hypothetically, "it would be to poetry." And I set out to write a poem. I showed it to him and he liked it. Then I didn't write any more. I folded it neatly and put it away.

My senior year came. The great poet Robert Lowell was going to give two small seminars—one a reading course in modern poetry, and the other a writing seminar for only ten people. I was sure that I could not be in a writing course; I wasn't good enough to be a writer. But, I thought, perhaps I could take the reading course. I went to the room where the course was to be held to apply. More than thirty students were already in the room, looking very tense, holding manuscripts—what looked like whole novels, whole volumes of poetry, three-act plays, in their hands. Lowell, looking weary and powerful, handsome and elegant, described the course. Those accepted would read modern poetry and their own work would be read.

Manuscript submissions for the course should be left in his office by 11:00 A.M. the next day. I was not at the first meeting of the reading class! I was at the first meeting of the poetry writing class! By mistake, I had gone to the right room on the wrong day—but I had nothing to lose in trying to enter the writing class. I took my single poem to his office in an envelope before eleven and put it under his door. The list of students admitted to the class—the most prized writing class at Harvard, the hardest one to get into—was soon published. My name was on it.

Lowell talked about poetry as none of my professors had. He helped us, students who had been driven tone deaf by overanalysis and competition, to hear and feel the voices of the poets. Being in Lowell's class was very much like having studied a foreign language for years and then, at last, going to the country where it was spoken. It was a delight and liberation. Once we had read the great poets, Lowell would read one of our poems, on which he did not spend so much time. "Here's one good line," he would say of the poems I wrote. One good line out of eight or ten! Sometimes, zero out of twenty. Yet somehow I was not dismayed. Poetry was great language, something it was an honor to aspire to. Poetry was important, and it was something I was moving toward. How far along I was, was not so important. I began to understand why the one line was good and the others weren't. "Sometimes," Lowell explained, "we need to re-imagine experience so that it can escape the wirework of conventional language." I started to understand what he meant, to visualize more clearly so I could write more richly.

"It is better," Lowell told us, "to have one hundred readers in ten years than to have a thousand readers today, and it is better to have one reader in one hundred years than to have ten thousand readers today." The goal of a writer should be to say what needed saying so well that people would read her words for a century—turn to them for a description of life that was exactly right, not just for its own time, but for always. Viewed in that long perspective, I forgot to worry about how I looked to other people, or even to Mr. Lowell, in the fall of 1964.

At the end of the course each of us received a grade with a comment from Mr. Lowell. I opened mine with eagerness. I had received

The author in Panajachel, Guatemala, 1990

an A! His note said, "You have already passed that point so triumphantly passed by M. Moore and E. Bishop, where the prose of good conversation becomes music." I had been blessed. I carried the little slip of paper with this note on it with me in my wallet for years, like an amulet. The only bad thing was that I was more interested in rereading his praise than in writing new poems. The point of being a writer is not "being a writer," but writing.

Still, I *was* a writer! Robert Lowell had said so. Besides that, I won the Radcliffe Poetry Prize (or half of it, someone else was named, too), and on the money, I went to Europe for the summer and then to New York. Robert Lowell had told me that after college, I ought to go to New York to work in publishing.

New York did not have Europe's beauty or history, but it was awesomely big. I roomed with two friends from college. We had a beautiful apartment next to the New School for Social Research. The apartment had hardwood floors, which, if you knew where to step, did

not put splinters in your feet. And, if you leaned out and to the right, you could see from the bathroom window to the New School sculpture garden. Because of the great respect for culture we three shared, everyone who came to our apartment was immediately pulled through all the rooms of the apartment and pushed partway out the bathroom window with us pressed closely behind them. We didn't let our guests back in the window until they'd spoken some well-chosen words of admiration.

I loved New York. In my hometown I had always felt I had to hold up my parents' reputation, do everything right, appear to be perfect. Often, because of my mother, I had felt myself a solitary figure being watched out of many windows. In New York, no one cared what I did. I was part of a crowd, huge, enormous, everyone purposeful, going somewhere important and glorious. New York was prosperous in 1965. There were no beggars and no homeless people in its streets. The idea that people might ever live there on the gratings over heating outlets was unthinkable. The idea that people might be buzzing along the street out of their minds talking to themselves was inconceivable. The great thing about New York in 1965 was that its people were from every country and of every color, practicing every art and profession and striving for perfection.

People from home, friends of my parents, came to visit me. They took me to dinner. I showed them the apartment, the bathroom, and the sculpture garden. Except when we got ready for large parties, our apartment was never in perfect condition. "In New York," I told my parents' friends grandly, "we don't dust." They looked a bit surprised, but appeared to be trying to believe me.

I didn't know exactly what to do with my freedom, but this did not prevent me from enjoying it. One clear fall evening I took my umbrella out and went round and round the block with it, opening and closing it rhythmically every two or three steps. I did this for an hour, waiting for someone to ask me what I was doing. No one did, so I never got to say, "I am walking my umbrella." But I was not disappointed. I had proved the freedom of New York.

By chance I became the assistant to an editor who had done graduate work at Harvard and who was a good friend of the professors I had worked for there. He set me to reading manuscripts. "Tell me if there's something interesting about these," he said. Another revelation. At Harvard you were supposed to read things, interesting or not, profess an interest in them in an interesting way—or fail. In New York you could give your own actual opinion and it would be taken seriously, so you could keep learning to express it better and more clearly. And you could learn to edit manuscripts the same way. And you could meet actual writers—talk to Lewis Mumford, get a letter from Leonard Woolf, and meet Anaïs Nin; talk to younger writers like the South African John McIntosh, whose first novel had just been accepted for publication. When his previous novel was rejected, John said he'd been so angry that he had torn the rejection letter into tiny pieces and stomped on it. It could be satisfying to symbolically stomp on one's rejecters—better than letting them crush one's spirit.

Besides the pleasure of my job, I was earning eighty-five dollars a week—plenty of money to live on in 1965. But what I wanted to be was a writer, not an editor. In 1967 I started

a novel. With five chapters of it and the recommendation of the editors I'd worked for, I won a fellowship to the Iowa Writers Workshop and invitations to the summer artist colonies of Yaddo and MacDowell. My father had died of cancer just a few months before, and I felt very empty and sad, but I was still interested in myself and my future. The artists' colony visits were at once fascinating, a great privilege, and perhaps a misfortune for me. The problem was almost everyone was much older than I. They knew so much more. They had read so much more. What they wrote and thought generally seemed much more complex than what I thought and wrote. Elizabeth Ames, the director of Yaddo, read my chapters and said my work reminded her of Carson McCullers. I had never read Carson McCullers, and when I looked at my chapters, I found them simpleminded. I stopped working on the novel and wrote poetry.

In Iowa City my life changed once more. I got married to a young poet. I was very happy in some respects but also very angry. The world I thought was basically fair and stable had been turned upside down. In the space of five years, the most important people in the United States had all been murdered. John F. Kennedy, Malcolm X, Martin Luther King Jr., and Robert Kennedy were dead. Lyndon Johnson had lied to me and all Americans about the provocation for enlarging the Vietnam War, inventing an attack that had never happened in the Gulf of Tonkin. And now the United States was pouring all its resources into that war, choosing to kill thousands of young men of my generation and sometimes whole villages of Vietnamese civilians. Like many people my age, I blamed everybody over thirty. I blamed all taxpayers. I blamed dentists. Or one anyway. When I went to consult him and saw he was in his fifties, I knew he was a villain. The poor man swore to me that if his own wife had teeth like mine he would recommend to her treatment XYZ, but I didn't believe him. Thirty years later my teeth are collapsing—an indirect consequence of the Vietnam War.

At the University of Iowa, I was the first reader of all the fiction manuscripts submitted to the Writers Workshop. I taught an undergraduate class in literature and actually got the class excited about poetry. I read all the writers I thought I ought to read before I wrote, and started a second novel about a movie star's trip to death on a yacht. The novel went well and convincingly until I got to Chapter Three, when I exhausted all I knew about movie stars and yachts. Nobody at Harvard had ever mentioned research as an activity of Great Writers. Greatness was supposed to come from the Imagination, and it was not coming from mine. I was crestfallen. My favorite teacher at Iowa, the novelist Gina Berriault, said to me, "You're afraid to dream." Maybe she was right, or maybe I hadn't found what it was natural for me to dream about. But I think my main problem was that I had no idea how hard writing was. I knew from working in publishing that novels often went through three and four drafts and could take years to write—but I never thought *I* was going to have to take so much time to achieve something. I hadn't grasped the difference in the level of difficulty between being a college student and an adult and a professional. I didn't realize the difference wasn't intelligence or talent, or even maturity. The difference was a commitment to hard work much greater than any I had ever made.

I got my master's degree but turned down a fellowship for a Ph.D. I felt I had spent too much time in universities, that if I didn't get out I would wind up as someone with no experience outside books, a person only fit for quoting other people, without knowing how I really felt about things myself. Once I had started working full-time, I realized that I was a very long way from having the time to complete an adult novel. If I wrote for children, I thought, I might at least finish something. I sent a story to Margaret McElderry, the head editor at Harcourt Brace where I'd worked, and she was good enough to not just reject it but to criticize it for me. Not long after that I looked at a baby squash plant growing on our window sill. It—or she—became the subject of my first published children's book, *The Seed,* about a seed in the dark earth, blindly waking, not knowing where she is, and deciding, when she hears a storm above her, that she will not grow. *The Seed* was accepted by Frances Foster at Pantheon Books. She has been my editor ever since.

My husband, Charles Harvey, and I moved to Berkeley, California, where I got a job working for an eight-employee scientific company, Humphrey Instruments, a place that was so improbably like paradise that even today I

can hardly believe it was part of my life. The chairman of the company, Luis Alvarez, whom I first mistook for a janitor, had won the Nobel Prize. Big corporations had bought the exclusive rights to manufacture some of his inventions; but in the end they had never produced them: their real intentions were to keep the inventions *out* of production, to prevent competition with the products they already had for sale. Luis wanted Humphrey Instruments to get his inventions produced and used. He wanted to have the pleasure of seeing his ideas change the world.

The president of Humphrey Instruments, an engineer, Jack Lloyd, became my friend. He agreed with me that human society was sociopathic—thus curing my rage at society in about ten seconds. Of course, I thought, the world never was the secure and fair place I thought it was! I had no reason to expect it to be.

Jack was an immensely busy person but took lots of time to get to know everyone who worked for him. In retrospect, I see that he must have set himself the job of straightening out my head.

One day he asked me, "Are you a cage rattler?" I asked what a cage rattler was. "A person in a cage who rattles the bars and protests, but who when the door is open won't come out."

"I'm not that," I said. "Good!" Jack said heartily. "I didn't think you were."

Once he gave me advice about friendship. "Always try to have friends who are at least as successful as you are—preferably more so." That sounded cold-hearted.

At other times he talked to me about creativity. "Luis Alvarez has had a lot of failures," he said, "but nobody remembers the failures, the successes have been so many and so great. Creative work is like throwing snowballs against a wall. If you throw enough snow, some will stick. In the end, it's only the successes that people remember." The snowball simile sounded very messy to me, but the designer for the company, Toshio Yamada, who was also a potter, backed Jack up. "When you're working," Tosh said, "the good stuff and the bad stuff both have to come out. The only thing you need to save is the good stuff." And he advised, "When you're working, don't think how hard the work is. Work just takes energy. And energy is infinite." One day I said self-deprecatingly, "Well, at least I'm a good worker." And Tosh responded, "The point of life isn't to be a good worker, the point is to be a beautiful person!"

Could it be that if you did some things well, the failures really didn't matter? And could it be true of life too—that if you kept trying to put out the best you could from your mind, heart, and spirit, eventually all your mistakes, misspent time, and angry youth wouldn't matter anymore?

Meantime, I had other problems. My marriage was wobbly—reeling toward its end. My husband's best friends, Fred and Janie, were a couple who had decided they didn't want to meet any major or minor life crisis unmedicated. Or perhaps the drugs they used—and not they—had made the decision. They used mostly legal drugs, muscle relaxants they got through a doctor who prescribed them like popcorn. Overdosing on muscle relaxants caused Fred and Janie injuries. Once Fred slumped against the grate of a very hot electric heater. By the time we dragged him off it, his whole back carried the fine zigzag print of the grate: his skin looked like a lizard's. Another time he wanted to develop photographs. He had a fear of failure even greater than mine. To subdue it, he downed some muscle relaxants but then spilled photographic chemicals on Janie. Photography was forgotten as we hurried to get the chemicals rinsed off Janie. These were just the smaller disasters that Fred and Janie brought upon themselves.

They came to visit me and my husband lots, and stayed for days at a time. The more often they came to our apartment, the more I tried to stay away from it. I went to work at Humphrey Instruments every day of the week except Sunday. The only reason I didn't go to work Sunday was that the door was locked, nobody was there, and I couldn't get in. Charles said I was a snob because I had gone to Harvard and preferred my friends to his friends. I told my best friend, Gwen Booze, the accountant for Humphrey Instruments, what he'd said—

"Our wedding day and my instant family": (from left) Angela Cherry, Ann Cameron,
Bill Cherry, and Cristi Cherry; (in front) Jessica Cherry, November 2, 1990

hoping she'd say I wasn't a snob. She said, "At least a snob has aspirations and a sense of direction."

One night at home, I told my husband and Janie I needed to talk. I didn't like having Fred and Janie with us so much, didn't like Charles's much greater interest in them than in me. "You're upset," said Janie, sounding very concerned. "You shouldn't talk now. Take a Valium first. Take two. Just wait a few minutes. Calm yourself." I swallowed and the Valiums went down. I waited. In a few minutes I couldn't talk at all. Not a word. I was astonished, open-mouthed—as if a giant hand had just reached into my head and pulled all the thoughts out of me. I knew there had been something important on my mind, but I had no idea what it was. Luckily for me, my mind came back in the morning. I was able to take it with me when my marriage broke up. It would have been a pity to have left it behind.

I returned to New York. There, in 1975, I met a new friend, Julian DeWette, who told me stories about his childhood in Cape Town, South Africa. The stories were charming and universal—especially one about a lemon pudding Julian's father had made. Little children of all countries and races would love them, I thought, and, with Julian's permission, I turned them into my first really successful book, *The Stories Julian Tells.*

Julian was a very fine poet and short-story writer at work on an adult novel about his life in South Africa. His father had wanted him freed from the burden of apartheid, and had sent him to university in England. Julian had moved on to New York and was about to become a graduate student in international relations at Columbia University. Later, he went to work for the United Nations. According to the all-white government of South Africa, though, he was nothing but a criminal. His crime was that the American woman he had married, a pianist and an artist, was white. This was against the law in South Africa because Julian was colored—a mixed-race person. Julian, married to Judy, could not go home to South Africa. (In Julian's life, apartheid, which segregated blacks, whites, and coloreds, had cut both ways. As a child, he had lost his best friend, Gloria, because she was black. When her family was discovered to be illegally living in a Colored Area, they were deported.)

To write my stories, I moved all the characters out of South Africa into an imaginary unnamed country where racism was not part of anyone's life. I didn't want to write for six-year-olds about the kind of brutality and injustice the real Julian had experienced. The real Julian hated segregation and anyone putting any kind of limitations on anyone's love or friendship. He said what made him happiest of anything in the United States was to see children of all races on a school playground, having a good time together.

The not-so-good things in my own past were still not settled for me. I entered psychotherapy to hash everything out. I also went to the free meetings of AlAnon, an organization where people who've lived with alcoholic or drug-using family members can talk about their angry and despairing feelings and learn to manage them. Both these therapies helped bring to an end the sense of isolation from other people that had troubled me most of my life.

In 1982 my mother died. Her old friends told me how much good she had done for Rice Lake, and how much they missed her. I had known another person—not the one they knew. I felt deeply sad—as if my mother had been an angry and disappointed child who never got to grow up. I am glad she was able to express other sides of herself with her friends.

I was becoming successful as a writer, but I didn't make enough money to just write full-time. I thought if I lived in a Third World country, I would be able to make a living from my books. Besides, I had always wanted to immerse myself in another culture, to learn its wisdom. The more you understand, I thought, the bigger your life is. With the inheritance my mother left me, I moved to Guatemala. I picked Guatemala because a good friend, who'd lived in the United States for forty years, a filmmaker named Pablo Zavala, had just moved back to Guatemala to develop film projects and be near his family. If I was going to learn a country, I wanted to learn it from the inside, from someone who belonged to it. On March 31, 1983, my plane landed in Guatemala City, and I was met by Pablo and about half of his many relatives. When Pablo realized I actually could speak Spanish, as I'd always claimed, he stopped translating for me. But he remained a guide to people's values, to what you said and what you didn't say, to nuances I'd never have understood without him.

Pablo Zavala, 1987

After a month traveling with Pablo, I settled in Panajachel, a town on the shores of one of the most magnificent lakes in the world, with three enormous volcanoes rising above it and casting great purple shadows on the water. It's the town I call "San Pablo" in *The Most Beautiful Place in the World*. The majesty of the volcanoes fascinated me—the way they radiated grandeur and completeness. I became quieter, more relaxed. I was living in a very poor country where just getting a family fed every day was a triumph for most people. Helping people when I could, enjoying the beauty of the world and the people in it . . . all that became more and more important to me.

In 1988 my friend Pablo died. I wanted to write about him and his welcoming spirit. When I wrote the description of Julian's mother in *Julian, the Dream Doctor*, it was Pablo I had in mind. He, like Julian's mom, was never in a hurry. If he asked someone "How are you?" he always waited for the real answer. He was like a cool green planet with forests and flowers and waterfalls. Anyplace around him was a good place to be.

In 1989 I was visiting a friend in Washington, D.C., when I met Bill Cherry, the staff director of a congressional committee. He was from Texas and had been a surveyor, a sailor, a soldier, a newspaper reporter and editor—and on the side he knew how to fix almost anything. He went out of his way—and still does—to help people all the time, without intruding on them or bossing them around.

In 1990, Bill and I married. In one very short ceremony I got a husband, two stepdaughters, Angela and Cristi, and a granddaughter, Jessica, who's ten and who likes my books. Shortly after the wedding, Bill moved with me to Panajachel, where he is now famous. This is because every single day he gives a piece of candy to every young child he sees. Some days he must hand out a hundred pieces. He keeps track of who has had his or her piece that day, who has or hasn't shared, as promised, with a younger brother or sister. Up and down the street kids are waiting for the first sight of him in the morning, speculating in awed voices about whether he's awake, if he's finished his bath, if he'll soon come outside . . . Don Guillermo, king of candy.

Guatemala has given me much. I wanted to give back, but I didn't know how. Then, in 1993, I saw the terrible condition of the town library, which had been closed ten years and only recently reopened. Children were inside trying to do homework using ten-year-old *World Almanac*s. Half the lights in the library didn't light, and the windows didn't open. It was very dirty. I didn't think any American children would have put up with the conditions in that library for two minutes—no matter how much they were interested in learning. But Guatemalan children were nevertheless in there, trying to learn.

When the mayor saw I cared about the library, he and the Panajachel City Council named me its unpaid supervisor. Bill and I went to work to raise funds to improve it. In the past two years American donations have enabled us to add fourteen hundred new children's books to the library—and to paint it and keep it clean and beautiful. I'm especially happy because donations from my hometown, Rice Lake, have been a significant source of the money. Schools and libraries all over the United States have helped us, too. We hope more Americans will continue to help Guatemalan children learn.

One of the children who used the library every day was a three-year-old Mayan boy named

"Bill and I with Yovany (center) and his parents, Victoria and Ramon,"
Public Library (Biblioteca Popular), Panajachel, Guatemala, 1995

Yovany Yoc. He got into the habit of "reading" to Bill—taking out a book, sitting down by him, and explaining all the pictures. Yovany adored Bill because Bill listened. In September, he asked Bill to be his grandfather, and Bill said yes—so I got to be a grandmother, too.

The books Yovany looks at have become part of his mental world. Last spring someone set fire to the hillsides around Panajachel: most of five thousand young trees newly planted by the town died in the fire. Yovany was very upset. "My daddy says the fire was very bad," he said. "It killed all the little animals on the mountain." He paused, trying to think of something good. He smiled. "But not the dinosaurs!" he said. "The dinosaurs got away."

Yovany is an unusual boy with unusual parents for Guatemala. Victoria and Ramon, Yovany's parents, don't believe in physical punishment as discipline, and they say they want to have few children so they have more time to devote to each one. So far, Yovany is an only child. His parents consult Yovany and explain things

to him as if he is as important a person as any adult. When she has something serious to say, Victoria kneels down to say it to him with her head right at his level. Often, Yovany's parents play with him as if they were children, too. He is a very happy and confident boy and very smart, with a new idea every minute. The other day he explained to me and to two little girls who admire him that he was hitting himself on the head because it's a good way to rid yourself of coughs. Then he said, "Oh! My hair is sticking up in spikes all over," and proceeded to comb it the same way, with his fist. He was so sure of his cough-curing and hair-fixing methods that it almost convinced me. (In fact, I've found myself hitting myself on the head lately, hoping my worst ideas will fall out.) Whatever Yovany does gives everyone else at least half a mind to try it. The mayor's wife, who's a dentist and just fixed Yovany's teeth, also thinks he's an extraordinary boy— the first child she'd ever treated who wasn't scared to take anesthetic from a big needle, and who got so relaxed he fell asleep in the dentist's chair. "He's going to be something special one day," she said. I think so, too. I'm paying for him to go to kindergarten in a private school, where there are two good teachers for fifteen kindergartners, the activities are fun, and school is not like prison. I think that with a good education Yovany could become a great leader for Guatemala. Grandparents, like children, are dreamers, and sometimes the dreams come true.

But nobody knows what the future will bring. What's beautiful is now—Yovany coming up the street, shouting *"Hola, abuela!*—Hello, grandma!"

I hurry to shout back *"Hola, nieto!*—Hello, grandson!" Whenever I see him, I am filled with joy.

BIBLIOGRAPHY

FOR CHILDREN

Fiction:

The Seed, illustrated by Beth Cannon, Pantheon, 1975.

Harry (the Monster), illustrated by Jeanette Winter, Pantheon, 1980.

The Stories Julian Tells, illustrated by Ann Strugnell, Pantheon, 1981.

More Stories Julian Tells, illustrated by Ann Strugnell, Knopf, 1986.

Julian's Glorious Summer, illustrated by Dora Leder, Random House, 1987.

Julian, Secret Agent, illustrated by Diane Allison, Random House, 1988.

The Most Beautiful Place in the World, illustrated by Thomas B. Allen, Knopf, 1988.

Julian, the Dream Doctor, illustrated by Ann Strugnell, Random House, 1990.

(Adaptor) *The Kidnapped Prince: The Life of Olaudah Equiano,* Knopf, 1995.

The Stories Huey Tells, illustrated by Roberta Smith, Knopf, 1995.

Contributor of stories to *Iowa Review* and *Northwest Review.*

Beverly Cleary

1916-

Early Memories

Mother and I stand on the weathered and warped backsteps looking up at my father, who sits, tall and handsome in work clothes, astride a chestnut horse. To one side lie the orchard and a path leading under the horse chestnut tree, past a black walnut and a peach-plum tree, to the privy. On the other side are the woodshed, the ice-house, and the cornfield, and beyond, a field of wheat. The horse obstructs my vision of the path to the barnyard, the pump house with its creaking windmill, the chicken coop, smokehouse, machine shed, and the big red barn, but I know they are there.

Mother holds a tin box that once contained George Washington tobacco and now holds my father's lunch. She hands it to him, and as he leans down to take it, she says, "I'll be so glad when this war is over and we can have some decent bread again." My father rides off in the sunshine to oversee the Old Place, land once owned by one of my great-grandfathers. I wave, sad to see my father leave, if only for a day.

The morning is chilly. Mother and I wear sweaters as I follow her around the big old house. Suddenly bells begin to ring, the bells of Yamhill's three churches and the fire bell. Mother seizes my hand and begins to run, out of the house, down the steps, across the muddy barnyard toward the barn where my father is working. My short legs cannot keep up. I trip, stumble, and fall, tearing holes in the knees of my long brown cotton stockings, skinning my knees.

"You must never, never forget this day as long as you live," Mother tells me as Father comes running out of the barn to meet us.

Years later, I asked Mother what was so important about that day when all the bells in Yamhill rang, the day I was never to forget. She looked at me in astonishment and said, "Why, that was the end of the First World War." I was two years old at the time.

Beverly Cleary, age two

Thanksgiving. Relatives are coming to dinner. The oak pedestal table is stretched to its limit and covered with a silence cloth and white damask. The sight of that smooth, faintly patterned cloth fills me with longing. I find a bottle of blue ink, pour it out at one end of the table, and dip my hands into it. Pat-a-pat, pat-a-pat, all around the table I go, inking handprints on that smooth white cloth. I do not recall what happened when aunts, uncles, and cousins arrived. All I recall is my satisfaction in marking with ink on that white surface.

Memories of life in Yamhill, Oregon, were beginning to cling to my mind like burs to my long cotton stockings. The three of us, Lloyd,

Mable, and Beverly Bunn, lived—or "rattled around," as Mother put it—in the two-story house with a green mansard roof set on eighty acres of rolling farmland in the Willamette Valley. To the west, beyond the barn, we could see forest and the Coast Range. To the east, at the other end of a boardwalk, lay the main street, Maple, of Yamhill.

The big old house, once the home of my grandfather, John Marion Bunn, was the first fine house in Yamhill, with the second bathtub in Yamhill County. Mother said the house had thirteen rooms. I count eleven, but Mother sometimes exaggerated. Or perhaps she counted the bathroom, which was precisely what the word indicates—a room off the kitchen for taking a bath. Possibly she counted the pantry or an odd little room under the cupola. Some of these rooms were empty, others sparsely furnished. The house also had three porches and two balconies, one for sleeping under the stars on summer nights until the sky clouded over and rain fell.

The roof was tin. Raindrops, at first sounding like big paws, pattered and then pounded, and hail crashed above the bedroom where I slept in an iron crib in the warmest spot upstairs, by the wall against the chimney from the wood range in the kitchen below.

In the morning I descended from the bedroom by sliding down the banister railing, which curved at the end to make a flat landing place just right for my bottom. At night I climbed the long flight of stairs alone, undressed in the dark because I could not reach the light, and went to bed. I was not afraid and did not know that other children were tucked in bed and kissed good night by parents not too tired to make an extra trip up a flight of stairs after a hard day's work.

When I think of my parents together, I see them beside this staircase. My big father is leaning on my little mother. Sweat pours from his usually ruddy face, now white with pain, as he holds one arm in the other.

I am horrified and fascinated, for I think one arm has fallen off inside his denim shirt.

He says, "I'm going to faint."

"No you're not." Mother is definite. "You're too big."

He does not faint. Somehow Mother boosts him along to the parlor couch. Later, after the doctor has gone, I learn that a sudden jerk on the reins by a team of horses has dis-

located the arm, an accident that has happened before in his heavy farm work, for his shoulder sockets are too shallow for the weight of his muscles. Mother's determination always supports him to the couch.

Those Pioneer Ancestors

When I think of my father without my mother, I think of him sitting with his brothers after a family dinner. They are handsome, quiet men who strike matches, light their pipes, and as Mother said, "smoke at one another." When their pipes are puffing satisfactorily, one of them begins, "I remember our granddad used to say . . ."

I pay no attention, for I am "being nice" to my younger cousin Barbara. This is my duty at family dinners.

Father was the grandson of pioneers on both sides of his family. All through my childhood, whenever a task was difficult, my parents said, "Remember your pioneer ancestors." Life had not been easy for them; we should not expect life to be easy for us. If I cried when I fell down, Father said, "Buck up, kid. You'll pull through. Your pioneer ancestors did."

I came to resent those exemplary people who were, with one exception, a hardy bunch. My great-grandmother Bunn was rarely mentioned. I pictured them all as old, grim, plodding eternally across the plains to Oregon. As a child, I simply stopped listening. In high school, I scoffed, "Ancestor worship." Unfortunately, no one pointed out that some of those ancestors were children. If they had, I might have pricked up my ears.

My grandfather John Marion Bunn married Mary Edith Amine Hawn on September 30, 1872. They bought land in and around Yamhill and a wheelwright's house that they enlarged into the first fine house in Yamhill. They had ten children, eight of whom survived—five boys and three girls. The farmhouse at the time of my father's boyhood held three generations and was a lively place.

My father told one story of growing up in Yamhill. When he was fifteen, his father sent him to the butcher shop to buy some beefsteak. Instead of buying the meat, he continued, by what means I do not know, to eastern Oregon, where he worked on ranches all summer.

When I once asked my grandmother Bunn if she had worried about my father when he did not return, she answered, "Oh my, no. We knew he would turn up sooner or later." Turn up he did, three months later.

All his father said was, "Did you bring the beefsteak?"

The Little Schoolmarm

Many words are needed to describe my mother: small, pert, vivacious, talkative, fun-loving, excitable, easily fatigued, depressed, discouraged, determined. Her best features were her brown eyes; her shining black hair, which grew to a widow's peak on her forehead; her even white teeth; and her erect carriage. She had a round nose and a sallow complexion, both distressing to her, but she made up for these shortcomings with her sense of style.

Mother was born Mable Atlee in Dowagiac, Michigan, and became a classic figure of the westward emigration movement, the little school-marm from the East who stepped off a train in the West to teach school.

Her father, William Slater Atlee, arrived in the United States from England in 1854, at the age of two, with his parents, Thomas and Jane, and a baby sister. The six weeks' voyage by sailing vessel with two infants was so terrible that Thomas and Jane, homesick for England all their lives, could never face the return trip.

Little is known of the family of my grandmother, Mary Frances Jarvis of Dowagiac, Michigan. Her father, Zeduck Jarvis, was well-to-do; she loved him, and all her life took pride in his having given the land for the local school. Her mother died of "the galloping consumption," and at the age of seventeen Mary Frances married my grandfather to escape her stepmother.

The marriage of William and Mary Frances produced three children: Guy, Henry, and Mable, my mother. In the beginning, the marriage of my grandparents, a poor young miller and the daughter of a prosperous landowner, must have been unhappy. Mother recalled that when she was a little girl, her father drank heavily. "There is nothing more terrible for a child than seeing her father carried home drunk," she often said. I believe her. However, my grandfather, after observing the deterioration of some of his drinking neighbors, concluded that no good

Mother, Mabel Atlee, and father, Chester Lloyd Bunn, during their engagement

ever came from liquor, and never drank again. Mother had a horror of any sort of alcohol.

Mother graduated from Dowagiac High School in 1903 after spending one unforgettable year living with an aunt and going to school in Chicago. She taught two years in Dowagiac, then emigrated west in 1905 to Quincy, Washington, with two cousins, Verna and Lora Evans, also teachers. They had been hired by mail to teach in what their teaching certificates called the "Common Schools of Washington."

One letter to her parents, written in round, upright penmanship, exists from this period of Mother's life. It comes from "School Marm's Hall." Mother's cousins had already begun teaching, and she was about to hire a livery to drive out to her school in Waterville, Washington, a school that she thought had about fifty pupils.

Her description of life in Quincy in 1905 is lively. All the bachelors and widowers had "taken to" the new girls in town. Word went around that the young women liked watermelon, and "the result was rather alarming. There are watermelons upon the floor, table and shelves, behind the doors and in the closet. We never venture upon the street, but what some designing fellow offers us one. We accept them all and do our best. . . ." The young teachers went to dances and took in "all the little one-horse shows going. We always tell everyone we are going, start early, walk slowly and never have to pay our own way in."

Mother saved from this period of her life a copy of *The Biography of a Grizzly,* by Ernest Thompson Seton, which had been sent by friends in Michigan. She told me that after she read the book aloud in Waterville, her pupils told their families about it. People began to come from miles around to borrow the book, which was read until its binding was frayed and its pages loosened, but Mother treasured it and in her old age wrote inside the cover in a shaky hand, "This book very soiled because it has been read by many many people, including boys and girls."

The three young teachers spent their summers trailing through the West in their big hats and long skirts, traveling by train in coach cars, marveling at San Francisco the summer after the earthquake and fire, the sea through a glass-bottomed boat at Catalina Island, the pin that drops silently in the Mormon Tabernacle in Salt Lake City. Those years were perhaps the happiest in Mother's life.

Mother took a side trip to visit her parents in Banks. There, sitting on the steps of the store, was a tall, handsome young man wearing a white sweater and eating a pie, a whole pie. This man was Chester Lloyd Bunn. He and my mother were married on December 26, 1907, in Vancouver, Washington.

The couple moved to Yamhill, where Lloyd, as he preferred to be called, was working the farm for the Bunn Farming Company, an attempt to hold together for the family the land left by their father, who had died, gored by a bull, the previous August.

The life of a farmer's wife came as a shock to my small, high-strung mother, ill equipped for long hours and heavy work. Three or four years later, Father saw that he was doing more than his share of the work on the farm, and the Bunn Farming Company was disbanded. My father's share of the farm, eighty-two acres, included the house and outbuildings. He was the only one of the five sons interested in

Beverly with her mother

farming. On April 12, 1916, I was born in the nearest hospital, which was in McMinnville. Mother traveled there by train and lived in the hospital for a week while she awaited my birth. It was wartime, and there was a shortage of nurses, so she busied herself running the dust mop and helping around the hospital until I was born. McMinnville was my birthplace, but home was Yamhill.

The Farm

An only child on a farm, I had freedom for self-amusement, for looking, smelling, examining, exploring. No one cared if I got dirty. My parents were much too hardworking to be concerned about a little dirt. At the end of the day, Mother simply had me climb into my enameled baby tub set in the kitchen sink and scrubbed me off. The tub in the bathroom was almost six feet long, too long for one small girl. Sunny afternoons, I sat among the windfalls under an apple tree that bore cream-colored apples with pink cheeks, sniffing the sun-warmed fruit, taking one bite, throwing the rest of the apple away, and biting into another. The first bite of an apple tastes best, and our tree was bountiful. Juice flowed down my chin. Nobody cared.

Freedom was permitted because Father had taught me rules of safety which I was trusted to obey. One cold morning, I had come downstairs to dress in the kitchen by the warmth of the wood stove. The heat felt so good I held out my finger to touch the stove.

"If you touch the stove, you will burn yourself," Father told me.

Defiant, I touched the stove and howled in pain.

Mother, who was dishing up oatmeal, was shocked. "Lloyd, how could you? Why didn't you stop her?"

"She has to learn sometime" was all Father said. Neither parent offered any sympathy. I had to learn.

In good weather, I followed my father around the farm, listening while he explained his work and taught me the rules I must obey.

Never play in the grain bin; the grain could slide down and smother me.

Never walk behind the horses; they might be startled and kick.

If I played in the haymow, I must always play in the center; if I played near the edge, I might slide into a manger below and frighten a cow or a horse.

Never enter the pump house below the windmill alone; the floor above the tank was rotting, and I might fall through.

Never walk uphill behind a load of hay; the hay might slide off the wagon on top of me.

Never lean over the pigpen; if I fell into the pen, the pigs would hurt me.

Always shut and fasten gates to keep animals from getting into fields.

All these rules, when explained by Father, seemed sensible and interesting. I understood and never disobeyed, not once.

I walked beside Father while he plowed, and watched the rumps of Pick and Lady, our plow horses, rise and fall in the sun as the blade of the plow laid back the brown earth, and the dogs, Old Bob and Scotty, trotted beside us. Father taught me the names of the flowers that hid the split-rail fence: Quaker bonnets, which some people called lupine; wild

roses; Queen Anne's lace, which looked to me like crocheted doilies on long pale stems. He taught me to sing songs about "Polly Wolly Doodle" and "The Bowery."

When he drove to the pasture for firewood, I sat beside him on a wagon seat polished by three generations of overalls while he named trees: maple, elderberry, alder, and cedar. He taught me, not very successfully, to imitate the whistle of the bobwhite. He sometimes climbed down to pick a purple thistle and a twig, which he magically turned into a tiny parasol for me.

When Father milked the cows, I stood beside him, watching his strong hands pull and squeeze the udders, making milk ching-ching into the bucket. My hands were not strong enough to bring down milk. Sometimes he squirted milk into the mouths of a waiting row of barn cats.

I stood on the fence, out of the way, to watch Father work with the threshing crew as the men caught in gunnysacks the golden stream of wheat from the threshing machine. In spring, I stood on the same fence to watch another crew shear sheep, run them through a vat of sheep dip, and release them, naked and bleating, while hungry lambs searched for their mothers.

Late sunny afternoons, Mother escaped the house, and I joined her on a walk to the pasture to bring home the cows. Old Bob, crouching low, nipping heels, was capable of bringing home the cows without us, but Mother was glad of the sunshine and freedom from endless chores. These walks, with the sound of cowbells tinkling in the woods by the river, and bobwhites, like fat little hens, calling their names, filled me with joy as I searched for flowers whose names Mother taught me: shy kitten's ears with grayish white, soft-haired pointed petals which grew flat to the ground and which I stroked, pretending they really were kitten's ears; buttercups and Johnny-jump-ups to be gathered by the handful; stalks of foxgloves with pink bell-shaped flowers which I picked and fitted over my fingers, pretending I was a fox wearing gloves; robin's eggs, speckled and shaped like a broken eggshell, which had such a strong odor Mother tactfully placed my bouquet in a mason jar on the back porch "so they will look pretty when Daddy comes in."

If we cut across a field, I picked bachelor's buttons, which Mother said were also called French pinks. Once when Father's sweater needed buttons, I picked some blossoms and, with a darning needle and thread, sat under the dining room table, where I sewed the bachelor's buttons to my father's sweater in place of the missing buttons. Although he disliked those flowers because as a boy he had been forced to weed them from the fields, he wore the sweater, buttoned with flowers, until the blossoms withered, crumbled, and dropped away.

Mother's work in the kitchen was so tiresome we were glad of distractions that took us, running, from the house. One day Mother thought she heard an airplane. We tore out to look. Sure enough, two army planes were flying right over our farm. We stood among the clucking chickens, watching in awe, until the planes disappeared into the distance. "Mamma, I could see the aviators," I said, almost not believing what I had seen—men up in the air.

Winter days belonged entirely to Mother and were spent in the kitchen, where it was warm. I stood at the window watching the weather, the ever-changing Oregon clouds that sometimes hung so low they hid the Coast Range, rain that slanted endlessly on the bleak brown fields, stubble stiff with frost, and, sometimes, a world made clean and white by snow.

Because we were lonely for companionship, Mother talked while she boiled clothes in a copper wash boiler, ironed, baked, or worked at her hated chore, washing and scalding the cream separator. She recited lines she must have learned from an elocution class in Chicago when she was a girl. "There it stands above the warehouse door"—dramatic pause, thump of the iron on the ironing board—"Scrooge and Marley." These words from Dickens's *Christmas Carol* to me were mysterious and filled with foreboding.

In spring, Mother shared Chaucer, as much as she could recall: "Whan that Aprille with his shoures soote the droghte of March hath perced to the roote . . ." I learned to imitate every word, every inflection.

Mother also told me everything she could recall about her childhood in Michigan—sleigh rides, sledding, gathering sap for maple syrup. The Oregon maples in our pasture were a disappointing lot when compared with Michigan maples that gave forth sweet sap to be boiled and poured on the snow to cool for children to eat. I longed for the deep snows of Michigan. If we had snow like Michigan's, I could coast down our hill, if I had a sled.

Never mind. I could find substitutes. I took the broom to the top of the stairs, laid it on the steps with the handle pointing down, sat on the bristles, and descended the steps with terrifying speed, bumping every step and screaming all the way.

"How on earth did you get such an idea in your head?" asked my weary mother as she ran to pick me up and wipe my tears.

At Christmas I was given an orange, a rare treat from the far-off land of California. I sniffed my orange, admired its color and its tiny pores, and placed it beside my bowl of oatmeal at the breakfast table, where I sat raised by two volumes of Mother's *Teacher's Encyclopedia*.

Father picked up my orange. "Did you know that the world is round, like an orange?" he asked. No, I did not. "It is," said Father. "If you started here"—pointing to the top of the orange—"and traveled in a straight line"—demonstrating with his finger—"you would travel back to where you started." Oh. My father scored my orange. I peeled and thoughtfully ate it.

I thought about that orange until spring, when wild forget-me-nots suddenly bloomed in one corner of our big field. The time had come. I crossed the barnyard, climbed a gate, walked down the hill, climbed another gate, and started off across the field, which was still too wet to plow. Mud clung to my shoes. I plodded on and on, with my feet growing heavier with every step. I came to the fence that marked the boundary of our land and bravely prepared to climb it and plunge into foreign bushes.

My journey was interrupted by a shout. Father came striding across the field in his rubber boots. "Just where in Sam Hill do you think you're going?" he demanded.

"Around the world, like you said."

Father chuckled and, carrying me under his arm, lugged me back to the house, where he set me on the back porch and explained the size of the world.

Mother looked at my shoes, now gobs of mud, and sighed. "Beverly, what will you think of next?" she asked.

Children

Children were part of everything that went on in Yamhill. In winter we went to dances in the Masonic Hall, where, after sliding on the dance floor, we fell asleep on benches along the wall and were covered with coats. We sang or recited in church programs, and afterward ate drumsticks at potluck suppers.

On May Day, we took part in a pageant at the high school and ran around with bunches of wildflowers, which we left at people's doors. On Memorial Day, we went with our families to the old cemetery at Pike, where the graves of our pioneer ancestors were pointed out to us. We played among their tombstones while the adults weeded their graves. On the Fourth of July, we took part in a parade with little girls, dressed in their best, riding on the bed of a truck disguised with bunting as a float. I recall a man nailing a board across our stomachs so we couldn't fall off. Each girl wore a ribbon bearing the name of a state. I probably brought disgrace to Ohio as the only state whose white stockings had dirty knees.

School did not open until after the prune harvest, when the whole town turned out with picnic lunches to pick prunes to be hauled off to the dryer. Children played among the laden

Beverly (right) with friend Elma, as flower girls during one of Yamhill's May Day festivals

trees but were careful to stay away from the yellowjackets. I stayed away from them but loved to watch them suckling at the plump purple bosoms of fallen prunes.

I went to birthday parties where boys wore sailor suits and girls wore their best dresses, with big bows held to their hair by metal clasps. The curly-haired girls were lucky. Their bows stayed in place. We were always accompanied by our mothers, also dressed for the occasion. Sedately, we played London Bridge, drop-the-handkerchief, and ring-around-the-rosy. I could have played all day. Mothers chatted, and those with straight-haired daughters darted out to adjust slipping hair ribbons. Ice cream and cake were served, and we all went home.

Once I received a written invitation to come to play with Elma, the daughter of the town electrician. Elma had a little electric stove in which we baked, with the help of her mother, a little cake. The stove was plugged into a fascinating electric socket near the floor. All the houses I knew had one electric bulb hanging from the middle of the ceiling. After the cake was baked and the stove unplugged, Elma's father cautioned us that we must not touch the socket, which in those days did not have a built-in plug but had, instead, a tiny metal door. I could not keep my eyes off that door, which hid a round hole lined with metal the color of the sun. Finally, when no one was looking, I opened the door and stuck my finger in the hole. *Then* everyone looked, for I received a terrible electric shock, a shock that made me shriek. Everyone was nice about it, and Elma's mother comforted me, but I was ashamed. I did not mean to be naughty; I was only curious and did not think anyone would notice if I stuck my finger in just once.

The Library

The summer I was five, farm life began to change. For the first time, the cookhouse did not come to our farm at harvest time. No burly man with a wood stove built in a shack on a wagon bed cooked for our harvest crew. I did not get to hang around hoping, but never hinting, for a piece of pie.

Instead, Mother and Grandma Atlee cooked for the crew. All the leaves were added to the oak dining table; dishes of jam, chowchow, and pickled peaches were set out. The two women

The Bunn home in Yamhill, Oregon. Enlarged from a wheelwright's house by the author's grandfather, John Marion Bunn, in the early 1870s, it was "set on eighty acres of rolling farmland in the Willamette Valley . . . the first fine house in Yamhill." This photo shows the author's grandparents, John and Mary Edith Bunn, on the porch.

worked frantically, peeling, mashing, frying, baking on the big wood range in the hot kitchen, trying to prepare dinner before the crew began to complain of hunger. Finally they rang the dinner gong to summon the sweaty, dusty, sunburned men, who trooped across the barnyard to wash at the sink on the back porch and wipe their hands and faces on the roller towel.

As the men seated themselves, Mother and Grandma rushed in with platters of fried chicken, mountains of mashed potatoes, great bowls of green beans simmered with bacon for hours, piles of biscuits, coffee. More chicken, more string beans, biscuits, and coffee, followed by several kinds of pie.

Finally, when the men had eaten everything in sight, they returned to the threshing machine. I helped clear the table, and when Mother and Grandma began to wash dishes in water heated on the stove, Mother said, "Beverly, never, never, serve mashed potatoes to threshers. They

disappear too fast." To her mother she said, "What will the men think of me, running out of potatoes like that?"

"Why didn't the cookhouse come?" I asked.

Mother sighed. "Because we simply don't have the money. Most farmers don't this year."

As my parents grew downhearted, I grew increasingly restless. "Tell me a story, Mamma. Tell me a story," I begged, or whined, until Mother was worn out. She had told me over and over every story she could remember: "Little Red Riding Hood," "Three Little Pigs," "Chicken Little," "The Little Red Hen." She had recited every scrap of poetry she could recall. On Sundays my father read me "The Katzenjammer Kids" from the funny papers. Grandma Atlee continued to read the "Burgess Bedtime Story" from the newspaper, even though I never went to bed afterward.

My picture books were a book of Jell-O recipes that showed shimmering pastel desserts, and advertisements in *The Saturday Evening Post, The Ladies' Home Journal,* and *The Country Gentleman.* I looked for the fluffy yellow chick in the Bon Ami advertisement. "Hasn't scratched yet," Mother read when I asked her what the words said. The Dutch woman who carried a stick and chased herself around the can of Dutch Cleanser was a character I admired. To me, she stood for energy and hard work, two qualities necessary to livelihood on a farm. My favorite magazine characters were the Campbell Soup twins, chubby and happy, always playing together. I longed for someone to play with and wished I had a twin.

I owned two books: the Volland edition of *Mother Goose* and a linen book, *The Story of the Three Bears,* in which Mother Bear, returning from her walk, carried a beautiful bouquet of purple violets. Mother read both books until I had memorized them.

Mother, too, was starved for books, perhaps to take her mind off her worries. "Yamhill needs a library," she said. "There is entirely too much gossip. People would be better off reading books."

Somehow, in spite of all her work, Mother summoned energy to start a campaign for a library. The editor of the *Yamhill Record* cooperated by writing articles expressing the need for a county library "because there is no place in Yamhill where books can be obtained free," and explaining that "a county library would cost a man whose property was assessed at $5,000 only $1.50 a year."

Mother, too impatient for voters to raise their taxes, and probably suspecting they wouldn't, plunged ahead. She asked for donations of books and a bookcase or cupboard that could be locked. A glass china cupboard was carried upstairs to the Commercial Clubrooms over the Yamhill Bank. The community donated books, boring grown-up books with dull pictures that were a disappointment to me. Mother reported in the *Record,* "Little folks come in eager for a book and have to go home disappointed."

The bank building where the author's mother organized her library in the Commercial Clubrooms on the top floor

At six

With this small beginning, Mother opened the library every Saturday afternoon, when country people came to town to shop and Uncle Ray put out in front of the drugstore his popcorn machine, where celluloid dolls bounced in the dancing popcorn. I looked forward to the walk uptown to the library, where, even if there were no books for children, I could sit in a leather chair with its stuffing coming out and be seen and not heard. I listened to talk with big words I did not understand, but I did understand when women spoke angrily about the high price of sugar and the cost of canning fruit and making jam when summer came.

Mother persisted. She arranged a silver tea to raise money for the library, and someone gave a luncheon at which a woman played a saxophone solo. The library now had sixteen dollars! Mother called a meeting for the purpose of securing a traveling state library for Yamhill. The *Record* reported, "Twelve ladies were present who made up in enthusiasm for a lack of numbers." Mother wrote that the library had sixty-four permanent volumes, including Dickens, Scott, Eliot, and Hawthorne, and concluded her

article with, "It is said that a young girl who reads George Eliot's *Adam Bede* will never give her parents much cause for worry." She also cautioned, "Let every person donating a book first ask himself if the book contains anything that might cause young people to form wrong ideas."

Next Mother reported that a hundred people had asked for books. Men wanted adventure, a boy asked for forestry, an old lady who was ill sent in for cheerful stories, women who lived in lonely places asked for books. She concluded this article by saying, "Our children need and are entitled to the use of a library just as much as city children are."

Crates of books began to arrive from the Oregon State Library in Salem. At last Yamhill had books for children—and what good books they were! The first I recall was Joseph Jacobs's *More English Fairy Tales,* which included a gruesome little tale called "The Hobyahs." I was so attached to that story that Mother had to pry the book out of my fingers at bedtime.

Books by Beatrix Potter were among the many that came out of those state library crates. My favorite was *The Tailor of Gloucester,* not only because I loved the story, but because of the picture of the waistcoat so beautifully embroidered by mice. I studied that picture and knew that someday I wanted to sew beautifully, too.

Mother wearied of reading aloud so much. "I'll teach you to read," she said.

"No." I was firm about this. Little girls who were to enter the first grade in the fall had spent a day at school in the company of big girls. I had such a good time that I wanted to learn to read in the real school with other children, not in our kitchen alone with Mother. I could hardly wait.

That brave little library brightened the lives of many of us that winter, and in the spring, when flowers bloomed again, the library had a hundred and forty-two books in addition to sixty-two state books.

That summer everything changed. Father was proud of his bountiful harvest of heavy wheat, laden fruit trees, woolly sheep, fat hogs, cows that gave rich milk. This was followed by bitterness because he could not sell any of it for enough money to meet expenses. We stopped subscribing to *The Oregonian* because, as I understood it at the age of six when I missed "The Katzenjammer Kids," the *Oregonian* did not say nice things about farmers.

Someone had borrowed money, Father had agreed to cosign, and when the person (perhaps an uncle) could not repay, my father had to assume the debt. Years later, Mother recalled that year with sorrow. "We had everything," she said, "everything except money."

Money was needed for things we could not grow, that mysterious, invisible mortgage payment, a pretty hat.

One day Father, looking worried and exhausted, came in from the barn. "I've had enough," he said. "I'm quitting."

Mother, who had been standing at the kitchen stove, dropped into a chair. "Thank goodness," she said.

Father found someone to lease the farm, and our livestock was sold at auction from the wagon in the barnyard. When the animals were being led away, and Mother learned the amount of money they had brought, she said, "Oh dear." I was sad, without understanding why.

Leaving Yamhill did not distress me, for home was wherever my parents lived. I looked forward to Portland, where I would have children close by to play with, school, a real teacher who would teach me to read. Even though adults had troubles, I was secure. Yamhill had taught me that the world was a safe and beautiful place, where children were treated with kindness, patience, and tolerance. Everyone loved little girls. I was sure of that.

The Big City

Portland, city of regular paychecks, concrete sidewalks instead of boardwalks, parks with lawns and flower beds, streetcars instead of a hack from the livery stable, a library with a children's room that seemed as big as a Masonic hall, buildings so high a six-year-old almost fell over backward looking at the tops. I loved elevators that lifted me, leaving my stomach behind, and escalator stairs that moved, so I did not even have to raise my feet. Mother patiently rode up and down, up and down, with me.

Standing (far right) with two Halsey Street sisters, about to enter the first grade

Grandparents William and Mary Frances Atlee in their general merchandise store.
Beverly is peeking out of the right of the photo.

On Halsey Street, we rented a six-room two-story house with a furnace instead of wood stoves; it seemed warm and cozy after the big farmhouse. The city lot had been part of a farm at one time, for old cherry and plum trees and a bramble of loganberries grew in the backyard. An acre or so of hazelnut brush flourished across the street, and beyond, in Sullivan's Gulch, railroad trains huffed and chuffed, dividing the city.

A plumber, who lived behind his corner shop, sang "O Sole Mio" into a washtub. A French widow, who took in boarders, lived next door. She had a fascinating accent and called me "Bevairly." Best of all, children lived in almost every house.

And toys! I had never seen such toys. A boy who, with his father, boarded next door, had an Uncle Wiggily board game, Parcheesi, and Tinkertoys. Girls had whole families of dolls. One girl, Elizabeth Ann, had a rocking horse, a tricycle, and, in the corner of her dining room, a large and completely furnished dollhouse.

Her parents owned a radio, the first I had ever heard. Everyone had roller skates. I sat on the front steps, longing for skates of my own and for a skate key on a string around my neck, hoping someone would offer to lend me theirs.

And then one day my father brought home a pair of roller skates of my very own, and I, too, became part of the neighborhood, skating up and down the gentle slope. My knees were constantly skinned, but I picked myself up, screwed my skates in place, and skated on with blood trickling into my half socks. Sometimes I squatted on my skates and, with my arms wrapped around my legs, coasted down the slope.

We made stilts out of two-pound coffee cans and twine and clanked around the block yelling "Pieface!" at children on the next street and bloodying our knees when the twine broke. When we tired of clanking, or someone said, "For heaven's sake, children!" we pounded rose petals with rocks and soaked them in water, hoping to make perfume. We hunted for old bricks among the hazelnut bushes and pounded them into dust in a game we called Brick Factory. With scabs on my knees and brick dust in my hair, I was happy. I had children to play with who could be summoned by standing in front of their houses and yelling their names. Telephones were for grown-ups.

There was one problem, however, in the midst of all this joy. Because the children of pioneers considered education unnecessary for sons, who were expected to farm the land and hand it on to succeeding generations, my father's education consisted of two years of high school—all that Yamhill offered at that time—and a few courses in farming at Oregon Agricultural College, which left him ill equipped for city life. He became a night guard, from 7:00 p.m. to 7:00 a.m., for the Federal Reserve Bank, his one Portland connection. At some time in his youth, he had worked guarding Federal Reserve gold shipped by train to San Francisco. Trying to sleep daytimes with all the neighborhood children skating, yelling, clanking, and crying over skinned knees was difficult. He moved a cot to the attic and sometimes yelled out the window, "Quiet down there, you kids!" We tried to be quiet, until we forgot.

The Platoon System

When school started in September, girls discovered that boys, awful in the sixth grade, had become terrible in the seventh grade. They said bad words, some of which we did not understand. They tucked small mirrors under the laces of their Keds and stuck their feet under girls' skirts.

Our class was supposed to be studying grammar, which included diagraming sentences from a tan book, *Grammar and Composition,* by Effie B. McFadden, with selections for seventh-grade study and memorizing. Many of us referred to this unpopular book simply as "Effie."

In the seventh grade, changes took place, not only in boys but in the school curriculum. The platoon system was introduced. This meant we were taught some subjects—"Effie," reading, arithmetic, and United States history—in our homeroom but marched off in platoons to other rooms for music, art, nature study, library, an oddly named class called "auditorium," and double periods for domestic science or manual

training. And, of course, gymnasium, where seventh-graders exercised with wands or marched while my friend Claudine Klum played "Napoleon's Last Charge" on the piano.

Girls sewed in 7A and cooked in 7B while boys hammered, sawed, and sanded in another basement classroom. Many parents objected to the platoon system; schools should stick to basics. Mother felt the new system too strenuous. "It's just rush, rush, rush all day long," she said. At PTA she complained to Miss Stone that my handwriting had deteriorated and was difficult to read. Miss Stone replied that before long most people would use typewriters.

We now had a school library with a librarian, Miss Smith, a young, brisk, well-tailored teacher who also taught reading. She taught us how to use the library and once made us line up alphabetically by our last names, as if we were books on shelves. After that, I found a place on the shelf where my book would be if I ever wrote a book, which I doubted.

Miss Smith introduced an innovation to Fernwood. Until Miss Smith entered our lives, our teachers forbade reading in the classroom, except for old copies of the *National Geographic.* No one enjoyed this except the terrible boys who knew, by ragged covers, which issues contained pictures of naked women in African tribes.

Not being able to read in school had frustrated me. During the first week, I held my reader under my desk and read it all the way through, even though teachers said repeatedly, "Do not read ahead." After that I hid books I wanted to read inside my geography, an ideal book, because of its size, for hiding other books. I was deeply grateful to Miss Smith, not only for letting us read but for letting me into the library first on the days when *St. Nicholas* magazine arrived. Miss Smith had standards. We could read, but we must read good books. Cheap series books, traded around the neighborhood, were not permitted in her classroom. Miss Smith was also strict. She once made me stay after school until I could write on the blackboard, from memory and in order, all the presidents of the United States. I do not recall what I did to deserve this judgment, but I do recall thinking it more sensible than writing "I will not talk in gymnasium" one hundred times—a penalty once meted out by Miss Helliwell, our gym teacher.

Miss Smith also gave unusual assignments. Once, without warning, she said, "I want you to pretend you live in George Washington's time and write a letter to someone describing an experience."

Write something we had not learned in a book? This was unheard of. "But that's not fair," some protested.

Miss Smith assured us that such an assignment was perfectly fair. We knew she was right. Miss Smith was always fair. Strict, but fair.

"You mean now?" someone asked.

"Now." Miss Smith was always firm. "But how?" someone else asked. "Use your imaginations," said Miss Smith, unconcerned by the consternation she had created.

I was excited. All my life, Mother had told me to use my imagination, but I had never expected to be asked, or even allowed, to use it in school. After a moment of pencil chewing, I wrote to an imaginary cousin, telling how I had sacrificed my pet chicken to help feed Washington's starving, freezing troops at Valley Forge.

The next day, Miss Smith read my letter to the class, praised me for using my imagination, and said everyone else in the class had to try again. At Fernwood any written work, even practice sentences, that did not measure up to teachers' standards was rewritten—sometimes more than once. Smugly I read a library book while my classmates struggled with letters about their sacrifices of pet lambs and calves for Washington's troops. Copycats, I thought with contempt. Mother had told me authors found their ideas in their own minds, not in the words of others. Besides, who ever heard of lambs and calves in the middle of winter? In Yamhill, they were born in springtime.

Next Miss Smith gave us homework: writing an essay about our favorite book character. This brought forth groans and sighs of resignation from most of the class. Nobody wanted to do homework, especially original homework.

That weekend, Mother happened to be visiting her parents in Banks, where Grandpa Atlee had bought back his store. (When he was seventy, after two years of retirement, he decided he was too young to be idle.) After I put together a Sunday dinner for my father, who gamely ate it and was enjoying his pipe and the Sunday paper, I sat down to write the essay. Which favorite character when I had so

many? Peter Pan? Judy from *Daddy-Long-Legs?* Tom Sawyer? I finally solved this problem by writing about a girl who went to Bookland and talked to several of my favorite characters. I wrote on and on, inventing conversations that the characters might have had with a strange girl. As rain beat against the windows, a feeling of peace came over me as I wrote far beyond the required length of the essay. I had discovered the pleasure of writing, and to this day, whenever it rains, I feel the urge to write. Most of my books are written in winter.

As much as I enjoyed writing it, I thought "Journey Through Bookland" was a poor story because the girl's journey turned out to be a dream; and if there was anything I disliked, it was a good story that ended up as a dream. Authors of such stories, including Lewis Carroll, were cheating, I felt, because they could not think of any other conclusion.

I was also worried because I had used characters from published books. Miss Smith had lectured us on plagiarism and said that stealing from books was every bit as wrong as stealing from a store. But how could I write about a favorite character without having him speak?

When we turned our essays in during library, I watched anxiously as Miss Smith riffled through the papers. Was I going to catch it? Miss Smith pulled out a paper that I recognized as mine and began to read aloud. My mouth was dry and my stomach felt twisted. When she finished, she paused. My heart pounded. Then Miss Smith said, "When Beverly grows up, she should write children's books."

I was dumbfounded. Miss Smith was praising my story-essay with words that pointed to my future, a misty time I rarely even thought about. I was not used to praise. Mother did not compliment me. Now I was not only being praised in front of the whole class but was receiving approval that was to give direction to my life. The class seemed impressed.

When I reported all this to Mother, she said, "If you are going to become a writer, you must have a steady way of earning your living." This sound advice was followed by a thoughtful pause before she continued, "I have always wanted to write myself."

My career decision was lightly made. The Rose City Branch Library—quiet, tastefully furnished, filled with books and flowers—immediately came to mind. I wanted to work in such a place, so I would become a librarian.

Eighth Grade

Our class was changing. A quiet boy who sat in front of me had so much trouble with arithmetic that he began to cry during an important test. The tears of a boy thirteen years old distressed me so much that, for the second and last time, I cheated in school. I slipped him some answers.

A bitter, scowling boy across the aisle from me spent his days drawing, in elaborate detail, guns and battleships. He made me uneasy, and perhaps made Mrs. Drake, our eighth-grade teacher, uneasy, too, for she left him alone. Teachers were there to teach, not to solve, or even discuss, personal problems.

The boys who were so awful in the sixth grade and terrible in the seventh grade became really *horrible* in the eighth grade. They belched; they farted; they dropped garter snakes through the basement windows into the girls' lavatory. In the days before zippers, a boy could, with one swipe of his hand, unbutton the fly of another boy's corduroy knickers—always in front of girls who, of course, nearly *died* of embarrassment while the red-faced victim turned his back to button up. Mrs. Drake said, "Something has been going on, and you know what I am talking about, that has to stop." When Mrs. Drake was not looking, "something" went right on.

The horrible boys, whose favorite epithet was "horse collars!" shouted "Hubba-hubba!" at any girl whose developing breasts were beginning to push out her blouse.

Some girls changed, too, and were considered "fast" because they took to wearing lipstick and passing around two books, *The Sheik* and *Honey Lou: The Love Wrecker,* books I scorned. These they ostentatiously read on "those certain days" when they sat on a bench in the gymnasium while the rest of us twirled the Indian clubs or marched while Claudine pounded away at "Napoleon's Last Charge" on the battered piano.

I was engrossed in *Jane Eyre,* but Claudine peeked into *The Sheik* and reported, "Gee, kid, there was this sheik who kidnapped this girl and carried her off to his tent in the desert. He laid her on a bed, and when she woke up in the morning, he was gone, and then she discovered a dent on the pillow next to her, and she knew he had slept in the same bed

with her. Wow!" Our innocent imaginations were incapable of filling in the crux of this scene. A dent in the pillow was shocking enough. Yipes!

That winter I became ill once more, with what was assumed to be influenza—in those days almost any sickness was called the flu or grippe. When fever, weakness, and sore throat persisted, Mother finally called a doctor. He examined me, felt my glands, leaned on the foot of the bed, and asked, "Mother, does she know about the moon?"

Weak as I was, I was infuriated. He spoke as if I were absent or deaf, he addressed my mother as if she were his mother, and he insulted my intelligence by his silly reference to "the moon."

I knew very well he was referring to monthly periods. Why didn't the stupid man say what he meant? And what business was it of his, anyway? The old snoop. Mother was angry because he charged five dollars for the visit, even though he had to pass our house on his way to his office, and because he did nothing to help me recover.

After I had been in bed two weeks, Mother sent me back to school because, she later ruefully admitted, she was worn out taking care of me. I felt so weak I paused to rest against every fire hydrant along the way and almost immediately had to return home for another two weeks of fever and weakness, lying in my great-grandfather's four-poster bed, looking out at rain and sleet. Mother began to read me *The Little Minister,* by James M. Barrie, because for once I felt unequal to reading. Halfway through, she laid it aside. I finished it a few pages at a time.

After my illness—whatever it was, it would be my last for many years—I looked so bedraggled that Mother bought me rouge for my pale cheeks and, every morning before school, insisted on curling the ends of my hair with a curling iron heated over the flame of a burner on the gas stove.

"Yow, you're burning my neck!"

"Stand still a minute, can't you?"

The odor of singed hair filled the kitchen when Mother overheated the curling iron. By the time I had walked to school, because bicycle riding was unsophisticated for an eighth-grade girl, the damp air had usually wilted my curls.

The lingering debilitation of illness subdued me to the point of studying harder, with the result that, on one report card day, Mrs. Drake announced that I was the only member of the class to earn straight E's for Excellent. No one at school held this against me, but Mother said, "You see? You could always earn straight E's if you would only apply yourself."

About that time, Mrs. Drake confided that she was taking a course in short-story writing. Because she was taking this course, we should write, too, a paragraph of description. The class groaned.

After some thought, I recalled the moment when the mule deer sprang out of the juniper trees and hesitated in front of our car as the sun was rising over the mountains. I handed in a short paragraph entitled "Sunrise on the High Desert."

My description was returned to me inflamed with red pencil corrections. Mrs. Drake had changed almost every word. This was a shock. After so much encouragement from Mrs. Weaver, I did not know what to think.

Mother, in a day when parents supported teachers, merely remarked that she did not agree with some of Mrs. Drake's corrections, but she kept the paragraph. Years later, after I had published several books, I ran across it. The morning sun in the clear, cold desert air I had described as "blazing"—not a particularly good word—as it rose above the juniper trees. Mrs. Drake crossed out "blazing" and wrote in "burning," apparently believing that "burning" was the only acceptable modifier for a desert sun, even the sun on a cold Oregon morning. Perhaps she had read *The Sheik.*

In a negative way, this experience influenced my writing. For years I avoided writing description, and children told me they liked my books "because there isn't any description in them."

Toward spring, Mother began to tell the neighbors, "Beverly has finally begun to perk up," and a good thing, too, for Miss Helliwell had us hang up our Indian clubs and begin to rehearse calisthenics, identical to those taught in gymnasiums all over Portland, until the important day when girls dressed in white middies and black gym bloomers and boys in white gym suits marched to the Grant High School Bowl. There we joined hundreds of pupils from all over the city and performed, under the leadership of the tan, muscular superintendent of physical education, the calisthenics in which we had been drilled. In a yellowing newspaper

Beverly Cleary, in the eighth grade

photograph, we look more like the youth of Germany than of Oregon.

Our eighth-grade graduation took place in our classroom without parents present. From my seat by the window I could see Mount Hood, which was out on that sunny June day. (In Portland we spoke of Mount Hood as being "out" on clear days, as if it had popped out of the ground like a gopher.) The class waited, excited and expectant, for Mr. Dorman, who finally arrived, carrying a handful of paper diplomas, to make a short, friendly speech. Fernwood had prepared us to be good citizens, he told us.

With forty and sometimes more pupils in a class, our teachers had taught us the fundamentals of survival in society. Every one of us could read. We had learned to speak distinctly and correctly and to cope with the arithmetic necessary for daily life. Girls were capable of making their own clothing—not that many wanted to—and to prepare simple, nutritious meals. Boys had learned basic carpentry, and some had even built tables with hand-rubbed finishes, which we all admired as they proudly bore them home on the last day of manual training. School was a businesslike place. Teachers and parents expected us to learn but not to think for ourselves; we expected to be taught. Our textbooks were practical-looking and of a size comfortable for the hands of children in the grades in which they were used. No one, not even ourselves, expected school to amuse us, to be fun, or to be responsible for personal problems. The appreciation of music and art would have been considered expensive and unnecessary by parents. As I listened to Mr. Dorman and walked to the front of the room to accept my diploma, I was already imagining myself in the long corridors of the Ulysses S. Grant High School.

With our diplomas, Mr. Dorman handed each of us a small buff card, our first adult library card, a symbol marking the end of childhood.

At the author's request, this essay is excerpted in its entirety from her book-length memoir *A Girl from Yamhill,* Morrow, 1988.

BIBLIOGRAPHY

FOR CHILDREN

Fiction:

Henry Huggins, illustrated by Louis Darling, Morrow, 1950.

Ellen Tebbits, illustrated by Louis Darling, Morrow, 1951.

Henry and Beezus, illustrated by Louis Darling, Morrow (New York), 1952, Hamish Hamilton (London), 1982.

Otis Spofford, illustrated by Louis Darling, Morrow, 1953.

Henry and Ribsy, illustrated by Louis Darling, Morrow, 1954, Hamish Hamilton, 1979.

Beezus and Ramona, illustrated by Louis Darling, Morrow, 1955, Hamish Hamilton, 1978.

Fifteen, illustrated by Beth and Joe Krush, Morrow, 1956, Penguin (London), 1962.

Henry and the Paper Route, illustrated by Louis Darling, Morrow, 1957.

The Luckiest Girl, Morrow, 1958.

Jean and Johnny, illustrated by Beth and Joe Krush, Morrow, 1959.

Leave It to Beaver (fictionalization of TV series), Berkley, 1960.

The Real Hole, illustrated by Mary Stevens, Morrow, 1960, Collins (London), 1962.

Emily's Runaway Imagination, illustrated by Beth and Joe Krush, Morrow, 1961.

Two Dog Biscuits, illustrated by Mary Stevens, Morrow, 1961, Collins, 1963.

Henry and the Clubhouse, illustrated by Louis Darling, Morrow, 1962, Hamish Hamilton, 1981.

Sister of the Bride, illustrated by Beth and Joe Krush, Morrow, 1963.

Ribsy, illustrated by Louis Darling, Morrow, 1964.

The Mouse and the Motorcycle, illustrated by Louis Darling, Morrow, 1965, Hamish Hamilton, 1974.

Mitch and Amy, illustrated by George Porter, Morrow, 1967.

Ramona the Pest, illustrated by Louis Darling, Morrow, 1968, Hamish Hamilton, 1974.

Runaway Ralph, illustrated by Louis Darling, Morrow, 1970, Hamish Hamilton, 1974.

Socks, illustrated by Beatrice Darwin, Morrow, 1973.

Ramona the Brave, illustrated by Alan Tiegreen, Morrow, 1975, Hamish Hamilton, 1975.

Ramona and Her Father, illustrated by Alan Tiegreen, Morrow, 1977, Hamish Hamilton, 1978.

Ramona and Her Mother, illustrated by Alan Tiegreen, Morrow, 1979, Hamish Hamilton, 1979.

Ramona Quimby, Age 8, illustrated by Alan Tiegreen, Morrow, 1981, Hamish Hamilton, 1981.

Ralph S. Mouse, illustrated by Paul O. Zelinsky, Morrow, 1982, Hamish Hamilton, 1982.

Dear Mr. Henshaw, illustrated by Paul O. Zelinsky, Morrow, 1983, MacRae (London), 1983.

Lucky Chuck, illustrated by J. Winslow Higginbottom, Morrow, 1984, MacRae, 1984.

Ramona Forever, illustrated by Alan Tiegreen, Morrow, 1984, MacRae, 1984.

The Growing-Up Feet, illustrated by DyAnne DiSalvo-Ryan, Morrow, 1987.

Janet's Thingamajigs, illustrated by DyAnne DiSalvo-Ryan, Morrow, 1987.

Here Come the Twins, Hamilton, 1989.

The Twins Again, Hamilton, 1989.

Muggie Maggie, Morrow, 1990.

Strider, Morrow, 1991.

Petey's Bedtime Story, illustrated by David Small, Morrow, 1993.

Other:

The Hullabaloo ABC (poetry), illustrated by Earl Thollander, Parnassus, 1960.

The Sausage at the End of the Nose (play), Children's Book Council, 1974.

The Ramona Quimby Diary, illustrated by Alan Tiegreen, Morrow, 1984.

The Beezus and Ramona Diary, illustrated by Alan Tiegreen, Morrow, 1986.

A Girl from Yamhill: A Memoir, Morrow, 1988.

Barbara Corcoran

1911-

Whenever I talk to people about my books, both children and adults have a few questions that they always ask. One of those questions is "When did you start to write?"

I still find it hard to explain that there was no starting point that I know of. I have been making up stories ever since I can remember. I don't suppose I was born with paper and pencil in my fist, but as soon as I was old enough to see myself as a person, I saw myself as a person who tells stories.

My father was a music lover, and from as early as I can remember, he would play classical music and famous singers on our Victrola, which used wooden needles that had to be resharpened with a little gadget after every few records. I began learning to read by figuring out the titles on those old Red Seal records so I could hear the ones I liked best.

If I was playing records with wooden needles on a Victrola that I had to wind up, you are thinking "This woman must have been born in the Dark Ages." It wasn't exactly that far back, but it was well before World War One. April 12, 1911.

I was three years old when that war began, and when the United States went into the war in 1917 I was in the first grade. Like most writers, I think I have a clearer than average memory. There are many things I remember about that war: for one thing, at school we were asked to save peach pits. We put them in a big box at school, and then we took the full box to Jim Crow, the bootmaker. I enjoyed all that, although I had no idea what it was all about. I knew it was "patriotic," so I was proud of every peach pit I saved. It was not until recently that I read somewhere that the peach stones were ground up and used in gas masks.

The other most memorable thing for me was that my cousin Ernest, whom I liked very much, joined the navy and went to sea on a "mystery ship." Long after the war I learned

Barbara Corcoran and her father at her grandparents' house, 1913

that a mystery ship was a ship that tracked down German submarines and blew them up. Because their locations were highly secret, the crew were not allowed to write to their families. We all worried about Ernest, but he came safely home at last and gave me one of his sailor caps, and we went back to playing duets of "I love coffee, I love tea" on our piano.

One of the other questions people ask is "Where do you get your ideas?" The answer is not so much that you go looking for ideas (although sometimes you do); it's more likely that they are already stored away in your memory. Sometimes they may be things that happened to you, or stories you have heard about other people's experiences. One advantage of a long life is that many things have happened, have come and gone, or have changed.

Seventy-one years after the end of the Great War, as World War I was called, I wrote *The Private War of Lillian Adams.* I made Lillian a little older than I had been at the time, but there are more "real happenings" in that book than in any I have written. Like Lillian's, my father was a doctor. Like her, I had my sailor cousin. And I had skipped the second grade, but they had forgotten to tell me. When I went into the second-grade room, I fell and cracked my head, just as Lil does, and a nice, dependable boy called Hot Dog walked me home.

Lillian is more adventurous than I was, though. I needed a plot to hang my story on, so I invented all the spy scare business. Other details, like the peach pits, are true to my life, and so is Crazy Harry, a happy man who was the town's photographer. He had been an honor student at Harvard until an attack of scarlet fever tilted his mind. People laughed at Harry for his odd ways, but I think everyone loved him.

If you ask a writer if his or her story is "real," they will often hesitate and say something like "Well, not exactly." What they mean is that they did what I did with Lillian: used some actual events and some real people, but real life is not organized into a neat story, so we wrap a story line, or a plot, around the real events, maybe change them a little, and we find that even if we don't intend it, the "real people" we have in mind change to fit the story as it develops.

When I think about the first ten years of my life, they seem to have been divided between snow and water. In the winter, when we weren't in school, my friends and I were usually on Ayers' hill trying out our new Flexible Fliers or piling onto my toboggan or skating on Miles River and some of the ponds around town. One of my friends was an expert fancy skater, and another was the best speed skater of us all. If I were to write a book about them, I would discover that those two quite different skills explained things about their different characters. But at the age of eight or nine or ten, I was not analyzing people's characters much.

About age three, with cousin Harry Wilcox, in the author's hometown of Hamilton, Massachusetts

Sometimes my father or my friend Bob's father would let us hitch our sleds to the back of his car for an exciting, slippery, swervy ride around town. Our mothers thought we would get killed, but cars didn't go very fast in those early days so there was very little danger.

I don't think I have used those winter experiences in my hometown, Hamilton, Massachusetts, but I set *Mystery on Ice* at Camp Allegro, the girls' camp in New Hampshire that I went to in my teens, and I used my old skating memories with the characters, who were on a short wintertime vacation at that lake, Silver Lake, in New Hampshire.

In the summers of my first ten years we always went to another New Hampshire lake, Lovell Lake, where my aunt and uncle and their two boys had built a cottage before I was born. (The cottage is still in our family.)

My favorite relative, next to my grandmother, was my aunt Alice, whom I called Aunta. Aunta got some water wings and taught me to swim with those and then by myself. I was never what you would call an Olympic-style swimmer, but I have enjoyed it all my life.

Aunta taught me to row a boat as soon as my arms were long enough to handle the oars. I longed to try paddling my cousin's big Old

Towne Canoe, but he wouldn't let me near it until I was in my teens, and then I usually took it out when he wasn't there.

The cottage is set back in a grove of tall pines, on a point where the lake narrows. It was always cool there, even when it was very hot in town. Sanbornville was the town, and it was then a big railroad terminal with many branch tracks and turnarounds. It seemed as if every man in the town worked for the railroad. You would see them striding along in overalls and those tall pointed visor caps that railroad workers wore. I liked to sit around the station and watch them switch engines.

Beside the cottage there is a very large boulder with a pine tree growing out of the middle of it. It was just a young tree when I was a child, but each year it had forced its way further up, enlarging the original crack where the seed had fallen. That boulder was a good place to sit and read or just to be by yourself.

In my book *The Sky Is Falling*, the story is set in that cottage at the time of the Great Depression. In another book recently finished and not yet published, *A View from Here*, I used it again, in the present time. The boulder, in both books, is a place to which the girl in the story likes to retreat. The people in those books are invented, although the older woman in each book has the kind of quiet strength that I associate with Aunta.

When I was eleven years old, my life began to change in a number of ways. I was in the sixth grade, which I remember mainly for the struggles I had in a kind of home economics class that we had to take. We were learning to sew, and I was not happy about that. In spite of all the fine needlewomen in my family, my connection with handwork that females are supposed to be good at, like sewing or knitting or whatever, is a disaster. Even patient Aunta gave up trying to teach me to crochet. I was saved, if you can call it that, from anything past the dish towel stage when I got sick, first with measles, then with double mastoids. Thanks to penicillin, hardly anyone gets ill with mastoids any longer. The mastoid is the bone just behind the ear that can get infected from other diseases like measles. I was out of school the rest of the year, having repeated major surgery and very painful daily treatment. Always there was the possibility that I

might be left totally deaf. In fact, after one operation I was completely deaf for a week or so.

For a long time afterward it was a year I was glad to forget, but some sixty years later I wrote a book that is the one I like best of all my books: *A Dance to Still Music*. The story has nothing to do with my bad year except that the girl in the story has had an illness that has left her suddenly deaf. I remembered from my own illness how it had felt, that time when I could hear nothing at all, so I could imagine how this girl, Margaret, would feel.

For a story line I used another quite recent experience I had had. Some friends and I had gone to Key West for a vacation. Key West, the tip of Florida that juts out toward Cuba, was unlike any place I had ever been. I loved it. So I had a character I could understand and a place that fascinated me. I thought up the woman who rescues Margaret, basing her partly on the talkative little woman who had cleaned rooms at the motel where we stayed. Then I tossed in a difficult mother, a few other characters, and a Key deer. Key deer are no bigger than a large dog. In this story the deer plays an important part in helping Margaret adjust to her difficult new life.

So two entirely unrelated experiences, one bad, one good, separated by sixty years, came together to make a book that sold about thirty-six thousand copies in hard cover, many more in paperback, and won some prizes. And gave me more pleasure than any book I have written.

After I recovered from my illness my parents decided to send me to a small private school in Salem, Massachusetts. And I do mean small. There were two of us in the seventh grade and five in the sixth. We shared some but not all our classes. I loved that school. Early in the morning I took the train by myself past Beverly Harbor through the pitch-dark tunnel into Salem. Then I walked up Chestnut Street, making up stories in my head about the sea captains who once lived in the handsome houses that still line the street. Then over to Essex Street to the house that was Tower School.

I liked my few classmates, I liked the teachers, and later on when I enrolled in a public high school, I realized what a lot I had learned at Tower School in those two years. I was also pretty proud of being the standing jump champion, although there was not a lot of competition. Tower School is in Marblehead now, and I have heard that it is still a fine school.

Does that sound like a commercial? Well, the only person from that school that I ever saw again after I went off to college was my eighth-grade buddy, Jane Kelsey, whom I met in a hotel in Tbilisi, then in the USSR, in 1973. The world is sometimes so small, it's hard to believe. Now Jane and I keep in touch.

During my second year at Tower School, however, my parents separated, and my mother and I had to move to another house in North Beverly. In those days divorce was not common, but whether common or not, the children of a broken home always suffer, I think, more than the adults realize. I have written several books in which the parents were divorced, but the one that pays the most attention to it is *Hey, That's My Soul You're Stomping On.* It is set in Palm Springs, California, where I had just spent a short vacation. Often I have used as my background a place I have recently visited, partly because the details of the scene are fresh in my mind.

When it came time for high school, I chose Beverly High School. If I had stayed at Tower School, my life at college would have been easier because of the intense academic preparation I would have had. Beverly was a big school and

The house where the author grew up, Hamilton, Massachusetts, 1930s

a good one, but many of the students were not college-bound. For the first two years I was taking the same French and Latin courses I had already had at Tower.

But I enjoyed the social life of the larger school. Dancing school one evening a week was a fact of life for me from the time I was six till I was in high school; not ballet or any of that kind of dancing, but social dancing. It was like a party every week. Most of my dancing school friends, both boys and girls, went to Beverly High School. And in Helena Cronin, not long out of college herself, I found the best English teacher I ever had anywhere until I was in graduate school many years later and had the luck to have author Walter Van Tilburg Clark for my teacher.

From the sixth grade through high school I always went to school on a train or a streetcar, until my last year when my mother bought a yellow Chrysler convertible that I sometimes drove to school. When it had been time to trade in our old Chevrolet, I did a lot of talking to persuade her to get a convertible. And yellow, at that. She had stopped driving some years before after we had persuaded her that she was a menace to the population. She had a tendency to give a small shriek and take her hands off the steering wheel when she saw another car coming toward her. The day she ran into the baby carriage containing her best friend's baby, she saw the point. Ben Robertson, the baby in question, bounced lightly out of the carriage onto our lawn and survived without a scratch to become a lifelong friend. His older brother, Bob, was like a brother to me as well. We were born within five weeks of each other and grew up together. I always felt deprived not having either brothers or sisters. My writer friend Sharon Barrett teases me about how often the girls in my books have wonderful brothers, some younger, some older, and always nearly perfect. I suppose they all add up to the brother I wanted and didn't have. (I have sometimes been told I was lucky, but I don't believe it.) Luckily I had some great boy cousins who taught me to fish, among other things, and even to bait the hook. Now I'm enjoying the second and third generation of cousins, both boys and girls. They seem to get better and better.

Wellesley College had been chosen for me by my father. He enrolled me almost as soon as I was born. Surprisingly, since I had my own ideas about most things, I never questioned that. I read a book called *Babs at Wellesley* that made it seem like the perfect choice. Babs, in the book, was a great success. I don't remember how her academic life went, but undoubtedly she was an *A* student; she was captain of the field hockey team, she was on the crew, she did everything perfectly.

Imagine my surprise when I tried out for the *Wellesley News* and didn't make it. And my horror when I was assigned to remedial gym. We were required to take two years of physical education, but I took four, not from choice, believe me, but because I hated the later physical education classes I was assigned to, such as archery and volleyball, so I frequently cut class. I'm probably the only Wellesley graduate who ever flunked volleyball.

College was a learning experience in every way. If you don't count math, I had never had to work very hard before, to get good grades. I made National Honor Society in high school, I was class poet at graduation, and I had been published in every school magazine or paper since elementary school. At Wellesley I had to work hard, and I learned how close to disaster you could come if you didn't. Humility was one of the lessons I learned before I graduated. It took a while. I got a very solid education, in many courses a brilliant education from brilliant professors, one of whom was the greatniece of my lifelong favorite poet, John Keats. Ella Keats Whiting made Piers the Plowman and the characters of Chaucer's tales vivid and real.

Poetry had been my particular enthusiasm in high school, and while I was in college I wrote some not very good poetry and took courses in most of the famous English poets.

I think, unless one has real talent, poetry is often just the first phase a writer goes through. Even if she has no particular talent, it is a good way to teach oneself to observe, to note details, and perhaps to see the world in a new light.

I did get a few poems published, and now and then I still write one for myself. But after college I got interested in writing plays. Getting out of college in the midst of the Depression gave a lot of us a big shock, after the protection of academe. I spent most of my time and energy job-hunting, along with writing school history books for the Works Progress Administration Writers Project.

I went to as many plays in Boston as I could afford; in those days you could usually sit in the second balcony for fifty cents or a dollar. You needed good eyesight and hearing from that lofty place to keep up with what was going on down on the stage. The actors looked very small.

Finally I got a summer job as assistant stage manager with a professional theatre in the Oceanside Hotel in Magnolia, within commuting distance. The Oceanside was one of those enormous summer hotels where wealthy people from New York and Boston and elsewhere ate very large meals and sat in rocking chairs on the block-long veranda, inhaling the good salt air from the Atlantic. Once in a while they played tennis, but vacations in those days were not very active.

We did one play a week. I was in charge of props, among other things, so I had to round up whatever was needed for the set. I worked from about nine in the morning till after midnight and then drove the ten miles home. My pay was five dollars a week and meals. But it was many other things as well: such as becoming friends with Broadway actors, some of them stars; learning what went on backstage; and most important for me, finding out what a good play was and how it was put together.

In the fall I tried to persuade my father to send me to the Yale School of Drama. He offered to send me to Katy Gibbs Secretarial School instead. Neither of us gave in, but he did let me have enough money to live a very Spartan couple of months in New York. For a person who cared about good theatre, the thirties were the ideal time to be in New York, in the glory days of Broadway.

The following summer I was the stage manager at Magnolia, where one of the company was Shepperd Strudwick, who invited me to join the Surry Players, a group of young, talented actors planning to do summer seasons in Surry, Maine. He had read a play of mine and liked it. It was very exciting to be asked to join the Surry group.

I spent four wonderful summers with them, doing props (ten dollars a week this time, but board and room as well!). In the winters I went to New York and found any job that would keep me housed and fed. The Surry director, Sam Rosen, taught me more about playwriting than I probably ever would have learned at Yale.

Along with my playwriting, I was selling occasional short stories and articles to women's magazines. In the same year, one of my plays was produced at Bard College in New York State and another at the Peabody Playhouse in Boston.

Audrey Wood, the best play agent in New York, took me on. Everything seemed to be going in the right direction for me. But in 1941 World War II broke out, and the world changed.

I was at home again, walking the chilly roof of the high school three hours at a time, plane spotting. An English woman was my fellow spotter. When we saw or heard any sign of a plane, we identified it as, for instance, an innocent trainer from nearby Beverly airport or perhaps an Army Air Force twin-tailed P38 streaking high up. Then one of us would go into the tiny shack to call the information into headquarters. We had learned pretty well to identify all the types of planes flying at that time. The air force needed to keep careful watch, because although the United States was not yet in the war, there had been reports of German subs near the North Shore and even rumors of landings, though they were never confirmed.

It was a lucky break to have a cospotter who was interesting to talk to, because often nothing happened for a long time. And the roof of the high school was cold on those windy days.

Then it was December seventh, Pearl Harbor. I went to the government employment agency in Salem and got a job as an electronics inspector at the factory the navy had just taken over in Ipswich.

We were put through several days of orientation, mostly trying to learn the art of soldering. The girl next to me was from Essex, the town where my father grew up. She had heard of me, Essex being a very small town famous for its shipyard and its wonderful fried clams. Rosalie Gosbee and I became lifelong, close friends. And we finally managed to avoid cold solders, that first week.

My job was to inspect the strange objects that the girls on my line had assembled. Co-inspector Mary Conley and I tried to figure out what this miniaturized radio could be for, but everything at Sylvania was top secret. There were three separate working areas, and one was not allowed into any area but one's own.

Only after the war we learned that the proximity fuze, which was what we had been mak-

ing, was a shell with our tiny sending and receiving set in the nose. Once it was fired, someone on the ground could direct the shell toward an enemy plane, even when the plane was in evasive action. Once the shell was close to the plane, it exploded.

Microchips had not yet become available. Like home radio sets, this radio required a tube. The navy found a small, nearby company called Raytheon which was able to make these tiny tubes. Now Raytheon is a large company, making, among other things, the cruise missile, a sophisticated grandchild of the proximity fuze.

The proximity fuze, which had been invented by the English, was so accurate it turned the tide in the Battle of Britain and in the progress of the war. One could feel pride in being even a miniscule part of the Allies' winning of the war, but at the same time I couldn't help feeling bad about the deaths of those skilled German pilots. In the First World War, air combat, in which one lone pilot matched his courage and ability against another, was perhaps the last echo of King Arthur's knights. With the second war we moved into the impersonal world of electronics.

After a year of forty-eight-hour weeks, I became ill and had to leave my navy job. Months later I became a civil service worker again, this time for the Army Signal Corps in Arlington, Virginia, on the edge of Washington. Codes are broken by computers now, but then it was done by brilliant human minds. The Americans had succeeded in breaking the Japanese code and in keeping that secret from the enemy.

We worked in small groups of five or six. Every day each section was given a tiny part of a Japanese message to decipher. Since we had the already broken code to work from, it was not too difficult. My particular section worked on the date and place of origin on a Japanese message.

We were under very tight security in our work. Most of us lived at Arlington Hall, a kind of dorm for government workers. We were told—and it was probably true—that there was always a government "listener" on the buses that took us back and forth to work, in case workers talked too much about their work. Posters like LOOSE LIPS SINK SHIPS were everywhere.

Most of the time I worked on the swing shift, which gave me time to see a good deal of crowded but beautiful Washington. Although I had had a little time for my own writing during the months between my two jobs, once I had started work, there was no time for doing a story or a play. I can't remember that I even thought about it. The war consumed everyone's time and attention.

Many years later, after I had started writing children's and young adult books, I used some of the navy experience in a book called *Axe-Time, Sword-Time.*

After the war I had a job as advertising manager for a small chain of New England stores. It was pleasant, and it gave me a chance to write. Along with the newspaper ads, I wrote two columns a week: personal, chatty columns advertising the stores' wares.

Also I was selling quite a few magazine stories. But it seemed to me that I was on a track going nowhere. Most of my Surry friends had gone to California. So in a world that was once again at peace but badly shattered, I set out for Hollywood with Rosalie, my mother, and my cousin Helen Tuck in a prewar Chevrolet with recap tires and no spare. We took a southern route, going straight down the Atlantic coast to Atlanta before we turned west. We left in a New England blizzard, but the farther we went, the warmer it got. My mother left a piece of

winter underwear in the trash basket of quite a few motels along the way. It took us exactly one month to make the trip.

Los Angeles in the 1940s was, to this small-town New Englander, paradise. Years in the future were the gangs, the crime, the overpopulation, the smog, the freeways. The climate was warm and sunny; life was informal and mostly friendly; and it seemed as if everyone I talked to, from waitresses and busboys to the long line of young people drinking Cokes or having a sandwich at Schwab's drugstore, was a real or wanting-to-be actor or writer or something creative. After growing up in a small Massachusetts town where writing was looked upon as a hobby, like knitting, I was at last part of a community where it was not only acceptable but praiseworthy. It was very good for my shaky ego.

For a short time I worked with some of my Surry friends at a theatre in Westwood, backed by Paramount Studio. But then I got a job at Celebrity Service, where Rosalie had already put the service on an efficient basis. We were a small branch of the larger company in New York. People with a professional reason to need information about celebrities subscribed to the service: a TV producer, for instance, who wanted to find an actor in a hurry for one of his shows; or, in one case that I remember, a concert producer who desperately

Raiding a cotton field with friend Rosalie Gosbee en route to Hollywood, winter 1946

wanted to find the retired diva Galli-Curci. We had up-to-date files on just about every famous or active person in the arts, but we had lost track of Galli-Curci until a friend spent a weekend in one of the coastal resorts and saw her. That was luck; usually it was a lot of telephoning. We were rather like telephone detectives. But only for professionals with good reasons for needing information.

The job was pleasant most of the time, and it left me with enough energy to write at night. I stayed in there eight years, a record time for me in one job.

I sold four scripts to a popular radio show called "Dr. Christian," and I placed a magazine piece now and then, but my screen "treatments," as they were called, never quite made it.

We met a lot of interesting people in Hollywood, some whose lives were on our file cards, but most of whom would not be familiar to young people today, unless possibly on late late TV reruns. Jim Arness, who starred in *Gunsmoke,* used to drop into our office quite often because his agent's office was next door. One day he told us he was going to give up acting if he didn't get a job in the next two weeks. A short time later he landed the *Gunsmoke* job, and the show ran for years.

When Rosalie left the office to get married, Lynn Bowers, who took over, became a friend and fellow aspiring writer. Together we wrote four scripts about Medal of Honor winners. We chose winners from earlier wars except for one about a young man from California who had risked his life to save his unit in the Korean War. That script was nominated for an Oscar in the documentary film category. It was under Lynn's byline because she had been the one who got the contract, but for me there was a lot of satisfaction—and the money was nice.

I have never written a children's or young adult book set in Hollywood. The city and the entertainment business have changed so much, and I have been so long away from it, any story I might think up would seem dated.

In 1953 I visited a friend in Missoula, Montana, and fell in love with the place. Los Angeles had already changed from the beautiful, relaxed place I had first known. I decided to make a move. I applied to the CBS-affiliate radio station in Missoula and got a job as copywriter. After a year I decided to get a master's degree with the possibility of teaching college English.

At Celebrity Service on Sunset Strip, 1948

Coming back to the academic world after twenty-one years was an interesting experience. Not many older students were enrolled at the University of Montana (then called Montana State), but the other English majors, mostly seniors and a handful of graduate students, never made me feel like the ancient mariner.

Working in my own field at last, and with such outstanding writers as Walter Van Tilburg Clark, I was able to concentrate entirely on writing and specifically on transforming myself from a playwright to a fiction writer. Playwriting is excellent training ground even for a writer who may eventually move out of it. You learn to be concise, to make your dramatic points strongly, and to build the action toward its climax. All those things are devices that are important in fiction, but there is a flip side: you have to create in the reader's mind the background, the action, and the appearance of the characters, all of which a reader needs to be told, whereas the member of an audience has it set out before his eyes. The short story is most like a play because it is brief and concentrated, but in a novel the writer has more room to be inclusive. More characters, perhaps; a more generous background. Walter Clark taught me how to use that much wider screen. "Images, Barbara," he would write on my stories, "Images!"

I finished my master's in a year and had been given verbal offer of a teaching job. But the legislature cancelled that pleasant prospect by cutting university funds.

A friend and I took a short vacation in Mexico, and then it was back to Los Angeles to find a job. It was too late in the season for teaching. Being broke by that time, I took what I could get, and that ended up being a clerical job at the Old Age Assistance Bureau. The only good thing I can say for that tedious interlude was that I met Naomi Gates, who became a fast friend.

An offer to do copywriting at a radio station in Santa Barbara appealed to me much more than filing case histories, so I moved some miles north to that attractive city. In time I took on two other part-time jobs as well, trying to build my bank account up to something besides a row of zeroes.

At noon I drove over to Goleta and taught a class three times a week at the University of California at Santa Barbara. I ate lunch as I drove. Also I took an evening job twice a week at Los Angeles State, two hours' drive away. Obviously it was not a relaxing life, although in many ways I enjoyed it.

I accepted an offer for the following year to teach English at the University of Kentucky's new Northern Center. The center could hold classes only after 4:00 P.M. since we were using the top floor of the Covington high school. The day before classes began, I broke my ankle. Climbing several flights of stairs with my ankle in a cast was not the ideal way to start a new job.

There were other problems as well. Covington offered no places to rent, so I rented part of a house quite a long way out in the country. My landlord was right out of Dickens. He would come banging on the door if he thought he heard the water running "more than anybody needed" and again when he heard the furnace "kick in." And he was the father of all snoops.

One night a week my classes didn't meet, so I took on a teaching job at the YMCA in Cincinnati just across the river. I enjoyed all my classes, but this was not quite the academic life I had imagined. And then there was the climate. Covington is on the river, and as one of my students said, "There isn't a healthy sinus in town."

Before I had left Los Angeles, I had been taking an excellent course in writing for TV. It was a UCLA evening course, with a very good teacher. While I was in Kentucky, I wrote several pieces on writing for television, which I sold to the *Writer's Digest* in Cincinnati.

I have never tried to write about that year in Kentucky, partly because remembering all the problems (including a brand-new car which had a tendency to get stuck in low gear when I was driving home at midnight) are too much to cope with even in memory. Kentucky, especially in the south where the great horse farms are, is a fine place. I drove down there once or twice when I had time and admired the countryside immensely. But that wasn't where I was.

So it was back to Los Angeles and a job in the story department at CBS. After two years I lost my CBS job to a returning veteran to whom it had belonged before he went off to Korea. CBS found me a job in the shipping department, typing labels. It was not exactly a writer's heaven.

I had been regularly applying for college teaching jobs and not finding any, when suddenly a different offer came out of the blue. My college placement bureau had recommended me to a private girls' school in Los Angeles. I had never considered teaching below college level, but if asked to, I would have taught chimpanzees; anything to get away from typing labels.

Teaching thirteen- and fourteen-year-olds, who came from old Los Angeles families and who had a tendency in some cases to be royally spoiled, was a new experience. Most of them were very bright, and they kept me on my toes. I think what they liked about me was my car. I had bought an old, decrepit Morris Minor from a friend. It would not go over thirty-five miles an hour, which was as good as making a try at suicide in Los Angeles traffic. Sometimes I had to pull off the road to keep the drivers behind me from going into hysteria. The girls would meet me in the parking lot every morning, happy to see that the indomitable Morris had made it over the freeway from the Valley one more time.

Although tuition was high, salaries were abysmal. I wasn't sure I could last, financially, another year. Especially since the Morris showed increasing signs of geriatric collapse. Also I was in disgrace with the principal because I had allowed a girl to do a report on a book by Daniel Defoe. I had not read the book, but it didn't occur to me that the author of *Robinson Crusoe* would endanger the morals of a teenager. But, alas, the heroine of this book, Roxanne, was no better than she should have been. The principal and I had a rather stormy session, and I know she would have fired me then and there if I had not had a contract.

My class heard about it and offered to picket on my behalf. I persuaded them not to do that, but I was touched by their loyalty. The girl's mother, a Wellesley alumna as it turned out, called me at home and offered to go to bat for me. She said she was delighted that I could get her daughter to read *anything*. I was almost glad the whole thing had happened because of getting to know that woman a little: the kind of gracious, courageous woman one thinks about many times during one's own life when things are difficult. A "role model" as the phrase is.

At the most fortuitous moment possible I finally got the offer I had particularly wanted: to teach English at the University of Colorado.

I abandoned the Morris to eternity, packed up, and took a slow train to Boulder, Colorado, the place President Lyndon Johnson once called the most beautiful city in America.

Teaching in a university was so close to what I had hoped for, I could hardly believe my luck. Not that it doesn't have its problems, but boredom is not one of them.

In all the various kinds of writing I had done, I had never thought of writing books for children or young adults. It should have occurred to me that in almost everything I wrote, from plays to short stories, there was always a child as one of the principal characters.

Somewhere between graduate school and Boulder, I had finished a short novel about a child and a young man who was almost a dwarf. I called it *The Runaways*. It is set in Montana, the first of what would be many Montana books.

Not having an agent, I sent it "over the transom" to *Redbook*. To my total astonishment

they bought it for five thousand dollars. Exactly the same amount that I was getting from the university for a year's teaching. I had never seen so much money!

I had had no car since the demise of Morris, so the first thing I did was to pay cash (one thousand dollars) for a brand-new Austin Healy Sprite, a baby blue convertible. Some of us never grow up.

Redbook bought quite a few short stories from me after that, as did *Woman's Day* and some of the other magazines.

My stay at Boulder was limited to five years since I didn't have a doctorate. I very much did not want to leave. But it was the midsixties, and everything seemed to be changing.

I had an offer at more than double my University of Colorado salary from Palomar College, a junior college, so it was back to California again.

The college was small then, and the town of San Marcos was what New Englanders would call a village. A bank, a few shops, and on the edge of town a large, affluent colony for adults built around an artificial lake. I rented a condo there for one of my four years at Palomar.

Although I was not conscious of it, the most important part of my life was beginning. I had a heavy teaching schedule, but I had found time to start a book called *Sam*. The main character is a high-school-age girl, but I didn't think of it as a book for children. I had not kept track of books for the young. I assumed that it was still Nancy Drew, Tom Swift, and the Bobbsey Twins.

When my agent sent it to Jean Karl, juvenile editor at Atheneum, and she bought it, I was astonished. And of course delighted. After all the different kinds of writing I had done, I was at last a book author.

Sam was published in 1967. Two years later I had sold two more. *A Row of Tigers* (adapted from the *Redbook* novel *The Runaways* that I had sold in Boulder), *The Long Journey*, and *Sasha, My Friend*.

A busy teaching schedule, along with writing, was proving to be hard on my health. My doctor persuaded me to give up that combination. I could have continued teaching; I had been offered tenure. But I didn't hesitate long in making the choice to write full-time.

The choice was risky. I had very little money saved and no assurance that I could go on selling books. But *Sam* had been well reviewed in two pieces in the same issue of the *New York Times,* one of them an essay on their front page by the naturalist Hal Borland. And *Sasha* is to this day my most successful book. Although *Sasha* has been out of print for several years, I get more letters and phone calls asking about it than about any book I have written. It won the William Allen White Children's Book Award in 1972, it came out in a British edition, Scholastic reprinted it for its Arrow Club, and it was anthologized in part in several school readers. A woman wrote recently to say she had read it in her teens and now her daughter had found it in the library. She wanted to buy a copy. I would like a copy myself. I gave mine to some pleading child.

After I had discovered Montana, most of my books were set there for quite a while. I was back in Missoula; and except for many trips all over the country to children's literature conferences and library association meetings, a year and a half in the British Isles and a year in Hawaii, this was home. Though I hasten to say that I think of myself as a New Englander. Where you grow up stays with you for life.

An old high school classmate, Bradford Angier, got in touch with me. He was doing very well with books about outdoor living and wildlife. We collaborated on two books, *A Star to the North* and *Ask for Love and They Give You Rice Pudding.* We worked together mostly by mail, and it was fun to do.

I am always asked about my pen names. They were my publisher's idea. The reason for it was that I was writing four and sometimes five books a year, too many for good marketing. I used the name Paige Dixon, and another name, Gail Hamilton. In the beginning, the Dixon books had a boy protagonist, though sometimes I used the name for other books as well. *Lion on the Mountain, The Young Grizzly, Silver Wolf, Summer of the White Goat,* and *The Loner: A Story of the Wolverine,* all animal books, are Paige Dixons. But so is *The Search for Charlie,* whose main character is a girl.

The girls I had known at the school in Los Angeles began to appear as my central characters or at least as the basis for those characters, who inevitably developed characteristics of their own as the story opened up. In *Sasha* I used a mixture of several of those girls merged into the character of Hallie. In *This Is a Recording* I used a specific person only slightly disguised. And even when I was not thinking

With the second-grade class of Washington School, Missoula, Montana, 1972

of a specific person, I found that my hectic year at that school had taught me a lot about how thirteen- and fourteen-year-olds think and act. So, like many experiences, that rather difficult year turned out to be rich with material.

With *A Trick of Light,* published in 1972, I began to use my own New England background for some of my books. Especially Essex, where I had spent happy times with my grandparents. They lived directly across the street from the shipyards, and whenever a ship was to be launched in the tidal river, I would spend the night in my grandmother's feather bed (the bed so high I had to be lifted into it and so soft it was like falling into warm clouds).

They were still building ships in Essex then. The partly finished structures standing outlined against the sky like the skeletons of creatures from long ago fascinated me. The air rang with the sound of hammer and saw, and smelled of sawdust and tar. Men busy everywhere.

My quiet, gentle grandfather had a small livery stable; his carriage served as the town taxi, and often he would take me with him. I never knew till I was grown up that he had been a sailor in the Civil War or that he had run away when he was twelve from the home in Prince Edward Island where his Irish parents had settled. I would love to know why he ran away and what he did till he was old enough to join the navy.

In 1972, when only the ghosts of those shipyards hovered in memory and the river sounds were the growls of pleasure craft, a marina where the biggest shipyard had been, I wrote a book called *All the Summer Voices,* set in the old days. It was one of the books I most enjoyed writing. In that case the answer to "Where do you get your ideas?" went back to my early childhood, as Wordsworth said, "recollected in tranquility."

I think the best of my Montana-based books are the ones I wrote when Montana was new to me. As a child I had read an autobiographical novel by a famous cowboy movie star of the twenties, William S. Hart, set in Montana. I was about ten years old when I read it, and I was enthralled by his tales of life on a Montana ranch. The place sounded like some other planet. I wrote him a fan letter and asked him if the story was true. (One of those other questions I now have to answer often.) He wrote me a letter that could be a model of how to answer fan mail. No condescension, no adult-to-child tone; just a friendly letter telling me a little about himself and explaining that although he had grown up on a cattle ranch as the boy in his book does, the story and the characters were a mixture of fact and fiction. Although I was far too young to know it, I was getting my first lesson in fiction writing: remembered reality tempered by the writer's imagination is probably what most novels are.

The word "Montana" still lingered in my mind as a magic land when, in my middle age, I finally got here. The reality was no disappointment. Part of it is the magnificent mountains and the endless space of the plains. Part of it is the small number of people compared to the size of the state. It is a place where you can begin to sort yourself out. Everything I saw, every place I went, from Butte to Great Falls to Glacier Park, was not only different from each other but different from any part of the country I had ever seen.

The excitement I felt for the first few years supplied energy for *Sam* and *Sasha* and *The Long Journey* and the others. In twenty-six years you gradually become accustomed to a place, not so struck with surprise, perhaps. A sense of familiarity takes over, although I never quite get used to Montana. I have been in every state in the union except Alaska, and I have lived at least six months, sometimes years, in thirteen states. But in spite of TV and McDonald's, Holiday Inns and Wal-Marts, each part of the country is somehow itself alone.

Too many people are moving into Montana, a lot of them discovering to their dismay that the winter temperatures really can go to forty below, and snow can pile up beyond belief. The state is five hundred miles wide, so if you want to go see someone in another city, it may take you hours to drive there. But to me, using Bill Kittredge's phrase, it is "the last best place."

My great-grandfather left his little farm in Massachusetts not once but twice, to go across the nation to try his luck in the California gold fields. The first time he went overland, the second time by ship around Cape Horn. He never did "hit it rich," but from what I have heard about him, I suspect that the travel and adventure were really what he was after. Ironically, he died at home on his farm when a plow horse shoved him against his fence.

If he had a travel gene, I seem to have inherited it. Some of the greatest writers never left home. Emily Dickinson, for instance, who not only stayed in her own town, and her own house, but her own room. Or Proust, who spent most of his adult life in bed, not because he was ill but because he liked it there. Then there are writers who are always moving around. I am one of those.

I longed to go to Europe when I graduated from college, but the Depression ended that hope. It was not until 1973 that I had both the time and the money to venture across the Atlantic. With some compatible travel companions I set out, not on one of those "today is Monday, we must be in Paris" trips, but for a year.

Our flight took us far north and landed us in Denmark. We had planned for a week in Copenhagen and regretted later that we hadn't allowed more time in that enchanting city. But we were booked with a Finnish travel bureau for a month in a holiday village. In the end we spent two months in Finland, which reminded us of Montana but was intriguingly different at the same time.

Another month in what was still the USSR, a long story in itself. Later I used material for two books, one set in ancient Samarkand called *Meet Me at Tamerlane's Tomb,* the other in Moscow, *The Clown.* We spent a week in Budapest,

As "guest author" with students, Richardson, Texas, 1981

and then on to England where we stayed nearly a year in Cornwall, with short trips to Ireland, Scotland, and Wales.

I had carried a cumbersome battery-operated typewriter with me only to find that although I didn't have to worry about the direct current used over there, I had to recharge the batteries often, and it could not be done on a direct current. Electricians shook their heads, probably at my stupidity in not thinking about the batteries needing a recharge. Finally an ingenious man in Wales put together a large, clumsy gadget that made use of the typewriter possible. However, I finally sold it to a Pakistani student in Canterbury, who seemed to think he could solve all the problems with ease.

On a small European typewriter, a manual whose keys had to be hit very hard, I wrote *A Candle to the Devil* after seeing a sign on a mysterious little building saying that Witches' Coven met on Tuesdays. (It was not a joke.)

Also while I was in England I wrote *May I Cross Your Golden River?* about a teenaged boy who contracts Lou Gehrig's disease. It was a

hard book to write because a dear friend had recently died of that incurable disease, about which so little is known. Also I was sure I would never sell the book because it ends in the death of the main character. In fact, it did very well.

Perhaps because my father was a doctor, I have a layman's interest in illness. Several of my books, what my friends call "Barbara's clinical books," deal with an illness or disability. In *Axe-Time, Sword-Time* the girl has dyslexia. The girl in *A Dance to Still Music* is deaf. In *Child of the Morning,* set in my Surry theatre background, the girl has epilepsy. Each time, the illness or disability is something that changes the girl's life, forces her to find new ways of living.

Child of the Morning has sold very well in Spain, better in fact than it has sold in this country. Quite a few of my books have had foreign editions: *Sasha* in England, *The Lifestyle of Robie Tuckerman* in Germany, others in Switzerland and Sweden. My most recent, *Wolf at the Door,* has just sold to Norway. I always try

At home with friend Kari-Lynn, Missoula, Montana, 1994

to figure out why a particular country is interested in a particular book, but I never can understand it. Perhaps Norway has a wolf problem? Or is epilepsy common in Spain?

The children's book market has changed during the last twenty-five years. I happened to come into it at a good time, when President Lyndon Johnson's Great Society plan was providing plenty of money for libraries. It was the public and school libraries that bought the largest number of children's books. The bookstores usually had the Newbery and Caldecott winners and the classics like *Anne of Green Gables* and the *Little House on the Prairie* books, but few current books except the sure sellers like Judy Blume and Beverly Cleary.

Now the situation is reversed. Library funds have been cut to the bone, and bookstores are paying more attention to children's books.

However, the publishing business has also changed. All the old distinguished houses, some of them, like Harper's, dating back to the early nineteenth century when trains ran along New York streets, are now owned by huge corpora-

tions whose interest is in making money, the faster the better. Some of the best books, both children's and adult, are not immediate best-sellers, but if allowed to they will go on being read for many years, perhaps ultimately making more money than a quickie that comes and goes within a year or two.

One can't fight the market, but in fact I think a writer is better off not to think about it. Trends can change almost overnight, and what is "in" today is "out" tomorrow. If a writer tries to hit a particular marketable topic, like multiculturalism, for example, by the time the book is written, revised, and published, considerable time has gone by, and the publishers may be saying "No more multiculturals, please!"

I truly don't think good books are written with market in mind. In the final analysis the writer writes for herself, out of her own mind and heart, hoping the book will touch the minds and hearts of its readers.

In the letters I get from readers, I can't see any basic difference from one generation to the next. Superficial things change: language, especially slang; social behavior; clothes. But a girl or boy growing up in 1968 had the same fundamental problems in self-discovery, in bridging the distance between childhood and adulthood, in relationships with others, as a girl or boy has today.

Sometimes a change in the external world can date a book, in one sense: the collapse of the USSR makes the plot of my book *The Clown* out of date. Still, the situation of a girl taking personal risks to help someone escape from tyranny is a valid subject.

Some books fail, and you never know why. Others succeed beyond your greatest hopes. You look for the pattern or whatever it is that makes the successful ones a hit, but I have never been able to figure it out. I suppose if writers and publishers knew the answer to that question, they would have nothing but hits. The uncertainty is part of the business. Every new book is a gamble.

One of the questions children often ask, sometimes shocking their teachers, is "How much money do you make?" I would be glad to answer that question if I could, but the fact is, a writer never knows how much money will come in. It's a little like skiing. You may be standing at the top of the slope, sun shining, snow perfect, everything going your way; or you may find yourself at the bottom of the run, flat on your face. A writer has to learn to take the uncertainty and survive the down times.

If you have someone sharing your life whose income will keep you on your feet if your own income does a nosedive, that is a great help. But if you are on your own, it can get scary out there sometimes. A writer needs faith in herself and a whole lot of optimism, some of it cockeyed.

The other question that makes teachers gasp when students are cross-examining me is "How old are you?" I happened to be talking to a school in Missouri on my birthday some years ago. A boy in the front row suddenly leaned toward me and said, "How old are you?" I told him that it was in fact my birthday. Not giving up he said, "Yes, but how old are you?"

I said, "Seventy-five."

He said, "Oh, my God!" and I swear he turned pale.

So now I say, "I was born in 1911. Get out your calculator."

I have written, so far, seventy-three children's books, eight adult historical romances, and many short stories, essays, and plays. I finished a new book recently.

Rosalie's grandson Geoff reminds me that I promised him a book dedicated to him. Get ready, Geoff. It's coming up soon.

BIBLIOGRAPHY

FOR YOUNG READERS

Novels:

Sam, illustrated by Barbara McGee, Atheneum, 1967.

(With Jeanne Dixon and Bradford Angier) *The Ghost of Spirit River,* Atheneum, 1968.

A Row of Tigers, illustrated by Richard L. Shell, Atheneum, 1969.

Sasha, My Friend, illustrated by Richard L. Shell, Atheneum, 1969.

The Long Journey, illustrated by Charles Robinson, Atheneum, 1970.

(With Bradford Angier) *A Star to the North,* Thomas Nelson, 1970.

The Lifestyle of Robie Tuckerman, Thomas Nelson, 1971.

This Is a Recording, illustrated by Richard Cuffari, Atheneum, 1971.

Don't Slam the Door When You Go, Atheneum, 1972.

A Trick of Light, illustrated by Lydia Dabcovich, Atheneum, 1972.

All the Summer Voices, illustrated by Charles Robinson, Atheneum, 1973.

The Winds of Time, illustrated by Gail Owens, Atheneum, 1973.

A Dance to Still Music, illustrated by Charles Robinson, Atheneum, 1974.

The Clown, Atheneum, 1975, published as *I Wish You Love,* Scholastic Book Services, 1977.

Meet Me at Tamerlane's Tomb, illustrated by Charles Robinson, Atheneum, 1975.

Axe-Time, Sword-Time, Atheneum, 1976.

(With Bradford Angier) *Ask for Love and They Give You Rice Pudding,* Houghton, 1977.

The Faraway Island, Atheneum, 1977.

Make No Sound, Atheneum, 1977.

Hey, That's My Soul You're Stomping On, Atheneum, 1978.

Me and You and a Dog Named Blue, Atheneum, 1979.

Making It, Little, Brown, 1980.

The Person in the Potting Shed, Atheneum, 1980.

Rising Damp, Atheneum, 1980.

You're Allegro Dead, Atheneum, 1981.

Child of the Morning, Atheneum, 1982.

A Watery Grave, Atheneum, 1982.

Strike!, Atheneum, 1983.

Which Witch Is Which?, Atheneum, 1983.

August, Die She Must, Atheneum, 1984.

The Woman in Your Life, Atheneum, 1984.

Face the Music, Atheneum, 1985.

Mystery on Ice, Atheneum, 1985.

The Shadowed Path, Archway, 1985.

A Horse Named Sky, Atheneum, 1986.

I Am the Universe, Atheneum, 1986, also published as *Who Am I Anyway?,* Field Enterprises.

When Darkness Falls, Archway, 1986.

The Hideaway, Atheneum, 1987.

You Put Up with Me, I'll Put Up with You, Atheneum, 1987.

The Sky Is Falling, Atheneum, 1988.

The Private War of Lillian Adams, Atheneum, 1989.

The Potato Kid, Atheneum, 1990.

Stay Tuned, Atheneum, 1991.

Family Secrets, Atheneum, 1992.

Wolf at the Door, Atheneum, 1993.

Under pseudonym Paige Dixon:

Lion on the Mountain, illustrated by J. H. Breslow, Atheneum, 1972.

Silver Wolf, illustrated by Ann Brewster, Atheneum, 1973.

The Young Grizzly, illustrated by Grambs Miller, Atheneum, 1973.

Promises to Keep, Atheneum, 1974.

May I Cross Your Golden River?, Atheneum, 1975, published as *A Time to Love, A Time to Mourn,* Scholastic Book Services, 1982.

Cabin in the Sky, Atheneum, 1976.

Pimm's Cup for Everybody, Atheneum, 1976.

The Search for Charlie, Atheneum, 1976.

Summer of the White Goat, Atheneum, 1977.

The Loner: A Story of the Wolverine, illustrated by Grambs Miller, Atheneum, 1978.

Skipper (sequel to *May I Cross Your Golden River?*), Atheneum, 1979.

Walk My Way, Atheneum, 1980.

Under pseudonym Gail Hamilton:

A Candle to the Devil, illustrated by Joanne Scribner, Atheneum, 1975.

Titania's Lodestone, Atheneum, 1975.

Love Comes to Eunice K. O'Herlihy, Atheneum, 1977.

FOR ADULTS

Historical romance novels:

Abigail, Ballantine, 1981.

Abbie in Love (continuation of *Abigail*), Ballantine, 1981.

Beloved Enemy, Ballantine, 1981.

Call of the Heart, Ballantine, 1981.

A Husband for Gail (conclusion of *Abigail),* Ballantine, 1981.

Love Is Not Enough, Ballantine, 1981.

Song for Two Voices, Ballantine, 1981.

By the Silvery Moon, Ballantine, 1982.

Other:

"Yankee Pine" (play), first produced at Bard College, Annandale-on-Hudson, New York, 1940.

"From the Drawn Sword" (play), first produced in Boston, 1940.

The Mustang and Other Stories (short stories), Scholastic Book Services, 1978.

Contributor of radio scripts to "Dr. Christian" program, and of short stories and other pieces to magazines, including *American Girl, Charm, Glamour, Good Housekeeping, Redbook,* and *Woman's Day.*

Helen Cresswell

1934-

Helen Cresswell, age five

It was Christmas Day and she was four years old. She doesn't now remember the stocking at the end of the bed, with the new penny and tangerine in the toe, though there must have been one. Her first memory is of the three of them creeping down the darkened stairs, opening the door of the living room, and going in. Peter switched on the light.

It wasn't there! She could see that at a glance. By the fireplace were three pillowcases, half-filled. But there was no doll's pram.

"You be good, and Santa will bring you what you ask for," that was what her mother had said.

The only thing she had asked for was the pram. Santa's birds, they were told, had been watching children for weeks now, spying, reporting back to him.

She doesn't remember anything about the pillowcases, only the moment when Peter suddenly pointed at the floor-length curtains, still closed against the December cold, and said "Look!" He ran and pulled the curtain back.

She remembers that. There, impossibly, was the pram! It was dark green, with a fringed hood and shiny spoked wheels. She was delirious with joy—she must have been, because of what happened next (or rather, the next thing she remembers).

They are at the breakfast table, her parents at either end, her elder brother Peter

101

"My father"

opposite, and herself and her younger sister Pauline side by side, herself immediately on Daddy's right. She can see the scene in detail, locked in tableau. She can see the gilt-framed picture of Highland cattle, the enamelled tea-pot stand with its pattern of vines and grapes. The wind and rain are lashing on the still-darkened windows. Behind her is the loud ticking of the clock on the mantelpiece.

She has pulled her pram right up to the table beside her and is already fidgeting to get down. She is too excited to have noticed the telltale signs, the pulse at the temple, the flushed face and neck, the almost murderous glare that mean that her father, in seconds, will turn into a monster. On and on she burbles, heedless of the danger. Then it comes. Her father drops his knife and his arm swings and there is a sharp blow to her head. She hears her mother's voice, "Leave the child alone! It's Christmas Day!"

Now the scene goes into slow motion. As she cowers back, her arms shielding off another blow, she sees her father's face contorted, the veins standing out and his blue eyes hot. She sees his hand seize his cup of scalding tea and hurl it, straight down on the table. She sees her mother's face wearing a curious look of surprise and watches as tea and blood together run down from the gash in her forehead. Then the scene freezes.

Memory works in strange ways. Ever since I knew I was to write this piece I have been trying to awaken it, to call back the far-off past. Another, deeper part of my mind was resisting. I did not want to remember.

Then one night as I lay in bed I had an idea. I would try to trick my memory. I decided to try to literally revisit my childhood home. Each night before sleeping I have gone in through the back door of our house and retraced my steps through it, room by room. The detail is still there, half a century on, and because I could see it so clearly I hoped that a stream of scenes, glimpses would be released.

It worked. It worked from the moment I walked between the peeling brown painted front gates, down the short drive between the house and the high privet hedge, and could suddenly smell the sweet white flowers. All at once I was there, with Pauline, and we are each throwing a ball against the brick side of the house and catching it—throw catch, throw clap once catch, throw clap twice catch, throw clap three times catch, and then throw it high, high as the landing window to clap four times before it rushes back to your cupped palms. I am wearing the blue, daisied dress my mother made, it has a scallop of white braid down the front and white buttons. Pauline has her slippery brown hair tied with a pink floppy bow and she seems small, much smaller than me, though she is only eighteen months younger.

So come with me now into the back porch, over the cracked red tiles and past the half-open coalhouse door. We step into the kitchen. The floor is covered with threadbare lino in greens and browns. To the right, as you step in, is the mangle, which folds down into a scrubbed table when not in use. If it is Monday my mother will be there, pounding the sheets in a dolly tub, her face flushed, hair plastered down by steam. If it is fine, washing will already be flapping on the line. Wet Mondays I dread. My mother will be bad-tempered, as if the weather were foul on purpose, to spite her. A whole week's washing for five has all to be dried indoors, on racks that pull up to the kitchen ceiling, on clothes horses before the fire. It is as if the whole house was a laundry. In winter we come home from school half-frozen and shiver behind the screens of gently steaming clothes. The smell hangs like a pall and sickens me.

But the kitchen holds good smells, too. There is a tiled range with an open grate that burns summer and winter alike to heat the little oven and the water. On the hobs kettles are boiled, flat irons heated. In the early days the only other way of cooking is a single gas ring to the side of the sink. This is where my mother cooks the rare treat of homemade potato chips in a shallow frying pan. Only a few can be cooked at a time, and the three of us watch hawk-eyed as they are scooped onto our plates.

"It's not fair—she's got more than me!"

"He's got eleven—I've only got eight!"

Pauline and I can tell, from the way my mother doles out the chips, that Peter is her favourite. "He's a growing boy," she says, and so he is—growing bigger all the time, the better to thump and bully us.

We eat most of our meals in the kitchen, especially in the winter when it is the only warm(ish) room in the house. It is always in a terrible mess. The shelf above the range is a clutter of unpaid bills, matchboxes, spills, herbal remedies for my father's asthma. In winter washing dangles from the rack—we wear woolly vests knitted by our mother and liberty bodices, and they take an age to dry. We know it is dangerous to wear them still damp, we might catch cold, and even die. If we cough, a layer of pinkish padding called Thermogene is placed between vest and skin, to keep our chests warm.

On the far wall is a great wide built-in cupboard that reaches right to the ceiling. The only interesting shelves are the higher ones, where things are put so that we children cannot reach. My parents do not believe in medicine—or so they say. They are Christian Scientists, and tell us that there are no such things as pain or illness. We only think there are, because of something called "Mortal Mind." It is quite hard to work out what this means, especially if you have just banged your head or grazed your knee and are quite sure that it really is hurting. What it seems to boil down to is that if you think the right thoughts you are never ill or hurt because you are then part of "Infinite Mind and its infinite manifestation." And if you *are* ill, then it is your own fault for not thinking the right thoughts. This is confusing enough, but what is even more confusing is that on those forbidden upper shelves

"*My mother*"

are rows of remedies and medicines. There is iodine (that fearful burning liquid for cuts and grazes), there are Beecham's powders (taken in a spoonful of jam for headaches and sore throats), there are Doan's pills for my mother, brown cough mixtures, cod liver oil, and Andrews Liver Salts.

The day comes when we children *can* reach that shelf—or rather, Peter can, if he drags out a chair and stands on it. It is a hot Sunday afternoon, and our parents are having their usual "five minutes." Mummy has gone up to bed and drawn the curtains. Daddy is in the living room, his newspaper spread over his head, snoring. He has come in bad-tempered and smelling of beer, and refused his dried-out dinner kept warm in the oven. That could have been one of countless Sunday afternoons. A weird, oppressive silence hangs over the suburban street and gardens. The whole world, it seems, is "having five minutes."

What we are going to do is make an explosion. All that iodine and cough mixture, mixed together with things from the pantry, is bound to explode. (A girl in my class has already told me that if I eat the orange I have brought for breaktime, and then drink my school milk, the two will curdle together inside me and make poison and kill me. I believe this. The milk is compulsory. I give her the orange, and never take one to school again.)

My brother hands down the forbidden bottles and packets. Pauline goes into the pantry and collects salt, flour, marmalade, milk, and egg, as if for some infernal omelette. We are not sure exactly which particular combination of ingredients will produce the almighty bang. We are going to make the experiment in the garden. (It is by now wartime, and we have recently seen the bomb crater in the park, into which you could put a bus. We are hoping for a rather smaller explosion.)

In the hushed garden my brother digs a hole by the privet hedge that divides the flower from the vegetable garden. Then, one by one, we tip in the ingredients. A dreadful, dark, smelly concoction forms. We peer in at it in horrified fascination, bewitched by our own daring. In goes the milk, a full half pint of it, and I flinch, remembering the orange. The mixture curdles, all right.

"When will it go bang?" Pauline whispers. She is squatting, and I can see her navy knickers.

Peter pries open a tin.

"Now!" he says, and tips white powder into the hole.

The deep suburban peace is shattered as Pauline and I scream and scream and scream. We run into the house, hands over our ears and still screaming. The Andrews Liver Salts has sent the concoction into a seething, frothing boil. The end of the world is probably coming.

It is, almost, when our parents are so rudely awakened. Daddy is usually in an even worse than usual mood when he wakes up from one of his naps. Pauline and I run upstairs and lock ourselves in the bathroom. Peter is not so lucky. We hear my father's shouts and screw up our faces as we picture the cuffs and blows. There is a pattering noise closeby. I look down at the lino. Pauline is wetting herself.

That tall cupboard is not the only one in the kitchen, there is another, and in it is a jumble of newspapers, books, and toys. It is full to overflowing, so what my mother calls "a corner" is started next to it. Soon that corner is a great mountain of clutter. It grows and grows and is never cleaned out. Damp, speckled patches appear on the wallpaper behind it. It is a great indoor rubbish tip.

Now we are back to the range. There is a rag rug my mother has made. This is rolled up and tossed in the corner on the day the chickens arrive. They are delivered in cardboard boxes punched with holes and printed boldly, WITH CARE—DAY OLD CHICKS.

Pauline and I are beside ourselves with joy. These boxes are alive with cheeping and the slithering of tiny claws. My father has built a henhouse and run at the bottom of the garden. These chicks should really be with the mother hen, under her wings. But we are to keep them warm by the grate and give them saucers of water to sip, and their own special seed. They are balls of yellow fluff on spindly pink legs and their tiny beaks open and shut incessantly. We pick them up and stroke them with one finger, make little rag-lined nests, run after them if they stray into the hall. It does not occur to us that they may not live. When we see the first one stand drooping by the fire, head nodding, we think it is merely sleepy. In the morning it is dead. We cry, and make a little cardboard coffin and bury it under the may tree. When we return, two more chicks are drooping. We try to nurse them, but nothing helps. By evening there are two more graves under the may tree.

In the end, perhaps half survive. They grow visibly, start to flap their wings and make little tiptoe runs with their heads craned forward. Now our main business is to find and clean up the droppings. The kitchen smells like a henhouse. Hygiene is not our mother's strong point.

The table is at the centre of the kitchen. There we eat bacon and our home-produced eggs. During the war the bacon is pale and salty. My father has bought half a pig on the black market, and my mother feeds us pork for every meal. She wants to get rid of the meat as soon as she can, and dreads the knock on the door, the policeman standing there. She buries the bones in the garden rather than dare put them in the bin.

My father is missing at most meals. He is in town, at the County Hotel, drinking with

Helen Cresswell (left) with her brother, Peter, and sister, Pauline

the American soldiers and boasting of his own exploits in the First World War. When he does come in, reeking of drink, my mother purses her lips, though she dare not speak. Often he will sit at the table, push away his plate, then lean his head forward on his folded arms and be asleep, with hateful, heavy breathing, mouth half-open.

But at that same table my mother serves glorious fruit dumplings for Sunday dinners, and Irish stews, and homemade fish cakes. And at that same table I sit and write some of my early poems while the kettle spits and simmers on the hob.

On that table, every Christmas Eve, my mother lays out the family silver that has been carefully wrapped away all year. There are little bowls to be filled with sweets, cutlery, and three bangles that were my grandmother's and are kept in an old black handbag on top of my mother's wardrobe. Pauline and I sit happily smearing on Silvo, while my mother plucks and draws the chicken.

There is one last picture of the kitchen, one separated by years and years from all the others. My brother is now fifteen and as tall as my father, who seems to hate him. He is, after all, my mother's favourite. Our parents have been arguing and my father, as so often, makes to strike my mother. Then suddenly Peter too begins to shout, and raises his own fists and aims a first, unthinkable blow at his father. They are in a group by the sink and Pauline and I watch, terrified, from the hall. My father snarls and turns on him, but Peter backs away, wrenches open the back door, and is gone. He is crying tears of rage and despair. He does not come back until after dark, when my father's car has gone from the drive.

The hall is perhaps the best place in the house. Families do not live and eat and sleep in halls. This one has lino made to look like parquet and the morning sun streams through the glass panes of the front door. On one side stands a great dark carved chest with a dragon, and on the other a matching bookcase. Both have been made by my mother before she married. There are two steps up to a wide landing with a handsome hall stand and another, smaller chest. This, like the other pieces, has my mother's initials carved on the side: A. E. C.—Annie Edna Clarke. She is now Annie Edna Cresswell, and we sometimes wonder whether she married our father so that the initials will still fit. We cannot think why else.

There are two thick, handmade rugs on the floor, and it is on these I sprawl as over the years I plunder the shelves of the bookcase. The bottom shelf is the *Encyclopaedia Britannica,* the one above a complete edition of Shakespeare in twenty-one volumes with full-colour plates and engravings. I know and love them all and weave my own sad stories about the floating Ophelia and transmogrified Bottom. There are the novels of the Brontës, Thomas Hardy, Jane Austen, Palgrave's *Golden Treasury,* and the collected poems of Wordsworth, Longfellow, Tennyson, Milton, Browning. The only shelf that does not please is that housing the novels of Walter Scott. I never read them, but I like the picture of Amy Robsart lying dead, her golden hair spread about her.

Two other doors lead from the hall, one to the dining room (or living room as it becomes later, as we grow older) and the other to the front room or lounge.

The dining room door is the one I find hardest to open as I go in search of my childhood. That Christmas morning is only the first of many such scenes. The atmosphere is one of violence or, what is sometimes worse, oppressive silence. Sometimes my father's face will set into a hateful mask and he will go for days on end without uttering a single word to any of us. When he is present we dare hardly speak to one another. It is here, at breakfast, that we have to ask our father for dinner money. We dread the moment. Many a morning we hurry to the bus stop trying to choke back our tears.

I see my mother kneeling at the grate, plating newspapers to light a fire as tears run down her face.

"If it weren't for you children, I'd leave him tomorrow."

That is the refrain of our childhood. She says it often, and we know it is true, and are filled with a helpless misery.

On the mantelpiece a large, wooden clock fills the silences with a heavy, oppressive tick. Above the sideboard hangs a large, gilt-framed painting of a Highland scene. There are two leather armchairs, one on each side of the hearth. I see my mother, on winter evenings, endlessly knitting—vests, socks, gloves—even bathing suits. The clicking of her needles is sometimes more than my father can bear.

"Click click click! Bloody nitwit!"

The veins stand out on his temples. Sometimes he asks me to stroke his forehead, and I do so, very lightly. I see the gingery moustache, the enlarged pores of his nose, smell the beer and tobacco on his breath. He calls me his little nurse.

There are some happy times in that room. We act out little plays, give concerts. Both leaves of the table are pulled out and covered with a cloth. Then out come the lead soldiers and fort, the cannons that fire matchsticks or caps, the farmyard, and elaborate games are played. Or Pauline and I sit for hours on end designing paper outfits for paper dolls. We draw and snip and paint under the centre globe that is the only source of light in the room.

The house is in darkness at night, even before the war starts, and the blackout. It is dark and cold—my mother sits so close to the fire that her legs are permanently networked with yellowish scorch marks. I try to wait as long as I can before having to make the dread journey up to the lavatory. I think there might be something terrible—a snake, perhaps—lurking in the bowl. I do not press the plunger till I am poised ready to run. I have a kind of superstition that if I can reach the bottom of the stairs before the loud climax of the cistern, I shall be safe. Down I tear, under the huge etching of the Death of Caesar, half-stumbling into the hall stand at the bottom.

Later, my mother starts a little dame school in the dining room. Four-year-olds come in the mornings and my mother teaches them to read and write and do sums. We sometimes help her rule the lines in their little books, or cut out sticky paper for them to make patterns. She is doing what she loves best, and is earning money not only to help keep us at school, but also to put away, so that one day at long last she can leave our father.

The front room only ever has a fire at Christmas, when it smokes and pothers so that we have to open the windows to the frosty air. We children are not allowed in there, though I sometimes sneak in and hide behind the sofa, to read in peace. The furniture stands stiff and formal, there is a faintly musty smell. But there is a piano, and my mother plays it, beautifully, and the house is filled with Chopin, Beethoven, Mendelssohn. At Christmas, at dusk when the candles are lit on the tree, we children stand round and sing carols as she plays.

This is the only clean and tidy room in the house. My mother rarely dusts or polishes, and our clutter lies everywhere. Sometimes, when Mummy goes into town on the bus, Pauline and I will try to clean up in her absence, to give her a surprise on her return. We dust and polish and put little bunches of flowers in egg cups, and are rewarded by her smile. She sometimes brings us a little surprise, too, a treat—a quarter of chocolates or a pea soup from the Health Food Shop. This is magically in the form of a small cube, and we can hardly believe that it will turn into thick, delicious soup.

Upstairs is even untidier than downstairs, and holds dark secrets. The beds are rarely made, and one of them is never changed. On your right on the landing is first the lavatory, then the bathroom. Both have green and cream lino squares, and both have frosted glass windows and no curtains. We children have only one bath a week, and on that same night we have our hair washed. During cold spells when the pipes freeze our mother brings jugs of hot water and leaves them on top of the stairs. We dread leaving the warm cocoon of our beds, but know that if we are not quick that water will soon be cold. Behind our curtains the panes are crusted with frost, beautiful swirls and plumes, infinitely mysterious. They have formed secretly and silently in the darkness as I slept. I resolve one night to stay awake and actually see them forming, but never do.

The bathroom and lavatory have the only doors that lock, and so we run and cower there when my father is in a rage.

The room next to the bathroom is Peter's. It overlooks the garden. The door is usually kept shut because of the smell. My brother wets the bed, he goes on wetting it, on and off, until he is sixteen. The sickly smell of stale urine permeates the room. It is a source of agonising shame and embarrassment. Pauline and I taunt him with it, it is one of our few weapons against his bullying. He punches us and twists our arms until we cry, but is careful to do it only when we are alone. My mother

does not believe our stories. Peter is her favourite, we know that. I manage to win her approval by being top of the class, writing poetry, winning scholarships. My sister is not so lucky. On the other hand, she is supposed to be "daddy's girl." He gives her the choicest morsels when he is carving the joint, and sometimes sits her on his knee and calls her "Marmaduke," because she loves marmalade. He does not even mind when she pulls the crusts from her bread and hides them under the rim of her plate. He does sometimes tell her that if she doesn't eat up her crusts her hair won't curl, and as her hair is straight and silky, perhaps this is true.

Next to my brother's room and also overlooking the garden is where my father sleeps. I do not remember my parents ever sharing it. This room is the real dark secret. It is literally foul. At some point in my parents' ongoing battle my mother must have sworn that she would not clean up after him. Perhaps it was one of the few weapons she had in that battle. My father is proud of his appearance, his moustache carefully trimmed, his hair brilliantined. His suits are always pressed and his shoes buffed to a high polish. He goes out into the world and leads his own life at work and in billiard halls and bars, while my mother struggles and toils at home and tries to make ends meet. The money he spends on drink and cigarettes and betting would help pay for our school fees and uniforms.

She pays him out by refusing to clean his room. The floor, carpets, cupboards are thick with dust. My father's snuff-stained handkerchiefs lie everywhere, and empty packets of Craven A or Potter's herbal cigarettes. There are fading newspapers, heaps of old clothes, betting slips, empty bottles. This room is disgusting, not just because of the filth, but because of the unrelenting hatred it embodies. I have been to other children's houses and seen neatly made beds, frilled curtains, dressing tables with dainty lace mats. Other people do not live like this.

Sometimes I feel sorry for my father, forced to live in such squalor. Once or twice Pauline and I creep in there, meaning to clean and tidy up. But the task is hopeless and we soon give up.

In the next double bedroom, overlooking the small front garden and the road, my mother and Pauline sleep in a deep feather bed that had belonged to my grandmother. There are prints of Pinkie and the Blue Boy, and a triple glass dressing table whose drawers hold, among other things, embroidered cloths and runners. We are told my father worked these, during the months spent in hospital after he was wounded in the trenches. Our house is called Dovercourt after the place where he was nursed, and we have seen the leg that was wounded, a huge shrunken hole by the shin, all shiny blue and green.

It is in this feather bed that Pauline and I are put when we are poorly. A fire is lit and if the disease is infectious a doctor is called, despite our being told that our illness is not real, merely the product of "Mortal Mind" (A doctor's certificate is needed for us to be allowed back to school). Mumps is the worst. We cry, and old woolly vests are warmed at the fire and held to our aching jaws. One evening my father comes back from work with presents for us—little decorated cardboard sewing boxes filled with coloured threads and bugle glass beads that shine like jewels.

The small front room is mine. It has a wooden floor and rugs, a built-in wardrobe, a

At Anderby Creek, age twelve

bookcase. There is a Margaret W. Tarrant picture of the boy Jesus under a flowering cherry tree, a picture of a girl in a blue frock sitting on a rock and gazing out to sea. Above my bed hangs a framed text by Mary Baker Eddy, the founder of Christian Science: "Father, Mother, God, loving me, guard me while I sleep, guide my little feet up to Thee."

My divan bed is against the wall and I sleep with all my dolls and stuffed toys in a long row against the wall, for company. Teddy I cuddle and tell my thoughts to. By the time I am eleven he is bald and the stuffing has gone from one arm and I have bandaged it. One day I come home from school to find him missing. My mother tells me I am too old now for teddy bears and that she has thrown him out. I rush to the bin and find it empty. It is dustbin day.

It is lying in that bed that I start to make up poems inside my head, and sitting on it that I write poems and stories. I have a passion for words, I play with them as other children play with bricks, I go into another world.

It is there I lie awake night after night trying to work out how the world began, and why. I ponder what my mother tells me about God and illness. I wonder why, if it is true, babies are poorly. Surely they cannot think beautiful thoughts, or any other? Why do the tiny, day old chicks sicken and die, and plants wither in the garden? It is a mystery.

At night I am often frightened. I think I hear breathing, deep and regular, and burrow deep under the blankets to escape it till my hair is damp with perspiration. Or I hear our parents downstairs, their voices rising, my mother weeping. During the war we three children start up singsongs from our separate rooms, across the darkened landing:

> It's a long way to Tipperary,
> It's a long way to go. . . .

Or we call out jokes to one another, or at Christmas, sing carols. We are united in the darkness as we never are during the day. On rare occasions when my father is in a good mood he will bring home fish and chips, and we will be called and each given a saucer of dips with salt and vinegar, to eat sitting on the stairs.

When I am very small there is a pale blue wooden doll's cot in my room. I am a jackdaw, and it is under its mattress that I store my treasures. I collect beautiful things—pieces of coloured glass like jewels, veined stones, a saucer painted with violets. One day at a friend's house we explore her mother's dressing table and find a powder compact of mother of pearl. I am enchanted. It joins my other treasures under the mattress, and I visit it from time to time to gaze and gloat. This is my undoing. The compact is missed, the treasure trove is discovered and dismantled, I am disgraced.

A little later we are left in a dark, poky house with someone called Aunt Dora who is my father's sister, while my parents go to a funeral. Aunt Dora has golden hair and sings contralto and has been on the wireless in the *Messiah*. They say I am like her, but I don't want to be. As soon as our parents have left she turns on me and says I am a thief. She pushes me down some steps into a tiny dark scullery and shuts the door. There is a sour smell of damp and old cabbage, and a budgerigar in a cage. I am left there, listening to the voices and laughter in the next room, until my parents return.

I find a safer home for my treasures. In the stone wall bordering the front garden and half-hidden by the privet hedge, I find a hole, a tiny cave, perhaps two fists in size. It is there I now conceal my finds in a nest of cotton wool. It is very important to me, my own private secret. It comforts me.

I lie in bed on long summer evenings and hear the whistling of birds and steady whirr of lawnmowers in the suburban gardens. There is no house directly opposite, it is a piece of open ground housing an electricity substation. When the war comes, and the Americans, they go in there at night with local girls and do unspeakable things. My mother spends whole evenings spying from behind my curtains. She keeps a close watch, too, on the next house opposite. The people who live there have a Jaguar car and seem to hold one long party. They go out drinking and come back late, banging car doors, laughing, and accompanied by Americans. This neighbour has bleached blonde hair and wears lipstick, and smokes. My mother says she is "common"—her favourite term of disparagement.

During those long evenings she reminisces about her own childhood, and later, makes me her confidante. She tells me her plans, how she is saving up to escape, how she suspects my father is "going with women" and probably has some terrible disease as a result. She warns us all not to drink out of his special cup, or use the lavatory without first wiping the seat.

Once, much later, when I am about thirteen (but am taken for much older), my mother has a telephone call confirming her suspicions. It is from a man who is ringing to tell her that her husband is "carrying on" with his girlfriend, a waitress at the Kardomah Cafe. They arrange for him to come and see her. My mother makes me wear lipstick, and sit in on the meeting.

Now we will go into the garden. There is a small terrace outside the French doors and a big laurel bush where each year a thrush nests. Beyond that, for most of my childhood, is the curved roof of the air raid shelter. Many nights during the war my father will go out in his smart uniform with flat officer's cap and short cane tucked under his arm. He is in command of the antiaircraft guns on Wilford Hill. We dread the long rising wail of the air raid sirens and lie listening to the steady drone of planes overhead. If we look out of the front windows we see the sky crisscrossed with searchlights on Wilford Hill, and are proud to think our father is in charge of them.

We wear coats over our night things to go down to the shelter. It is bitter cold and dank and smells of earth. Our only source of light is candles, and of warmth a paraffin stove. Old Mrs. Cinammon from next door, and Miss Rankin from next door but one, join us down there. We children have bunk beds of canvas, the grown-ups sit on cane chairs. We all take our gas masks and there are flasks of tea and sometimes biscuits. We are not allowed to suck the barley sugar that is kept in our gas mask tins. It is for emergencies. I try to imagine what such an emergency would be, and pray that it will not be being trapped in this foul dungeon.

Beyond the shelter is a lawn, overhung by may and lilac, and borders with hollyhocks, lupins, roses. Beyond that is a privet hedge. You go down two steps to a rockery, abandoned and overgrown, and beyond that are the fruit bushes and strawberry bed, the greenhouse and hen run. During the war my father has an allotment to grow vegetables, "Digging for Victory" the posters call it. Later, he starts to grow chrysanthemums for show. He sets us to work dropping lighter fuel down the hollow canes that stake the flowers, to kill the earwigs. These flowers are beautiful, perfect—the incurved, whose petals he tweaks with eyebrow tweezers, and the great shaggy heads of the Japs. The night before the big Nottingham Show of the Chrysanthemum Society the flowers are cut and stand everywhere in buckets—even in the bath—reeking of autumn. My father sweeps the board year after year and great silver trophies and cups adorn the sideboard.

Beyond the greenhouse are the fruit trees, cordon apples and pears, and the chicken house. If we clamber onto the flat roof we can climb the poplar tree behind it. From here we have a view of the allotments and the back gardens of the street beyond. The people who live there do not know that we are watching them, and this gives us a kind of power.

There is a wider world beyond our house and garden, and I begin to take my first steps into it. When I am four my mother teaches me to read from a series of books called *The Radiant Way*. One day I am playing on the carpet and look up at the newspaper my father is reading and realize, with astonishment, that it is no longer a dizzying expanse of black and white squiggles. It contains words, and I can read them.

From then on my mother takes me every week to the local library. I love the smell of the polished parquet, and of the books themselves. My favourites are the Andrew Lang fairy tale books—*Red, Green, Yellow, Violet* . . . with their marvellously detailed line drawings of dragons, princesses, helmeted heroes.

The first lie I ever tell is about books. At four I go to St. Margaret's School and have a swan on my blazer pocket and hatband. We have a teacher called Miss Hickling, and we make the house of the three little pigs out of coloured paper, and violet-strewn bookmarks for Mothering Sunday. Each day, near home time, she reads us a story called *The Wizard of Oz*. She tells us about a film of it which she has seen, and it sounds so ravishing that I ache to see it too. I have never been to a cinema, and can only guess at its magic, if it really does bring Dorothy, the Tin Man, and the Scarecrow to life. I tell my lie.

"Miss Hickling says we've all got to go and see *The Wizard of Oz* at the Tudor."

My mother takes me. I am duly enchanted. Encouraged, no doubt, by my success, I tell my next fib. There are two very pretty fair girls in my class, the Dutton twins, with blue eyes and golden ringlets. I long to be friends with them but don't know how.

"My mummy says will you come to tea tomorrow?" I invite. She has, of course, said nothing of the kind, and I see her horror when these two prissy and befrilled children turn up with their smart mother at our house—a house where no one is ever invited.

From the very first I love school. Here is a world of calm and order, a predictable world with its own framework. I love reading and writing and words, above all, words. I move from St. Margaret's to the Modern School, a mile away. Peter is already there and soon Pauline will join us, the three of us often walking together in our neat black and red uniforms, gas masks slung like satchels over our shoulders. We dread that an air raid warning will sound when we are caught halfway between home and school.

The journey holds other terrors, too. There is a great tall house at a junction called The Three Lamps, behind a high stone wall and with an overgrown garden. A witch is said to live there, for years it haunted my nightmares. To reach our school we have to pass the rough children from the elementary school—they jeer and taunt and throw stones and call us "Modern monkeys." I am frightened of dogs and will hide for hours behind gates and walls to escape them. I am frightened, too, of an old man who wears long black robes and a black hat. He carries a curved stick and will use it as a shepherd uses a crook, catching at our legs to trip us up. One day I am by myself and see him coming up behind. I run into the garden of a house and crouch there among the bushes, waiting for him to pass. Shamingly, I wet myself. I hear his footsteps retreat, but wait for ages before I dare come out. Then I run, run for home, but as I turn the corner into our road I see that he is standing at our gate, talking to my mother! The Enemy, in cahoots with my own mother!

By the time I am eight I am learning French and Latin in a class with children much older than myself. My teacher is so delighted with the stories I write that she lets me out of school early as a reward. At ten I win a scholarship to the Nottingham Girls' High School. My mother takes me. We are two bus rides away. I am wearing my conspicuously new uniform, the rough tweed of the coat rubbing my neck. Clutched in my hand is a large shoe bag with my name embroidered across it in white letters two inches high. I don't like strangers to know my name. It gives them power over me.

I join my new class, and we read aloud a poem by Walter de la Mare called "The Scarecrow." I love it. I copy the words with infinite care into my book and draw a picture of that marvellous, stoical scarecrow, and am happy.

Most of my happiest childhood hours are spent in school, but there are other delights in the world away from our house. From my bedroom window I can see a green hill and woods beyond the roofs. Whenever I can I escape up there and lie for hours in the long grass watching the sky change. Then there are expeditions to the spinney, which is dark and thrilling with rich odours of earth and moss. In spring it is full of bluebells and even the air becomes a faint blue haze. We find whitened bones and are deliciously scared. There is a whiff of danger.

At the end of our road there is a farm, not yet swallowed by suburbia. We play in the haystacks and find litters of kittens, and dodge among the scratching hens to peer in at the snuffling pigs. The fields that stretch away towards the river are often flooded. In winter, when it freezes, we spend whole days slipping and sliding on the ice until the sun is a huge red ball in the whiteness. We run home along the darkening streets and warm our numbed fingers by the fire and feel the exquisite pain of "hot aches."

Most evenings we play in the streets. There are few cars and the road itself is part of our playground. "What time is it, Mr. Wolf?" we chant as we tread warily, awaiting the dreaded "Dinner time!" We play long after the street lamps are lit and our shadows fly at our heels. I invent games and tell stories, and a neighbour calls at our house to complain that I am frightening her children. When the evacuees from London arrive they bring with them new games and new words, too, words that have never been heard before in these prim streets. We are warned not to play with them, told they have fleas and nits in their hair—and perhaps they have, but we play with them anyway. They are wizards with the skipping rope and tireless scrumpers. They chalk enormous hopscotch squares on our tame streets and leap across them like gnats. They are mean and skinny and defiant as we dare never be, and it does not occur to me to feel sorry for them because they are away from their families.

There are people I feel sorry for, though. At the bottom of our road appears a row of what look like giant cardboard boxes with windows. They are called prefabs, and are meant as temporary houses for the homeless. The neighbourhood is outraged, petitions are got up. But the prefabs go up. We begin to see their inhabitants in the row of shops that stands between us and them. They are often unwashed and ill-looking, their clothes shabby. One day in the newsagent's I see a mother and small child and they fill me with such pity that I buy a cheap colouring book, push it into the hand of the little girl, and run off. I don't run far enough. The woman comes out of the shop, waving the book, screaming abuse. I cower before her, afraid that she will strike me, but in the end she simply flings the book down on the pavement and pulls the sobbing child back into the shop.

I do not learn from this. Later, when I am at the high school, I regularly see a poor old shuffling woman, dressed all in black, on South Parade, where we catch our bus home. Sometimes she just stands there, muttering to herself. I weave a story around her, decide that she has no family or home and no money to buy food. She must roam the streets of Nottingham by night and day. Perhaps she is a leper, or a crone like those in fairy tales, who beg for crusts to test the woodcutter's youngest son, or the prince. There is a health store nearby. One day I go in and buy a nut cutlet. Then, just as our bus pulls up, I run to the old woman and push the paper bag into her hand. As the bus draws off I look out and see that she is peering into the bag, but cannot tell if she is glad or sorry.

When I am about twelve I am sent for elocution lessons to a lady called Mrs. Humber, who lives in Carlton. I go there straight from school and she gives me tea and sandwiches and cakes before the lesson starts. I love it, because it is all to do with poetry. I love the sound of her voice reading the lines and I love the sound of my own.

> The wild duck, stringing through the sky,
> Are south away.
> Their green necks glitter as they fly,
> The lake is gray.
> So still, so lone, the fowler never heeds.
> The wind goes rustle, rustle, through the
>   reeds.

Line upon line I learn, verse upon verse, until my head is crammed with it. I am in heaven.

But in order to reach heaven I have first to go through hell. The bus that takes me to Carlton takes me first through a district called Sneinton. It is a slum, a close-packed network of mean alleys, houses back to back, their bricks pitted and blackened. Grey washing hangs in the yards, pale children squat in the gutters, women in turbans and slippers stand in doorways. I sit on the top of the bus and look down on the ugliness and squalor and tears of helpless misery roll down. I do not really know why I cry. I cannot understand how poetry and all this can exist in the same world.

There are other lessons after school. Pauline and myself are sent to Arnold Baths to learn how to swim. I am determined not to. I hate swimming baths with their chlorinated water that makes your eyes sting, with their crude echoes and rough boys who push you in. I dislike the changing cubicles, and trying to pull my clothes back onto my still half-wet body. Each Thursday we travel to Arnold by bus. Once there, I give the instructor the money and tell him that we have colds, or sore throats, and my mother doesn't want us to go in the water today. We then secretly dip our bathing costumes into the water and roll them in our towels. We dampen our hair, thorough in our deception. Back in town, we spend an hour or so wandering around Woolworth's, then go home. Our mother can never work out why we cannot learn to swim like the other children, and in the end gives up.

There are not many holidays, because of the war. The coastline is a literal minefield and fenced off with barbed wire. Before the war starts we go to Filey for a holiday in a caravan called the Rip Van. It is high on the cliffs in a large field. Each morning we go through the dewy grass to fetch milk from the farm and when we get back our father is frying bacon over the paraffin stove. Sea birds nest in the cliffs and the sky is threaded with their wings and cries. I dare not go to the edge of the cliff even holding my mother's hand. The rocks and the waves far away below seem to rush up to meet me, to pull me down.

After the war I go regularly with a school friend and her parents to stay at their bungalow in Anderby Creek. We have to fill the tank by pumping, and in the room we share is a washstand with enamel bowl. This is filled each morning with heated water taken from the rainwater butts. In it float strange specks and insects that we call pollywogs. Behind the bungalow are the sand dunes and we can run, barefoot, straight from garden to beach. The sands are wide and bare and the great North Sea rollers come sweeping in, bursting in foam. I am exultant, jubilant. I write endless poetry.

There are holidays with my mother, Peter, and Pauline first at Skegness, in private apartments. My father drives us to the station and carries the luggage down to the platform where the steam train is hissing. As we draw out we wave to him and I wish, ridiculously, that we were not leaving him alone. At the apartments there are whispered conversations with landladies as my mother explains about Peter's bedwetting.

Later, we go to Llandudno, and I have my first glimpse of mountains. We go in early September when the rates are lower, and Peter does not go with us, he now spends each summer working on a farm. Each evening we walk to the end of the pier to the pavilion, where an orchestra plays nightly. I am sixteen, and I fall in love with the handsome second violin. Our eyes meet and he evidently falls in love with me, too. His name is Robert and he is twenty-two and smells thrillingly of something musky. My mother is alarmed, but cannot prevent our meeting, first in cafes and cinemas, then in little shelters on the Great Orme where we kiss till I am dizzy. When we go home I feel literally sick at the thought of leaving him. He writes me a letter, calling me "la Belle Dame sans Merci" and quoting from the poem. He will pay for me to return for a few days to Llandudno and stay in a hotel. There is, of course, no question of this. I pass the letter round my envious classmates, awed by my conquest of a real man. Their own encounters are only with schoolboys. There are monthly dances with the boys from the high school, heavily chaperoned by staff from both schools. We giggle beforehand in the cloakroom, jockeying for the mirror, lending one another unsuitable shades of Pond's Angel Face. But I am too in love with the heroes of Thomas Hardy and the Brontës to be interested in mere schoolboys.

When I am twelve I am still in a class with girls a year older, though I am the tallest. I play hockey and netball for the school, I

*With Peter and Pauline on holiday
at Skegness*

produce the form play, an extract from *As You Like It*. At home I try to make scenery, painting on wallpaper. My back hurts. It has been hurting for months now, but my mother tells me it is "growing pains." I am to recite Mary Baker Eddy's Scientific Statement of Being. This is not real pain, it is a product of "Mortal Mind." It feels like real pain to me. Week after week, month after month, it gets worse. Now I have searing pain down my right leg and can hardly stand upright. Sometimes I lie awake all night until at last I hear the first birdsong and see the dawn lighten behind the curtains. My mother writes to a Christian Science Practitioner in Kent, and reads out the lengthy responses, which are all to do with "holding the right thoughts."

At last school steps in. A letter is sent to my parents. The teachers have noted my pallor, my red eyes, my evident pain in trying to move. For good measure, they have also noticed how pale and ill Pauline looks, that she has developed facial twitches. My mother's first response to this is to visit Woolworth's and purchase a little round cake of rouge powder called Bourgeois, with a strong scent I have sometimes noticed on buses or in church. This is applied daily before we set off to school.

The day finally comes when I cannot move without crying out in pain. The doctor is called. He is mystified by such symptoms in a child and suggests a visit to the hospital. He will make an appointment, and in the meantime I am to stay in bed. I am put in the double feather bed and lie propped up on pillows, reading and sketching to keep the monster pain at bay. When the day of my appointment comes we go there on the bus, then walk up the hill to the hospital, every step torture. By now I am bent double and cannot straighten. I am brought before an orthopaedic consultant surgeon. He takes one look and orders a wheelchair. How, he wants to know, did a child come to be in this condition before action was taken? I am wheeled across to the hospital and admitted to a Women's Ward—I am too tall for the beds in the Children's Hospital. My mother's fear of hospitals and doctors has communicated itself to me and I am now in a state of terror as well as pain.

But the nurses are kind. They put me in a bed on a balcony with five other beds. I am to lie absolutely flat on my back, with no pillow. They give me a strange little gravy boat affair with a spout to drink from. I lie for an hour or two, dazed and shocked. I feel a warm trickle between my legs and a great rush of fear and shame. It is blood, and it will be staining the spotless hospital sheets. This had happened only a few weeks previously when I had been horrified on a visit to the lavatory to see blood in the bowl. I had called my mother. She told me it was nothing to worry about and gave me a pad of torn sheet. I could not imagine what was happening, and was relieved when after a day or two the bleeding stopped.

The nurses have told me to call if I want to "go." I wait, desperately, until I am almost bursting. When the nurse comes I burst into tears of shame and fear. But when she sees the bloodstained sheet she is not angry, she smiles, raises me gently onto the bedpan, and goes to fetch a clean sheet. Two nurses roll me from side to side to change the sheet, they have strict orders that I am not to be moved in any other way. They fit a soft pad and say, "Poor child, poor child."

"College days"

And I come to see that I am in another world like school, a world of order and predictability, calm and nonjudgemental. Despite the constant pain I am happy to be there. I am spoilt by patients, nurses, and doctors because I am the only child in the hospital. When my thirteenth birthday comes the nurses make me a cake, with candles, and give me cards and little presents. Every afternoon my mother comes to visit, bringing with her books. She has obtained a reading list from school, so that I will not fall too far behind. She engages an elderly clergyman to come in and teach me Greek.

A woman in the next bed dies. She has diabetes and has already lost a leg. She has come in to have the other amputated. She is smiling and friendly and talks to me, telling me about her family. Then there is a sweet, sickly smell, the smell of gangrene. The screens go round her bed and next morning she is gone. Later another woman dies with terrible, strangled cries.

For months I lie in that ward, my only view that of the sky and the chimney of the hospital incinerator. Then comes the day when the consultant orders me to be put into a plaster jacket. I am wheeled down to a basement room and suspended on a kind of pulley while layer after layer of plaster is wound from armpits to the top of my thighs. The pain is excruciating, I am a prisoner in a dungeon, being tortured. All day I lie under a hooped cage lined with electric lightbulbs, to dry the plaster.

Then I am taught to walk again. At first even being raised to sitting position makes me giddy after lying flat for so long. The sciatica in my right leg has shortened it and I am sent daily to physiotherapy, and make weekly visits for years afterwards. The pressure of the cast makes my ankles swell like balloons. My skin itches intolerably and I vainly try to relieve it by scratching with a knitting needle.

By the time the cast is finally sawn off I have missed so much school that it is decided that I should stay down a year. For the first time I am with girls of my own age.

For the latter part of my childhood I am two people. I am the popular class clown, one of the top clique. But my real, secret self is the one who sits up into the early hours to finish poems. When I am with other people I am wearing a mask, I am the spy in the camp. I do not really accept the daily round and am constantly aware of a mystery beyond the banalities of everyday life. I can mark the moment when this begins. I am around nine or ten and walking, on a very hot day, down Davis Road. It is straight and long, possibly half a mile or more, and lined with neat houses with small front gardens and dusty hedges. The tar on the road is melting, I can smell it. Suddenly I stop, overcome by a powerful sense of displacement. The world about me is suddenly foreign. I think "This is not real," I think it, and I know it. Then "I don't belong here— what am I doing here?" I think it, and I know it, and am transfixed by the knowledge. It is at once terrifying and comforting. At that moment the boundaries of reality are irrevocably shifted. I have a new secret treasure and it is hidden, not under a mattress or in a hole in the wall, but within my own self.

This, then, was my childhood, or at any rate the parts of it that have risen in my mind as I write. When I was first asked to write this piece, several years ago, I refused. I had no wish to dredge up painful memories, and was afraid that to tell the truth would involve disloyalty to my now dead parents. When I was asked again, recently, I was again tempted to refuse. Then I thought that perhaps I could skate swiftly over my childhood years and get on to the later years of fulfillment, family life and creativity.

But that is not what has happened. As soon as I had hit upon the trick of revisiting my childhood home the memories flowed, and as I wrote I became aware of their true power and how deeply they have formed me. The most interesting part of any writer's life is her childhood. They are the only years that count in the sense that they hold the key to what she writes, and why. As I wrote I was constantly hearing echoes from my own books, found myself thinking, "Ah, *that's* what I meant, *that's* where it came from."

And so I am going to spend the last few pages not describing university, marriage, motherhood, friendships, but looking back on that childhood from the perspective of my adult self and trying to make sense of it. This, after all, is what writers really do—try to make sense of the world.

As I wrote I *have* been conscious of disloyalty to my parents. They would certainly have cringed to see what I have written. But I now see how damaged and wounded they were, too, how locked into their destructive marriage.

When I first read D. H. Lawrence's *Sons and Lovers* I was amazed, it was as though the writer had lifted the roof of our own house to find his characters. My mother had come from one of the foremost families in the area where she lived. She would tell me of her father's thriving business in agricultural machinery, of the property he owned. He had one of the first cars in Nottinghamshire and would go visiting at nearby Annersley Hall. She would describe visits to the dressmaker, her piano lessons, a visit to Paris. She was sent by train each day to the Queen Elizabeth School in Mansfield, and loved it, despite the fact that it set her apart from other local children. As long

"Wedding day—on my left are my father and sister"

as I remember, my mother never had any friends or confidantes who might have supported her, and this isolation must surely have originated in her own childhood. She was, I now see, a born teacher, and this too was part of her tragedy. She longed to go to college and become a teacher, and in fact did do some teaching before her marriage. But in those days families like hers did not send their daughters to university. She had two brothers, but neither had any interest in doing so, and went straight from school into the family business. I was aware, even at the time, that when I went to university I was largely doing so for my mother's sake, fulfilling her own ambition. From this sprang her obsession with the importance of education, the sacrifices made to send the three of us to the best (fee-paying) schools. And she was right. I thank her for it.

My father was born in the same area but in a very different background. His father was a miner. The family lived in a terrace with a narrow passage to a backyard and closet. (This was the house where Aunt Dora shut me in the scullery.) I know virtually nothing of his childhood because he never talked about it, except to tell us with relish of the time the tip of a finger was accidently cut off and the doctor managed to stick it back on again. What he did talk about, endlessly, was the First World War, when he had fought in the trenches. He told in particular, over and over, obsessive as the Ancient Mariner, the story of how he had shot an old French peasant who had wanted money for water. He told it because he was pleading for someone to say, "That's all right. It doesn't matter. Anyone would have done the same." But it was wrong, and he knew it was wrong, and it stayed wrong however many times he told the story. It was not war, it was murder. It was then that my father developed the asthma that was to shadow the rest of his life. He had fearful attacks when his breathing seemed to take him over until he was helpless and I was sure he was going to die.

Helen Cresswell with her husband, Brian, and their daughters Candida and Caroline

He met my mother at the local tennis club. I have snapshots of him in his whites and can easily see how attractive he must have seemed to my mother. He is tall, handsome, dashing, and confident. He must have been ambitious—sons of miners did not usually join tennis clubs—and to him my mother was a good catch. Though it can scarcely have been only her social standing that attracted him. There are snapshots of her, too, ravishingly pretty and demure under a Japanese parasol, her Pekingese dog curled beside her.

They were probably both equally determined to escape the narrow confines of their village. They married on Christmas Eve and went straight, in heavy snow, to their first home in Nottingham. I suppose my grandmother must have given them the money for this, and also to set my father up in his own business in wholesale fruit and vegetables. Just as my mother was a born teacher, he was a born salesman, a charmer. He worked long hours, and by the time Peter was born they had moved to a handsome detached house in West Bridgeford, the most sought-after suburb, and had a maid. It was then that they both became Christian Scientists and began to attend the church in Nottingham.

I have thought long and hard about this, and think I can see what attracted them. Partly it may have been in the hope of a miraculous cure for my father's asthma. But beyond that was the philosophy of self-help, the promise that if you put your own thoughts in order, all will be abundantly well, you can conquer the world. There is little in Christian Science about humility, or helping others, making sacrifices. The testimonies of healing in their journal are just that, testimonies of how health and lives have been improved—all, no doubt, perfectly genuine. Both my parents were fiercely competitive and ambitious and this must have held enormous appeal. In their struggle to achieve, Christian Science was an extra weapon.

I think Mrs. Bagthorpe in the "Bagthorpe Saga" is based (albeit unconsciously at the time) on my mother. She was "the greatest Positive Thinker since Canute." Mrs. Bagthorpe is not only strong on Positive Thinking but also keen that her offspring should be high achievers. They all (except ordinary Jack) have several "Strings to their Bows." We were given lessons in elocution, violin, piano, swimming, trumpet, and urged to enter competitions. I remember winning several—ten shillings for a poem called

"The Gull" in the *Mickey Mouse* comic, then a poster competition for which I was awarded a watch. At sixteen I won an adult poetry competition organised by the Poetry Society and my photograph was in the local paper (of which my mother ordered numerous copies).

Tragically, the positive thinking of Christian Science was to fail—for my father, at least. During the recession of the 1930s he was made bankrupt, the grand house and maid went, we moved to a semidetached house in another part of West Bridgford where no one knew us. This was not in fact because of my father's inability to "think the right thoughts," but because he was in a business of rapid turnover and if his customers did not pay him on time he had no money to settle his own debts. This left him permanently embittered. Not only had his religion been found wanting (at least in his own eyes), but he used later to say that none of the members of the church had offered him any assistance. He broke with them completely. The bitterness spread to my mother—it was her mother's money that had started the business and it was all lost. Because my father remained an undischarged bankrupt until a few years before his death in his seventies, he was left permanently in the financial power of my mother. The house we lived in was in her name, he could not have a bank account. The blow to his male pride was enormous, he resented it bitterly and in the end came to resent her.

I did not find out about the bankruptcy till I was in my late teens but had always been aware that some kind of shameful secret dogged our family. At all costs the neighbours must be kept in the dark. They must not know of the bankruptcy any more than they should know of my father's violent and abusive behaviour. The suburb where we lived was known as "bread and lard island." This meant that its inhabitants would rather live on bread and lard than let the world know that money was short. Appearances were everything. Shabby clothing would be dried indoors rather than hung on the line for the world to see. Our family must be seen to be happy and successful. If you look at the studio portraits of myself and Peter and Pauline as children there is nothing at all to suggest what lay behind them.

The other major rift and source of resentment between my parents was education. My father had left school at fourteen, my mother

The author with her daughters, 1994

was grammar school educated, accomplished, and well read, the great passion of her life was education. My father was quick-witted and probably at least as intelligent as my mother, but his aim in life was to get rich quick, and he was full of harebrained plans that came to nothing. He filled in the football pools every week of his life in the vain hope of realising his dreams. It cannot have been easy for him to see my mother scrimping and saving to spend every spare penny on books and school fees and uniforms, and even less easy to find himself overtaken by his own children and left feeling more inadequate than ever. He loved to boast of his three clever children at the best schools in Nottingham, but had he held the purse strings the money that sent us there would have gone into half-baked ventures or even, literally, to the dogs.

I now feel an enormous sadness when I think of my parents living out their lives locked in such helpless misery. My mother was probably more fulfilled than my father, because she was able to live vicariously through the achieve-

ments of us children. Her sacrifices were justified.

I see now that most of the stories I have written have their roots deep in my childhood. My early fantasies, in particular, have at their core the sense of two worlds coexisting, the ordinary life of every day and another, more significant dimension. These have their roots in the experience I had on that hot day in Davis Road and countless following similar glimpses. *The Night-Watchmen* and *The Bongleweed,* in particular, crystallise this. Over and over, in book after book, I assert this sense of the thinness of so-called reality compared with the richness of life lived in the light of the imagination. Most writers repeat themselves. They tell the same story over and over again in different ways, as if they were driven (and indeed, I suppose they are).

There is little point in describing the rest of my life. It is vain to try to give the sense of one's own daily life, it is rather like showing one's holiday photographs—they never capture how it really was and everyone is concealing yawns. But we were *there*, and can evoke again the sights, sounds, smells, and indefinable something that goes even beyond the senses.

But I must mention my daughters. Caroline now lives in Kenilworth with her partner, Colin, and works as a TV producer. Candida read zoology, got a First, and has just gone to Oxford to read for a D. Phil. We went there last week to celebrate her Halloween birthday and sat in a restaurant where a pumpkin glowed on every table. My daughters are what I love most in the world and are my greatest achievements. You might not think so, from what I have written. When I look back on the first pages, that world of my childhood seems light years away, another life. But whatever I am now is contained in those years, and whatever I have written. And that is that. You can't give up on your childhood.

BIBLIOGRAPHY

FOR CHILDREN

Fiction:

Sonya-by-the-Shore, illustrated by Robin Jane Wells, Dent, 1960.

The White Sea Horse, illustrated by Robin Jacques, Oliver and Boyd (Edinburgh), 1964, Lippincott (Philadelphia), 1965.

Pietro and the Mule, illustrated by Maureen Eckersley, Oliver and Boyd, 1965, Bobbs Merrill (Indianapolis), 1965.

Where the Wind Blows, illustrated by Peggy Fortnum, Faber (London), 1966, Funk and Wagnalls (New York), 1968.

A Day on Big O, illustrated by Shirley Hughes, Benn (London), 1967, Follett (Chicago), 1968.

The Piemakers, illustrated by V. H. Drummond, Faber, 1967, Lippincott, 1968.

A Tide for the Captain, illustrated by Robin Jacques, Oliver and Boyd, 1967.

The Barge Children, illustrated by Lynette Hemmant, Hodder and Stoughton, 1968.

The Sea Piper, illustrated by Robin Jacques, Oliver and Boyd, 1968.

The Signposters, illustrated by Gareth Floyd, Faber, 1968.

A Game of Catch, illustrated by Gareth Floyd, Chatto Boyd and Oliver (London), 1969, Macmillan (New York), 1977.

A Gift from Winklesea, illustrated by Janina Ede, Brockhampton Press (Leicester), 1969.

A House for Jones, illustrated by Margaret Gordon, Benn, 1969.

The Night-Watchmen, illustrated by Gareth Floyd, Faber, 1969, Macmillan, 1969.

The Outlanders, illustrated by Doreen Roberts, Faber, 1970.

Rainbow Pavement, illustrated by Shirley Hughes, Benn, 1970.

The Wilkses, illustrated by Gareth Floyd, BBC Publications (London), 1970, as *Time Out,* Lutterworth (Cambridge), 1987.

The Bird Fancier, illustrated by Renate Meyer, Benn, 1971.

Up the Pier, illustrated by Gareth Floyd, Faber, 1971, Macmillan, 1972.

The Weather Cat, illustrated by Margery Gill, Benn, 1971.

The Beachcombers, illustrated by Errol Le Cain, Faber, 1972, Macmillan, 1972.

Bluebirds over Pit Row, illustrated by Richard Kennedy, Benn, 1972.

Jane's Policeman, illustrated by Margery Gill, Benn, 1972.

The Long Day, illustrated by Margery Gill, Benn, 1972.

Roof Fall!, illustrated by Richard Kennedy, Benn, 1972.

Short Back and Sides, illustrated by Richard Kennedy, Benn, 1972.

The Beetle Hunt, illustrated by Anne Knight, Longman, 1973.

The Bongleweed, illustrated by Ann Strugnell, Faber, 1973, Macmillan, 1974.

The Bower Birds, illustrated by Margery Gill, Benn, 1973.

Butterfly Chase, illustrated by Margery Gill, Kestrel, 1975.

The Winter of the Birds, Faber, 1975, Macmillan, 1976.

Awful Jack, illustrated by Joanna Stubbs, Hodder and Stoughton, 1977.

Donkey Days, illustrated by Shirley Hughes, Benn, 1977.

The Flyaway Kite, illustrated by Bridget Clarke, Kestrel, 1979.

My Aunt Polly by the Sea, illustrated by Margaret Gordon, Wheaton, 1980.

Dear Shrink, Faber, 1982, Macmillan, 1982.

The Secret World of Polly Flint, illustrated by Shirley Felts, Faber, 1982, Macmillan, 1984.

Ellie and the Hagwitch, illustrated by Jonathan Heap, Hardy, 1984.

Petticoat Smuggler, illustrated by Shirley Bellwood, Macmillan (London), 1985.

Greedy Alice, illustrated by Martin Honeysett, Deutsch, 1986.

Whodunnit?, illustrated by Caroline Browne, Cape, 1986.

Dragon Ride, illustrated by Liz Roberts, Kestrel, 1987.

Moondial, Faber, 1987, Macmillan (New York), 1987.

Trouble, illustrated by Margaret Chamberlain, Gollancz (London), 1987, Dutton (New York), 1988.

Hokey Pokey Did It!, Ladybird, 1989.

Rosie and the Boredom Eater, Heinemann, 1989.

Whatever Happened in Winklesea?, Lutterworth, 1989.

Almost Goodbye Guzzler, Black, 1990.

Giant!, Cambridge University Press, 1994.

Polly Thumb, Simon and Schuster, 1994.

The Watchers: A Mystery at Alton Towers, Macmillan, 1994.

Mystery at Winklesea, Hodder and Stoughton, 1995.

Stonestruck, Viking Penguin, 1995.

"Jumbo Spencer" series:

Jumbo Spencer, illustrated by Clixby Watson, Brockhampton Press, 1963, Lippincott, 1966.

Jumbo Back to Nature, illustrated by Leslie Wood, Brockhampton Press, 1965.

Jumbo Afloat, illustrated by Leslie Wood, Brockhampton Press, 1966.

Jumbo and the Big Dig, illustrated by Leslie Wood, Brockhampton Press, 1968.

"Lizzie Dripping" series:

Lizzie Dripping, illustrated by Jenny Thorne, BBC Publications, 1973.

Lizzie Dripping Again, illustrated by Faith Jaques, BBC Publications, 1974.

Lizzie Dripping and the Little Angel, illustrated by Faith Jaques, BBC Publications, 1974.

Lizzie Dripping by the Sea, illustrated by Faith Jaques, BBC Publications, 1974.

More Lizzie Dripping, illustrated by Faith Jaques, BBC Publications, 1974.

Lizzie Dripping and the Witch (play; produced in London, 1977), BBC Books, 1991.

"Two Hoots" series; illustrated by Martine Blanc:

Two Hoots Go to Sea, Benn, 1974.

Two Hoots and the Big Bad Bird, Benn, 1975, Crown (New York), 1978.

Two Hoots in the Snow, Benn, 1975, Crown, 1978.

Two Hoots and the King, Benn, 1977, Crown, 1978.

Two Hoots Play Hide-and-Seek, Benn, 1977, Crown, 1978.

"Bagthorpe Saga"; illustrated by Jill Bennett:

Ordinary Jack, Faber, 1977, Macmillan, 1977.

Absolute Zero, Faber, 1978, Macmillan, 1978.

Bagthorpes Unlimited, Faber, 1978, Macmillan, 1978.

Bagthorpes versus the World, Faber, 1979, Macmillan, 1979.

Bagthorpes Abroad, Faber, 1984, Macmillan, 1984.

Bagthorpes Haunted, Faber, 1984, Macmillan, 1985.

Bagthorpes Liberated, Faber, 1989, Macmillan, 1989.

Bagthorpes Triangle, Faber, 1992.

Bagthorpes Besieged, Hodder and Stoughton, 1995.

"Posy Bates" series:

Meet Posy Bates, Bodley Head (London), 1990, Macmillan, 1990.

Posy Bates Again!, Bodley Head, 1991, Macmillan, 1991.

Posy Bates and the Bag Lady, Bodley Head, 1993, Macmillan, 1993.

Other:

Rug Is a Bear, illustrated by Susanna Gretz, Benn, 1968.

Rug Plays Tricks, illustrated by Susanna Gretz, Benn, 1968.

Rug and a Picnic, illustrated by Susanna Gretz, Benn, 1969.

Rug Plays Ball, illustrated by Susanna Gretz, Benn, 1969.

John's First Fish, illustrated by Prudence Seward, Macmillan (London), 1970.

At the Stroke of Midnight: Traditional Fairy Tales Retold, illustrated by Carolyn Dinan, Collins, 1971.

The Key, illustrated by Richard Kennedy, Benn, 1973.

Cheap Day Return, illustrated by Richard Kennedy, Benn, 1974.

Shady Deal, illustrated by Richard Kennedy, Benn, 1974.

The Trap, illustrated by Richard Kennedy, Benn, 1974.

Nearly Goodbye, illustrated by Tony Morris, Macmillan (New York), 1980.

Penny for the Guy, illustrated by Nicole Goodwin, Macmillan, 1980.

The Story of Grace Darling, illustrated by Paul Wright, Viking (London), 1988.

(Editor) *Puffin Book of Funny Stories,* Viking (New York), 1992.

(Editor) *Classic Fairy Tales,* Golden Books, 1993.

Television plays:

The Piemakers, BBC, 1967.

The Signposters, BBC, 1968.

The Night-Watchmen, BBC, 1969.

The Outlanders, BBC, 1970.

"Lizzie Dripping" series, BBC, six episodes, 1973, five episodes, 1975.

"Jumbo Spencer" series, five episodes, BBC, 1976.

"The Bagthorpe Saga," BBC, 1981.

"The Secret World of Polly Flint" series, seven episodes, ITV Central Television, 1986.

"Moondial," series (six parts), BBC, 1987.

Also author of television plays *Dick Whittington,* 1974; *For Bethlehem Read Little Thraves* (for adults), 1977; "Five Children and It" series (adaptation of Edith Nesbit's book), 1991; "The Return of the Psammead" series, six episodes, 1993; and "The Watchers" series, 1995.

Contributor to several children's anthologies.

Kevin Crossley-Holland

1941-

Kevin Crossley-Holland, age eight, sitting with Bruce, the family's bullterrier

I f I were to ask you to tell me your story and to begin at the beginning, you might tell me first where and when you were born, and you might not. . . .

Once upon a time I travelled by overnight train and then by boat to the desolate island of Eigg in the Hebrides. One day I went scrambling on the mountainous dark hunk of pitch-stone porphyry known as the Sgurr, and for the first time in my life I got vertigo.

I couldn't go up; I couldn't come down. White-knuckled, I leaned into a silver tumbling burn, I clung to the rocks in the bed of the stream, I tore my nails. I closed my eyes. Swill and rush and chuckle. All around me the sounds of the stream, and I was safe again. For a long time. Safe. And at home. For I believe what I heard at that perilous moment awoke in me memories of another time: the sound of blood coursing round my mother's body and her heart thump-thumping. I was remembering the time before I was born.

I've always had more sympathy for the hare than the tortoise but the truth is that throughout my childhood and early adulthood I was in many respects a slow starter. My first slow start was in being born. My mother was some two weeks overdue before I was ready to face the world.

I was born in a nursing home in the little village of Mursley in north Buckinghamshire at 9:30 A.M. ("late for breakfast," my mother used to say) on February 7, 1941. My mother's father jokingly suggested I should be called "Benghazi" after the Libyan town that day wrested from the Germans. But in the event my parents mercifully settled on Kevin John William. Kevin, because my father was enamoured by the saint and sound of that name and because my mother was one-quarter Irish (descended from the Keoghs and Swinneys and de Veres). John, after the man who was supposedly my earliest known ancestor. And William, after my paternal grandfather, Frank William.

The staff in the nursing home had other ideas. They nicknamed me the "Professor." Why? "Because he looks so worried."

From time to time during my twenties and thirties, while I was reading a book or listening to a discussion, someone would ask me, "Why are you looking so worried?" "I'm just concentrating," I'd reply. So I expect Kevin John William, newly hatched, was just concentrating on the life-journey in front of him.

During the war years of my early childhood, my family was often on the move. Ruled ineligible for all three services because of a gastric ulcer, my father took up a post in 1943 with

123

Whiteleaf Hill and Cross, which rose above Crosskeys, the little cottage
where the author was born, in the Chiltern Hills

the Ministry of Food and with the CEMA (Council for the Encouragement of Music and the Arts, which later became the Arts Council of Great Britain) as director of the northwest counties, and my mother and I followed him from Colwyn Bay to Whaley Bridge to Wilmslow. At this last stop my sister Sally (actually christened Zara Irene Mary) joined the show. She was born at Stockport on January 24, 1944: a constant, fair thread—good-humoured and generous and willing and resourceful—in the fabric of my story.

In exasperation hurling my "Noser Ark" at a stubborn friend; shaking an entire box of baby powder over a red-haired, red-faced Welsh baby; running to catch a bus with my mother, and crying out because the top of a toothpaste tube was lodged inside my right shoe, and still I had to keep running: these are some of my earliest memories.

I think I have only one recollection of the war. I was a page at a London wedding, dressed in gold satin trousers. At the wedding break-

fast at the Savoy, I trundled off to get the bride a piece of wedding cake. Then everyone heard it: a flying bomb—first the whine, then the silence. There was a huge, muffled thump. No one moved; no one spoke; nothing. And then the music—was it an orchestra?—started up again. The guests began to move, to talk . . . "Swa swa hit ne waes": that's what the Anglo-Saxons say. As if nothing had happened.

When I was six, my mother and father returned to the house from which I was born: a little cottage called Crosskeys in the Chiltern Hills. At its shoulders stood the beechwoods, so feminine in spring, so brassy in autumn; above its head reared Whiteleaf Hill and the mighty chalk hill-carving known as Whiteleaf Cross.

First I shared a room downstairs with Sally; we slept on bunk beds, I on top, she on the bottom. We had a green blind with rather splendid yellow tigers stalking across it; when the wind got up, an elderbush flapped at the window-panes and the tigers began to sway and prance.

But later I had my own bedroom—and my own desk at the window, with a view of Bledlow Ridge (where in a field ploughed for the first time in generations as a result of wartime pressure to increase food production, my father discovered the remains of an Iron Age settlement) and half the Vale of Aylesbury. From the hilltop the view was immense. In the foreground, the villages of Whiteleaf and Monks Risborough; the ancient hedgerows flanking the Neolithic track known as the Icknield Way, the ever-growing sprawl of Princes Risborough, a little train puffing its way from halt to halt on its slow journey to and from Marylebone. In the midground, the cement works at Chinnor, and a wide, intricate tapestry of fields, some of them arable, some dotted with cattle and sheep. And far, far off, a shimmer—a dream of Oxford; and even further, the faint blue of the Cotswold Hills. "And on a clear day," said my father, "on the clearest day, you may even be able to see the mountains of Wales."

As for Whiteleaf Cross, the white badge on the chest of the hill, one hundred fifty feet high and just as broad at the base: Sally and I spent half our childhoods scaling it or sliding down it. Its steep face was the quickest route to the hilltop and our climbing trees, our hides and glades; we made primitive carvings from hunks of its chalk; we found fossils embedded in it; we watched as troops of Boy Scouts spread out across it and weeded it; sitting in the back of the battered old blue Morris Ten (BTM 812), we spotted it, a gleaming beacon, from twenty miles away, and knew we were almost home.

I can see two children. Look! There they are, sitting on the wiry grass near the hilltop, almost eight hundred feet high. They're swinging their legs over the apex of the cross and talking, talking, talking . . . Almost the whole of their lives is waiting in front of them. Now, far below, a woman walks into her cottage garden. What is she carrying? An Alpine cowbell. She rings the bell. Again she rings it. Up there, the two children hear her. They scramble, they slither. In five minutes they'll be standing and panting on the cottage verandah. With flat hands, their mother will wallop their chests and backs and bottoms, and the chalk dust will fly. . . .

After we had returned to the Chilterns, my father joined the Music Division of the BBC in 1948, and he stayed up in London during the week. My mother, meanwhile, who had been a well-known potter and designer for Doulton before her marriage, worked for the Central Office of Information, first conducting Social Surveys, and later on in London, in Baker Street.

But at the weekends, until I was nine and went away to school, Crosskeys burst into life. In his study, my father played the piano and warbled as he worked on his own compositions; my mother, caught I think in a difficult marriage, filled the house with tides of friends—ours as well as hers—and filled the air with aromas from the Aga; Bruce, our bullterrier, galloped around not doing good. (Alas! he was eventually put down after burying every inhabitant of a nearby henyard between our rows of cabbages; but Sally and I were told he had gone to live on a farm, a long way away, on the other side of the country. Oh dear! How many times did I ask my mother if we could go once, just once, to see him?) We all went out walking in the high woods and dragged back branches which my father chopped and sawed and stacked against one wall of the cottage right up to the eaves; and at bedtimes my father sometimes came with his Welsh harp and sat by our bunk beds, and said-and-sang (as the Anglo-Saxons called it) folktales to Sally and me.

Not only humans beautiful and ugly and rich and poor and ambitious and lazy and brave and cowardly (and most of us are a mixture of those) but seal-women and ghosts and dragons and boggarts visited that little room. Above all, though, my father loved the Celtic stories of fairy folk. In the gloom, I saw pookas and pipers, changelings and the Banshee, dark horsemen, Tam Lin and (my father's favourite) the bewitching lady who walked out of the lake up on the mountain of Fan Fach. I haven't the slightest doubt that the seeds of my lifelong interest in folktale, legend and myth were sown there, in the blue hour between day and night, waking and sleep.

Sometimes I accompanied my father when he went walking over archaeological sites—and from that day to this I don't suppose I've walked past a molehill without kicking it over. Together we found potsherds: Iron Age coarseware, medieval brown glaze and green glaze. And now and then, two pieces actually fitted together: part of a Romano-British cooking pot, a little medieval jug broken and chucked away by someone like you or me.

One day my father said, "Today we'll find a coin." And I believed him because he has the gift of serendipity. We walked, we stooped and scrambled, we used our eyes. . . . Small and dark as the top of a cartridge case, it lay under a little bush on Cop Hill: a bronze coin, small as a penny or a dime. On one side was the head of the Roman emperor Constantine; on the other, two soldiers at attention, each holding a spear. I was electrified. Who dropped it? Why? What was his name? Her name? What colour eyes? Where was he going? What did her mother say? Who and what and when and why? That was the place and moment at which I was first fully conscious of the presence of the past: that mysterious, challenging, enriching, shared dimension which has underpinned so much of my writing for adults and children.

There was a garden shed at Crosskeys and, with my father, I cleared it out and turned it into a little museum. We henched the walls with shelves and tables; we laid out potsherds, coins, tiles, fossils, shells, ores, Egyptian scarabs and figurines. There, with my father, I cleaned and sorted and enquired and catalogued.

"My sister, Sally," 1949

Again and again I turned over in my hands one of our *pièces de résistance:* a Crusader coat-of-mail and helmet and a Saracen shield with a fierce moustachioed face on it (all three donated by my father's father and later sold to the Tower of London); a little Roman perfume bottle, made of glass, pale blue, lustrous; beads from Ur; and my Constantine . . .

Always something of an opportunist, I soon "opened" the little museum to the public. That is to say, I propped up Sally's and my blackboard on its easel at the end of the lane. Museum, it proclaimed: Entrance Free.

On our garden gate, a few yards down the lane, I posted an altogether smaller sign: "Museum: Entrance One Penny."

Undeterred by this petty deception, weekend visitors began to call in. The very first (she lived in Whiteleaf) astonished me by leaving in the till—a lead box with a Negro's head on the top of it—not one penny but half a crown. A fortune! And this visitor? The author Rumer Godden.

That museum! How wonderful it was. Musty; dusty; cobwebs at the window: of all the rooms I have ever stepped into, this is the one I return to most often. Was my father the ringleader? Was I? I hope the truth is that we egged one another on.

My mother (Joan Mary) was brought up in the Manor House at Leighton Buzzard, the only child of a doctor (Claude Cowper) and his wife (Mary nee Collard, the ninth of ten children) who initiated, funded and ran a hospital supply depot, and was decorated for it, during the First World War.

Children like to know what's what, even if they sometimes bridle at it, and my mother did not disappoint us. With spirit, a strong sense of organization and savoir faire, she taught us how to lay the table in the right way, required us to eat whatever was on the plate set in front of us, allowed me to make up to four telephone calls a week to friends, ensured we wrote thank-you letters before we played with our presents, had us make our own beds and make them properly, spurned the local hairdresser and drove me into Oxford so that I could have a "decent haircut," made me responsible for polishing the family's shoes. . . .

For her part, my mother was eager for us to have not only as secure but as rich and varied a childhood as possible. She enthusiastically organized a succession of dancing lessons and riding lessons and golf lessons; with the help of her uncle, she arranged for me to have cricket coaching (from county and test cricketers, at Lord's); and, herself an ex-county player for Bedfordshire, she gave me regular tennis lessons and entered me for a number of county tennis tournaments.

At the first of these, in Norfolk, I didn't fare too well! Eager and very nervous, I spent most of the time helping my opponent retrieve the balls with which he beat me 6-0, 6-0. But I did somewhat better at subsequent tournaments, came to love the game dearly, and to play competitive tennis in my teens and early twenties at Bryanston (my public school) and Oxford.

My resourceful mother also got Sally and me to many of those marvellous set piece occasions that are part of the English sporting and social calendar: a test match at Lord's, where I saw Bill Edrich and Denis Compton bat against South Africa; the British Grand Prix at Silverstone; the Royal Tournament at Olympia.

It was my father, meanwhile, who sat Sally and me either side of him in the BBC box at the Promenade Concerts, and who first took me to opera when I was eight or nine—*Carmen* at Sadler's Wells and then the very next night to *The Magic Flute* at Covent Garden.

Such a plethora of activities suggest that my parents were rather well off. They were not. Rather, each had a clear sense of what was worthwhile, and worth making sacrifices for. And chief of these was their shared belief in the value of private schooling.

"Does he know the three R's?" the headmistress of Sumach School asked my mother.

"Well. . ."

"Yes," I chipped in. "Yes, I do."

In truth, I hadn't the faintest idea what the three R's consisted of. But, in a hurry to get on to the next stage of my life, I wasn't about to make a poor showing at my interview. I figured I could ask my mother about the mysterious trinity on the way home, so as not to be caught out on my first day at school.

Our sharpest memories of early childhood—and they are usually images, seldom sounds or tastes or smells—are of moments of emotional intensity. And so I suppose it is typical that I can remember my interview with the headmis-

"*My mother: a studio portrait by Madame Yevonde, taken two or three years before I was born*"

tress but virtually nothing of the humdrum hours during which I developed my skills in reading, writing and arithmetic, as well as getting underway with subjects beginning with other letters of the alphabet.

What I recall from my pre-preparatory school days between the ages of six and eight is distinctly non-curricular: slowly regaining consciousness after a friend had knocked me out with the backswing of his croquet mallet (I still have the semblance of a scar on my forehead) and seeing, out of focus, my sister's face white and weeping—she was quite sure I was dead; and I remember being dragged in to school by one ear, an ear twisted by Mrs. Boulting (and thus hating all members of the Boulting family, and their inane films, from that day to this); playing hide-and-seek in the school hall, and peeking through my fingers before the lights were put out, and seeking Karen Thomas under the piano, and kissing her there, and being flushed and excited at doing so. I remember leading the flat race on Sports Day, and slowing down as I looked for my mother in the crowd of admiring mothers, and being overtaken. (For the last forty years, my mother has seldom missed an opportunity to impress on me that a game is never won or lost until it is actually over. "Think of Big Bill Tilden," she says. "At Wimbledon, and leading Cochet 6-2, 6-4, 5-1. And then he took his eye off the ball. . . .") And, sharpest memory of all, I am trying to sing the first verse of "The Holly and the Ivy," solo, at the school Christmas concert, and my sore throat is hurting. "The holly and . . ." Croak! The audience laughs. I stick out my chin. Tears, hot and unshed, sting the insides of my eyelids. "The holly and . . ." Three times, with the help of the pianist, I try to reach that high E . . . "Well! I did practise this morning," I announce as loudly as I can. And everyone laughs again.

When I was eight, my parents decided nothing would be lost by entering me for a choral scholarship to the Chapel Royal at Windsor. I don't think my father was particularly convinced by the timbre of my voice but maybe he thought my habitual eagerness might make up for what I lacked in natural talent.

For weekend after weekend we rehearsed—one of my set pieces was that singularly dreary hymn, "There is a green hill far away"—and then, just before Christmas, my parents drove me over to Windsor. Well prepared and optimistic, I sang at full throttle before the examiners—perhaps a half dozen men sitting in low slung armchairs and settees in a softly-lit, oak-panelled room.

The choirmaster telephoned my parents that same evening. He was sorry, he said, not to be able to offer me a scholarship; very sorry; but, well, the examiners did wonder whether I perhaps had a bit of a sore throat. "However," said this choirmaster, "we were all impressed by Kevin's manners and his confidence. He walked round," he said, "and shook each of us by the hand, and wished us all a happy Christmas!"

Unable to afford a place for me at a boarding preparatory school, my parents reluctantly sent me to a private day school at Prestwood. There, I got cut on the forehead (again) after being hit by a snowball with a stone in it, and ripped one leg open while trying to climb over a barbed wire fence, and failed my eleven-plus exam. . . .

Probably even more unhappy than I was, my mother contacted an old tennis partner, now owner-headmaster of Swanbourne House preparatory school, some twenty miles away in the north of the county. And in the name of friendship, this kind man immediately offered not only to make room for me but, I believe, to reduce his fees. "I'll put up a camp bed for him if it comes to it," he is reported to have said.

So in September 1950, aged nine-and-a-half, I went away to school. It has long been intellectually fashionable to talk about what children at boarding school are deprived of (above all, of course, of the daily interplay of family) and what they have to endure. But such talk is partial and often deliberately exaggerated to score social or political points, or simply because horrors always make a better story than the humdrum. When I think of my four years at Swanbourne and then five years at Bryanston, I have much more mixed feelings.

In the classroom, sitting behind my ink-stained desk deeply incised with the names of

"Get that leg across! Playing cricket in the garden at Whiteleaf," 1952

"My father playing the Welsh harp," 1949

former tenants, I just about held my own. That is to say, in a score-based and competition-conscious system, I was under average without being bottom of the class.

"Floppy" Wright, the master in charge of Latin and cricket, was the terror of the school: he used to tower menacingly over us, and yell, and slam our desk lids. Once, I incurred Floppy's wrath of wraths, and he hurled a pile of new hardback textbooks at me, one after another. Over my head they sailed, dark blue frisbees with sharp corners, and smack-smack-smacked into the classroom wall. But this man: he knew the language spoken by the emperor and two soldiers on my Roman coin; and with the sweetest patience that was the antithesis to his vile temper, he showed me how Latin could underpin my knowledge of English and French. To him, I think, I owe part of my lifelong delight in language.

But what amazes me is that I could have come away from Swanbourne, and away from childhood, without any particular love of reading. I believe I only once borrowed a book

from Whiteleaf library. Keeping it for one week too long, and reluctant to pay the small fine out of my pocket money, I kept it another week. And then another year. Then I kept the book another forty years! When I finally took it back, with a complete set of my books by way of penance, I was mortified to discover the library had long since burned down.

The one book that enthralled me as a young boy was *Our Island Story,* an account of such key episodes in British history as Boadicea's last stand and Alfred's treaty with Guthrum and the Battle of Hastings and the sinking of the White Ship. . . . Fired by this patriotic and highly-coloured book, and nothing if not ambitious, I decided at the age of eleven to embark on a major literary enterprise of my own: a *History of the World* which, somewhat later, and rather reluctantly, I scaled down to a *History of Britain.* I resumed work at the beginning of each holiday, and managed quite a number of chapters before eventually losing heart.

At Swanbourne, though, we were seldom encouraged or given time to write stories or

*The Crossley-Holland family: parents Peter and Joan
with Kevin and Sally—and Bruce, 1949*

poems. How teaching practise has changed! What importance we place on stimulating children to recreate the world with words and images and movement. I think the only thing I wrote during my years there was one highly-derivative ghost story.

On the other hand, Swanbourne did much to develop my love of games. There was no tennis but I shot in the rifle range and ran cross-country (rather well), I played rugby (rather timidly) and football (in the 1st XI, at right halfback), I swam (unenthusiastically, and only after being dragged round the pool countless times, like a flapping fish on the end of a rod), and I played cricket. . . .

I am eleven again and sitting on the grained bench in the pale green changing-room in front of my locker: Number 29. I'm glad it's a prime number. It cannot be reduced. It's something singular. I can hear shots from the rifle range, and flushing cisterns, and bumping and clumping and muffled laughs in the scout-loft overhead. But I have a job to do. I have to oil my cricket bat for the first time this season.

I open my locker and there at the back is my sticky-and-dusty bottle of linseed oil. I pour a glob onto the top of the bat, just under the splice, and another near the bottom. Then I begin. Fingertips first. My whole left hand. Round and round in small circles, opening the pores of the willow.

The back of the bat is angled. It's less easy to stop the succulent oil from trickling and dribbling . . . Now the front again . . . The willow drinks. And drinks. Until it becomes quite plump and juicy. Then, all at once, it's saturated. Satiated. The job is done.

My fingertips, pink and tingling: the blade of the bat, mottled, surprisingly rough to the touch, with bruises and abrasions and faded cherry echoes of blows well struck; the rubber handle, slightly sticky; and year after year, at the back of my locker, the miraculous cruse—the supply, seemingly self-replenishing, of sweet, thick, nourishing linseed oil. . . .

I admire the modern Renaissance man/woman: the self-reliant all-rounder equally at home painting a watercolour or penning occasional verse, discussing new developments in the sciences, tinkering with the boiler or the car. . . .

Alas! There is not the least chance of my living up to this ideal. I am not at all practical, and it was as cub and then scout at Swanbourne that I first realised this was the case. The reef and the granny were the only two knots I mastered; and I couldn't put up a tent without it leaking or sagging or listing. To light a fire with no more than the regulation two Swan Vestas; to cook porridge of an even texture: these skills were quite beyond me.

Consequently, scout camp after the end of the summer term represented an unpleasant hurdle and a whole week of holidays gone to waste. The dismal proceedings began with the digging of horrible, huge shit-pits; and they continued with terrifying wide-games in which it seemed I was always the hunted, never the hunter: I remember hiding in a blazing cornfield, carrying our team's colours; I remember my heart beating so loudly I was certain it would give me away. The hunters came closer. And closer . . . When I see a combine harvester threshing a field, I always think of the rabbits cowering in the ever-diminishing uncut corn, too afraid to make a run for it, and imagine the panic rising within them.

One evening during my first scout camp, our parents joined us to eat barbecued sausages and sing camp songs and play rounders. Great was my delight when both my parents showed up, and great was my amazement when my father, playing barefoot, proved to be the star of the game. With quite explosive force, he whacked and welted the balls over the tents and across the scrub and into the woods, and ran pink and smiling from base to base as if he actually liked the game! As young children, we are so eager for our parents to excel, and so proud when they do.

Aged seven or eight, I found a viola in the attic at Crosskeys. It was quite beautiful, chestnut and gleaming, lying slim-waisted in its black velvet bed, and I took possession of it and pressed my father to arrange lessons for me. That he did, with the composer Phillip Cannon, and these lessons continued after I went to Swanbourne. But I was no good. No good at all. I couldn't even play decent scales. I kept trying, though, until I was fifteen. . . .

Sometimes I still ask myself why. A belief in persistence? Filial piety?

The music I enjoyed most at Swanbourne were the hymns we sang each morning at assembly and in chapel twice each Sunday: Abide with me . . . From Greenland's icy mountains . . . Praise the Lord, ye heavens, adore him . . . I still remember their numbers in the Public School Hymn Book.

But evensong on those Sundays when I had been out with my parents (just three times each term) could be painful. After giving me a delicious day at Whiteleaf, with my favourite lunch of shepherd's pie and rice pudding, and after driving me back to Swanbourne—miles sometimes forlorn, sometimes quite oppressive—my parents would stay at my behest for the evening service. I sat with the choir, they in the congregation. Hymn number 25: "The day thou gavest, Lord, is ended . . ." My tears lolloped onto the page.

Some writers have described their preparatory schools as being hives of sexual activity.

The creek and maltings at Burnham-Overy-Staithe, "only a minute's gallop from my grandparents' cottage"

"Gun Hill and the island of Scolt Head: then, now, and forever"

Swanbourne was not really like that. True, our first dormitory captain was something of a Queen Bee:

> Licker Lonsdale could tap dance.
> His hot eyes stripped us
> naked so Murdoch the Mole used to
>   burrow
> beneath his blankets before
> lights out . . .[1]

And so did I! True, Jack Ramply levied three weeks' worth of sweets (we were allowed two and one-half ounces each Sunday) as a price for certain information. But our more formal instruction was saved for our very last afternoon at school.

"Right! Now you have this Thing . . ." began the headmaster.

<hr />

[1] Lines of verse from "Preparatory School" in *New and Selected Poems: 1965–1990,* by Kevin Crossley Holland. London: Hutchinson, 1991.

At that point, I still wasn't completely clear about the function of this Thing. I knew it was tender and private. I knew I peed with it and had taken part in "Who can pee the furthest?" contests . . . I knew it had something to do with making babies . . . I knew how to masturbate . . .

". . . this Thing," continued the headmaster. "I call it a Tool . . ."

All around me, I could hear the silence deepening; fifteen school-leavers clutching their thighs, backs and lips stiffening.

". . . Tool. And there's no need to be ashamed of it. Every man needs a Tool."

Humane and witty though our headmaster was, I found my first sex lecture absolutely excruciating. As soon as it was over, all fifteen of us ran away into the school grounds, and climbed tall trees (strictly one boy per tree) and, keeping companionable silence, sat on high for a long time to cool off.

Swanbourne! Mixed feelings. I think of preparatory school as the time of first separation from my parents and sister and home, and don't think it can do any child good to regard separacy as the norm. Then I think of Swanbourne as a place where it was essential to learn to hide some of my feelings, and develop some grit. It wasn't much fun to inherit the nickname Morbus (Disease) from a boy called Holland, who had a pocked face and had just left the school; it wasn't fun as a squit[2] to have to dance on the table in front of jeering top-formers, or to have my arm locked in a half nelson by Grummet, or to be beaten with the cane. But I don't believe that such experiences have left deep psychological scars.

But the sunlight . . . I also think of prep school as a time when I first made wonderful friendships, and as a time of intellectual and sporting challenge and rapid development, a time when almost everything seemed possible and there was still all the time in the world. It's not difficult to isolate and criticise absurdities and authoritarian elements in the English private school system, but to suggest that there is something sinister in its moral and social milieu is to overstate the case.

Two-thirds of the year for school, one-third of the year for holidays. Holidays! At large in beechwoods; ensconced with Sally in the ancient beech that was "our" climbing tree, its bottommost branch a magnificent, kicking swing, its topmost deeply graven with the initials KJWC-H and ZIMC-H—and petrified once because the "wild boys" gathered under the tree and, unaware of us, held a war council right below our feet; bicycle rides through the dopy lanes and villages of rural mid-Buckinghamshire, Askett and Hampden (the sometime home of John Hampden) and Meadle and Denton and Stone— from time to time I used the same Swiss penknife that carved initials in the beechwood to prise shining cat's-eyes out of their rubber casings; occasional light-headed afternoons with my first girlfriend, Ann Hellings, who lived nine miles away; and, most longed for of all, sometimes at Easter, always in summer, the visit to our grandparents (my father's parents) on the north Norfolk coast.

How Sally's and my spirits soared as, year after year, we drove out of the dapper Home Counties. In the back of the Morris Ten, we counted down the approaching towns with chants

repeated over and over again. "Swaffham," we sang, "Swaffham, Swaffham, good for nawthen." And then, "Fakenham, Fakenham, where they're maken 'em." And at last, with Swaffham and Fakenham safely behind us, we sang a simple third almost ad infinitum, just a couple of semi-quavers and a couple of quavers: "Burn-ham Mar-ket, Burn-ham Mar-ket, Burn-ham Mar-ket . . ."

At Burnham Market, my mother and father wound down the windows so that we could all smell the salt air. And that was when, just as my sister and I thought he had forgotten, my father offered "a penny for the first person to see the sea . . ."

My father's father (Grandpa Frank) had moved from Bedfordshire to a little cottage at Burnham-Overy-Staithe in 1945 after a quite remarkable career as physician (he invented the healing cream known as Iodex, in common use during the Second World War and still widely used in some Third World countries) and barrister, practising on the Midland Circuit. He had been High Sheriff (1940) and Deputy Lord-

Walking companions: Grandmother Neenie and Kevin in Switzerland, 1947

---

[2]A small, insignificant person.

Lieutenant (1940–52) of Bedfordshire and, in his seventies, he took a doctorate (written in French) from the Université de Nancy.

But of course such achievements scarcely impinged on me as a young boy. What I knew was that Grandpa Frank was the most wonderful carpenter alive. In his little workshop, orderly to the last shaving, he made me a windmill. When I wound the handle at the base of the mill, beneath the little painted sign saying KEVIN MILLER, the sails of the mill turned and the miller came out of his house and glided on a pathway of green tape towards the mill. . . . I knew my grandfather drove his grey Hillman much too slowly for Sally's and my liking, and enjoyed visiting decrepit churches and playing church organs:

> I was the bellows-boy. And in corners
> decorated with curious tidemarks
> or up against grey walls frosted with salts
> I pumped and monsters with twenty
>   throats
> or forty throats shuddered and wheezed.
> Then the old sorcerer showed them his
>   palms
> and soles: they hooted and began to
>   sing.[3]

I knew my grandfather relished a course of cheese after his dessert, and liked singing hymns after supper (preferably in harmony with my father), and I knew he could be severe. Aged ten, I once began a sentence with "Er . . ." and he gave me a fearsome lecture on never opening my mouth until I knew precisely what I wanted to say. But I also knew Grandpa Frank was kind, and he invariably sent Sally and me away at the end of our holiday clutching bank notes (a green one-pound note for me and a brown ten-shilling note for Sally). He was, I suppose, a latter-day paterfamilias.

My grandmother Neenie—the name I gave her when I was two and unable to say "Irene"—always made it clear to me that she and I had a special relationship. She preferred boys to girls, she told me; and I was her eldest grandson. For year after year, and largely unknown to Grandpa Frank, she sent me money and food parcels at school; she wrote me weekly letters—I have kept them, an enormous stack; in Norfolk, she not only cooked wonderful meals

and forgave us for getting back hopelessly late for them, but delighted Sally and me by telling us stories about our father (and his younger brother Dick) when they were children, and endlessly obliged us by boiling our catches of shrimps and washing bunches of muddy samphire and paddling around the creek, helping us push our little boat *Mallard* over sandbars. In return for this sweetness and selfless patience and generosity, I gave my grandmother unconditional and lasting love. As the years passed, there was very little I did not discuss with her. She lived until she was ninety-four, and I suppose my relationship with her, almost forty years long, was within the family the least intense and uncomplicated that I have had.

It is only a minute's gallop from my grandparents' cottage to the creek at Burham-Overy-Staithe: the little waterway where the murky tide rises for three hours and ebbs for nine; where a few sailing dinghies tug at their anchors, then rest on their shoulders; where the austere black-eyed Maltings overlook the water,

Just home from hitchhiking in Finland, 1958

<hr>

[3]Lines of verse from "Generations of Air." Op cit.

and the great stanchions of the old jetties slowly rot and moulder.

A screeching and mewing overhead; the smell of ozone and the stench of iodine-rich marsh mud. But look up! There! There is the huge stark theatre of saltmarsh and serpentine creeks; and beyond this great, palpitating emptiness, on the quivering skyline, the North Sea and the tidal island of Scolt Head:

There it was, the island.

Low-slung sandhills like land-waves,
    fettered by marram.
One hut, a dark nugget. Across the creeks
    gleaming like
tin, like obsidian, across the marshes
    almost rust,
olive, serge, fawn, purpled for a season,
    the island.

We shoaled on the Staithe, stared out and
    possessed it;
children who collar half the world with a
    shout, and
share it in a secret . . .

In a coat of changing colours it awaited
    us. In the
calm seas of our sleep it always loomed,
    always ahead.
We woke, instantly awake. As if we never
    had been
tired, and all things were possible . . .[4]

The north coast of Norfolk is my imaginative heartland. The acres I walked and waded and rowed over, and so came to love as a boy, have become the ground—I think that's the right word—for much of my writing. Many of my early poems arise from the fierce nature of the place ("Here alone I cannot sham. / The place insists that I know who I am.") and from the hammering sustained by the sea-defences during the Great Flood of 1953. And in a long sequence of poems called "Waterslain" (an old Norfolk word meaning flooded and my fictional name for Burnham-Overy-Staithe), I celebrated many of the villagers I came to know in my childhood: Miss Disney, who always went for a swim in the creek before breakfast, and sometimes caught her breakfast with her feet; Billy Haines, who took his little boat *Rosemary* round

the coast and over to Dunkirk; Mason, who gave us thrilling rides on his amphibious vehicle know as the Duck (DUKW). Waterslain turns up again in my lucky little story, *Storm*: it is my heroine Annie's destination on her perilous night journey.

Crossing places are potent. Think of midnight (when coaches turn into pumpkins) and New Year's Eve and bridges (several folktales begin on London Bridge) and beaches. Quite apart from their fierce beauty and hard crystalline light, I think the marshes of East Anglia appeal deeply to me precisely because they are the daily battleground of earth and water; and yes, I suppose it is paradoxical to feel most at home in a place that is in a state of constant crossover and change:

This flux, this anchorage.
Here you watch, you write, you
    tell the tides.

        You walk clean into the
            possible.[5]

In the summer of 1947, my mother scraped up enough money to take my father and Neenie (aged sixty) and me (aged six) to Switzerland. Sally was not invited, and has taken a dim view of being left behind from that day to this. This was a great expedition, away from the ration-book austerity of postwar Britain: a flight from Northolt (at that time London Airport), then successive trains into the Bernese Oberland and up to the village of Wengen, which members of our family have now regularly revisited over a period of fifty years. My grandmother and I were walking companions and, in the early evening, I used to eat in solitary state in the hotel dining room. I soon fell in love with the waitress. And up in my bedroom, with its commanding view of the Jungfrau and Eiger, I wrote her a passionate eulogy in red crayon: page after page of it, containing every possible permutation of the words I LOVE THE WATRIS, all of them surrounded and decorated with leaping and springing crotchets and quavers and semi-quavers.

When I was twelve and Sally nine, my parents arranged for a French boy to stay with us for a fortnight during the summer holidays.

---

[4]Lines of verse from "The Island." Op cit.

[5]Lines of verse from "Sounds." Op cit.

Laurent. We didn't get on very well. In fact, we soon had so heated an argument about Nelson and Napoleon that Laurent packed his case and, unnoticed, slipped out of the house. My mother picked him up halfway down the hill to the station, tearful, penniless and on his way back to Paris . . .

But Jean-Pierre, who came the following year, seemed much worse. He was scornful of the museum, and he fancied Sally. Sally liked him, too, and I suppose this made me rather jealous.

In the third year, Sally and I not only entertained Laurent and his sister Pascal but went to stay with them in the Alps and Paris. On our first evening, Laurent's mother served us a rare delicacy—and rare is the word: fillets of steak, still bleeding. I was appalled. I couldn't even bring myself to nibble at the edges. Then Sally took over. "Excusez-moi!" she said, and she raised the little glass of red wine allowed to her. "This is what we do in England!" And with that, she poured the whole glass of wine over my steak. "Go on!" she urged me under her breath. "Eat it!"

These first exchanges may have been difficult but they were also habit forming. It became natural to go abroad, and I was soon possessed of a great wanderlust. Aged seventeen, I embarked on a hitchhiking holiday through Belgium and Germany and Denmark and Sweden to Finland; and before I was twenty, I had visited almost every country in western Europe. Love of abroad still burns fiercely in me. A few years ago, I edited *The Oxford Book of Travel Verse;* I long to return to India; and I have worked and lived for two years in Bavaria and five years in the American Midwest. . . .

Grandpa Frank died when I was sixteen. His death upset me and a few days after his funeral, which I was deemed too young to attend, I wrote a poem: a kind of psalm about life as a prelude to death.

Within a couple of weeks, I wrote two more poems: an impressionistic account of a concert at the Royal Festival Hall, and a sonnet about the windmill at Burnham-Overy-Staithe. This sonnet was published in the termly Bryanston *Saga*: and other than a letter about the English penny, written at Grandpa Frank's bidding and printed in *The Times* when I was just nine, it was the first time I had seen words of mine in print.

There was the highly-coloured *History of Britain* when I was eleven; and between the ages of twelve and fourteen, aided and abetted by my mother, I rubbed dozens and dozens of church brasses and completed a descriptive inventory of *The Church Brasses of Buckinghamshire.* But the chief intention of these works was to inform; really it was in drafting the three poems described above that I first felt excited by the risk and possibilities of imaginative writing.

My father was the first person to whom I showed drafts of my poems. A contributor to *Encyclopaedia Brittanica* and *Grove's Dictionary of Music and Musicians*, he knew precisely how to write clean, quick, musical prose, and his quiet advice and steady support were the best possible encouragement:

> You thinned my words like seedlings. *And*
>   *avoid*
> *long words where short suffice.* (work; will do.)
> For vogue and buzz and all-too-commonplace
> you wrote in almost timeless substitutes
> (ex-Yeats, ex-Graves). *Revise and then revise.*
> *Our second thoughts strike deeper than the first.*

I also have cause to remember the fathers of two semi-girlfriends! The first was Alan Ross, at that time not only poet and deputy editor of the *London Magazine* but also cricket critic for the *Observer.* When I was seventeen, Alan gave me some of his manuscript poems to type out—I remember going home with them, flushed and anxious—and then he sent me a wonderful letter about the writing of poetry. First, he commended me for making a start; he pointed out that, young and inexperienced, I still had a limited amount of things worth saying; then he argued that I should play games with different metres and rhyme schemes, and use my time to discover the function and magic of poetic form, so that, having valuable things to say, I would also know how to say them.

The second father was Terence de Vere White, novelist and at that time literary editor of the *Irish Times.* One night, he went off to bed, taking a clump of my poems with him. He delivered his verdict next morning, after breakfast. "I think you could make a good prose writer," he said. Kindly meant, no doubt, but the very last thing I wanted to hear, and absolutely crushing.

For all that, I did begin to write prose as well as poetry during my very early twenties.

Kevin Crossley-Holland, with daughter Eleanor, 1986

and games of squash and rounds of golf, and the winning of a tennis tournament; to describe my long love affair with the Anglo-Saxons and the literature of the early North-West European world: to write of my work as a publisher and teacher and my love of broadcasting; to tell at last of my marriages and my own four children, Kieran and Dominic, and Oenone and Eleanor: these parts of the story must wait for some other time and place. For here, I have chosen largely to write about my childhood, quite sure (and even more sure after writing these pages) that the child is mother to the woman or, in my case, father to the man. Look into one and you will see much, maybe most, of the other!

Let me, however, undermine my own position. Childhood is not an end in itself. Not long ago, an eighty-eight-year-old priest snorted and said to me, "Childhood! Yes, childhood's all very well. But it's what you go on to do that's interesting. It's what you make of it that counts."

*

First an autobiographical and unpublished novel called *Debendranath*, about the friendship of a young Englishman and an Indian; and then the first fifty pages of a second effort, *The Breaking of the Circle*, before I got hopelessly stuck. . . . At this point, aged twenty-two, I read the medieval romance *Havelok the Dane*. I thought it rather trite and colourless as a poem, but also recognized that it told a rattling good story; and I began to wonder whether I could retell it in prose, fleshing it out, throwing in all the medieval verve and detail I could think of. I remember deciding to abandon my second novel, and feeling very reluctant, very relieved. And I remember, one spring day, setting out on that joyous part of my story which has been and is to write books for children. . . .

To write of how I resolved, aged fourteen, to become a priest, and did not waver until I went up to Oxford; to describe how we moved from the village of Whiteleaf to Hampstead; to recount Sally's years at the Ballet Rambert School; to speak of my deep and abiding love of classical music, and collaboration with Sir Arthur Bliss and William Mathias and the writing of two libretti (*The Green Children*, for children, and *The Wildman*, for adults) for the composer Nicola LeFanu; to record hockey tournaments

When I was a young editor in the London publishing house of Macmillan, I bought a leather-bound Visitors Book. The first writer to inscribe his name in it added the comment, "How difficult to begin!" A couple of days later, a second writer came to my office. He duly inscribed his name and he, too, added a comment: "How difficult to follow!"

I like that. I like the wordplay, combining respect and a touch of arrogance. And not long ago I copied it out and stuck it on the wall behind my desk. There are several other sayings alongside it. "Never mind the song—it was the singing that counted." *"Festina lente"* (Latin for "hurry slowly"). "I made it out of a mouthful of air." And *"Eard gemunde"* (Anglo-Saxon for "he remembered his home country").

There is another saying stuck up on the wall behind my desk, the astonishing first sentence of St. John's Gospel: "In the beginning was the Word, and the Word was with God, and the Word was God." What does St. John mean? I think his seventeen words (sixteen of them monosyllables in the inspired Authorized Version) express the nature of God in terms of sound and speech, and imply that the power of sound actually generated matter. It follows, doesn't it, that each artist (permitted one breath, one sip of this divine force) has a share in the process of constant renewal—a responsibility to sing this world to life.

BIBLIOGRAPHY

FOR YOUNG PEOPLE

Fiction, except as noted:

Havelok the Dane, illustrated by Brian Wildsmith, Macmillan (London), 1964, Dutton (New York), 1965.

King Horn, illustrated by Charles Keeping, Macmillan, 1965, Dutton, 1966.

The Green Children, illustrated by Margaret Gordon, Macmillan, 1966, Seabury Press (New York), 1968.

The Callow Pit Coffer, illustrated by Margaret Gordon, Macmillan, 1968, Seabury Press, 1969.

(With Jill Paton Walsh) *Wordhoard: Anglo-Saxon Stories,* Macmillan, 1969, Farrar, Straus (New York), 1969.

(Translator) *Storm and Other Old English Riddles,* illustrated by Miles Thistlethwaite, Macmillan, 1970, Farrar, Straus, 1970.

The Pedlar of Swaffham, illustrated by Margaret Gordon, Macmillan, 1971, Seabury Press, 1972.

The Sea Stranger, illustrated by Joanna Troughton, Heinemann (London), 1973, Seabury Press, 1974.

The Fire-Brother, illustrated by Joanna Troughton, Heinemann, 1975, Seabury Press, 1975.

Green Blades Rising: The Anglo-Saxons (cultural history; part of "The Mirror of Britain" series), Deutsch (London), 1975, Seabury Press, 1976.

The Earth-Father, illustrated by Joanna Troughton, Heinemann, 1976.

The Wildman, illustrated by Charles Keeping, Deutsch, 1976.

Beowulf, illustrated by Charles Keeping, Oxford University Press, 1982.

The Dead Moon and Other Tales from East Anglia and the Fen Country, illustrated by Shirley Felts, Deutsch, 1982.

(With Gwyn Thomas) *Tales from the Mabinogion,* illustrated by Margaret Jones, Gollancz (London), 1984, Overlook Press (Woodstock, New York), 1985.

Axe-Age, Wolf-Age: A Selection from the Norse Myths, illustrated by Hannah Firmin, Deutsch, 1985.

(With Susanne Lugert) *The Fox and the Cat: Animal Tales from Grimm,* illustrated by Susan Varley, Andersen Press (London), 1985, Lothrop (New York), 1986.

Storm, illustrated by Alan Marks, Heinemann, 1985.

British Folk Tales: New Versions, Orchard (London and New York), 1987, revised edition published as *British and Irish Folk Tales,* Orchard (London), 1990, and as *The Dark Horseman,* Orchard (London), 1995.

Boo!: Ghosts and Graveyards, illustrated by Peter Melnyczuk, Orchard (London), 1988.

Dathera Dad: Fairy Tales, illustrated by Peter Melnyczuk, Orchard, 1988.

Piper and Pooka: Boggarts and Bogles, illustrated by Peter Melnyczuk, Orchard, 1988.

(With Gwyn Thomas) *The Quest for Olwen,* illustrated by Margaret Jones, Lutterworth Press, 1988.

Small-Tooth Dog: Wonder Tales, illustrated by Peter Melnyczuk, Orchard, 1988.

Wulf, Faber (London), 1988.

Sleeping Nanna, illustrated by Peter Melnyczuk, Orchard, 1989, Ideal (New York), 1990.

Under the Sun and Over the Moon, illustrated by Ian Penney, Orchard, 1989, Putnam (New York), 1989.

Sea Tongue, illustrated by Clare Challice, BBC/Longman, 1991.

Tales from Europe, BBC, 1991.

Long Tom and the Dead Hand, illustrated by Shirley Felts, Deutsch, 1992.

(With Gwyn Thomas) *The Tale of Taliesin,* Gollancz, 1992.

The Labours of Herakles, illustrated by Peter Utton, Orion, 1993.

The Green Children (no connection to the earlier publication in 1966 of the same title), illustrated by Alan Marks, Oxford University Press (London), 1994.

The Norse Myths, illustrated by Gillian McClure, Simon and Schuster (London), 1993, Barnes and Noble (New York), 1995.

Editor:

Running to Paradise: An Introductory Selection of the Poems of W. B. Yeats, Macmillan (London), 1967, Macmillan (New York), 1968.

Winter's Tales for Children 3, Macmillan, 1967, St. Martin's Press (New York), 1968.

The Faber Book of Northern Legends, illustrated by Alan Howard, Faber (London and New York), 1977.

The Faber Book of Northern Folktales, illustrated by Alan Howard, Faber (London and New York), 1980.

The Riddle Book, illustrated by Bernard Handelsman, Macmillan, 1982.

Northern Lights: Legends, Sagas and Folk-Tales, illustrated by Alan Howard, Faber (London), 1987.

FOR ADULTS

Poetry collections:

The Rain-Giver, Deutsch, 1972.

The Dream-House, Deutsch, 1976.

Between My Father and My Son, Black Willow Press, 1982.

Time's Oriel, Hutchinson, 1983.

Waterslain and Other Poems, Hutchinson, 1986.

East Anglian Poems, Jardine, 1988.

The Painting-Room and Other Poems, Century Hutchinson, 1988.

New and Selected Poems: 1965–1990, Hutchinson, 1991.

Poetry as single works (limited editions, booklets, and broadsheets):

On Approval, Outposts, 1961.

My Son, Turret, 1966.

Alderney: The Nunnery, Turret, 1968.

Confessional, Sceptre Press (Frensham, Surrey), 1969.

A Dream of a Meeting, Sceptre Press, 1970.

Norfolk Poems, Academy, 1970.

More Than I Am, Steam Press, 1971.

The Wake, Keepsake Press, 1972.

Petal and Stone, Sceptre Press (Knotting, Bedfordshire), 1975.

Above the Spring Line, with an etching by Malte Sartorius, Francis Kyle Gallery, 1986.

Oenone in January, Old Stile Press, 1988.

The Seafarer, with woodcuts by Inger Lawrance, Old Stile, 1988.

Eleanor's Advent, Old Stile Press, 1992.

Other:

Pieces of Land: Journeys to Eight Islands (travel), Gollancz, 1972.

The Norse Myths: A Retelling (mythology), Deutsch, 1980, Pantheon (New York), 1980.

The Stones Remain: Megalithic Sites of Britain (history), photographs by Andrew Rafferty, Rider, 1989.

Translator:

The Battle of Maldon and Other Old English Poems, edited by Bruce Mitchell, Macmillan, 1965, St. Martin's Press, 1965.

Beowulf, Macmillan, 1968, Farrar, Straus, 1968.

The Exeter Riddle Book, Folio Society (London), 1978, as *The Exeter Book of Riddles,* Penguin (London), 1979, revised edition, 1993.

The Anglo-Saxon World, Boydell Press (Woodbridge, Suffolk), 1982, Barnes and Noble (New York), 1983.

The Wanderer, Jardine, 1986.

Beowulf, Boydell, 1987.

The Old English Elegies, Folio Society, 1988.

Editor:

Winter's Tales 14, Macmillan, 1968.

(With Patricia Beer) *New Poetry 2,* Arts Council, 1976.

Folk-Tales of the British Isles, Folio Society, 1985, Pantheon, 1988.

The Oxford Book of Travel Verse, Oxford University Press (Oxford and New York), 1986.

Medieval Lovers: A Book of Days, Century Hutchinson, and Weidenfeld and Nicolson (New York), 1988.

Medieval Gardens: A Book of Days, Rizzoli, 1990.

Peter Grimes: The Poor of the Borough, Folio, 1990.

Writer and presenter of documentary television features: "The Seven Burnhams-by-the-Sea," BBC, 1978, "The Lambton Worm," BBC, 1983, "Waterslain," Anglia, 1987, "The Painting-Room: Three Artists in Constable Country," Anglia, 1988; co-writer of scripts for television series for primary schools: "Tales from Europe," BBC, 1991, "The Anglo-Saxons," BBC, 1992, "The Labours of Herakles," Channel 4, 1993; writer of numerous programmes for BBC Radio 3 and 4, including "Arthur's Knight" (six-hour drama series), and of the recordings "Beowulf," "The Battle of Maldon and Other Old English Poems," and "British Folk Tales."

General editor, *The Mirror of Britain,* ten volumes, Deutsch (London) and Seabury Press (New York), 1974–79. Also librettist for Nicola LeFanu's operas *The Green Children,* 1990, and *The Wildman,* 1995. A collection of Crossley-Holland's poetry notebooks is housed in the Brotherton Collection at the University of Leeds. The manuscripts of his books for children are housed in the Osborne Collection, Toronto. The Kerlan Collection, Minneapolis, holds material relating to *Under the Sun and over the Moon.*

Arthur Dorros

1950-

Arthur Dorros, sitting on the tail of an alligator, about age four

By age nine I had traveled the world. I crossed the Pacific on a raft with Thor Heyerdahl. I cruised around the globe in trains and cars, on horseback and the occasional burro, by air and on foot. I was venturing into new lands and discovering home, all the while digesting words. I liked books. I even ate a few. There is a photograph of me at age sixteen months with a page in my mouth. My son Alex ate a few pages when he was about that age too. Maybe it's a genetic thing.

I did get lost in the pages. Also found. Baseball, radio, and my parents insisting I go to bed early all made me do it. I enjoyed reading. When I was eight or nine, I was going through a book a day, the day including a night. That reading rate might have been because I was tired of the Washington Senators baseball team. At least listening to the games on the radio. To me, listening to baseball on the radio was and is not an exciting participatory sport. But good for me came out of baseball. Reading, and an appendectomy.

After a bag of peanuts and a seventh inning soda at a Senators' game, my stomach began to ache in a way I'd never felt before. I was doubled over with a pain that made it hard to even hobble down the ramp and out of the stadium. When it was discovered that I had both a fever and my appendix aflame, I was rushed to the hospital. After the appendectomy, a nice slice having been made across my lower belly, it only hurt when I sneezed or laughed. So my friends came into the hospital and cracked jokes, including some about baseball. Later yet, I went to what I was told was the only high school named after a major league baseball player, and then without figuring out who she was, started dating his granddaughter. I never thought of my life as wound up with baseball, but there I am. I guess it's not always possible to tell at the time what will be important in the future.

Now I have to take a minute to try to explain the Washington Senators, though it has been said that no one could explain the Senators. They were moved to another city and then no one could explain that, either. And I still haven't figured out how baseball could have been on the radio all year long, because I thought baseball had a season. But I know it was on all year, because that's what happened when I was eight. I know it did. I tried tuning my radio for what had to have been a year of nights, and I only got one station. The one with the Senators' games. I'd been given a crystal radio shaped like a small red-and-white rocket ship. It was a kind of science experiment for a little kid. It didn't need a battery and had a magnet inside that slid around to run and tune it, and besides that you had to clip a wire to something metal. I found out that the springs under the mattress on my bed worked great to clip to, and you could only hear the radio through an earphone that fit in one ear. So if I laid my head on the pillow with the earphone ear down, when my parents looked into my room to see if I was asleep, they thought I was indeed sleeping.

That was it. I really got into reading. My parents had bedtimes for me they insisted on. When I was very young it was 7:00 P.M., then worked up to eight. I never seemed to be able to fall asleep until about eleven. I'd lie in bed, thinking my way into the light and dark corners of the universe as I knew it. Or there was the crystal radio rocket. After radio, I discovered batteries and flashlights. After my parents had checked on me and gone to bed, I'd continue reading by flashlight. I threw the covers over my head to make a kind of a tent. That could have been so the light wouldn't bother my little brother, David. But he was a lot younger than me and usually asleep in his crib early in

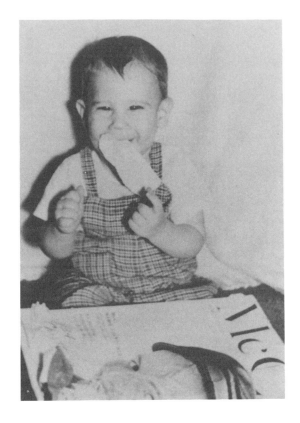

At sixteen months, enjoying some early reading material

those years (unless he stayed up late to throw his bottle). It was probably in case my parents came back, though I can't remember them commenting on the glow from beneath the covers. So this was what I considered a "bad thing," early bedtime, turning out to be something good—I read more and more.

One of my favorite types of books to read was adventures, mostly the exploring type: up the Amazon, or books like *Kontiki* by Thor Heyerdahl. I wrote to Mr. Heyerdahl, asking him if I could go on his next trip. I didn't get an answer to my letter for about two years. By that time I thought I'd never hear from him. The card came one day out of the blue, and I was elated to get it. He said that it would be awhile until his next voyage—it took time to organize the kind of expeditions he made, and the next one would be in about eight years.

I could have written to him in eight years, but by that time time had a different meaning. I didn't realize eight years had passed, I'd forgotten about the card, maybe didn't think he'd really take me. I only found the card again a couple of years ago, in a pile of old papers that had been stuck away in the attic of my parents' house. When I found the card, it made me realize it would be nice to answer as quickly as possible any letters that I now get from people who read my own books. I never thought when I was a child that I would be a writer. In fact, I never met any writers of books, and so it seemed a distant thing, people writing books. Getting correspondence from Thor Heyerdahl was a very kind act on his part, I realize, for he was definitely extremely busy with many projects. But getting the letter back two years later added to the feeling of distance, that a writer was not knowable, a person. That's one reason I like going into schools these days, so that people can see that whoever I am, a writer is just another person, and could be anybody.

Though I didn't know I would someday be a writer, my childhood connection with stories, books, and written words was extremely strong. From the time I could read on my own, at about age six, until I got my driver's license when there was a teen after the six, books and my bicycle were my main path to other worlds. My bicycle was a heavy, red metal thing, the kind people had 'in the old days'. If it fell over, it was too heavy to pick up. So I learned to ride well enough that it wouldn't fall over. Sometimes with friends, sometimes alone, I biked around the Washington, D.C.,

On the streambank, about four years old

area, down to the C & O Canal and Great Falls, and around town.

A friend and I rigged up a rope between bikes for really long rides, so that we could take breaks by towing each other. Farther afield, D.C. was full of sights to grow on. I saw inaugurations and funeral processions, a city burning, a city elated with cherry blossoms. The Smithsonian Museum was one of my favorite spots with its dinosaurs, inventions, and historical oddities. I once ended up riding around the halls of Congress not on my bicycle, but with a congressman on a golf cart. Congress definitely can take strange turns.

Often, I'd bike to the library. Inside, I'd find my way around the walls of books. Country, city, forest, field, California, New York, sidetrips to the Sahara, Himalayas, and South Sea Islands, and stops underseas and in outer space. Again, part of this was just because of my own interests, and partly was fueled by the odd bits of life that floated by.

In the same bedroom where I spent so many early childhood hours reading, there was a huge map. The map covered a whole wall, an entire side of the room. A family named Castro had owned the house before our family, and a colonel or general who'd worked at the Pentagon had owned the house too. I guess it wasn't General Castro who put up the map, but it was General Somebody. Every day when I woke up, and before I went to sleep, I'd look from my bed and see parts of the world I'd barely or never heard about, Quito to Kathmandu. There were a lot of places around the equator because that's about how high my bed was on the map. I'd move my bed around to different continents from time to time and dream about the places I might someday visit.

Besides reading, what I liked to do was walk, run, or bike, to explore the tangible world around me. I had a few friends in my neighborhood, and a couple a mile or two away that I had to pedal over to. Often I ventured forth with those friends, but if not with my sisters or brother, I spent a fair number of afternoons alone. I enjoyed the solitary time, if it meant being able to observe and experiment. I had attributes that I've since found many scientists, detectives, and writers share: I was curious, had theories, liked observing, investigating, and searching for what might be "true." I made a hole in the sidewalk with the help of a neighbor in one experiment, and on

A beaver chewed the tree to cut it down.
Beavers drag branches away to build their
round lodge home and a beaver dam.
Behind the dam is a beaver pond.

Who lives among the tall grasses by the beaver pond?

From Animal Tracks, *written and illustrated by Arthur Dorros*

my own thought I'd invented plastic in another. Discovering how things are put together still interests me.

I never did understand how my third grade teacher was put together. I started the third grade ecstatic that I was going to be under the tutelage of Miss Rowe. In second grade I'd had a teacher who had been at work many years. She was kindly, but I cannot remember her opening her mouth. She must have, at least to tell us what pages in our workbooks to do. We did a lot of workbook pages in second grade. That year passed silently, especially the

spring when I had an operation to remove a growth that on the skin surface was marble-sized and was marble hard when lifted from my arm. The growth turned out to be like a root, growing much deeper than had appeared, but it was removed in time. I was lucky that my mother, in her usually determined way, had persisted, getting the opinions of three surgeons, the last of whom decided to investigate immediately. He was a great surgeon with an off-beat sense of humor. To remove my stitches he whipped out a flashing, chromed, foot-long bowie knife, the type Davy Crockett might favor. Fortunately, after he laughed, he used

another, smaller tool to take out the stitches. On school days, while I recuperated, I watched from inside the building, climbing up on a bathroom stall so I could look out the high window and watch my classmates play at recess. Perhaps I should have considered myself fortunate, as prior to the operation a crew of three or four bullies used to pursue me every recess. Being a recent arrival at the school, not being the greatest baseball or kickball player, and not yet having developed many allies, I was solo enough for the bullies. Bullies always seemed to travel in groups, or were much larger than the rest of the class if they dared oper-

ate alone. There weren't any bullies my size. Part of the nature of bullies—try to ensure that you have the edge. Anyway, our second grade teacher seemed to evaporate away in times of peril.

But in third grade I was going to have Miss Rowe. Someone who talked, who was exciting, who was there. For three weeks. Then she slipped a disc in her back and was put in traction. We were told she would return to us in a month or so, but we never saw her again. She was replaced by a teacher whom I saw as distant and cold, particularly after the warmth of Miss Rowe. I resented this Miss Rowe re-

Arthur, age six, and sister Ellen with grandparents, Harry and Irene Dorros

placement. This was the first of a chain of teachers in elementary school, teachers from another planet, who hailed me through an asteroid-filled fog of far-off space. This teacher's specialty was keeping me after school. I was not a good printer, and we were starting into script. I held my pencil in an awkward grip and tried to make the letters the best I could. My teacher, however, decided that I and I alone merited staying after school to practice the alphabet. She would sit me at my desk and command me to write the alphabet one hundred, two hundred, three hundred times while she went out into the hallway, closed the door, and discussed vacations, cars, and other-planet deeds with her friends. After a week and a half of my lonely scribbles, I noticed the windows open wide enough to the spring air for me to climb out of. I made my escape and ran home. Shortly thereafter, my teacher called asking if my parents knew where I was. The teacher had apparently searched the multitudinous cabinets and closets of our old classroom

and, having been right outside the door, was mystified as to how I could have escaped. My mother said I was at home. She was surprised that the teacher didn't know where I was. Guarding my shame at being the only one to stay after school, I had told my parents that I was staying to practice a school play. My parents were not happy that I'd lied, nor with the teacher's lack of communication with them, but seemed to understand my shame and the teacher's side too. Being a little stubborn, my inability to form letters in the third grade didn't stop me from writing many years later.

For all that I didn't think I was learning in elementary school, I stumbled into bright lands with several great teachers in junior high and high school. One teacher was a real scientist who surprised the unwary with skeletons and dissections, another an English teacher who tried to get us sweaty students to think, another a studier of people who looked like Ichabod Crane but had the heart of thousands, another an art teacher with whom everyone could be an artist. I hadn't drawn since I was in the fifth grade. Like most children I meet of that age, I thought I could not draw as well as I should be able to. At sixteen I started to draw again for biology class (that teacher was well known for drawing cartoons every day on the blackboard, his cartoon rat gave us helpful tips). I drew planaria, amoebas, cells, the insides of frogs and fish, and continued with other drawings and paintings in the art class where almost everyone felt they could make pictures.

And I had many more turn-arounds when I became a teacher. As a teacher, I learned. At first I was a substitute teacher in Seattle schools. I decided at age twenty-eight, while as a carpenter talking to some of the children whose homes I'd remodeled, hearing their stories and me hearing theirs, and having kept alive interests in drawing and writing during various jobs, that I would like to make picture books. I'd been in schools as an adult, acting as a photographer, clicking my way through classrooms doing filmstrips on reading and volunteers in the schools. I'd then volunteered myself to make a lot of noise—banging, sawing, drilling, teaching children carpentry. It occurred to me that while I got started making picture books, being a substitute teacher might mesh better than a hammer, and that I'd learn more about children through getting a teaching certificate and teaching. All of that proved to be true.

Substitute teachers need special skills to survive. I learned to remember thirty-some names in the first ten minutes of a new class. No one had responded to my earlier shouts of "Hey, you in the yellow shirt," when I saw an exploding star streak across the back of a room. I learned to step out in front of the favorite state of classrooms when a substitute enters, chaos. To focus, we'd have a drawing lesson or practice telling stories. These activities saved me from a number of spitballs.

Since I spoke Spanish to some extent, I had been classed as a bilingual teacher. The district would assign me to a class of Chinese-speaking students: "Well, you're bilingual, aren't you?" My protestations about "in which language" fell on ears to which that didn't matter—they needed me in the classroom twenty minutes ago. I did learn about all kinds of students, and about myself. I've noticed that I am especially sympathetic with small students, the kind that are in elementary schools.

I moved from Seattle to New York to learn more about the publishing world and to live in the big city. Then, Seattle was still more like a small town in feeling. Cast into the sea

Early travels, age thirteen

of New York rent-payers, I took up familiar instruments. I dragged a bag of tools that weighed at least four or five tons on the subways and up and down elevators until the strap of the bag cut into my shoulder and I didn't need to show or talk a resume, people just looked at my shoulder and said: "Oh, you're a carpenter." I built walls and beams, and hanging doors made from old Empire State Building windows. A struggling musician worked with me from time to time (I now see him on national concert tours—creativity is one part of being an "artist," hard work another), and we cemented a friendship. Soon I realized I wanted to look for work more directly involving artwork, and/or writing. Out of the phone book I called the right place. Teachers and Writers Collaborative sent writers and other "artists" into the schools. It was an opportunity to work with teachers and writers far wiser than myself. It was and is an intriguing group, bringing energized innovations into teaching, particularly writing. For a couple of years I was sent to schools around New York City, for weeks or months, as an artist in residence. I saw the richest and poorest, the lost and the dedicated. Outsiders and insiders often hear about death in the South Bronx, in Harlem, in Brooklyn. The richness of the voices that rise 'here is not always so readily heard. I was surprised by the strength, the amazing freed imaginations, the dreams, the best and hopeful humanity that appeared so often in the young students I worked with in the most desolate of neighborhoods. When I was growing up around Washington, D.C., I'd seen neighborhoods like this erupt in flames just a few blocks from the White House. Now I saw other kinds of sparks that could shed light, whether internal or turned to the outside. I was usually given either the best classes in the school to reward them with an "art project," or the classes of the untouchables, the unreachables, for whom I was a last-ditch effort. The "difficult" classes were often the best. Students who had the kind of strong energies which could burn out of control could also ignite in the classroom when we got to where the students lived.

A class in the South Bronx stood out. All of the blocks around the school were brick rubble—the buildings had been bulldozed. There was no cafeteria school lunch for teachers. The old and dedicated Irish-American teacher I worked with took me to "Helen's" for lunch.

From Alligator Shoes, *written and illustrated by Arthur Dorros*

"Helen's" was the local restaurant. We knocked on a heavy steel door. A voice I could barely hear called out, and the teacher responded with familiarity. A small metal window in the door slid open. Then we were in "Helen's," a few formica tables in a room with bare walls and mismatched chairs. But there was Helen, who was known for good food and so had lunch and a couple of dollars on hand. It was not a friendly neighborhood. Dangers lurked outside lunches. There were posters on light poles around the school warning the children about a local murderer who had done in eight or ten people recently. And we'd found that every child in our class of fourteen teenagers had had someone in their household die, had mostly seen the deaths that were too young, too close. The teacher I worked with was afraid of unleashing a torrent, a tidal wave of emotion, if we started to talk about these experiences or let them write about them if they wanted to. They wanted to. The most die-hard student, a fifteen-year-old who I was told could usually be found not in school but down in Times Square dealing dope, started to show up in class every writing day. I missed him once when he didn't show. Then he showed up the next week with a story about the pact his father and he had made, the day before his father was murdered, to decorate the Christmas tree. The teen's story told how he put the star on the top of the tree at Christmas, and how he felt. It was definitely a tearjerker and a story with feelings his classmates knew, and they embraced the possible gangster afire with liquid, warm, quiet looks.

I have no illusions that those students are saved from or are safe in the rubble. Yet I can hope that they have retained some of the energies that caused faces to split with smiles. Those who'd known the greatest sadnesses knew well what it meant to see the other side. That class had the best smiles. Some may have escaped, some don't need to, some can't. Some may have moved North, or South, or East, or West like I did. There are people from the Bronx in Seattle. There are worlds outside the worlds we daily see. I wanted to show one I knew of to Sandra, whom I'd met in New York.

By now I'd met many people during my life. Sandra and I gravitated toward each other quickly and with a force known only to comets and sometimes to lovers. On our first evening together, when the chairs were being put up on the tables so the floor could be mopped, Sandra and I were the only ones left dancing. She still tries to get me to dance that late when the music is good. Meeting people in life is not always easy, not always good. But we felt an understanding that was immediate in many ways. Later we began to understand that understanding could always be developed further. We did both immediately agree in our understanding that the view out the windows of my Brooklyn apartment was not the most enlightening. As Sandra said, we had to leave all of the lights on during the day to keep the place lit enough to see. Across the street was Prospect Park, designed by the Olmsted brothers, but we could not see it. Through the windows out one side we looked at a brick wall. Out the other side we looked at a brick wall.

We were somewhat walled in. I remembered trees and mountains and a garden beside my house out West. I described them to Sandra, and she agreed that we should head out beyond the walls. She was a little hesitant, as she'd never crossed the country before. I figured we'd better drive so she could see what was between New York and Seattle. Some New Yorkers seem to think there's nothing. One New York editor, a very fine editor it turned out, had suggested I start writing science books. "You're from Seattle," she said, "you know, nature and all that." I wasn't so sure what "all that" was. Sandra wasn't either. Her family had immigrated from South America not many years before. Though she was in the process of becoming a citizen, she hadn't had as much of a chance to see the new country she was becoming a part of. I have to admit, I editorialized a little. We didn't stop everywhere.

Our first stop was way out west. Western New Jersey, my grandmother's house. When I first introduced Sandra to my grandmother, I was nervous. How would they get along, having originally come from two different continents, two supposedly different cultures? My grandmother's first question to me had been a surprise. "Does she have an accent?" I hadn't realized before how much my grandmother felt like an outsider. I'd always taken her accent to be just an endearing tune that hearkened back to her roots. Yet she knew it as something used to separate her from being fully accepted by some. An accent could bring out fears about immigrants, about other languages. Europeans, like my grandmother, often learn and enjoy two, three, four languages. When our son Alex was born, some of the native-English-speaking side of my family voiced worries that Sandra and I would confuse him by trying to have him learn two languages, that his English might suffer, that he could have an accent. His first word was "agua," which did not quiet the worriers. However, as soon as he started talking, he sorted out the two languages easily. Like all children I've met who are bilingual in this country, he quickly recognized that English is the predominant language and needed no prompting to adopt it fully. He did so with great facility and no accent. Learning two languages at a young age seems to open channels in the mind, can actually facilitate learning language in general. My family ceased worrying, especially after having Alex regale us with his own stories or songs starting at age two in either language.

But back to the possible culture clash between my grandmother and Sandra. When they first met we ate, with relatively little conversation, the ten-course meal that my grandmother had spent weeks sculpting. Finally I trapped my grandmother in the narrow kitchen as we brought dishes to the sink. "What do you think, Grandma?" "About what?"

"About Sandra?" Grandma thought for just a brief moment.

"She eats good." Sandra was accepted. Each culture puts weight on various things. Many we accept and adopt graciously, as my grandmother has done with Sandra and Sandra with her. They've never had harsh words. Sandra's family also welcomed me. All of the names in *Abuela* are from her family, and the characters and relationships are part of what we've both known. In subsequent years, Sandra's university-level teaching and study of Spanish and her innate good sense about how stories should go have been turned not only to my books, she's translated six into Spanish for publication as well as those of a number of other authors and has become a well-recognized translator.

When we set out from New Jersey to the West, past roads opened before me and new ones to both Sandra and me. Telling you about that trip alone could fill more than the pages of this volume. So I'll skip all of the stops and just mention a couple of the surprises. Kansas. We got off the main highway, took back roads, entered different time zones, got invited to lunch in the center of a summer town. Colorado. Even higher than expected. Maybe because it's after the ancient sea-level altitude of Kansas. Deserts beyond, pastel and coral tinged rock spires, a road where we didn't pass a vehicle in either direction all day, and at night we could not see one house or city light—the sky provided the only lights on our horizon in any direction. It was so quiet when we stopped the car that these recently ex-New Yorkers were overwhelmed with how the silence filled and weighed space. We rode on with only the wind in waves and radio stations that bounced from all over the world crackling in the night as we drove into the sky.

Again the sky. For a few springs and falls back in the days of elementary school, when someone said "go fly a kite," that's exactly what I might do. Until the kite was a tiny dot that I could barely see in the sky. Baseballs fell at me in right and left field, baseballs that I could not see, they had been invisible in the skies. When the wind whipped wild and storm clouds gathered, I remembered the story about Benjamin Franklin at the end of a kite string discovering electricity in a thunderstorm. I imagined Ben more than slightly frazzled, but was more concerned about losing my kite. Sometimes even in milder winds—*tunk,* the string snapped, and gone was the small sky ship of paper and sticks. When I could tell where the wind had carried the kite, I'd climb a tree and bring the shredded or not-so-shredded kite down. My greatest triumph in locating a kite was when I found one that had disappeared into the clouds, having broken the long long tether of three rolls of kite string I'd tied together so that it could reach the stratosphere.

It escaped. I estimated the length of the string, the wind strength, biked to the street where I thought it had landed, studied every tree, and was lucky. There was the kite, dangling from a branch. I felt as if I had navigated to the North Pole.

When I didn't bring down a kite from a childhood tree climb, maybe I'd find birds' nests with speckled or blue eggs, or squawking chicks. I'd look for animals in explorations of the forests below and wade in streams. I searched under rocks for crayfish, found frogs and turtles, and brought some home. They were all escape artists. The frogs leaped to freedom and the turtles dug their way out in the cover of night. The turtles were usually kept in a chicken-wire pen in the backyard. At one time I had thirteen of them, each named Bobby as all looked similar. I discovered turtles are good diggers. They tunneled out under the wire. Trees were tamer and didn't run around so much. The big ones were great for climbing and, when I held onto the thin branches at the top, swayed like boats on the ocean. My brother, sisters, and I rode a high-wire tram we'd made from a wooden box and a rope strung between two huge willows. We didn't quite have the design right— the box kept flipping over and we'd be riding upside down. To build a swing, my brother David had sister Carol sit on a board, sawed around her, and suspended the board from a branch. These were among our many adventures up trees. I brought home seedlings I'd find sprouting from cracks in the sidewalk or along the edges of the forest. I planted the sprouts in our yard, watered them, and imagined them growing. One did. After a few years it was as tall as our house. Besides trees, I'd bring home animals that weren't well, like baby rabbits that were wandering dazed near the yard, and try to bring them back to bouncing health. My parents were generally patient with my patients and helped me build pens or find food when I needed help. My mother, a nurse, showed me how to clean out the animals' wounds. This early natural interest in fauna and flora has continued and often finds its way into my books, for example, *Animal Tracks, Elephant Families,* and *A Tree Is Growing.*

Now my son Alex loves to fly kites, and I have etched in my mind his confidence and smile as at age four he flew one higher than anyone on a hill. He's fascinated by and keenly observes the natural world—he spots small creatures high above and low below, looks for tracks, and though I can already see our differences, there are these echoes. On the other hand, he's curious and thoughtful and likes to draw. As an honest three- and four-year-old he would walk into my studio while I was painting and say "Nice elephant, Dad," or "I don't like that one so much," or he'd break up a serious moment with "Dad, why aren't you smiling?" Fatherhood has proved to be the great surprise joy (people warned me about the agonies) that it seemed no one had mentioned, filled with reflections, returns, and goings on.

We search in tide pools and Alex, still at a young age, wants to bring home buckets. Crabs, starfish, rocks, sticks. We've seen what goes belly up and aim at keeping creatures alive, giving them the right food. Recently, Alex didn't want to feed an earthworm to a newt. "Dad, it's a part of nature." My own interactions with animals were not always the most humane. Like many kids, I poked at ant hills, and sometimes stomped on scurrying escapees. Ants were at the same time fascinating and pests. My relationship with ants changed over the years, as have other relationships. My book *Ant Cities* is dedicated to my grandmother Irene Dorros. Her main relationship to ants was to step on them, set out traps for them in the kitchen, and pour boiling water on them through cracks in the sidewalk. I don't mean my grandmother was a generally cruel person—she can be one of the kindest people I know. Both her and my interactions with ants changed over time. Especially through my doing the book about ants. The dedication just kind of happened, as I had told her my next book would be dedicated to her, and with my grandmother's interest in ants that seemed somehow appropriate. She never again poured hot water over ant colonies, at least not in front of me.

I changed my views of ants as I learned more about them, reading every book I could find in the Brooklyn (where I was living at the time) Library. I found out that there is an incredible amount one could know about these amazing tiny social creatures. And I found, surrounded by piles of books about ants, that there were about as many scientific opinions about the "facts" of ant life as there were experts in the field. I wrote letters to experts on ants and called with questions. I discovered that science is not a set of facts agreed on by all scientists. On any given matter, different scien-

tists may have different opinions of what the "facts" are, and I would have to sort them out before I could decide which to present in my books. In researching how ants communicate, I called one of the foremost ant researchers. At that time she was with the Harvard Museum of Comparative Zoology. She, as have been most people I contact to find out more about their fields, was glad to share what she knew. Several days later I unexpectedly received in the mail a small box addressed to "Doctor Dorros." I had become a doctor of ants. I had to tell her I was not an ant doctor, not even a doctor for that matter, though my sister Carol is, as are my great brothers-in-law Boris and Dave. In almost all of the scientific areas I study to write about, I know little when I start and don't see myself as an expert as I go along, just know more than I did when I started. I got to know more about the harvester ants that were sent to me as those ants, hitherto unknown in Brooklyn, had soon escaped and were running around my apartment.

As a child I'd spent a lot of time practicing looking for animals. Two highlights from my earliest explorations were finding a duck's nest with eggs under a bush at the edge of a Maryland red clay clearing in the woods, and getting stuck in quicksand. Streambanks were a favorite haunt. They were winding trails through the forest, and in the soft mud or sand along the streambed I found animal tracks, as in the much later book of that name. I could see where raccoons had come to catch or wash food, where frogs had hopped or turtles crawled on their way to or from a swim. I left my own tracks along many a streambed, particularly near a house where we lived in Baltimore. I also left one of my shoes.

They were heavy leather shoes, before the days of running shoes, the kind of shoes my mother would buy a little too big for me so I'd grow into them and I'd have for a year or so and then they weren't really worn out, just got too small. So my mother noticed one day when I came home with only one shoe. I couldn't think of a really good story about how it happened. One of my sisters, Ellen, had recently tried "It just flew down the sewer" when she lost a boot while playing in a water-filled street gutter. Since her explanation hadn't appeared to be a hit with my parents I tried my own truth, that I had gotten stuck in quicksand. That wasn't a big hit either, and I went on to say I had just been looking for frogs, stepped on what looked like sand, and started sinking in, and sinking in, and sinking in until the sand was above my knees. I grabbed onto a bush and barely pulled myself out for which I was grateful and my parents seemed to be too. But the shoe had been slurped deep into the quicksand as I pulled my foot out.

My parents weren't thrilled. Either that I'd lost a shoe, or that I'd played in quicksand. My father quietly (I thought) went to the ga-

rage with me and found a set of golf clubs, which up to that time I don't think I even knew he had as I'd never seen him use them. He took a couple of clubs and had me lead him to the quicksand. We walked along without talking. I was afraid to ask him why he was bringing golf clubs. When we arrived at the quicksand, he asked me to point out just where I'd been stuck. One thing I'd learned from being in the woods and trying to locate animals and keep myself from getting lost was to remember where things were. So I looked

Have you ever been to a rain forest?
If not, you've probably heard of rain forests.
Sometimes people call them "jungles."
In rain forests you can find
colorful birds calling,
monkeys leaping through trees,
giant flowers—
more kinds of plants and animals
than anywhere else on earth.

From Rain Forest Secrets, *written and illustrated by Arthur Dorros*

around, looked at the quicksand, and pointed to a spot.

My father took one of the clubs and prodded into the sand. We were both somewhat amazed when he struck something solid a couple of feet down, hooked it with the club, and pulled up my soggy shoe. I remember that night I spent time in my room alone, with the idea that I'd think about what I'd done. I also remember that night my father didn't tell stories as he often did. Usually he told stories with characters he made up like Cookie, Cakey, and their little brother Stanley, also known as Stinky, and stories about his own growing up. He was a good storyteller. One of the three tales in my first book, *Pretzels,* is based on a story my father told me about the worst cook on any sailing ship. The cook's name was "I Fry'em Fine," called that because he would chase the sailors who insulted his cooking out of the galley yelling: "I Fry'em Fine." I Fry'em Fine ultimately invented the pretzel. I got several somewhat positive responses to that first manuscript by sending it to publishers, yet their answers boiled down to different forms of no. So I went to New York and carried my stories around to publishers, an unorthodox technique. The third editor I met had an urge to surprise me. As I sat in her office and she speed read the tales of I Fry'em Fine, she looked up and said "We'll take it." My family's stories have provided me lots of writing ideas. I often use things I've heard, seen, or done to make stories. I've heard—be careful what you say to a writer. You may read it later.

When I was grown and traveling and writing in South America, I met someone else who had gotten stuck in sand, when he was lost in the Amazon for a month. He lost more than his shoe on that trip. He ended up with just his shorts, a tee shirt, a pocket knife, a map, and a hammock, and survived a month's walk alone. I wondered what he'd eaten. Fruits, he told me. I thought maybe bananas, mangoes, other tropicals that I knew. No, he encountered only fruits that he'd never seen before and I'd never heard of. I learned later, in doing the research for a book about rain forests, that for every kind of tropical rain forest plant we know about, there are perhaps ten more that are unknown. Most flora in the rain forest is yet to be carefully studied. He ate some of the unknown, waded in swampy water up to his nose, swept away spiders as big as

The author in the rain forest,
Costa Rica, 1989

his fist in the moonlight. But that's another story.

My own interest in the tropics was enlivened at an early age. At age four and a half I sat on the tail of an alligator. There weren't many alligators near our Washington, D.C., area home, so I had to travel far to find one to sit on. This happened on our first long family trip, a drive to Florida. We stopped at an alligator farm and there in pens were dozens of alligators. Sleeping gators, I thought, as my sister Ellen and I climbed over the low pen fence. Times were different then—it seemed like climbing in with the alligators was okay. Until we were among them, ten- to twelve-foot-long creatures with mouths big enough to swallow the odd dog, cat, or four-year-old that wandered by, I thought. Sleeping gators now appeared ferocious or hungry gators to me. Fortunately, they were not hungry, and both my sister and I walked among the gators and were able to tell about it later.

Alligator talks to writers, Indiana, 1991

I sat on the tail of one of the sleepy giants while my father took a picture. I tried to keep still so the gators wouldn't notice me and reached down discreetly just long enough to touch the tail of my alligator chair. It felt like tree bark. My smile was not very obvious in the expression of my face, but some of my fear was. I remember my father being on the outside of the pen fence to take the picture, and I was on the inside. My parents knew something that I wasn't fully convinced of at the time, that alligators only need to eat every few weeks or even months, and the particular alligators we met had just been fed a huge meal that morning. So they were resting full and groggy in the sun, ready to give us exciting toothy grins.

That afternoon held more excitement. "Get off of there!" I heard a mad yell as my parents carried the contents of our car into a motel room for the night. It wasn't my parents yelling to me though. It was an old, skinny man with white hair, yelling at me from the doorway of his motel room. I was just stand-

ing on a pile of rocks next to the parking lot. I couldn't figure out why he might be yelling at me, so I kept standing there. He yelled again that I should get off the rocks, then he added: "There are poisonous snakes in there!" Thank you for telling me. I jumped off the pile of rocks and snakes and hit the field running while his yell still hung in the air. He continued to glare at me. It was hard to be grateful to a grouchy old guy, but I was. Sometimes it's important to be grateful to grouchy old guys.

Thirty-five years later, when I went to a rain forest research station in a lush Costa Rican forest to prepare for *Rain Forest Secrets,* snakes still hung in my mind if not on the vines and branches around me. The first day I arrived, I walked gingerly along the trails and looked nervously at anything long, slender, and potentially wriggling. I saw lizards scurry along the trail, but no snakes. I saw leaves walking down tree trunks and on closer examination found that they were bits of leaves being carried by leaf-cutting ants to their underground gardens. I heard rustling in the tree branches overhead and spotted a troupe of spider monkeys swinging, dangling, and leaping. Soon though, there was a louder rustle throughout the treetops. Wind was picking up, gusting and bringing in dark, dark rain clouds. I knew that this was the rain forest, and I was here in the rainy season. I had been told that quite predictably every afternoon during an hour or two it rained. But I was not ready for the deluge that followed, or for the speed with which it arrived and inundated me.

Branches started to bend further and further. This was a strong wind, a storm, not just a few light gusts before a rain. I heard cracking of branches. One fell with a tremendous *womp* just feet away from me. It was not just a branch, it was a giant piece of the forest. A branch that had been a piece of the tree canopy so covered with plants—epiphytes, bromeliads, orchids, an entire treetop garden, that it was elephant heavy and shattered into chunks of greens and yellows as it thudded close to me. I thought I might be crushed by the forest itself just for having dared come out in the rain knowing so little.

A tree smashed other smaller trees as it was blown over and tumbled to the forest floor, opening a clearing to the now thick, black sky. Cloud heads raged in and spouted rain, emptied all water that had ever evaporated skyward back into the forest. The narrow trail I'd been walking on became a knee-deep, reddish muddy torrent, then was waist-deep, swirling along. I almost forgot about the snakes, then imagined them swimming around me. I struck for higher ground and stopped under a tree, then not under the tree, as it swayed. Now I could see that there were light patches among the clouds, the storm was breaking and blowing off almost as quickly as it had arrived. Within minutes the water on the trail started to subside, and though the forest would be full of the drumbeats of water dripping from leaf to leaf for hours, the sky had ceased to pour into the forest.

By nightfall I was still tuned to the jungle with all of the senses I could muster. Especially because after dinner I had to walk part of a mile back from the central dining room and kitchen where the scientists at this research station had their meals, to the cabin in the forest where I would be sleeping. The trail through the forest was littered with sticks, large quantities having been blown down in the daily rain squalls. Each curving twig lying across the trail looked like a snake in the glare of my flashlight. All the more, as during dinner conversation one bit of information I'd gleaned was that snakes are most active and hunt at night.

Each careful step I took on the trail was made in agony. By the time I got about a hundred yards from my cabin in the forest, I was sweating not just from the hot, wet night, but from the sweat that rolled from trying to keep my whole body focused in concentration. I was not relaxed. Particularly when I saw two bright beady eyes glittering at me from a few feet ahead. Another stick, this one with eyes. Eyes attached to a head that was attached to a long curving body which I was certain would soon be attached to my own now-not-moving legs.

The snake glared at me and continued glaring, not moving.

I remembered seeing animals: deer, raccoons, possums, become transfixed in the beam of a bright light at night. But I knew about batteries. The batteries in my flashlight would not last until morning. I decided I would have to do something besides standing there holding the snake fixed in my beam. So I did what any brave, thinking person might do under the circumstances—I screamed for help. After a few seconds that did not seem like such a great idea. No one answered nor arrived. Standing in the rain forest at night yelling for help was awkward. I was the only one listening, it seemed, other than all of the animals of the night now frozen in the silence between my yells.

I decided to take further action. I thought it was best to try to keep the snake glued to its spot in the middle of the trail. While I kept the light pointing into its eyes I walked off the trail and around the snake, through the forest. My philosophy was, and I needed a philosophy at the time, my comforting philosophy was that snakes do not travel in packs, so there wouldn't be another snake close by to tread on as I tromped the dark forest floor. Finally I got around the snake and loosed my flashlight onto the trail ahead. When I reached the cabins, I knocked to see if any of the scientists staying in the cabin next to mine were at home. One American botanist was sleeping. A Costa Rican biologist was awake and had heard me yelling but could not tell what was going on from the noises I'd made. Next time I call out, I'll have to provide more specific details. I told the biologist about the snake across the trail, and she asked me what kind it was. I didn't know, snake in the night was enough for me. She insisted that I show her where the snake was. These were among the rules of this forest: that if anyone saw a snake it was important to tell what kind it was and where it was then mark the spot, because snakes often find a place and stay there waiting for prey for many days. They may not slither around hunting. So someone could unknowingly walk by and have a problem in a day or a week. (Years later when I took Sandra, Alex, my sister Ellen, and her son Brian to see the rain forest I'd enjoyed so much, there was some apprehension about what we might run into or onto. I assured them that there was a good chance we wouldn't see any snakes. Within the first thirty yards into the forest you can imagine what we saw. Turned out to be the most dangerous snake of the region, a fer-de-lance, disguised as a pile of dead leaves, waiting patiently by the trail for lunch. Much to the brave

credit of all involved except the serpent, my family decided to continue their first walk, around the snake and into the forest.)

My first night in the rain forest, having protested that I'd just gotten away from the snake I'd yelled about, we walked back toward it. Standing cautiously about twenty feet away, I pointed with the flashlight. Barefoot, the biologist walked up, bent her head to within striking distance of snake eyes, and assured me that it was not a poisonous snake but a blunt-headed snake that eats insects, with a body pencil thin and a mouth big enough for grasshoppers. Humbled but still wary, I returned on the trail to the cabins. Just as we arrived, I saw a tiny snake.

"That one's probably not poisonous," I said.

"Oh no, that one is very poisonous," she said, just as it slithered into a muddy boot among those left outside the cabins. That night I took my boots inside the cabin, stuffed my socks in the tops, and after listening to howler monkeys practice their own jungle screams, slept.

On a trip through the Andes years before, I had tried to sleep on a truckload of rocks. That had not been my first choice for a bed, but on that night there was no choice. I was heading across the Andes Mountains after traveling for much of a year in Latin America observing, absorbing, writing notes for what would become magazine articles and letters, and sketching to help me remember what I'd seen. I'd seen incredible sights, met all kinds of people from farmers of the altiplano, the high mountain plains, who waved and invited me to share what little they had in smokey huts, to not-so-friendly secret police in tweed jackets who burst with arms ready into my hotel room in Chile to search the room (and everyone else's in the hotel) just because the dictator of the time, someone who many of the normally democratic and free Chileans wanted overthrown, was coming through town. Almost everyone else was welcoming. They would invite me to visit for a day, a month, no limit. That was Latin American hospitality, which took many forms.

Being a foreigner, I was able to cross a street or a town and visit the plush neighborhoods and homes of the monied and privileged or the thatch-covered dwellings of hard-working farmers who got up in the middle of the night to start gathering water and firewood for

Parents, Dorothy and Sidney Dorros, 1977

Sister Ellen holding Brian, Art, sister Carol, brother David, 1983

the next day. From all that I've seen, people whether rich or poor, whatever language they speak, have more in common in basic humanity than what is superficially different. People share needs, desires, though with a lot of possible twists in the forms lives take and the styles to be seen on the surface. It had taken me almost six months to learn why many of the people of the high Andes region did not readily talk to me when I approached them in Spanish. I was discovering that people usually appreciate attempts to understand who they are. I found that to the Indian peoples, Spanish was still the language of invaders who had come and with their words and deeds done more than occasional harm to the locals. When I learned just a few words of Quechua, like "hello," "thank you," "what's your name?" and "what a cute baby," I saw a total change in the way people related to me. Long bus rides without talk became animated conversations, often easily drifting into Spanish once the ice had been broken with Quechua. The "cute babies" would often end up sitting on my legs, and riding in

the open backs of trucks we could laugh and dodge water balloons thrown by young boys who leaped from behind boulders in the middle of nowhere during Carnaval.

Careening across the altiplano, few things were more amazing than seeing little bands standing in open fields (imagine finding a band playing in the middle of an Iowa cornfield) with the wind and mountains sweeping around them, the notes of panpipes—*zampoñas,* flutes—*quenas,* drums—*bombos,* and occasional trumpets or rattling goats hooves thudding towards us and I knew in a few minutes we would reach another village. A band would later dance into town and, when they did, costumed and masked villagers would dance in a line, winding through the village, shuffling and stepping to the music for three days and nights. The strength people had earned working fourteen-hour or more days, seven days a week much of the year was now turned to dancing in the release of this Carnaval time. Work and worries were obscured for a few days in clouds of dancing dust and the repetitive rhythms of songs played full force.

Years later, I would remember that trip and what I'd seen of the Andes life and put some of those memories into *Tonight Is Carnaval,* which Sandra, a native Spanish-speaker much better with the language than I who learned as an adult, translated into Spanish for the edition titled *Por fin es Carnaval.* That story was illustrated by people the story was about. With the help of two Peruvians generous with their time and energy and whom we could reach by phone and mail, we found a co-operative of around thirty women and one man who made the artwork—brilliant-colored cloth pictures called *arpilleras.* The bright pictures were sewn in the drabbest of shacks on a Lima hillside and carried their maker's memories and dreams of their own mountain lives, before they had moved to this distant satellite edge of the city where, like in the mountains, they had no phones, no mail service, no buses, no running water. Yet, as people had waved me to their houses in the high Andes, these people gathered all their resources to be able to offer us lunch, graciously, in Spanish. Language had begun to stick in my mind connected to the people who spoke it.

Meanwhile, I was sleeping temporarily on a bed of rocks. Or about to. I had been traveling long enough, had slept in old, elegant, wood-and-iron steam trains built in the eighteen-hundreds, chugging through Bolivia until stopped by the mud and rock-covered tracks of landslides, slept on buses with signs that said in Spanish "Only God knows our destination," which seemed likely, or "God is my co-pilot," which the passengers certainly hoped as we bounced along, taking days to cross muddy, potholed roads that would have been a few hours' trip on highways. And now I was stuck in a cold, unheated hotel on the freezing shores of Lake Titicaca. The trains down to the Peruvian coast were on strike, or at least the workers on the trains were on strike. Since the trains were the main transportation through the mountains to the coast, the hotels were full of edgy people trying to figure out how to continue their journeys.

One of the only alternatives was to hire what were normally town taxis to drive over the muddy mountain road that eventually wound down to the warm coastal valleys. Renting a taxi for such a trip was a relatively expensive proposition, so small groups of people got together and split the cost. I ended up with a crew of people about my age, in their twen-

ties, who all had pressing reasons to continue their travels as soon as possible. There were two women from the U.S. on their way home after years in the Peace Corps in Brazil, a Peruvian going back to his job in Lima, and a Bolivian student returning to a Peruvian university. The arrangement seemed reasonable as the taxi driver had a newish, large American sedan that would accommodate us, and which we thought he wouldn't risk on the mountain roads unless he knew what he was doing. Besides he must have driven the car up here from somewhere. We began to suspect otherwise as the five of us passengers piled with our luggage into the car along with the driver and his assistant dressed in a suit, who sat in the front seat helping to navigate. The assistant's job was obviously important, and it became clearer why as soon as we came to the first big, muddy pothole on the road out of town. The assistant got out of the car, walked toward the puddle, gingerly touched his shoe to the pool, careful not to get his suit pants wet, and stood studying the water for minutes. He returned to the car to report that the pothole was not too deep, that we could drive through it rather than try and make our way around it. That was important to know, as I had seen many a pothole on Andean roads which could swallow a car, and in which even trucks and buses got stuck up to their axles in mud. Driving around such holes had other dangers. The roads were often cut into the sides of hills and mountains and we watched dirt and rocks tumble downhill as the road gave way underneath our vehicle. Our assistant climbed out of the car many times to check whether the road would hold us. It did hold us up, but not onto itself.

After a few hours of driving, we knew that our driver did not know how to handle the slippery mountain roads. He was driving too fast for the conditions, then slamming the brakes on when we came to curves, which caused the car to fishtail. It appeared that someone else had driven the car up to deliver it from a coastal port, that he had never driven outside the town. Various members of our crew tried to give him quick tips on handling the road and, when those went unheeded, comments shifted to requests, also unresponded to, then escalated to louder objections, after which began threats to end our journey with him. He did that for us.

Just as we passengers had agreed that it would be best to have him deliver us back to town and start over in other transport, we came to a good muddy bend in the road, our driver slammed on the brakes, and we slid towards space. The car came to a stop hanging halfway out over the road and cliff edge so that our driver was now in the front half of the car navigating the sky, while we crammed in the backseat were in the part of the car still on earth. Our portly driver and his heavy-set assistant, looking into the heavens, reached for the door handles and started to open their doors, ready to plunge back to earth. This caused a unanimous exhortation from the backseat as the car was already teetering on the edge of the cliff, barely balanced. We finally took our power as passengers to its limit as we said that we would get out first, one at a time, keeping our weight on the car and then sitting on the trunk to balance the vehicle. We did that, carefully, while the driver and his safety assistant wiggled their feet in the air, testing their way back to *tierra firma*.

After awhile a truck rolled up, rumbling under the weight of a load of Bolivian tin ore bound for the coast. This was not a well-traveled road, and the only vehicles we'd seen were these Bolivian trucks that chugged by once every couple of hours. The truck driver fortunately had a chain and pulled the taxi back onto the road, leaving all of our crew standing in the road inspecting the damage. Amazingly, there was no visible mechanical disorder, just a little scraping where the car had rested on the cliff edge. But after a short drive uphill in a cloud of steam, we discovered a small puncture in the radiator. The car was immovable, the assistant started walking for help to a town which appeared nonexistent, and we knew that we could be here for days. We flagged down the next tin ore truck that came by.

The truck driver was not excited about taking on passengers, but he agreed not to refuse us on this lonely road. This driver had an assistant too and, with the two of them in the cab of the truck, the only place to ride on their dump truck was in the open back, on top of the load of tin ore. Being picky was not an option, so the five of us now ex-taxi passengers clambered up on top of the rocks. At first it wasn't bad up there. We watched our taxi driver and his marooned vehicle getting smaller and smaller as we pulled away. The

afternoon was sunny, and the snowcapped Andes passed by us at a steady pace. Both this driver and his assistant seemed more reasonable and knew how to handle this road. They had done it many times, and it was obvious they wanted to make the journey as quickly but as safely as they could. This meant they kept driving steadily and did not stop. Even when it started to rain, and the cold winds started to chill us damp, outside passengers. Then, as the sun went down, the rain turned to snow and the cold lashed us and with the hours the rocks showed us their thousand points of hardness. But then it was beautiful again. I've rarely seen anything as beautiful or dream-like. When I stood to get off the rocks and peered through the snow with ice particles hitting my face, I saw llamas dancing. They were dancing, a herd of white llamas, ballet in white snow. Lit by moonlight the llamas tiptoed, pranced, leaped, pirouetted through the snowflakes. They were in their element and their own silent snow-starred night.

"Alex and I tracking a raccoon,"
Olympic Peninsula, Washington, 1990

Alex, Arthur, and wife, Sandra, on a rooftop in Colombia, South America, 1995

Our truck made no noise. We passed unnoticed.

The truckers stopped for soup at a tiny inn which was not an inn but the only building we had passed in hours and which had no soup. We had a bit of tepid water that mountain greens had been boiled in. It was not enough to warm us, the building itself was not heated, and the owners of this cold, empty place were also cold. So the truckers and their crew climbed back onto and into the truck. It was becoming longer, this night, and colder. We five wet passengers huddled under a piece of canvas that the truckers found for us. All five of us huddled in our rock-floored frozen shelter with the only other cover we had, my now damp and opened-up sleeping bag. We piled closer and closer until we were a small mound in the snow as I'd heard sled dogs sleep·in the arctic to keep from freezing, which is what we were trying to do. Feeling or imagining the warmth from any part of someone else's body that might touch was less and less comfort, all of us saying later that our bodies

had been so cold they were barely functioning, our hearts had almost stopped moving, and we were almost stopped completely by the cold. We rattled and rocks struck our bones all night as we rumbled, drifting between dark cold and trying to sleep. When the sun broke through the night and the first weak rays struck our faces, we were warmed even by thoughts of the sun and, having survived, enjoyed that we were now stuck in a line of trucks waiting to cross a river where the bridge had washed out in a flood the night before. We sunbathed for our lives and, still stiff from the night, helped as everyone threw rocks into the river in one spot to make the river shallow enough to drive across. The first truck that tried got stuck in the middle of the river, waves washed through its doors, and the engine died. With more rocks the crossing became shallower and trucks could ford. We crossed and cruised out of the mountains into the blessed warmth of the coastal desert and into Arequipa. Any warm town looked like a good town. It was one of those times that I remembered to be grateful for life.

My father also periodically reminded me about making the most of life. We only get so many opportunities to do the things we want to do, say the things we want to say to people. When I was a young child my father was in good health, but at age thirty-six he showed the first symptoms of Parkinson's disease, which ultimately can leave someone completely paralyzed and soon forced him to have to quit working. This was a shock of the unknown, as was my mother's death at a youngish age not many years later. Life is definitely not predictable, cannot all be neatly arranged, though certainly my family tried to make it that way. At first my father was saddened, then angry at the unexpected and seemingly unacceptable physical limitations and struggles he faced each day just to be able to walk or talk. When I was younger we had gone on family camping trips and fished. Now he collapsed with the tent when he tried to set it up, and the fishing line was tangled in bushes or trees much of the time. But he found new ways and new activities. He was optimistic about what people can do. He learned how to do the best possible with his abilities and managed to help others do the same with their daily struggles. He wrote a widely acclaimed book, *Parkinson's, a Patient's View: Accommodation without Surrender,* which coincidentally was published the same year as my first book. His early stories to me, with all of their humor, were still alive. He added to them and made new ones as he took on his own life with general good humor. My brother and little sister hardly knew my father before he got sick. My own childhood with my parents was not always easy, but most children think that about their own growing up—I feel lucky in who my parents were. I lost a close friend when my father died recently.

There were lots of stories in our family. Stories of towns and gypsies and giant fish that flopped under beds, of cities and countries that I'd never been to, of escaping across borders, of wars that came too close to home, of trips on ships, on carts, on trains. All of my grandparents made their ways from Europe. My grandmother Irene once showed me an old family picture of twenty-six people, all except one with little pencil *x*'s on them. The one without the *x* was the only one to live through the terrors of Europe during World War II. The rest had died. My grandfather, Irene's husband, after being unable to enter Canada once entered, how else,

as a member of a baseball team. All it took was a cigar and a baseball cap and he looked like part of the team. He'd crossed the Atlantic, made the trip across many borders alone as a teenager. He'd grown up in a small town in rural Europe and only went to school through the third grade, when he was apprenticed to a tailor. Yet I saw that same grandfather read three newspapers every morning. He had taught himself ways to know the world. He could look into a store window, see a coat, and go home and identically re-create what he'd seen. And in letters to me he would draw a bird, always the same bird in the letters. But that let me know that even adults might be able to draw, and so when my mother readily provided paints though I might spill them on the floor, or I saw the set of pastels she had kept for years in a dresser drawer, or I met an eighty-five-year-old neighbor who climbed trees when branches needed trimming and made sculptures from roots he found, I knew that art was a possible if not probable part of life at least for some people. As children, my sister Carol and brother David were better drawers than me, but they chose other directions. My sister Ellen molds clay into fantastic shapes. Art takes many forms. All of my grandparents had their own art forms. My ant-loving grandmother showed me how to put a watermelon into a small jar, wove her own stories, and I eventually wove grandmothers from my wife's and my families into *Abuela,* where children and grandparents fly.

It was in my twenties, during and after college, that I set feet out of the Wisconsin hills and physically started to travel extensively to far-off lands as well as around North America. It was a time of experiments, for me and the country. Friends or family would comment on the extent of my travels, sometimes saying that they wished they could do the same. When I looked carefully, I thought they could. Where they might have chosen to spend the money they had on cars, stereos, or other things, I had bought no stereo and I drove a seventy-five-dollar car into the trunk of which I could easily pack all of my belongings. When what I owned could no longer fit into the trunk of a car, friends and family kindly stored the excess in basements and attics. I was not always happy, and for this my family would sometimes point to my travels. But the travels were not the cause of such unhappiness, they were a search for another road. I took jobs in which

I could work for awhile, then make time to look and search again. I worked as a carpenter starting summers during high school, then as a longshoreman, farm worker, photographer, short-order cook, greenhouse worker, substitute teacher, magazine article writer, at various times. I could not seem to find work that was enlivening for the long term. Then I found it. I didn't work, I became a writer and illustrator.

Writing and illustration I did know would take hard work. I'd kept painting and writing on my own, outside of "work" hours, throughout stints at different jobs. I'd sat or stood at my desk painting, trying to get an image to work out, for six, eight, ten, twelve hours a day. But that time was unnoticeable, usually passed in an instant. Unlike in an office job I tried for three days. Minutes were days, one day took months to pass. Then I ached for work I knew passed quickly, like carpentry or painting, where I became involved in making something. Well actually, the first summer, as a carpenter's helper I spent most of the time destroying. I was given just a crowbar and a hammer to take apart mistakes the carpenters had made. Harold, the carpenter I worked with, tried to help me too, but he had no front teeth so I rarely could understand what he said. Maybe just as well. One day a hammer fell on my head. It was a pure accident. That's what hard hats are for. I should have been wearing one. It's a good way to learn, to look at mistakes. It can help you figure out how to do something right. I try to remember that when I'm painting or writing, that making mistakes is a great chance to learn. Since we all make mistakes, we may as well take advantage of them. In writing and painting, what may look like a mistake often opens the door to unexpected creations better than the original plan.

These recent years have been different but better than the course I thought I was mapping out. I've been surrounded by a lot of great people, including friends and an expanding family. I think I've learned to look more to the present, with glances to hopes for the future. Goals may stay the same, the road does change. With writing and illustration I've felt fortunate to be able to pursue all kinds of interests. I have left out much. If you've read this far, perhaps you can imagine. More about people; places, from Australia, the tip of South America, villages of Bali, Asian jungles, Himalayan inns, to truck stops in Nebraska. There are stories you might want to hear, and others not. I can't easily decide for you.

I am in the middle now. In the middle of writing, of illustrating, of watching Alex grow up, of a family, of a life full of changes. I try to remember that I am not only a teller of stories, but a learner. Much of what I've done and experienced has found its way into my books. I've heard writers, when asked if a novel or story they've written comes from their own experiences, say "no." I see my life and writing intertwined. Each of us brings our own being to stories and our particular stories into our lives. Last night Alex told a short story to me, in part: "You know why old people walk with those sticks?" (He imitated using a cane.) "So they can balance on one leg. Maybe kids should use them too, to help them balance." A pen, pencil, words, help me balance, make connections between what's around me, between us. A friend said everyone should write an autobiography. I agree. Everyone has stories to tell.

BIBLIOGRAPHY

FOR YOUNG PEOPLE

Fiction written and illustrated:

Pretzels, Greenwillow, 1981.

Alligator Shoes, Dutton, 1982.

Splash Splash, Harper, 1987.

Yum Yum, Harper, 1987.

Fiction; Spanish translations by Sandra M. Dorros:

Abuela, illustrated by Elisa Kleven, Dutton, 1991, translated as *Abuela,* Dutton, 1995.

Tonight Is Carnaval, illustrated by Club de Madres Virgen del Carmen, Dutton, 1991, translated as *Por fin es Carnaval,* illustrated by Club de Madres Virgen del Carmen, Dutton, 1991.

(And illustrator) *Radio Man/Don Radio* (bilingual), HarperCollins, 1993.

Isla, illustrated by Elisa Kleven, Dutton, 1995, translated as *La Isla,* Dutton, 1995.

Nonfiction written and illustrated:

Ant Cities, Harper, 1987, translated by Daniel Santacruz as *Ciudades de hormigas,* Harper-Collins, 1995.

Feel the Wind, HarperCollins, 1989.

Me and My Shadow, Scholastic, 1990.

Rain Forest Secrets, Scholastic, 1990.

Follow the Water from Brook to Ocean, HarperCollins, 1991.

Animal Tracks, Scholastic, 1992, translated by Sandra M. Dorros as *Las huellas de los animales,* Scholastic, 1993.

This Is My House, Scholastic, 1992, translated as *Ésta es mi casa,* Scholastic, 1993.

Elephant Families, HarperCollins, 1994.

Other:

The Day the Pigs Took Over, Scholastic, forthcoming.

A Fungus Ate My School, Scholastic, forthcoming.

A Tree Is Growing, Scholastic, forthcoming.

Also illustrator of children's books *Charlie's House, Magic Secrets,* and *What Makes Day and Night.*

Scriptwriter and photographer for filmstrips, including "Teaching Reading, A Search for the Right Combination," released by the National School Public Relations Association, and "Sharing a Lifetime of Learning," released by the National Education Association. Writer and director of *Portrait of a Neighborhood* and other videos. Contributor of articles and illustrations published in periodicals and purchased by Dodd-Mead Publishers and *USA Today.*

Mary Elting

1906-

Mary Elting with her mother and father, 1908

Here is a riddle: My life has been lived in three centuries, although I'm less than a hundred years old. How can that be?

Perhaps you can begin to guess the answer when I say that the house where I was born had no electric lights until I was ready for first grade, and in almost every detail it was like the house where my mother was born in 1873. Like her and her brothers, my brother and I bathed in a big round tub that was used for washing clothes on Mondays. We never heard the word "baby-sitter" because it hadn't been invented yet. So in those and other important ways I started life in a nineteenth-century world.

The twentieth century really began for me in 1917 when I was eleven years old. That year my father bought his first automobile, and the day after he brought it home he began teaching me how to drive it. I have driven and loved cars ever since.

Then, just the other day, a news story told me that inventors have built experimental automobiles that don't burn gasoline or any other kind of fuel. Instead they turn sunlight into electricity to make the wheels go around. By the year 2001, said one inventor, electric cars will be on the market for people like me. So here I am, thinking how wonderful it will be to drive a twenty-first-century car.

Back to the old days. My mother and father met and were married in a little town called Creede, high in the Colorado mountains. Gold and silver had recently been discovered there, and hundreds of people began to crowd the narrow mountain valley. Some worked in the mines. Others, like my father, started businesses. (He sold hay and grain for horses and coal for cookstoves in town.) There were thieves and crooks, too, and because bars and saloons never closed, people sang a song that ended: "It's day all day in the daytime, and there is no night in Creede."

Life had settled down a good deal when my mother came to teach in the four-room schoolhouse. She and my father belonged to a very proper group of young people who often went bicycling together. It is hard to believe that they could pedal their heavy one-speed bikes on the rough dirt roads out of town. Even a small hill was a problem for the women in their long skirts and petticoats. But in case they had to admit defeat, their young men came equipped with rope to give them a tow.

My parents, after their wedding, moved into the two-story white clapboard house where I was born June 21, 1906. The last time I visited Creede my old home was still there but fancied up with a new reddish brown outside and a closed-in vestibule where we had only a windy front porch. Does it still have the kitchen I loved, with the enormous cookstove that left little room for anything but some stools, a large worktable, and a sink for washing dishes? Water for dishwashing, as well as for laundry and baths, came from a pump on the back porch, which is still there. The barn and chicken shed have disappeared. So has the playhouse that my father made for me from a large box. For some reason he had saved the box from which he had taken a piano, his wedding gift to Mother.

The three upstairs bedrooms and a long, very dark closet under the eaves were what I considered my domain, although I shared it with my younger brother, Roelof, and Grandmother Shawhan, Mother's mother. They say I was a wakeful child, but it was easy to persuade Mother to play her beloved piano in the living room and sing us children to sleep. (Sometimes I still find myself humming "The Last Rose of Summer.") If I begged hard enough, she would sing the sad Stephen Foster song, "Oh, my darling Nellie Gray, they have taken you away, and I'll never see my darling any more."

The song always made me cry, because Mother had told me Nellie Gray's story. Like many other black slave women, she had been sold to a new master who lived far away. Slavery was terrible, Mother said. She hated any kind of oppression, and she was always glad her father had been an officer in the Union army during the Civil War.

Eventually I outgrew my tears for Nellie Gray, but I have continued to share Mother's anger at what we now call racism. She would have rejoiced with me when my husband became one of the founders of the Council on Interracial Books for Children, and later when I began to find the growing list of books about African Americans and other minorities that I have read as a member of the Jane Addams Children's Book Award Committee.

There were no such books for children when Grandmother Shawhan came to live with us. She had a certain dramatic sense, and she liked reading aloud. Listening to her for hours on end, Roelof and I spent winter days close to the tall stove, called a base burner, in the living room. The business part of this remarkable invention was a large cylindrical chamber that sat high on a base supported by feet shaped like animal paws. Coal, poured into the chamber, was fed by gravity into the burner at the base. The fire in it lasted all night, and each morning Dad simply shook down the ashes and poured in more coal. The wonderful thing about this stove was the little doors with windows made of mica through which I could see the red fire. The mica fascinated me. Dad said it was a mineral that miners removed in sheets from under the ground. How big were the sheets? How did they get buried? Why didn't mica burn or break like glass? Nobody could tell me, and in those days there were no children's science books for Grandmother to read to us.

The first book I remember was *The Tale of Peter Rabbit*. Grandmother used it to teach me to read when I was about four. From that time on I sensed, though I couldn't have told why, Beatrix Potter's elegant style. Today my advice to young people who want to write is that they should study her magic.

After *Peter* and the other Potter books, Mother bought us two sets of myths and fairy tales, about six volumes each, and Grandmother took us through them, cover to cover, more than once. Then came *Tom Sawyer* which I read to myself so many times that I could recite page after page by heart. Later we had a subscription to *The Youth's Companion* which I shared with my fourth- and fifth-grade classes at school.

I was not sent to first grade, and I don't know why. Perhaps Mother thought it would be too hard for me in winter to walk, all bundled up, to the schoolhouse along paths shoveled through snow three feet deep. A more likely reason is that during those long, frigid housebound months, I served a useful purpose as companion for my little brother. At any rate, the year when I would otherwise have started school turned out to be memorable. First, electricity came to our end of town and a streetlight went up on the corner, just outside my bedroom window. At that same time *Tarzan of the Apes* was being published serially in a periodical that my parents took. For some reason I thought Mother would not consider *Tarzan* proper reading for a little girl. Perhaps she even said so. At any rate, I sneaked the paper upstairs with me at bedtime, shut the door, crept to the window, and read each installment by the dim glow from the streetlight.

Before long we had our own lights in the house. A bare bulb hung from the ceiling at the head of my bed, and by that time *Tarzan* had come to an end. Now I could lie and read *Tom Sawyer*, blameless and comfortable.

One day something went wrong with the hanging light fixture. Always curious, I lay on my bed watching Mr. Charlie Herkert, who was learning to be an electrician. He was a tall man, so he could simply reach up and tinker with the light socket. He had explored it only a moment or two before he sailed across the room yelling swear words, some of which I had never heard before. A bad shock had knocked him over, because nobody had told him to turn off the current before he stuck a finger into a socket. I would have another encounter with Mr. Herkert later.

What was this mysterious thing called electricity? How could it make a little glass bulb glow harmlessly—and then topple a strong grown man? I had to wait—and keep on asking questions—for ten years before my high-school physics teacher astonished and delighted me with the answer.

Meantime something else—something just as important—happened to Roelof and me.

Our father bought a small ranch about five miles from Creede on the bank of the Rio Grande River. Originally the ranch had been a tourist resort called Antlers Park, built at the time when wealthy fishermen began bringing their families north from Texas for the summer. Dad simply wanted to use it as a ranch. In addition to barns and an icehouse, there were two main resort buildings set in a grove of tall aspen trees. One building had housed tourists in thirteen bedrooms stretched out along the river. In the other, a vast kitchen with two pantries adjoined the dining room and sitting room used by everybody and living space for the owner's family.

The ranch was going to be our home only from May through September. The snowy months we would spend in Creede. Roelof and I explored the new place with joy and wonder. It had a bathroom! We had been in bathrooms before, because Dad took us to the stock show in Denver every winter, and we stayed at an up-to-date hotel. But this room at the ranch was different. It had only a tub.

Water for baths and for the kitchen, when Roelof and I grew bigger, depended mostly on us. It was our job every morning to pump the day's supply through a pipe to a big tank on the roof of the kitchen. From there gravity pulled it to the hot water tank and faucets below. Pumping was a chore, and we might well have been glad about the lack of a flush toilet.

We were asked to share an easier chore as soon as we moved to the ranch. It was our job to fill the wood box in the kitchen and keep it filled. To haul the sticks from the yard behind the cow barn we had a small wagon, onto which Dad had rigged a basket like a hayrick. It didn't hold much, and often we had to make several trips if Mother needed to keep a fire going in both of the cookstoves in the kitchen.

I had a third duty that did irk me. Every morning and night, after the three or four cows were milked, either Mother or Bruce, the "hired man," ran the separating machine. First they poured the milk into a large bowl at the top of the apparatus, then turned a crank at one side. Almost immediately yellow cream began to flow out of a spout on one side of the separator, and pale white skim milk streamed from another spout. My chore was to clean the machine after each use. The heart of this ingenious device was a stack of graduated metal cones that had to be treated with absolute attention. Each cone had its proper place in the stack, and after I washed them all they had to go back into the machine in just the right order. A sort of large safety pin was supposed to hold the cones together, but sometimes it came apart, and I had to reassemble the pieces of metal correctly. Once I got careless. A misplaced cone carried its own penalty—a cloud of milk sprayed out of the separator all over the kitchen. And, of course, I had to help clean it up.

Annoyed though I was, I tried to find out how such an improbable contraption worked. Somehow the cones' rapid whirling flung the heavy cream outward so that it abandoned the milk and flowed down its own tube to the spout. My uncle Charlie said it worked by centrifugal force. And what was that? A mystery.

Aside from the milk, wood, and water duties, Roelof and I were pretty much free to do anything we pleased in summer at the ranch. Especially on rainy days we scurried down a short lane to the "pavilion." This had been an open-air dance-hall in the tourist days, and it still had a fine, smooth floor. Mother had seen immediately that it was a place to keep us occupied, at least some of the time. She got us roller skates and tricycles and a small handcar that we could pump round and round the spacious pavilion. Since the building had no side walls, it was kept foursquare by turnbuckles attached to long, thin iron rods that criss-crossed just above the height of a tall man. Those rods were our gymnasium where we hung by our knees or "skinned the cat" or raced each other hand-over-hand.

Late in summer Dad cut hay in the meadows and stored it in the pavilion. After haying time we spent hours balancing on the rods and tumbling down into the soft bed below. By the next summer the cows would have consumed all the hay, and we could skate and ride our kids' vehicles again.

Our next-best playground was on the other side of the river. There two castlelike piles of sandstone rock became theater for some of the imaginative games my brother thought up. The king of the mountain held court there. Or we were detectives hiding from robbers. The sandstone itself was a source of wonder. Millions of years ago it had been sediment deposited in thin layers at the bottom of a lake. Now,

high and dry, turned into thin stony sheets, it broke apart easily, and like the pages of a book it held pictures of leaves and seeds and ferns. How could such things get inside a rock? No one I knew could have told me the secret of these fossils, but the excitement of discovering them was still with me when I began, years later, to write about dinosaurs and other ancient prehistoric life.

To reach our castles, Roelof and I had to cross the river. For the first three or four summers at the ranch that was no problem. A swinging bridge hung between tall pines on either side, and we could run and bounce across. Then one day a cloudburst up the river brought whole trees hurtling downstream. One of them hit the bridge and ripped out the footboards, but the two heavy cables that supported them were not pulled loose. There they hung, stretched from bank to inaccessible bank. The only way to get across now would be hand-over-hand on one of the cables.

"I dare you," Roelof said.

I might not have done it except for the dare. It wasn't hard actually. The river was wide and deep, and it roared beneath my dangling feet, but for some reason it didn't scare me. My arms were very strong because of all the exercising we did on bars in the pavilion. Roelof had a lot of muscle, too. Probably both of us had also profited from the water-pumping we did.

From then on, we scarcely missed the vanished swinging bridge. Our parents didn't forbid our dangerous coming and going, and I suspect now that they may have taken a certain pride in our skill and self-confidence. Or perhaps our mother was just too busy to notice. She cooked, baked, washed and ironed, made children's clothes and her own everyday dresses, had a big vegetable garden, and raised chickens—some for eggs, some for Sunday dinners. Once she tried rabbits, but she did not know that the buck had to be separated from the doe, and when the babies came, he ate them. So much for rabbits!

We had pigs, too. They came in the spring from somewhere else and spent the summer growing big enough to be butchered in the fall. For details of this butchering process I suggest Laura Ingalls Wilder's account in *The Little House in the Big Woods.* It was just like that on our ranch, and our mother, like Laura's, made sausage for the winter.

At times Mother did have a "hired girl," to help care for the flow of people in and out of the park. One or another of our grandmothers or other relatives came for frequent visits. Friends of relations turned up often. There was plenty of space in those thirteen former tourist rooms. Sometimes cowboys stayed a while, too. They looked after a small herd of cattle that Dad had on the range higher up in the mountains. So it was no wonder Mother often had two cookstoves going in the kitchen. And tourists appeared now and then, thinking that the Antlers Park Hotel still operated. If they pleaded, my kind-hearted mother said they could stay and have potluck with us.

I didn't like the tourists very much. They chucked me under the chin or pulled my pigtails and made me feel as different from them as I actually was. I was especially offended when they offered me tips. Just once a pleasant old gentleman asked Roelof and me if we wanted to take a spin in his Stanley Steamer. (Dad didn't have a car yet.) Soon after that my cousin Claribel's boyfriend gave me a ride in his Stutz Bearcat, and with those two glorious events I was prepared to embrace the automotive world. But it was a while before my father was ready to let an automobile replace the buckboard he drove every day from the ranch to his office in town. In the meantime he surprised Roelof and me with something new. A great herd of sheep had passed by on their way to high pastures up the river, and the herder had a burro he didn't need. Dad bought her for five dollars. She was docile, and Roelof and I could take turns riding her. We named her Ribbon because of a stripe over her shoulder.

Two days went by after her former owner moved on up to the range with his flock. On the morning of the third day we discovered that another adult burro, a teenaged colt, and another very young one had joined Ribbon. Obviously they were her offspring, and they were lonely without her. Roelof and I were delighted. We had to keep them, we told Dad. I could ride Ribbon and Roelof could have her grown-up son. We called him Shadrach, and the two younger ones became Meshach and Abednego—named for long-dead triplets in Grandmother Elting's family. Our canny father agreed. He knew it would cost him nothing to feed the four of them in our meadows until fall. Then he could give them back to the sheepherder when he made his way with his flock

Mary and her brother, Roelof, with their burro Ribbon, at the family ranch, 1915

back to their winter pasture fifty miles down the river.

Ribbon turned out to be easy to ride. She did not object when I stood on her back to be photographed—in stocking feet so I wouldn't hurt her. (The stockings, long and black, were part of my everyday outfit. We were not allowed to go barefoot.) Shadrach was not his mother's type. Unlike her sleek brown coat, his white hair stood out aggressively, and he had a challenging bray. Often he wouldn't go more than a few feet when Roelof got on his back. One day our hired hand Bruce said, "Somebody ought to light a fire under that donkey." I took him literally. The blazing newspaper that I put on the ground under the burro's belly had only one effect. He bucked Roelof off, and that was the last time either of us tried to ride him. Ribbon and her family departed with the sheepherder at the end of the summer.

The next year Dad thought it was time for me to have a horse of my own. From an ac-

With Roelof, 1916: "The dress, decorated with blue lace, was designed by my great-aunt Carrie"

quaintance he bought a little blue mare named Maude. Maude was indeed blue. She had just that combination of black and white hairs in her coat that gave the illusion of a washed-out denim color. Her former owner said she was gentle, but we discovered that she had other characteristics he did not reveal. She hated the saddle, and you had to pay attention when you put it on her. If she was in a contrary mood she would take a deep breath, swelling up her abdomen. Then when the rider put foot into stirrup to mount her, she deflated her middle. This loosened the cinch, the saddle slid sideways, and the would-be rider was spilled on the ground.

For my first long ride Mother said I could go to town, five miles away. Halfway there Maude began to limp. The limp grew worse. Finally I couldn't bear it. I slid out of the saddle and led her the rest of the way. Of course she was simply playing one of her tricks. After that I rode her bareback, often to bring in the cows from a pasture half a mile away. One day a

sudden Colorado rainstorm caught us. The wind was at our backs, so we didn't mind too much until we came to a hill where the path wound back and forth in a gentle climb. The first switchback brought us around with wind and rain in our faces. Maude snorted in protest. The next time we had to turn into the gusts, she rebelled. I'm sure she knew what she was doing. Instead of staying on the gently sloping path, she made a dash straight up the steep hillside, and I slid off over her rain-slick rump. Without a glance behind her, Maude turned and took off for the dry barn, and I had to bring the cows in on foot.

Eventually Maude disappeared from our lives, but not from my somewhat grudging affection. I had completely forgiven her mischief when, many years later, I wrote a small picture book about her called *Lady, the Little Blue Mare.* (The editor didn't think Maude was a romantic enough name.) I must confess that my story gave her a more heroic role than she deserved.

Milking a cow was a skill I admired, but Bruce didn't have the time or inclination to teach me how he did it so deftly. Another enthusiast for his craft was our cat, Old Lady. She and Bruce had worked out an agreement. If she positioned herself close to where he sat on the milking stool, he would squirt a quick drink into her open mouth. This maneuver never interrupted the rhythm of his squeezing on the teats, and it spilled not a drop of milk.

Old Lady, growling and protesting, had come with us in a cardboard box when we moved to the ranch the first time. The next morning she was gone. Sadly we thought a coyote had made away with her. But several days later, when Dad went to get something from our house in town, there she sat on the front porch where she thought she belonged.

Dad had heard that cats possessed a sort of built-in sense of direction, and he thought perhaps he could outsmart it. That evening he managed to box Old Lady up, but he didn't come straight home with her. He drove up and down and back and forth on Creede's streets, then took a detour on the road back to the ranch. The trick worked. Old Lady settled down, and from then on, as long as we made our seasonal moves from one home to the other, she accepted the arrangement.

Old Lady's fur had a special smell—not an animal smell such as our dogs and horses had, but a sort of vegetable odor. I suppose it came from her frequent naps in the hay in the pavilion or her hours crouching in the meadows full of mice and flowering grasses. The flowers and shrubs and trees around the ranch interested me, and from someone—probably my uncle Charlie—I learned the names of a good many of them. This led to a curious event in my later life, after I was a grown woman with a job in New York City. The whole thing started one summer when another of my uncles brought a friend named Mr. Lowery to the ranch. Mr. Lowery liked to go for walks, and he often asked Roelof and me to accompany him. Along the way I told him the names of the flowers we saw—columbine, Indian paintbrush, butter-and-eggs . . .

"Wait a minute!" Mr. Lowery said sternly. "Don't make up a silly name like butter-and-eggs when you don't know the proper one." I insisted I was right. He persisted in disbelief, and my feelings were hurt.

At Christmastime, however, I got a wonderful surprise—a package in the mail from Youngstown, Ohio. With apologies, Mr. Lowery had sent me a copy of *Colorado Wildflowers* in which there was a painting of the creamy and yellow flower called butter-and-eggs. I never saw him again, but that is not the end of the story. Mr. Lowery had no children of his own. When he died in 1929, he left Roelof and me each $1000. How amused that old gentleman must have been, when he wrote his will, thinking of the amazement and pleasure he would create. Perhaps he wondered if I still had the book he sent me. I did, and I used it later when I wrote *Flowers and What They Are.* I think he would have approved of the way I spent his gift. I quit my job and took off for a year in Europe. First I bicycled with a friend around France, then studied for two terms at the University of Strasbourg. Because a thousand dollars bought so much more in those days than it does now, I still had enough money left over to travel for several months—thanks to butter-and-eggs.

Thanks to Uncle Charlie, the world beyond our village began coming to me in small, powerful flashes. Uncle Charlie worked in the mines. Not that he had to. My father had offered him a desk job more than once, but the notion of doing business bored him. What he might have done if he had had formal education I can't judge. It certainly would have been

something that exercised his mind, not the muscles that came from hard-rock mining. Bookshelves covered one wall of his living room and they held, among many other things a multivolume history of the world. On one long bottom shelf sat piles of the little Haldeman Julius *Blue Books.* These were pocket-sized paperbacks that cost five cents, designed to educate working people.

Uncle Charlie came to our house often. He and Mother talked endlessly in the evenings when Dad was at the Elks Club or the Masonic Lodge or on town business of some sort, and I was allowed to listen. From some of his books Uncle Charlie had acquired a strong curiosity about unexplained phenomena—Tommyknockers, for example. These were special loud noises that warned miners there was going to be a cave-in. Most people, he said, thought

Mary Elting, 1936

that Tommy-knockers were made by the spirits of people who had been killed in mine accidents. He didn't believe in spirits. There must be a sensible reason for the noises, and someday scientists would discover it. Of course they did.

One day Uncle Charlie talked to Mother about the universe. It was a word I had never heard before. My idea of the heavens was based mainly on the doings of the Greek and Roman gods. Now, suddenly, the Sword Belt of Orion was transformed for me. Those small bright spots that made a picture in the night sky became a very real array of huge glowing objects on the edge of infinite space. I was enthralled, a little scared, and I wanted to be alone with this awesome new thing, or non-thing, the universe. Quietly I excused myself, went upstairs and lay down on the floor of the dark closet under the eaves. Staring into total blackness I tried to imagine the cosmos. I often wondered about it as I grew up, but somehow I've never felt comfortable with the science of astronomy. Flowers, bugs, fossils, all the sciences of earthly nature have lured me into exploring and writing about them. A friend who has written for young people about the stars says I've just been lazy. Perhaps.

Soon after I discovered the universe, Uncle Charlie moved away from Creede, and adult talk lost its spark. For new ideas, I had to depend more on teachers and books. The teachers in our four-room school were pleasant women who managed two grades each, and until I was in seventh grade, they presided over a peaceful institution. How that peace was broken I'll explain later. Until that time, we had the usual three R's with an unusual reward: Our teachers read aloud to us after lunch every day. I heard *Huckleberry Finn* that way and a popular novel called *Penrod* and a parcel of Greek and Roman and Norse myths.

Miss Hunt, who taught fifth and sixth grades, introduced us to the *Just So Stories.* She also borrowed and read from my *Youth's Companion.* One of these stories, laid in Civil War times, had a lasting influence on me. A long section in it recounted the battle of Gettysburg in gory detail. After that, a passionate rejection of warmakers never left me, even when the cause was just. It was rage at the military that I felt then and still feel when conflict is resolved by killing.

The First World War was still to come when my days were so largely filled with books. After school I often visited my great-aunt Carrie, who not only read to me but also shared her copies of *Vogue Magazine.* Every month she and I marveled at the French designer Erté's pictures of the outlandish costumes that made him famous. Aunt Carrie sewed well from patterns she found in *Vogue.* Unfortunately she liked to sew for me, too. It was creations, not dresses, that she made, and I wanted to hide when other girls asked where in the world I got those weird garments. Actually I loved them, though I hated to put them on.

Aunt Carrie and Mother shared political opinions—both were Democrats. In 1916 they voted for Woodrow Wilson. (Women in Colorado already had the vote by then.) As usual, on election day the Ladies Aid Society held a fund-raising trout dinner in the public hall. In its attached kitchen Mr. Charlie Herkert, our part-time electrician, was at work that evening cooking the trout. Before dinner started, my best friend and I wandered out there. I watched Charlie for a moment and then cried in anguish: "Mr. Herkert! You can't fry trout in flour! They have to be rolled in cornmeal!"

He stopped, with a floured fish in the air above the crackling bacon grease, and gave me a fierce stare. Then he said, "Just because you females have the vote doesn't mean you can tell me how to cook." He was wrong, of course.

I have always thought that Charlie Herkert got what was coming to him a few years later. The kitchen gods had justly sentenced him to stomach ulcers. Charlie suffered such pain that he finally decided to end it all. He swallowed what he thought would be a fatal dose of lye. But it was hardly down when he changed his mind, rushed to the doctor and had himself pumped out. Charlie had served his sentence. The lye apparently burned away the ulcers, and he lived on for years, a pain-free and unrepentant cook.

With Democrat Woodrow Wilson in the White House, my Republican father decided he had better change with the times. He took the train to Denver and bought a 1917 Dodge touring car. The salesman explained what the gear shift and emergency brakes were for, how to crank the engine, how to use the clutch and brake pedals, and that was that. Dad had never been behind the wheel of a vehicle before. He just drove off as best he could. Luckily the car

*The author visiting the Artek summer camp for children in
the former Soviet Union, 1964*

shop was on the edge of the city. By the time he had completed the 250 miles home, he was an expert.

The next day, Mother and I had driving lessons. After a few trips up and down the ranch lane, we were ready for the road. In those days no one had to have a driver's license—at least not in our part of Colorado. I still find it curious that my father trusted his eleven-year-old daughter with that dangerous machine, even though the roads were so rough that you could go no more than ten or twelve miles an hour. I suspect that he had no idea how dangerous it really was. Few people had cars, and so there were few disasters. In fact, years went by before I knew anyone who had an accident. He was an elderly cowboy who rode his horse to town for a few drinks every Saturday night. On the way home he often slept in the saddle but the horse got him safely back to his ranch. The Model T Ford that he bought had no such skill and, when he dozed at the wheel one Saturday, it crashed into a ditch.

After the United States entered the First World War, even though Woodrow Wilson had promised to keep us out of it, my classmates and I had a curious glimpse of that dreadful conflict. An appalling number of young Englishmen had already been killed in the three years since the war in Europe began. Now, hoping to replace them with British subjects who were not yet U.S. citizens, British recruiters visited this country. One of these agents came to Creede, and for a while he stayed with us at the ranch. As a sideline to his duties he gave a talk to school children. We squirmed in our seats while he described the itching bites of "cooties"—the lice that fed on soldiers in the trenches.

It was a cruel performance. Perhaps the recruiter, a disabled veteran, was taking out on his helpless listeners his own feelings of frustration. I gave him no encouragement, pacifist that I already was, and he must have sensed that there was something more than impoliteness in my attitude. He insisted that it was my

Mary and her husband, the author Franklin Folsom, at her seventieth birthday party, 1976

patriotic duty to knit for the Red Cross. He would teach me, starting with wash cloths. They were boring. So he brought me a lot of wool and the small needles for knitting socks. His stay at the ranch lasted long enough for him to keep me at the task until I could turn the heel and "toe-off" properly. I have no idea whether he got any recruits for Britain, but I do remember delivering socks to the Red Cross with a certain pride in my new skill. I never practiced it afterward.

This first year of the war I was in seventh grade, feeling rather strange in the same room with the big eighth-grade boys and a male teacher for the first time. He was a husky young man, handsome and popular with the boys. Unfortunately he left us at Christmastime, probably because he had been drafted into the army. His replacement was a somewhat older man, less vigorous, but very earnest and to my mind more interesting. The big boys had a different opinion. He was Jewish and intellectual and not athletic, and they put together the usual

stereotype to whisper loudly during class. What difference did Jewish make? I wanted to know. Our best friends, Rosa and Albert Moses, were Jewish. The big kids jeered. Our teacher pretended not to notice.

Then one morning what sounded like a battle suddenly broke out in the potbellied stove in our classroom. The big boys, who had the job of bringing in the fuel for the fire, had stuck rifle bullets into cracks in the wood. When the bullets got hot enough, they went off. We innocent ones were terrified, but our screams weren't much louder than the laughter of the perpetrators. Our teacher picked up the poker and threatened to use it on the boys if they didn't get out and stay out of his class from then on. Soon afterward he resigned, but the school year was almost over anyway.

My parents and many friends were outraged. On the whole, bigotry seems to have played only a small role in Creede affairs, though the town had its share of cliques and rivalries. Of these I remained somewhat innocent because, from now on, I spent my school days elsewhere. My young brother's heart had been affected by influenza, and the doctor insisted it needed a rest from Creede's high altitude—9000 feet. Mother reluctantly agreed to take him first to Independence, Missouri, where she had relatives, then to Denver. Of course, I went along.

Our little mountain school had taught me well. I already knew more than many of the kids in eighth grade in Independence. A cousin in my class did beat me in math. Unreasonably I held this against him, but he had some really disagreeable traits as well. I was not surprised when he grew up to be a rather shady politician. Remembering him thirty years later, I made him into an unpleasant character in my book called *Patch*.

In Denver we lived in a house near North High School. This was the luckiest possible place for an awkward teenager from a little mining town, eager and full of curiosity, brought up without many social graces. North was not Denver's fashionable high school. I loved everything about it—well, almost everything. Science classes, first in chemistry, then in physics, especially delighted me. My only problems were nonacademic. Twice in sewing class the nail of a finger got stitched by the electric machine. In mechanical drawing I could never keep the special pen from unloading its ink in blobs. Art class left me in total despair. I could not make even a milk bottle look like what it really was. This disability affected me even more a few years later. If I had been able to draw I might not have become a writer. More about that later.

Small muscle control seems to have been my weakness. Big muscles worked better—best of all in the ballroom dancing class Mother sent me to one evening a week. The girls learned to waltz and two-step wearing simple blouses and skirts, but the boys had to sweat out the lessons in coat, tie, and white cotton gloves.

Except for the dance classes, and a very rare movie or a night at a concert or a theater, regular entertainment came only from the books that Mother read aloud to Roelof and me. Our sitcoms were in such works as the Charles Dickens novels, one after another. I do remember one concession Mother made. She shared an E. Phillips Oppenheim mystery story with us.

In my third year at North some evenings were a bit different. I belonged to the Latin club drama group and, dressed in togas, we put on plays. (How stuffy that sounds now, but it really was fun.) That was also my movie year. By now the piano music I had been practicing ever since I was a little kid caught the attention of the minister at the Congregational Church. He had arranged to show wholesome films every Saturday night—silent films, because this was 1923, long before the days of sound. Like the regular movie houses, the church basement was to have a piano player—me—to accompany the action with appropriate tunes. For cowboys furiously riding I gave the audience "The Charge of the Uhlans." Serious scenes called for "Berceuse" or the opening of "Moonlight Sonata."

When high school graduation came, Mother took almost unheard-of exception to my father's wishes: she insisted that I go to college. Fortunately, in spite of my poor performance in art, I got a scholarship to the University of Colorado—sixty dollars each quarter to pay my tuition for four years, provided I kept up my grade average. Studying was no problem. First came the Latin I had already come to love. Then the literature of other countries, which meant learning French, Spanish, and Italian. It happened that a woman who taught biology was a member of the sorority I joined. She

Backpacking in the Grand Canyon, 1980

had recently been in Latin America researching chromosomes in the intestinal cells of mosquitoes. I could hardly wait to take a course in her department.

Lectures and text in introductory zoology were all I could have wished for. Then I discovered that I had to draw pictures of everything I observed or dissected. Impossible! Plainly, I could never be a scientist. That was a shock, but not a devastating one. I could always read what had been written by those with the visual sense I lacked. So I added an occasional science book to the list—from Catullus to James Branch Cabell—that my friends in literature studies were reading. Some of us by 1926 felt compelled to do writing of our own, and we began reading our efforts to each other every Sunday afternoon. We called ourselves the Sunday Sympathizers.

Three of us in that earnest group went on to be professional writers, and ten years later its organizer, Franklin Folsom, and I were married. He in the meantime had published poetry and won the Harriet Monroe Poetry prize. I had made a new translation of *Manon Lescaut,* which ran serially in the magazine for which I was assistant editor, and I was doing book reviews for another publication. Frequently I had a chance to review a new book designed to make some aspect of science understandable to us ordinary readers, and like the elephant's child, I was finding answers. In my enthusiasm I sometimes got carried away and told my husband more than he wanted to know about my discoveries. He wasn't antiscience, but he found literature and politics more absorbing.

When our son Michael was still in his stroller, he and I began to share a lifelong fascination with the workings of big machines. It was hard to get him past the holes alongside New York's streets where diggings for new buildings went on. He was fifteen years old when I wrote *Machines at Work,* and many of his questions and mine had already been answered by my research for other books in the "At Work" series.

Before that, Mike and thousands of other children had wanted to know what their fathers were doing in the services during the Second World War. With the help of a retired army officer, I wrote, and Jeanne Bendick illustrated, *Soldiers, Sailors, Fliers and Marines.* I had to change some of my strong feelings against armed conflict which had already been somewhat numbed during the civil war in Spain. I had been frightened by the part the Nazi military played in defeating the elected Spanish republican government. With many other writers in this country, I helped to send aid to antifascist teachers and writers who had to escape from Spain. They were in danger of prison or death because they were opposed to the new fascist dictator. We also aided antifascist writers who escaped ahead of Hitler's armies before the United States entered the war. So I was already well aware of the Nazi danger to everyone—not just to writers—when I had to answer children's questions. At that time young people had been spared the scenes of killing that movies and television now bring them. My book left to parents the difficult task of explaining what weapons do.

A report about my book from the publisher's salespeople puzzled the editor and me for a while. The Navy Department had ordered three thousand copies. Why? Because at least that many boys who joined the navy could not read

Bird-watching with son Michael and grandson Jamie, 1989

or write. Our book was to be their first easy reader.

After the war, when Mike wanted to know how the lead got into pencils and the sticks got into lollipops, Jeanne and I did *The Lollypop Factory*. Meantime our agent persuaded the publisher, Franklin Watts, to start a series of "First Books" with my text and Jeanne's pictures.

When Mr. Watts looked at my manuscripts he said: "Dandy. But of course we can't put your name on them."

"Why not?"

Mr. Watts seemed surprised. "Can you imagine a father buying for a little boy a book about airplanes or boats that was signed by a woman?"

What about the artist? Reluctantly Jeanne and I agreed that Frank could use Campbell Tatham as the author's name but that Jeanne could sign her delightfully cartoony drawings. Soon the list of "First Books" by me and other writers became immensely popular, and Mary Elting quietly put her name on *The First Book of Nurses* manuscript.

More and more publishers began finding out that children had a very real need not only for stories but also for information books. A few editors were dismayed by this notion. At one children's book luncheon I heard an emotional argument between the publisher of a talented science writer and an editor who wailed that books about electricity or the human body "were not literature." Fortunately for me a number of other editors felt that young readers would welcome both kinds.

When I was gathering material for *The First Book of Nurses*, my husband was researching a book about Native Americans. So we set off with our young son and daughter on what would be the first of many camping trips in the West. At the hospital on the Navajo reservation I heard an unusual story about Miss Whitecloud, an Indian nurse. Later I found out about Mary F. P. Mahoney, the first African American nurse. Both of them appeared in my manuscript, and the artist, Mary Stevens, put their portraits in her illustrations. Otherwise, however, she managed only a hint of a few nonwhite faces.

Frank Watts listened politely to arguments that "First Book" pictures as a whole did not reflect the ethnic makeup of their audience. At last, in exasperation, he said, "All right, get me a writer and I'll publish *The First Book of*

With daughter, the artist Rachel Folsom, and granddaughter Lizzie, 1989

Negroes." My husband immediately called Langston Hughes and got him to write it.

Children's book writers were pioneers in a quiet—and unfortunately still not finished—campaign to have illustrations reflect reality. Most white artists I have known are sensitive to facial differences and try hard to draw them. There have been exceptions. In the sketches for one of my books I found not a single illustration of passages where black children appeared. I complained and the editor ordered additional pictures. The artist illustrated the scenes—but arranged them with the children's backs to the reader. When my husband and I collaborated on *Flags of All Nations and the People Who Live under Them*, we connived. That book was illustrated with photographs of beautiful faces from around the world. Since then I have had to apologize only twice for artists who refused to answer my pleas for representative portraits.

By the time our son and daughter were old enough to do their own research, I had filled my head with children's questions. The day had come for an answer book which would introduce young readers to simplified general science. So I wrote it. *The Answer Book* was the first of a whole lot of similar question-and-answer titles by other writers that various publishers brought out. For two years mine was a best-seller on the *New York Times* Christmas list of books for children.

One volume didn't begin to take care of everything that needed discussing. Over the years six more "Answer Books" have appeared, and some have been published in eight foreign-language editions. For two of the books I had the collaboration of my husband. On two others I worked with my daughter, her husband, Rose Wyler, and Rose's daughter.

Writers sometimes say that theirs is a lonely occupation. Not mine. Working with enthusiastic collaborators has been a delight. My son and I researched and wrote together *The Mysterious Grain,* the story of botanists who traced the ancestry of the corn plant. Ann Goodman and I did *Dinosaur Mysteries* to which was named an "Outstanding Science Book for Children, 1980" by the Children's Book Council and the National Science Teachers Association.

In these and other books I have tried to stir young readers in two ways. First, I want them to find excitement in the discoveries that scientists make, and then in the stories of how men and women went about solving the endless puzzles in their fields.

When my husband and I were asked to write *The Story of Archeology in the Americas,* we had for background only an anthropology course in college. So we began talking to archeologists and reading their books. We watched them at work excavating ancient dwellings and were invited to help at a dig in Colorado. We visited museums and sites in many places, and archeology became a habit. My husband wrote several young people's books with backgrounds at sites and digs. With our son Mike I wrote *The Secret Story of Pueblo Bonito.* Still we had more ideas and information than we knew what to do with—until we decided to write for adult readers *America's Ancient Treasures,* a guide to sites and museums. Our daughter Rachel, now an artist, did many drawings for the book. One of the best things about it is that it has to be brought up-to-date once in a while. This means we have had to read and visit and find out the ongoing news about the ancient world. The

Sharing a meal with grandson Raphael, 1994

fourth revised expanded edition came out in 1993.

In between these recurring archeology sprees there was time for me to explore other fields: spacecraft and helicopters, dinosaurs and other prehistoric creatures, snakes, the amazing human body and how it works, math games and math history. I even worked with my son-in-law, a professor of computer science, on a paperback *Answer Book about Computers.* But I typed the manuscript on my 1938 Royal portable. My clumsy fingers haven't managed to give up their old-fashioned ways—yet.

One day when I was having lunch with Mike and his two young sons, all four of us collaborated on a book. The boys were at the age for riddles. We had heard them all before, but once again I pretended I didn't know the answer was "oinkment" when one of them asked "What did the pig put on a sore toe?"

"Enough, kids!" Mike said at last. "I've got one for you: Q is for duck. Why?"

They guessed in a moment: "Because a duck quacks." Then they began tossing follow-ups at us. "B is for dog," "C is for rooster," and on through the alphabet. Before the end of it, I said: "Stop! Write this down. We have a book."

I was right. *Q Is for Duck* has gone through many printings.

"If you aren't writing, what's your favorite thing to do?" a girl asked me once when I gave a talk at her school. My favorites, I told her, were different at different times. Thirteen times, the best possible thing to do in September was to spend five days backpacking with my husband and several friends, all the way down one side of the Grand Canyon and up the other side. Many times we traveled to distant places. We went to archeological sites in Mexico and Peru, Egypt and China. We visited children's camps in Russia and Uzbekistan. One year, when most countries were at peace, we journeyed by bus all the way from Europe to Nepal in the Himalaya Mountains. Later I saw those mountains from their opposite side in Tibet.

Sometimes, when I'm not away in winter, I've been invited to share in a program with girls and boys who may one day be writers. A number of fifth graders from all the schools in Colorado's Boulder County write a special story or poem or nonfiction article for the occasion. This is not a contest. It is just doing their best for fun. Then a group of us Colorado writers divide the manuscripts up, and each of us meets with eight or ten of the young authors to talk about their work. This is a very rewarding thing to do when I'm not writing. What a joy to find a young person whose funny piece makes me laugh out loud! I've found striking images in poetry manuscripts and a talent for observation in science stories. Once in a while I have to fuss at someone who has just imitated a TV murder mystery. More often I find young folks with ideas and insight who are eager to learn about form and style—and about what professional writers are like.

Best of all—I learn from them, too.

BIBLIOGRAPHY

FOR YOUNG PEOPLE

Nonfiction:

(With Robert T. Weaver) *Soldiers, Sailors, Fliers and Marines,* illustrated by Jeanne Bendick, Doubleday, Doran, 1943.

(With Robert T. Weaver, in collaboration with Margaret Gossett) *Battles: How They Are Won,* illustrated by Jeanne Bendick, Doubleday, Doran, 1944.

(Under pseudonym Campbell Tatham) *The First Flying Book,* illustrated by Jeanne Bendick, F. Watts, 1944.

(Under pseudonym Campbell Tatham) *The First Book of Boats,* illustrated by Jeanne Bendick, F. Watts, 1945.

(With Margaret Gossett) *We Are the Government,* illustrated by Jeanne Bendick, Doubleday, Doran, 1945, revised edition illustrated by Angia Culfogienis, Doubleday, 1967.

(With Margaret Gossett) *The Lollypop Factory—and Lots of Others,* illustrated by Jeanne Bendick, Doubleday, 1946.

Trucks at Work, illustrated by Ursula Koering, Garden City Books, 1946, revised edition, Harvey House, 1962.

Trains at Work, illustrated by David Lyle Millard, Garden City Books, 1947, revised edition, Harvey House, 1962.

(Under pseudonym Campbell Tatham) *The First Book of Trains,* illustrated by Jeanne Bendick, F. Watts, 1948.

(With Margaret Gossett) *Now You're Cookin',* Westminster, 1948, published as *Now We're Cookin': The Book for Teenage Chefs,* illustrated by Karen Bendick, Harvey House, 1968.

(Under pseudonym Campbell Tatham) *The First Book of Automobiles,* illustrated by Jeanne Bendick, F. Watts, 1949.

Who Lives on the Farm?, illustrated by Pauline Jackson, Wonder Books, 1949.

Wheels and Noises, illustrated by Elizabeth Dauber, Wonder Books, 1950.

The First Book of Nurses (also see below), illustrated by Mary Stevens, F. Watts, 1951.

(Under pseudonym Davis Cole) *The Real Book about Trains,* illustrated by David Millard, Garden City Books, 1951.

(Under pseudonym Campbell Tatham) *The First Book of Trucks,* illustrated by Jeanne Bendick, F. Watts, 1952.

Machines at Work, illustrated by Lazlo Roth, Garden City Books, 1953, revised edition, Harvey House, 1962.

Ships at Work, illustrated by Manning de V. Lee, Garden City Books, 1953, revised edition, Harvey House, 1962.

Wishes and Secrets, illustrated by Mary Stevens, Bobbs-Merrill, 1956.

The Answer Book, illustrated by Tran Mawicke and others, Grosset, 1959, abridged edition published as *Arrow Book of Science Facts,* Scholastic Book Services, 1960, British edition published as *Why? What? Where? Answers to 300 Questions Children Ask,* Odhams, 1962.

(With Franklin Folsom) *The Story of Archeology in the Americas,* illustrated by Kathleen Elgin, Harvey House, 1960.

Answers and More Answers: Answers to Questions That Every Child Asks, illustrated by Tran Mawicke, Grosset, 1961, abridged edition published as *Arrow Book of Answers,* Scholastic Book Services, 1962, British edition published as *Every Child's Answer Book,* Odhams, 1963.

Flowers and What They Are, illustrated by Carl and Mary Hauge, Whitman, 1961.

Question and Answer Book, illustrated by Elizabeth Dauber, Grosset, 1963.

(With Michael Folsom) *The Secret Story of Pueblo Bonito,* illustrated by Kathleen Elgin, Harvey House, 1963, with additional photos, Scholastic, 1963.

Aircraft at Work, illustrated by Janet and Alex D'Amato, Harvey House, 1964.

(With Franklin Folsom) *The Answer Book of Geography,* illustrated by Barbara Amlick, Grosset, 1964.

How Animals Get to the Zoo, illustrated by Stefan Martin, Grosset, 1964.

Water Come, Water Go, illustrated by Janet and Alex D'Amato, Harvey House, 1964.

Spacecraft at Work, illustrated by Ursula Koering, Harvey House, 1965.

(With Franklin Folsom) *The Answer Book of History,* illustrated by W. K. Plummer, Grosset, 1966, British edition published as *Every Child's Book of Why and When,* Odhams, 1967.

(With Franklin Folsom) *Flags of All Nations and the People Who Live under Them,* Grosset, 1967, revised edition, 1970.

(With Michael Folsom) *The Mysterious Grain,* illustrated by Frank Cieciorka, M. Evans, 1967.

(With Franklin Folsom) *If You Lived in the Days of the Wild Mammoth Hunters,* illustrated by John Moodie, Scholastic, 1968.

What's Going on Here?, illustrated by Dierdre Stanforth, Grosset, 1968.

All Aboard! The Railroad Trains that Built America, Four Winds, 1969, published as *All Aboard! The Trains that Built America,* Scholastic, 1969.

The Hopi Way, illustrated by Louis Mofsie, M. Evans, 1969.

(With Robin A. McKown) *A Mongo Homecoming,* illustrated by Moneta Branett, M. Evans, 1969.

Still More Answers, illustrated by Glen Fleischmann, Grosset, 1970.

How Many Legs, How Many Toes? A Beginning Book about Animals, illustrated by Cynthia and Alvin Koehler, Wonder Books, 1971.

What Happens to a Drink of Water? A Beginning Book about You, illustrated by Mac Conner, Wonder Books, 1971.

(With Judith Steigler) *Helicopters at Work,* illustrated by Ursula Koering, Harvey House, 1972.

(With Rose Wyler and Robert Moll) *A New Answer Book,* illustrated by Rachel Folsom and Ferd Sondern, Grosset, 1977.

(With Rose Wyler) *The Answer Book about You,* illustrated by Tony Tallarico and diagrams by Robert Engman, Grosset, 1980, revised edition, 1984.

(With Ann Goodman) *Dinosaur Mysteries,* illustrated by Susan Swan, Platt & Munk, 1980.

(With Michael Folsom) *Q Is for Duck: An Alphabet Guessing Game,* illustrated by Jack Kent, Houghton Mifflin/Clarion Books, 1980.

Gorilla Mysteries, illustrated by John Hamberger, Platt & Munk, 1981.

Mysterious Seas, illustrated by Fiona Reid, Grosset, 1983.

The Answer Book about Animals, illustrated by Rowan Barnes-Murphy, Grosset, 1984.

(With Robert Moll and Rose Wyler) *The Answer Book about Computers,* illustrated by Rowan Barnes-Murphy, Grosset, 1984.

(With Michael Folsom) *The Answer Book about Robots and Other Inventions,* illustrated by Rowan Barnes-Murphy, Grosset, 1984.

The Macmillan Book of Dinosaurs and Other Prehistoric Creatures, illustrated by John Hamberger, Macmillan, 1984.

The Macmillan Book of the Human Body, illustrated by Kirk Moldoff, Macmillan, 1986.

Snakes and Other Reptiles, illustrated by Christopher Santoro, Simon & Schuster, 1987.

Dinosaurs, illustrated by Gabriele Nenzioni and Mauro Cutrona, Golden Books, 1987.

The Big Golden Book of Dinosaurs, illustrated by Christopher Santoro, Western, 1988.

(With Rachel Folsom and Robert Moll) *Volcanoes and Earthquakes,* illustrated by Courtney, Simon & Schuster, 1990.

(With Rose Wyler) *Math Fun: Test Your Luck,* Julian Messner, 1992.

(With Rose Wyler) *Math Fun with Money Puzzlers,* illustrated by Patrick Girouard, Julian Messner, 1992.

(With Rose Wyler) *Math Fun with a Pocket Calculator,* illustrated by G. Bryan Karas, Julian Messner, 1992.

(With Rose Wyler) *Math Fun with Tricky Lines and Shapes,* illustrated by Paul Harvey, Julian Messner, 1992.

Fiction:

Smoky, the Baby Goat, illustrated by Veronica Reed, Whitman, 1947.

(With Margaret Gossett) *Patch,* illustrated by Ursula Koering, Doubleday, 1948.

Runaway Ginger, illustrated by Zillah Leskow, Whitman, 1949.

Speckles and the Triplets, illustrated by Mary Stevens, Whitman, 1949.

The Big Red Pajama Wagon, illustrated by Betty Anderson, Whitman, 1950.

Lady, the Little Blue Mare, illustrated by Florence Sarah Winship, Whitman, 1950.

Wishes and Secrets, illustrated by Mary Stevens, Bobbs-Merrill, 1956.

The Helicopter Mystery, illustrated by John J. Floherty, Jr., Harvey House, 1958.

Miss Polly's Animal School, illustrated by Lisl Weil, Grosset, 1961.

The Mysterious Milk Robber: And Other Stories, illustrated by Ursula Koering, Harvey House, 1970.

Other:

(Adaptor) *Arrow Book of Nurses* (based on *The First Book of Nurses*), Scholastic Book Services, 1963.

FOR ADULTS

Nonfiction:

(With Franklin Folsom) *America's Ancient Treasures,* drawings by Rachel Folsom, University of New Mexico Press, 1983, revised edition, 1993.

(With Franklin Folsom) *Ancient Treasures of the Southwest,* drawings by Rachel Folsom, University of New Mexico Press, 1994.

Translator:

(From the German, with E. I. Holt) Ferenc Kormendi, *Escape to Life,* Morrow, 1933.

Member of editorial staff of *Forum* magazine, 1927–29 and *Golden Book* magazine, 1931–35.

NOTE: Although the Library of Congress lists Mary Elting as the author of several titles under the pseudonyms Benjamin Brewster and Michael Gorham, the author has affirmed that these titles were written by her husband, Franklin Folsom. The incorrect attributions resulted from a publisher's error in filing copyright information.

Max Fatchen

1920-

SUNLIGHT, SEA AND COUNTRYSIDE

Many factors shape the way we write; where we live, what we experience; the urgency within ourselves. We can be erratic or meticulous; cool or passionate, but we must be ourselves with our own intimacy of thought, our own way of expression.

Our childhood is one of the most powerful influences and certainly it has been mine. We are affected by our lives as children; we don't leave our childhood behind us because it's there inside us. For when one writes for children and young people, one remembers that one was a child too. One can be surrounded by all the learning, conclusions of teaching, of literature and the wisdom that adults are supposed to acquire, but it is the way one was as a child that may help those of us who write, to understand the young people for whom we write.

So I want to begin by writing about my childhood because I was so lucky to have a happy one. I will tell you about falling rain and the sound of a plough turning the earth; of wide hot Australian landscapes; about the wonder of light and space and the experiences of a solitary, country child and how they became poems and books.

Where I lived, on the Adelaide plains north of South Australia's capital Adelaide, was a farming area although much of its southern part is being covered by the houses of new suburbs. The hay farms of my youth have also become market gardens of people of many ethnic backgrounds . . . Bulgarian, Greek, Italian and latterly Vietnamese.

The plains are flat with ranges behind them and small rivers across them, the rivers shaded by big gums and dry much of the year, but likely to flood if we have big rains.

Life on the plains in the late twenties and early thirties was simple and uncomplicated, although it was sometimes a struggle when the droughts came and brought the red dust on

Max Fatchen at age three, Adelaide, South Australia

the hot winds from the north. The nearest sizable town was Gawler, where we did our shopping. Its main street on Fridays was busy with farmers and farmers' wives attending markets, shopping or chatting, and there I went for my periodic haircut and sat in a remarkable barber's chair that could be elevated and rotated by a series of handles while around me farmers were shaved and trimmed. Beards weren't popular, although the moustache was a sign of some dignity.

There were no supermarkets, just general stores with white-aproned shopkeepers; men and women who knew each customer; who knew how to inquire about family, or whose cow was sick or whose child had the chicken pox.

And they packed the boxes of customers with health salts that fizzed, cochineal for coloring cakes, rice and sago for puddings, bread loaves with high tops, packets of tea and self-raising flour, cheese in cloths, long yellow bars of soap and the inevitable small bag of boiled sweets. The shopkeepers would then add the figures in their docket books, and placed the money and the bill in a small overhead container that whizzed along a wire to the cashier in a raised platform in the centre of the store.

The cashier presided over a veritable terminus of wires and containers whizzing their way while we children watched fascinated. We also noticed that she had a new hairdo each week. She was indeed the queen of cash, the goddess of accounts.

The final call would be the newspaper shop for my comics; most of them from England, and they were always rolled and placed in the corner of our grocery box so that they somehow smelt of new bread. Then home in the old tourer car with its flapping fabric hood and its side curtains if it was a wet, windy day. I liked to collect the names of cars with their distinctive symbols and radiator caps: the Indian chief on the Pontiac, the huge Dodge, the popular Chevrolet, the Model T Ford, the Overland, the Hudson, the Chrysler with its winged radiator cap. The undertaker had a great, dark Packard in which were borne the mourners; the doctor had a Sunbeam Talbot which he drove at great speed, often in the dead of night to deliver babies, or to help some poor child with croup, a terrible coughing affliction, while the family gathered around anxiously by lamplight, or boiled water while yawning children listened fearfully to the racking cough.

My home at Angle Vale had four rooms and a pantry and bathroom. The pantry contained the separator with a great bowl on the top, and one would turn the handle while this Scandinavian machine spouted cream from one spout and skim milk from the other. My mother would sometimes make her own butter, working it with wooden paddles after the cream had been placed in a wooden churn, until the butter appeared in a yellow, undisciplined mass.

My father rose at daybreak to feed our Clydesdale horses before they were harnessed into the agricultural implements to till our farm. This became my task as I grew older, and I

Father, Cecil Fatchen, on his haywagon, "with his faithful dog"

would go shivering across the paddocks to the stable in winter, and the horses, huge, gentle beasts, would hear me coming and begin beating their great hairy knees on the mangers, much as you would ring a dinner bell. The stable was reached from the adjoining barn by little windows, and I would slide back their wooden shutters and tip in tubfuls of chaff while the horses snorted with satisfaction and there was a great munching and clearing of nostrils. In the paddock on my return, I would see my friend the hare standing on its hind legs, its ears, like two pointed fingers, probing the frosty air at sunrise and about whom I would write a poem years later.

There was always a bad-tempered cow to milk before I went to school, a cow with a hefty kick, with a habit of tossing her horns and kicking the bucket over my head. But, as I became a better milker, I would lean my head against the cow's side and sing songs I'd heard on the radio, and the cow would chew her cud.

Then a quick breakfast and my schoolbag packed: the essay book with its homework; the grease-proof paper wrapped around the egg and jam sandwiches. And a pannikin to get a cool drink from the great water bag that hung under the peppertree in the schoolyard, a water bag with a snout like an elephant.

Our school was small. I walked there, about a mile, along the dusty country road: in winter with small water holes to avoid; in spring the wildflowers coming out among the tussocks; in summer sometimes a big brown snake, deadly and beautiful whipping across the road. The school had small windows and thick walls. The gum trees outside were full of predatory magpies, ready to swoop and puncture small heads. My guardian against magpies was a tall, pigtailed girl of the seventh grade who was determined that I should be mothered. She escorted me in the afternoon from the school, holding over my head a tin basin used for washing. The magpies would come arrowing down, their heads striking the basin a glancing blow.

I liked this girl. I liked her exotic chutney sandwiches. It was muttered among the older members of my sex that I was keen on her and that I was also the "teacher's pet" for, from the beginning, I loved words and books, and we had precious few; just a couple of dozen in cupboards made from kerosene cases lying on their sides.

There were *Alice in Wonderland, Treasure Island,* poems by the South Australian poet C. J. Dennis, Mark Twain's *Huckleberry Finn* and *Tom Sawyer,* books by Mary Grant Bruce and L. M. Montgomery's *Anne of Green Gables.* My own preferences were books about the Red Indians by Edward S. Ellis, such as *Deerfoot of the Prairies* and *Lost in the Rockies;* and others such as the *Swiss Family Robinson* and *Robinson Crusoe.* I was an only child, and in a way books became my brothers and sisters, and soon I was reading Sir Walter Scott and Jack London and, as I grew older, Henry David Thoreau's *Walden.*

The shelter shed at our school was a lean-to against the main building with rough wooden benches and rusty hooks on which to hang schoolbags. Move into the school and you would find thirty children sitting at long wooden desks with inkwells and smudgy surfaces and a small shelf underneath into which books were thrust— copybooks for handwriting, arithmetic books, exercise books covered with various cloth and even wallpaper. Each desk had a small furrow for holding pens. The pens were much chewed and the nibs irascible and easily crossed. On the walls were maps.

There was a marvellous print of the Saxon king, King Alfred (he of the famous cake burning), repelling the Danes, a graphic picture which all the children with shining bloodlust in their eyes loved because there was much mayhem, waving of swords, brandishing of spears and wielding of battle-axes on the longships with their dragon heads, staring eyes with ferocious Nordic beards being trimmed to size by Saxon swords and rough justice for all. Alfred was clearly getting the upper hand and we would lift sly eyes from our reading books and silently sigh in hope when the school inspector came in his roaring Dodge and gave us hard sums that he would meet King Alfred whirling a punishing battle-ax and then there would be no stumbling mental arithmetic, no trauma for the teacher watching her classes arrayed against this stern man of education.

Our teacher cared about her craft and cared for us. She taught us poetry and she taught us about words. She made words live and lilt. And I sat there wishing I could write such things. I did indeed write little poems of no great skill.

I was particularly moved by the Longfellow poem

> It was the schooner Hesperus,
> That sailed the wintry sea:
> And the skipper had taken his little
>   daughter,
> To bear him company.

Then the second verse:

> Blue were her eyes as fairy flax,
> Her cheeks like dawn of day,
> And her bosom white as the
>   hawthorn-buds,
> That ope in the month of May.

This caused much sniffling and the producing of none-too-clean handkerchiefs because everyone knew what would happen to the poor child.

The teacher tried bravely to teach us a little music. We had singing on Thursdays. She struck her tuning fork on the blackboard and we sang the scale. I seem to remember we sang "Sweet and low, sweet and low, wind of the western sea" very sweetly but we had awful trouble singing rounds such as "John, John the boatman, call, call, again / Loud roars the tempest and fast falls the rain." Everyone became hopelessly lost and the teacher would say in a resigned tone, "I don't think John can hear us, children."

Our sole musical instrument was a cracked gramophone which played a few records with a scratchy needle. Most of them were Sousa marches to which we stamped into school except when the needle stuck on the record and we marked time until the teacher set it working again. We had one link with musical celebrities. One day a tall eccentric-looking man in shorts and with a rucksack on his back went striding by accompanied by a tall fair woman.

There was a rumor that they had arrived on a square-rigged sailing ship and that they were going to relatives who lived on the other side of the Gawler River. The name didn't mean much to us then but it does to me now, for this was composer, arranger and pianist Percy Grainger, who had walked, we incredulous children learnt, from Adelaide nineteen miles away.

We children particularly looked forward to night country weddings in the small square country church with its adjoining hall. There was no electricity and the church and hall were lit by pressure lamps, hissing and throwing a brilliant light from their mantles on orange blossoms and filmy veils while the local organist did her musical best with the harmonium and the bridal march, the church cleaner hovering to see that not too much confetti was thrown.

There was a ferocious welcome for the young couple just moving into their home. As evening fell with its country tranquillity, stealthy groups of parents, children and others would approach and, at a given signal, beat upon kettles, tubs, tin trays and anything that made a noise, causing poultry to squawk, every dog in the district to give tongue and the young couple, embarrassed and giggling, to appear. Everyone trooped inside for everyone had brought food—pies and pasties and cold chicken, lamingtons, cakes and even fruit and jellies. There would be much happy uproar and singing to the accompaniment of an accordion, although the young couple cast longing glances at their bedroom as the moon climbed and the noisy hours went by.

We children would go home early because it was school tomorrow. We wondered about weddings and love and things, and there were various discussions in the schoolground; things whispered behind furtive hands.

I had no brothers or sisters but I peopled my world with invisible friends as I went home from school, much of my imaginings coming from books I had read and a growing desire to be a writer and not a hardworking farmer, for which role I was never suited although my kind father tried hard to make me one. On my way home from school I was Long John Silver limping along with a gum tree bough and my imaginary parrot crying for "pieces of eight." There were real parrots and sulphur-crested cockatoos sometimes flying over with harsh cries. Indeed my mother had a cockatoo as a pet, a bird that sometimes used unfortunate words that once shocked a meeting of local women discussing the next church social.

Like most children I liked rhythm and rhyme. I noticed that when the rain beat on a roof it had a rhythm and it was a sweet sound on a dry farm. When our rackety windmill began hauling up the subartesian water from underneath the plains, its clanking had its own rhythm as with each pump it delivered the water into the tank and the water would gush and then die away to a tinkling trickle and then, with the next drive of the pump it would gush again.

There was the discovery of sounds. My mother, who was imaginative, would call me on a still moonlit country night to come and listen to sounds because she said the night was always alive and we would hear the far cry of a fox or, on a winter's night, the quack of wild ducks, swift silhouettes against the moon until they plunged into our water hole. Sometimes on a moonlit night my mother would call me to hear a farmer who helped us in harvest, singing in his fine tenor voice as he stooked the sheaves of hay, erecting them in little wigwams in the paddocks. And the wind would rustle through our peppertrees and the peppertrees would sigh as if they had all the cares of the world.

For me, an only child, a country childhood could be full of small wonders. I had a lively, liberated mother who felt women were deprived of some of their rights and later, as a justice of the peace, she sat on the bench with magistrates in cases where young women and beaten wives were involved. She also established with her loyal band of voluntary workers a civilian relief depot where hundreds of needy people

Mother, Isabel Fatchen, "who received an MBE from the queen for her work with distressed and underprivileged people"

were helped. She had a tough practicality, and when a young woman was beaten badly and came to my mother for help which was given, my mother said, "If he beats you, beat him back." The young woman did and came back smiling and said, "He cried like a baby and now we get along." Rough justice perhaps but my mother had an overpowering sense of justice.

She also loved animals and birds. There were bird catchers who came to trap the little wrens and waxbills that nested in bushes along our roads. The bird catchers would mark the nests in the daytime with white pieces of paper and return at night to trap the birds and sell them to pet shops. My mother went down in the evening and removed the white paper and placed the pieces instead in the hearts of boxthorn bushes with their savage thorns. Howls of anguish came later as the bird catchers thrust their hands into the spiny bushes.

One thing I discovered as a country child was the wonder of light. I suppose this was because farming started early in the morning when the farm depended on its horses and inevitable milking of the cows. There was the way birds and animals always stirred with the coming of light. There was an almond tree outside my bedroom and it was my alarm clock, for its small choir of birds always began singing at daybreak. The roosters began challenging each other across the countryside, joined by the other sounds of sheep or a cow with her udder heavy with milk or a sleepy pig inspecting its trough and finding nothing but disappointment. There was the rattle of the wood stove as my mother stacked it and the smell of kindling and the thump of a filled kettle going on the stove.

There was the softer light of evening and particularly the lamplight. It's remarkable how lamplight can make a room into a kind of oil painting. I remember our kitchen lamp, how its light would catch the array of tins on the shelves; those with sugar, flour, tea, coffee, sago, rice and the little jars of condiments and the plain-faced alarm clock with its big figures and shrill bell that was sometimes even used to time cakes. The lamplight would touch the easy chair my father liked in front of the stove with its threadbare arms and the slight dip in the seat where the springs had given way.

I liked the wood fire in the open hearth of the living room. The wooden roots burned with a slow friendly warmth in winter. Our dog and I would sit staring at them and having our modest private dreams. My parents were very fussy about their fire and they resented visitors who came and poked it. We had one pair of visitors who were notorious pokers of other people's fires. They'd no sooner come into the room than they'd be saying, "That fire needs a bit of a stir" and, before you could stop them they would be jabbing the coals. The sparks would fly in a vengeful cloud and my mother would shriek, "My carpet!"

Then I knew that the visitors would not only get the second-rate teacups for supper with the hairline crack in the saucers, that they would have to be content with the failed cake that had been put aside for soaking as poultry food.

On a farm you are close to the earth and to the animals and the seasons. You see the creatures born, chickens hatch, young lambs come, calves clamoring to be fed; and you see creatures die, the sheep in the paddocks sometimes, in fact, the whole cycle of life. This made an impression on me and although it was a matter-of-fact feature of farm life I often thought about it and questioned it. Years later I came to write *Closer to the Stars,* published originally by Methuen in London and Sydney and short-listed in the Children's Book of the Year Award in Australia and later published by Penguin in its Puffin series. It is about a young boy's experience in war and death in World War II. Paul, the boy, and his sister live on an Australian farm near an Australian Air Force unit training young pilots. A young pilot has an affair with a girl who bears his child. He is killed later over Britain during the war. Paul, who fiercely defends his sister against local prejudice, ponders life and death with his friend, the farm worker Curtiss, an old World War I soldier.

"But how is it with us?" Paul wondered. "Everyone gets buried in a cemetery. It would be better to be buried in the paddock and they'd plough you in and grow wheat on top of you and that would be more sensible," he thought. "Out in a wide free paddock." He'd spoken to Curtiss about it, about dying, and Curtiss had given him a quick look and a short answer, "People die and people are born, lad. Old grass withers and new grass grows. . . ."

So I grew into the simple routine of country life.

One country highlight was the annual agricultural show and fair in a small nearby town. This was a time of challenge: lights burning late with country women making competitive cakes; young riders taking their mounts over improvised jumps ready for the show events; pocket money rattling into moneyboxes. "How much have you saved for the show?" we children would ask each other. Some were fiercely secretive; others openly boastful.

My mother always entered decorated fruit salads and always won. It was said that judges looked for her fruit salads with towers of jelly and fruit, so finely cut and arranged that some judges had to be dragged away before they devoured the whole exhibit.

My father always entered a sheaf of green hay. He'd select the part of the paddock which had the highest growth and then we'd go out with a lantern in the cool of the evening before the show and he would painstakingly cut each stalk with a pair of shears and lay them on the hessian sack until we had enough for a sheaf. He was as painstaking about this as

he was about everything. He taught me that the land was a living thing, to be cared for and not to be raped; that everything that came from it was to be treated with respect; that land was to be nursed; that there was a rhythm to it: day and night, rain and shine, seed time and harvest, the sowing and the reaping. I can see him now in the lantern light as he selected the stalks of wheat there under the evening stars with the wind rippling the wheat. The impressions I formed would permeate my writing and especially my poetry. In *A Paddock of Poems,* published by Omnibus/Puffin in Australia and as *The Country Mail Is Coming* by Little, Brown in Boston, I wrote about the wind, how it cooled the farmer's brow and set the long-eared wheat dancing in the paddocks.

Our Sunday school picnics were a great event. We went to a nearby mangrove-fringed beach with muddy flats where the tide went out into the gulf and didn't return until late afternoon when its bubbling, frothing verge would be escorted by hordes of excited children. Here and there an armored crab rode the tide, its fierce claws extended.

We went on our picnic in horse-drawn trollies with high sides and bags of chaff for we children to sit on and sing our way to the beach.

Parents and teachers went in their cars and, under tarpaulins supported by pitchfork handles, would lay out the trestle tables covered with food.

We all sang grace in a loud, heartfelt fashion, our faces sticky with sunburn cream, and we smelt strongly of citronella, generously applied to ward off marauding mosquitoes.

There was a view of the ships going up the nearby river to Port Adelaide and at the Outer Harbor were the funnels and decks of the great ocean liners there. When darkness came and the horses were harnessed and the buggy lamps lit, we children would stare at the harbor where the liners would be festooned with lights and the sound of a ship's siren drift across the water. Little did I dream that one day one of my sons would be captain of one of these liners.

High school was a new challenge for me. For the first time I boarded away from home. Our landlady, Miss Amy Pederick, was strict but motherly. Each night, without fail, we had banana custard for tea and listened to an Australian bush radio program "Dad and Dave."

The teachers at Gawler High School helped to change my life. One of them, Mr. Alfred Higgins, known as "Alfie," was an immaculate English teacher with a love of Latin and poetry. As I explored poetry and listened to the word music of Shakespeare (even in the tragedy of murderous *Macbeth*), I was stirred to explore language and would lie awake at night, planning my essays. Perhaps it was the stimulation of banana custard, or the long cool glasses of frosted ginger beer after a sports afternoon, but mostly it was my teachers. It was also the Gawler librarian Mr. C. C. Mazzarol for I had come second in an essay competition and the prize was a year's free subscription at the municipal library.

There, amid its long tables, its shelves bulging with books, the smell of newsprint from its newspaper files, I discovered books like P. C. Wren's *Beau Geste* and James Fenimore Cooper's *The Last of the Mohicans,* the great Australian writer Henry Lawson's *While the Billy Boils* but also classics such as *The Last Days of Pompeii, Ben Hur* and Jack London's short stories and novels that became my meat and drink. London struck a chord in me with his *Call of the Wild, White Fang, Turtles of the Tasman, John Barleycorn* and short story after short story, a challenging literary form.

After my first year at high school there began a tug-of-war between my teachers and my father. The teachers wanted me to continue my studies and my father wanted me, as an only son and child, home to work and inherit the farm. So there was a compromise.

I worked on the farm four days a week but studied English, French and history at home, driving a little horse-and-buggy to the high school once a week to have my papers corrected and to be tutored in the three subjects.

I studied when I was driving the plough, not the best preparation for a farmer. The plough horses were very knowing and one horse walked in the furrow and guided the other horses as they toiled line abreast hauling the six-furrow plough.

If I turned each corner properly with the reins, the furrow horse would take over while I hung up the rope reins and got out my textbook to study while the horses plodded up the half-mile paddock. One day my father discovered this ploy and switched the furrow horse. The result was some terribly crooked ploughing and my father sadly decided that I would

never become a farmer and so I went back to school. But my experiences on the farm would later permeate much of my writing for children . . . the hawks, the haystacks, the simple life, the march of the seasons and the country characters would all be a part of the poems and stories that I would one day write.

A newspaper friend of the family, Mr. Don Stevens, got me my first job as a copyboy on the *Adelaide News,* the evening newspaper. This was the paper on which young Rupert Murdoch would make his first appearance as a newspaper executive, for his father was the newspaper proprietor. Sir Keith Murdoch I would come to know. He was tall and distinguished and interested in his young journalists. He had made his mark in World War I with his reporting of the Gallipoli campaign where Australian and New Zealand soldiers landed at Anzac Cove and gave their countries the moving celebration of Anzac Day.

At this time my uncle Reg Foster had been a celebrated Australian newspaper representative in London. He nearly lost his life on the ill-fated British airship the *R101,* which had crashed in France. His seat had been taken by an official at the last moment. Reg Foster was now associate editor and lead writer of the *Sydney Morning Herald,* and later a famous columnist. He was my mentor and inspiration in my life as a journalist.

Copyboys were humble beings on a metropolitan newspaper. We ran copy for the reporters and subeditors to the composing room, which had clicking linotypes with magic-fingered operators setting the columns of lead type. This was before the days of computerised newspapers, and everything was urgent noise: the rattle of reporters' typewriters; the subeditors shouting "copy," which we also stuffed into cartridges and put into pneumatic tubes that whisked it away to the composing room. We copyboys also made tea for thirsty journalists. It was some of the worst tea ever brewed. One copyboy actually dried the tea leaves and used them again to save money from his tea club payments. This terrible deed was eventually discovered and he was banned from tea-making.

We copyboys all wrote small paragraphs to supplement our meagre earnings of fifteen shillings (just a few dollars) a week. We wrote about anything that might attract a subeditor's critical eye.

*"My bride, Jean, a young teacher, in the
wedding dress she made herself
after school hours"*

Many of our efforts finished on the reject
spike but it was the only way we could bring
ourselves to the notice of the editor, that mysterious and powerful man sitting at his crowded
desk, surrounded by proofs and a battery of
telephones.

Each morning the chief of staff gave assignments to reporters whom we would summon and we watched enviously as they were
briefed, hoping for the day when we could be
reporters too. There were clever women journalists, one of them, Nancy Cato, was to write
a famous book, *All the Rivers Run,* about our
River Murray that would become my own field
of literature.

I at last had a success (so I thought) with
a story about our notable poet A. B. (Banjo)
Paterson, the author of the poem "The Man
from Snowy River" and our famous ballad "Waltz-
ing Matilda." But I had made an unforgivable
error. I had spelt his name with two t's
(Patterson) and it was only discovered just as

the half metal cylinder of lead containing the
page was already clamped on the printing press,
the great rollers ready to start the first edition. The angry subeditors were determined to
teach me a lesson. It was all prearranged, all
ready to roll. A huge machinist was waiting
for me and my escorting subeditor. The machinist had a screwdriver in his hand and glared
at me ferociously.

"Is this the lad who wants to be a journalist and can't get the name of a great Australian poet right? We have this extra *t* and here
is the whole metropolitan newspaper, with thousands waiting for the first edition and everything held up by a *t* and a copyboy who doesn't
check names. I will now use this screwdriver
to gouge out the unwanted *t* from this metal
plate," which he did with much ceremony. Then
the presses began to thunder. I hung my head.
I never got a name wrong after that. I had
learnt my lesson.

World War II came and I joined the Army
Service Corps, taking supplies to the AIF forces
training in the Adelaide Hills for the battles
to come . . . the Western Desert, Crete, Greece
and New Guinea. I wasn't much of a soldier
and I transferred to the ground staff of the
Royal Australian Air Force, in the signal section, and for awhile was at the training station
of Point Cook in Victoria. One night in
Melbourne I met a dark-eyed, dark-haired young
student teacher called Jean Wohlers. She wrote
me a letter containing quotations from "Omar
Khayyam":

Ah moon of my delight that knowst no wane
The moon of heaven is rising once again.

Here was indeed a heavenly person, I
thought, and a girl who could quote the great
Persian poet might even be interested in an
ineffectual young airman who sometimes wrote
verse. Jean finished her teacher's course and
went to teach at a little bush school in Victoria.
We decided to be married.

The way ahead was unsettled, the Japanese
driving south through Malaya and Singapore
into New Guinea. The first American troops
had arrived and Australia welcomed its allies
because so many of our men were fighting
overseas in all branches of the services.

So our wedding day came in Melbourne
on May 15, 1942. Jean had made her own wedding dress, working over her sewing machine

to complete it. On the day of the wedding I realised I had a badly creased pair of pants for my uniform. In Melbourne I noticed a small clothing factory which also pressed garments. I presented myself to the sympathetic women there and while I sat in my underpants in a small alcove they pressed my pants and then gave me a kiss for luck on my wedding day.

Jean looked wonderful, and still does. In gloomy Collins Street, its lights dimmed because of the wartime brownout, we alighted from our car to have our pictures taken by a commercial photographer. There were many homesick American soldiers on leave and they cried, "Hey, look, a bride" and formed an unofficial guard of honor for us in the street. We never forgot them. Some of them were to die in the grim jungles of New Guinea alongside our men. But that moment in our lives, in a gloomy wartime street, became a poignant memory.

Jean went to teach in her country school. I went back to my base at Point Cook. Jean's friend, Heather Brown, another teacher, also married a sailor, Hugh Scott. One morning Hugh and I were waiting at Spencer Street station in Melbourne for our young teacher wives who were arriving on the express. We noticed many barricades on the station with military police. The express from Adelaide would be crowded, with people standing in the corridors and even sleeping on the parcel racks.

The big train pulled in with its hissing steam engines and Scottie and I climbed the barricades, not wishing to miss a moment with our girls. Suddenly from the other end of the train and from a special carriage emerged a tall military figure and the band struck up the American national anthem. General Douglas MacArthur had arrived at the end of his perilous journey from the Philippines. At a little station called Terowie in South Australia one of my journalist friends had earlier heard him make the famous statement that he would return to the Philippines, as indeed he did.

At last our young wives came from the carriages. They were excited about having the general on board. They were more excited to see us for soon Scottie was at sea in his ship and I was in the Northern Territory and our girls were back teaching. Jean, as I later discovered, was expecting her first baby, our daughter Winsome.

Wartime meant service in New Guinea and the Admiralty Islands; in signal stations in flimsy palm-roofed shacks in hot jungles or small coral islands, but nothing compared with the hardships and dangers of the servicemen fighting their way through razorback ranges or landing on lethal beaches as they drove north. There was much of the atmosphere that James Michener created in his wonderful *Tales of the South Pacific* and one stored one's impressions sometimes by sending a short story in a weatherstained envelope to an Australian newspaper. I wrote short stories about service life on the island, about the yearnings for home, the malaria, the huge mist-shrouded mountains, the fighter planes taking off on sorties. The censors allowed my stories and even enjoyed them. A veteran newspaperman, "Gunner" Pryce of the *Sydney Sun,* published them in his feature section. He was a World War I man who had written moving poetry about trench warfare. He knew about the loneliness of young servicemen and he sent encouraging letters for which I looked eagerly, as well as letters from my young wife. Our second child, Michael, had been born; the pictures came a little blurred and I wondered about this small son. Photographs were important for servicemen, little precious pieces of home taken out and scrutinised and sometimes disintegrating in the relentless jungle damp and decay.

But wars end, our old flying boat labored towards Australia. New Guinea went back into the past and finally I was clambering out of the train, shedding my equipment as my wife rushed forward and the two small children eyed me warily.

It took time for us to come to know each other, but soon came rowdy intrusions into bed in the mornings, stories at night, often of my own invention, and then finally a job on the *Adelaide News* as a journalist and with it the daily suburban train journey, the ordered family life, the saving of a little money, the equipping of our flat.

My newspaper years with the *Adelaide News* and later the Adelaide morning paper, the *Advertiser,* were lively days with lively colleagues.

On the *News* I had a variety of assignments. It was there one of my editors, John Hetherington, a famous war correspondent and later author of many books including one on Melba, the famous Australian opera singer, gave me my first column which led me into feature writing and, later on the *Advertiser,* a column of light verse as well as my journalistic duties. On the *News* I would see fresh-faced, dynamic Rupert Murdoch begin his long career as a newspaper tycoon.

On the *Advertiser* a brilliant young cartoonist, Pat Oliphant, illustrated my humorous stories and we published a small paperback together of my *Advertiser* pieces. Pat Oliphant later went to America to join the *Denver Post* and become one of America's most notable cartoonists, winning the Pulitzer Prize. And he was responsible for my writing light verse for the *Denver Post* for several years, and a visit to Denver when we journeyed into the Rockies to see Pike's Peak that had once beckoned the wagon trains across the prairies.

I had some memorable newspaper assignments. I stood on the plains of Maralinga in South Australia's outback with other international journalists, our backs turned to a tower seven miles away that suddenly exploded into an atomic bomb test, the flash of the nuclear bomb lighting the arid plains.

I rode the tea and sugar train that supplied railway settlers and families along the great East-West railway line across the featureless Nullarbor Plains. I accompanied the flying doctor into the outback to see him at work in his clinics in Aboriginal settlements and on the verandas of cattle stations.

And when the great floods came from the torrential tropical rains and flooded the outback around the little Queensland town of Birdsville, I flew in to photograph the scene and write a story about the great inland sea that the outback had become. There, a little band of Aboriginal and white children took me one night to watch the Australian cranes, the brolgas, dancing in the sunset on the banks of the flooded Diamantina River and the children and I sat together, enchanted by the wild choreography of this bird. Then I photographed the children and the brolgas and their pictures appeared in Australian papers, to the children's delight.

I was forty-six when I wrote my first children's book, *The River Kings,* a story about riverboat life on Australia's greatest river, the Murray, which drains much of the Australian continent and is the lifeblood of South Australia and particularly its capital, Adelaide, which draws its water through a system of pipelines. My life as a journalist and columnist took a new direction.

I was feeling sad about the loss of a close friend, and my editor, Harry Plumridge, sent me to write a story on the Murray and the plan to build a great dam. This dam never eventuated but I made my river journey with a friend, Spen Ogilvy, in his little launch, the *Waterhen.* The river, which has now many reconstructed riverboats, mobile houseboats and a busy tourist trade, was quiet then. Along its banks stretched the great irrigation settlements but the river itself had its own personality, its own mysterious beckoning. At the turn of the century it had been a main transport artery with scores of wood-burning river steamers hauling wool and wheat and stores. There were hard times and rough men on the riverboats. According to legend, one sly grog hut which had refused some tough rivermen their liquor had a rope placed around it and was dragged into the river. There was a church boat which conducted services, and floating stores. There were women engineers as well as men, and the crafty river with its shifting sandbanks and submerged trees awaiting unwary captains. Then came the railroads that took away the river trade.

Onto this wide river came Spen and I in our small launch. One night we pulled into the bank, I still grieving over the loss of my friend. I remember the moment well. Water lapped gently on the sides of the boat. A night bird called down the reaches of the river, the dark mass of river gum trees crowding on each side, and at the end of the long reach in which we were moored was the dark brow of a great cliff. Suddenly there was a rising glow in the east and then a full moon rose that transformed the river into a great sheet of silver. It was at this moment I felt as if a hand had suddenly lifted my great weight of grief. The river came alive for me, not just as a stretch of water but something else besides. I was aware of sounds I hadn't heard before: the slow passage of the great river along its course, the dark movement of the trees and other sounds I couldn't identify, but the whole effect was as if the river was talking to itself and that I had been permitted to eavesdrop and take comfort from it.

Other events intervened and it was in America that I finally decided to write *The River Kings.* In the meantime I had gone to Britain with two other journalists as guests of the British government on a background trip and then flew to New York in 1963.

"Aboard the Lazy Jane, *the riverboat that played a lead role in the TV series* The River Kings, *filmed on Australia's biggest river, the River Murray,"* 1990

In Washington two of my American friends arranged for me to be an onlooker at a press conference of President John Kennedy, in the auditorium of the State Department. I was very interested to see the Washington Press Corps at work but fascinated by the president himself. He was a golden-haired, vital young man, sure of himself, with a flashing smile and easily handled his questioners. Little did I and those present know that this would be one of his last press conferences. He preceded me on his tour down to the south and to Cape Canaveral, where I went a few days later, fascinated by the great spires of space and especially by a Saturn rocket tucked beneath its gantry, while nearby the bulldozers worked on what would become the site of the moon project.

The National Aeronautics and Space Agency people showed me the little control room from where Colonel John Glenn's flight had been monitored. The sea broke gently nearby on Cocoa Beach and the shrimp boats sailed along the horizon and I felt an awe to be on this sandy cape, this doorway into space.

I suppose a writer's mind is a kind of modest mental mansion, furnished with experiences, and this was a rich one.

It was at New Orleans that rivers came into my mind again as I stood on Algiers Bend and watched the Mississippi's great volume of water like a moving muddy plain, flowing by, its surface busy with barge traffic. At a luncheon my American hosts sat me next to a Mississippi historian whose name I can't remember but I remember his words. He understood rivers and river people and when I told him of my Murray experience, he said, "Go back and write a book. Put it all down. Make it live." And this is what I would try to do.

But there was one more American experience that would provide my most memorable and saddest newspaper story. As our plane flew towards Dallas on that November day, November 22, 1963, we learned that President Kennedy had been assassinated. I interviewed some of

"Ketches and squarerigger at the old windjammer port of Port Victoria on Spencer Gulf, South Australia. This is the scene of some of my books."

the Dallas people on the plane and shared their sense of shock. As we landed at Dallas, the airport was under guard and during my fifty minute stopover, President Kennedy's body was brought to the airport and the new President Lyndon Johnson sworn in by a woman judge. I felt I was in some overwhelming dream; the grief of people, the bewilderment. Our plane taxied to the end of the runway and we waited there as *Air Force One* came down bearing the former president's body and the new president and took off for Washington.

I felt a sense of unreality as I sat at a typewriter in the office of Western Union in Market Street, San Francisco, and wrote my story for my newspaper, *The Advertiser,* each page being transmitted as I wrote it.

Later I sat in a little restaurant and the waitress came and sat beside me and wept. I came to understand something of the American people in those hours. Later I would write for their newspapers and come again to their diverse country. But these memories were burned in my mind.

So I went home to Australia, my mind crowded with impressions: the day in Dallas; the day by the Mississippi; the tug and turmoil of history of which I had been a tiny part. And the words of that historian in New Orleans: "Go back and write. Make your story live."

Why I decided to write for children perhaps was caught up with that childhood remembrance of long-gone days but also with the challenge that young readers set for a writer: to interest them; to inform them; to touch their hearts; not to be patronising but to be a guide; to share some of their young wisdom and honesty. And perhaps they provided a new world for me after writing for adults as a journalist.

So one night in my Smithfield home, north of Adelaide, I began to write *The River Kings.* Suddenly all the emotions, the experiences began to come together as I wrote about Shawn and an old riverboat and its crew of characters. I had some interested help. Our Italian-born neighbors were cheerful, generous people and very interested in my career as a journalist and my wife Jean's as a teacher. Our children were all good friends. Eleonora, the seventeen-year-old daughter next door, had a new portable typewriter and offered to type my manuscript in presentable form. So I fed her the chapters. As she typed she translated the text verbally to her curious family. They fell around laughing at some of the incidents. I felt reassured, for I am always uncertain about my books. I worry about them. I said to my wife, "If the Iacopettas like it, it can't be all that bad."

It took nearly two years, after a round of publishers, before the English publisher Methuen took the book. I would come under the wing of Olive Jones, their editor, and publisher Marilyn Malin. They would have a great effect on my life. Editors and publishers do. Olive Jones had a great wit and her letters discussing my editorial failings were always full of fun, with an underlying intensity that I could do better and this I tried to do. Good editors are remarkable people. They cajole, they criticise but they are always supportive. The editor-writer relationship is the reason for countless good books. We writers sometimes lose our way. We fall into pits of despair. We brood over countless cups of coffee. We eat more than is good for us while we search for a lost theme or try to share a character. But one day the book is finished. The editor was right, we find.

All my editors (with one exception) have been women for my fourteen children's books, six of them novels and seven of them verse. My editors have been in New York, London, Boston, Sydney and Adelaide. Most of them have been young, lively, enthusiastic and watchful over this chubby, irresolute man who sometimes sneaks out for a takeaway with his young friends instead of meeting a deadline.

Olive Jones particularly knew how to handle me even at a great distance and certainly on the rare occasions we met in London.

Olive Jones had been the secretary for Walter de la Mare, the famous English poet. She understood the beauty and power of the English language. And when I stayed with her in later years in her historic little cottage in Sussex, she decided that not only did I need to get into mental shape but physical trim and she took me tramping around the South Downs. We climbed quarries to see badger lairs or "setts." We sat and watched the cloud pattern on the Downs as they scurried over mounds that had once been ancient settlements. Little cottages trickled smoke in the valley, the green of England stretching beneath us with its ever-busy streams. Those were wonderful moments for a writer, being with a wise editor; being encouraged to go on writing; talking over new plans until we went home under our umbrellas as the English rain pelted and we could warm ourselves in the cottage parlor and eat raisin cake and muffins.

So *The River Kings* was born . . . a journey on the Murray with a friend and a spiritual experience . . . an American riverman talking enthusiastically in New Orleans . . . a young Italian girl typing the manuscript and entertaining her family . . . a wise, amused editor in London.

The River Kings was published first in London and Sydney in 1966 and later in New York, Warsaw, Copenhagen and Stockholm. It was commended by the Australian Children's Book Council in the Children's Book of the Year awards. There were a number of paperback editions. Many years later, after several attempts, it was made into a TV mini-series by Prospect Production of Adelaide. It was put to air by the Australian Broadcasting Corporation.

The mini-series has been screened in many countries, including Ecuador, Barbados, Canada, Scandinavia, Germany, Greece, Israel and Kuwait. So one's life as a children's author began. It would be one of the happiest periods of my life and still is.

My experience as a newspaperman provided the setting for most of my novels and especially *The Spirit Wind,* which was published by Methuen in 1973 and was runner-up for the Australian Children's Book of the Year Award. It is a story of the square-rigged sailing ship days. These ships came to Port Victoria on South Australia's Spencer Gulf to load grain and they sailed home around Cape Horn to Falmouth in Britain to receive their orders for their cargoes. There were three-masted barques and four-masted sailing ships and life on them was rough and challenging and the wild seas around Cape Horn claimed some of them and their crews. On the shore at Port Victoria were big stacks of bagged grain. From these stacks wheat lumpers loaded small trucks that rolled by gravity towards the loading jetty, with a wheat lumper handling the primitive brakes. There a little man, "Froggy" Hart, and his horse took over, trundling the small trucks to the jetty where the wheat was slid down chutes to waiting ketches which carried it to the big sailing ships in the bay. These ships made a great spectacle when they shook out their sails and headed down the gulf, the farmers pausing to watch the ships out of sight in the blue gulf. I went holidaying to Port Victoria for many years and became caught up in its folklore and stories of the sea.

One night my ten-year-old son Michael and I talked to ketch master Doug Godleman in his cabin of the ketch *Stormbird.* Michael listened raptly to these sea stories; he was later to become a master mariner himself and is now captain of P & O cruise liners, one of his commands being the *Pacific Princess,* (the Love Boat of the TV series). Doug Godleman, sadly, was lost in the China Sea while bringing a new ketch from Hong Kong to Port Adelaide. It is believed the ship was taken by pirates.

So my love of the sea became very strong, particularly as some of my assignments were with the navy and especially the Commonwealth Lighthouse Service, landing from its ship the *Cape York* on the wild islands of the South Australian coast; swinging up perilous handholds while curious seals watched from the rocks or encountering the sea fury as the ship sheltered behind an island while the waves beat on rocks that sounded like a great gong. But there was also the gentleness of the sea and its creatures.

I especially liked the dolphins because there was a mystery about them and their intelligence. One of my friends who loved the sea was killed in an accident and his sad wife went to his favorite beach and sat there mourning him. Suddenly she felt a presence and she looked up and there out in the water just offshore was a dolphin, perfectly motionless, watching her. She said she felt an overwhelming sense of comfort.

A story began to take shape in my mind. *The Spirit Wind* is about a Norwegian boy who jumps ship to escape from a brutal mate obsessed with his struggle against the sea with an ailing ship.

The boy saves an old Aboriginal who, in turn, with some young friends ashore, helps to save the boy. The Aboriginal, Nunganee, understands the great tempests of the coast and particularly "the spirit wind," the sou'wester whose arrival signals the climax of the book in a shipwreck.

My aboriginal character of Nunganee came from the opposite end of Australia, from the shore of the great Gulf of Carpentaria and on the banks of a river in Arnhem Land. I had gone with the army and navy who were surveying the coastline, and one day I flew with a helicopter across the vast distances, past swamps where magpie geese rose in living clouds, and over rivers where the crocodiles were drawn up on the banks like scaly canoes. That night we slept beside our helicopter on the banks of the Koolatong River, and a songman from a

nearby Aboriginal camp came down for a chat. He was a handsome, lively man and we settled down for one of the best evenings of my life. As a songman he knew the legends of his tribe and he spoke of the playabout corroborees, not the important sacred corroborees, but the song times when he would tell the legends of why rain fell, how fish swam and the interpretation of this great silent land around us with its rugged escarpments and its glittering swamps, and its thunderstorms of the wet season with their enormous pillars of clouds. As he talked it seemed as if the land was listening. The helicopter, the rising moon glinting on its sides, seemed an intruder. I listened to the storyteller, fascinated by his gestures, his word pictures. When I came to write *The Spirit Wind* he was the powerful figure in my mind. He became Nunganee and *The Spirit Wind* became a living experience.

I like to write late at night or in the early morning when everything is still, when the dawn is appearing over the nearby ranges. Late at night I sometimes walk up and down my driveway under the brilliant sky of stars. *The Spirit Wind* required a certain state of mind, particularly the dramatic parts, and I walked up and down until I could hear the roar of the wind in my mind and feel the desperate men fighting the enormous strength of the sea. So another book was born.

And another shipwreck at the bottom of Yorke Peninsula, of the barque *Ethel,* only a rusty smear on the beach when I saw her, took a strange hold on me.

It was late afternoon, dark shadows on the beach and a sunlit patch where I could see footprints, and this gave me the idea for a children's poem, "Children Lost," about shipwrecked children who had been taken by the sea kings and were allowed on shore on moonlit nights. The poem was published in *A Paddock of Poems* and in the beautifully illustrated American edition *The Country Mail Is Coming.*

Here again I tried to express the mystery of the beckoning ocean.

It was a visit to the little town of Normanton under the Gulf of Carpentaria in Queensland that the seeds for another book *Chase through the Night* were sown. Normanton had wide, deserted streets; a little motorised train; the Gulflander that ran between it and the ghost mining town of Croydon; crocodiles in the

Norman River and the air of a colorful past hanging over it. One night I sat talking to an old Aboriginal drover, long retired, who had been crippled by a fall from his horse. He told me of the droving days and how at night he dreamed of his old dogs running beside him and his horse when he was young and strong and agile and rode so well that he seemed part of his horse. As we talked, the monsoonal wet season storms rumbled and flickered on the horizon. Sixteen years later I wrote *Chase through the Night*, the story of three men kidnapping a girl witness in their escape from a bank robbery. In a little outback town they are pitted against a few white and Aboriginal people and against the wisdom and the mysticism of a blind Aboriginal man which prevails in the end.

I could hardly contain my excitement when Independent Productions of Sydney wanted to film the book for a TV mini-series and telemovie. My London agents, John Johnson, and particu-

larly my personal friend Edna Wighton and my delightful personal agent, Elizabeth Fairbairn, were delighted too.

So Jim George, the producer, and Howard Rubie, the director, went in search of a small inland Australian township. They followed single railway tracks in Queensland and there was one last track they took to find at its end the little township of Kaimkillenbun, which received the shock of its life to be suddenly propelled into being a little Hollywood.

The Queensland Railways brought a small old-fashioned railcar like the one at Normanton out of retirement and supplied a crew. The film crew repainted the railway station. Farmers uprooted their windmills and brought them in to give the town more atmosphere. Schoolchildren were screen-tested for bit parts in the film. Alan Fitzsimmons of Casino, New South Wales, brought horses, three dogs, bulls and a snake, which all had parts in the film. The snake played the role of Slide, and being a

"On the streets of Normanton, a tiny outback township under the Gulf of Carpentaria in Queensland, where I got the idea for Chase through the Night, *which later became a TV mini-series. The steer in the photo became a character in the book."*

nonvenomous carpet snake had a mild temper and was cooperative with the nervous actors who handled him.

Vamp, one of the dogs, a gentle, intelligent animal, tried hard as she played the central canine character in the story. One of the bulls had plastic tips placed on its horns to make them longer (it played a bull called Heavy Horns), a process it didn't enjoy, and expressed its displeasure by chasing some of the crew.

Rob George, who wrote the script and later would produce the mini-series of another of my books *The River Kings,* kept faithfully to the story line. And the actors assembled. Paul Sonkkila played the chief crook, with John Jarratt as one of his blundering accomplices. A rising young actor, Brett Climo, played the hero, Ray. Aboriginal actor Alan Dargin played his friend Bindaree. Aboriginal Steve Dodd was the old, mystical Aboriginal Narli. Also included were Justine Saunders, a fine Aboriginal woman actor who later became a top star; and, as the young kidnapped teenager, Nicole Kidman, then

sixteen, tall and accomplished, already showing the vivacity that would make her a world star.

Nicole was studying for her school certificate and took every chance to work with her tutor, Joanne Kennedy from Sydney. As new scenes were set and the crew moved busily about Kaimkillenbun, Nicole and Joanne would bend their heads over *Romeo and Juliet.* Nicole did everything properly, including her studies.

In the storm scenes where the little railcar races through blinding rain, the special effects men used huge pumps to draw water from the creeks along the railway line and the rain machines sprayed the little train as it rushed past towards the climax of the story. So the film went its busy course with its mischievous bull, its conscientious dog, its slightly bored snake, its lively human actors and a stuffed crocodile for which the property master had to tour the country. He found a crocodile eventually, although some owners of stuffed crocodiles wanted more for their immobile beasts than was paid to some of the actors.

With young school friends, Elizabeth West Primary School, 1981

I saw a little of the filmmaking, mostly in Sydney, but it was highly enjoyable seeing it made; the completed series was purchased by a leading German television network and the book published by a German publisher.

Both animal and human actors gave very satisfactory interpretations of my characters. It's wonderful for a writer to see his work come alive and see it handled with sensitivity and flair.

I understand Vamp the dog and Slide the snake took a rest after production.

Strangely, it was a dog that set me writing poetry for children. We had a small white poodle called Butterfly, an astute canine with large mellow eyes who was always pirouetting around me to be taken for walks. One night as we walked together, with her looking back with her huge eyes to see if I was following, I had an idea for "Night Walk," the first poem for children that I ever wrote. I tried to interpret a dog's feelings when out walking.

The poem was the genesis of *Songs for My Dog* published by Kestrel in London and later as a Puffin book by Penguin. It was followed by *Wry Rhymes for Troublesome Times,* also published by Penguin, and then, in Australia, *A Paddock of Poems, A Pocketful of Rhymes* and *A Country Christmas.* A new book, *Peculiar Rhymes and Lunatic Lines,* has just been published by Orchard Books in London.

In my poetry for children I have experimented with different rhyme patterns and word shapes on the page and written about many aspects of childhood, from unruly hair to worrisome dogs; from country lunches to school reports. It has been my idea to make ordinary things sometimes extraordinary, to find humor even in cockroaches; to create quick little images.

> You put out the cat
> That sly lump of fur
> Then why is my pillow
> Beginning to purr?

I am grateful for my publishers and editors. I am grateful for my wife, Jean, as my helpmate and for our daughter, Winsome Millane, our sons, Capt. Michael Fatchen and Dr. Tim Fatchen, and their families who have all been so supportive. There are six grandchildren, most of them grown up; although we are scattered around the world we keep a loving contact.

I am fortunate that my verse now appears in more than one hundred anthologies through-

The author posing as life patron of the Dalkeith brigade of South Australia's bushfires service, 1994

out the English-speaking world. It has all been a rich experience. My belief in young people does not waver. They have given me lessons in life too, have made me search myself. While I am elderly there is still the spirit of childhood somewhere inside of me and children rekindle it and my faith in myself and in them. I set out to capture them with words but somehow they have captivated me. If my books are left on the shelves, so be it. This is something a writer must face. Sometimes children come to my study and peer over my shoulder as I write, making their comments.

One young reader said that my new book was enjoyable but that I could do much better. It was, however, quite promising.

I hear the pop of a Coke tin by my ear and look around at some small girl, saying accusingly, "You haven't written about dogs lately."

But as a writer I am trying to say this to young people.

"This is my book. I have created it, its setting and its people. But I can only present it to you to activate it, to bring it to life, to make its characters real, to make its events credible. You are the travellers I have invited on a journey through its pages. It's in your hands. It's your mind I want to borrow for just a little while. It's your enjoyment and interest I want to kindle. Perhaps after you've closed my book something of it will remain; a word picture, a phrase, a character. Because in my book or in my poem I have put my treasures. I hope that you will find them."

BIBLIOGRAPHY

FOR CHILDREN

Fiction:

The River Kings, illustrated by Clyde Pearson, Hicks Smith (Sydney), 1966, Methuen (London), 1966, St. Martin's Press (New York), 1968.

Conquest of the River, illustrated by Clyde Pearson, Hicks Smith, 1970, Methuen, 1970.

The Spirit Wind, illustrated by Trevor Stubley, Hicks Smith, 1973, Methuen, 1973.

Chase through the Night, illustrated by Graham Humphreys, Methuen (Sydney and London), 1977.

The Time Wave, illustrated by Edward Mortelmans, Methuen, 1978.

Closer to the Stars, Methuen, 1981.

Had Yer Jabs?, Methuen (Sydney), 1987.

Poetry:

Songs for My Dog and Other People, illustrated by Michael Atchison, Kestrel, 1980.

Wry Rhymes for Troublesome Times, illustrated by Michael Atchison, Kestrel, 1983.

A Paddock of Poems, illustrated by Kerry Argent, Omnibus (Adelaide), 1987, published as *The Country Mail Is Coming: Poems from Down Under,* illustrated by Catharine O'Neill, Joy Street Books, 1990.

A Pocketful of Rhymes, illustrated by Kerry Argent, Omnibus, 1989.

A Country Christmas, illustrated by Timothy Ide, Omnibus, 1990.

(With Colin Thiele) *Tea for Three,* Moondrake, 1994.

Peculiar Rhymes and Lunatic Lines, Orchard Books, 1995.

Poetry; illustrated by Iris Millington:

Drivers and Trains, Longman (Melbourne), 1963.

The Electrician, Longman, 1963.

Keepers and Lighthouses, Longman, 1963.

The Plumber, Longman, 1963.

The Carpenter, Longman, 1965.

The Transport Driver, Longman, 1965.

FOR ADULTS

Other:

Peculia Australia: Verses, privately printed, 1965.

Just Fancy, Mr. Fatchen! A Collection of Verse, Prose and Fate's Cruel Blows, Rigby, 1967.

Forever Fatchen, Advertiser, 1983.

Fatchen's poetry has been printed in more than one hundred British, American, and Australian anthologies as well as broadcasted on BBC radio and performed at English festivals. He has contributed light verse to the *Denver Post. Chase through the Night* was filmed for the Australian Broadcasting Corporation and *The River Kings* was made into a mini-series by Prospect Productions and ABC in 1991. The manuscripts for his books are housed in the South Australia State Library, Adelaide.

Charles Ferry

1927-

I wet the bed until I was fourteen years old.

An indelicate way to begin an autobiographical essay? Perhaps. But my enuresis, and the reason behind it, was the definitive fact of much of my life.

To understand me, to understand my entire family, one must first understand my father. He was a troubled, complex man, who sought comfort in alcohol and found only turmoil.

He had fought in the Great War (World War I), that unspeakably horrible, senseless war, in which soldiers lived in trenches that were infested with rats and roaches. He came out of that war so shell-shocked, he couldn't talk. At a veterans hospital in Wisconsin, he met a pretty high school senior, who taught him how to talk again. That pretty girl became my mother.

On October 8, 1927, the legendary Babe Ruth hit three home runs to help the New York Yankees defeat the Pittsburgh Pirates and sweep the World Series.

At 11:30 that night, a rainy Saturday night, I was born at St. Anne Hospital in Chicago, Illinois. I was named Charles (after my paternal grandfather) Allen (after my maternal grandfather) Ferry. I was the fourth child (and only son) of Ignatius Loyola Ferry, age thirty-two, of Philadelphia, Pennsylvania, and Madelyn Anne Bartholomew, age twenty-three, of Fond du Lac, Wisconsin.

In 1927, the Roaring Twenties were still roaring. Flappers were still dancing the Charleston, speakeasies were still flourishing, and "Lucky Lindy," who had flown the Atlantic, was a national hero. Times were good. General Motors had paid the largest stock dividend in American history. The country was on a roll.

Against that exciting backdrop I was taken home, where I would join my three elder sisters: Virginia, age two; Patricia, age three; and Mary June, who would become my sole confidant in life, age five.

Charles Ferry, 1994

Home was a first-floor flat at 1701 N. Mayfield Avenue, which was in a new subdivision on the city's West Side. It was a block north of North Avenue, a commercial thoroughfare with a streetcar line, and five blocks from St. Angela Roman Catholic School, which I would attend.

It was a nice flat, with new furnishings throughout: living room, dining room, kitchen, a walk-in pantry, two bedrooms, a bathroom with an electric wall heater, and a sun-room. There was a small backyard, a garage (we owned a used Essex), and a porch, with stairs leading to the upstairs flat and down to the basement.

201

(Before long, I would be hiding under those stairs, fearful of a strapping from my father.)

And so, in 1927, life was good at 1701 N. Mayfield Avenue. My father had a secure job at a sheet-metal firm; talking movies had arrived; and with the birth of a long-awaited son (I was called "Sonny Boy"), the future looked brighter than ever for the Ferry family.

But I never really knew any of this; I was too little. My earliest memory of that flat is of a foul smell and flecks of dried tomato skins on the wallpaper in the sun-room, where my father had vomited one night after coming home drunk.

You see, two years after I was born, on October 29, 1929, "Black Tuesday," the stock market collapsed. The Great Depression had begun.

Almost overnight, millions of men and women were thrown out of work. Soon, men without jobs were selling apples on street corners. Hungry families were forming lines to get a loaf of bread or a bowl of soup. In some cities, the unemployment rate was as high as fifty percent. Something had gone wrong, tragically wrong, with the country's economic system.

My father was one of the first to lose his job. Thus began seven long years of hardship and deprivation; it would be that long before he found a steady job again. During that time, our only income was the few dollars Daddy made from an occasional odd job and his monthly check from the government for his war wounds. It wasn't for much, forty-two dollars, but it paid the rent and kept the household going.

There was no welfare back then, no unemployment insurance, no health insurance. Nothing. (Never knock progress!) Life was a continuing struggle. Karo syrup on a slice of day-old bread was our after-school treat. Our father tried to give us each a dime every Saturday morning for the children's movie at the Manor Theater, with a penny for candy. But sometimes there were no dimes for movies or pennies for candy. Sometimes there was only oatmeal for supper.

But poor as we were, we were rich in a very special way. Thanks to our maternal grandfather, who had been a conductor on the Soo Line railroad, we got to spend our summers at Birchwood, in the wilderness of northern Wisconsin. We stayed at a cottage called "Baraboo Lodge" on a beautiful lake, Lake Chetac. Those wonderful summers at Birchwood had a lasting impact on our lives. I would write about them in my first novel, *Up in Sister Bay.*

You see, the cottage had been built as a communal vacation retreat by Gramps and a few of his trainmen friends. The others had all passed away, leaving Gramps free to grant us summer-long privileges.

Birchwood was kerosene lamps and a tin dipper hanging from the well pump. There was an icehouse and an outhouse that we called "The Office." I spent each summer barefoot, in a pair of tattered overalls and a straw hat. I hated to go back to Chicago, especially after I started school.

My first-grade teacher at St. Angela School was, fittingly, Sister Angela. On the first day of school, she gave each of us a complimentary wooden ruler from the Coca-Cola company.

THE GOLDEN RULE
Do unto others as you would have others
  do unto you.
COCA-COLA

I never forgot those words. I was able to read them because I was already a pretty fair reader. I had read several Big Little Books and was good at figuring out words in newspapers and on signs and labels. In future years, I would read avidly, including the Bobbsey Twins, Tom Swift, Nancy Drew, Frank Merriwell, and Horatio Alger books. By the fifth grade, I was reading Mark Twain and Jack London stories.

After a demonstration of our reading skills, we were assigned seats. The first row was reserved for the best readers. I was assigned to the first seat in the first row, the best of the best.

School work came easily to me. My only problem was bladder control. I was very shy, too timid to raise my fingers for permission to go to the lavatory. As a result, I was sent home a few times with my short pants soaked (or filled).

As I grew older (and my bladder larger), my enuresis grew worse. My mother despaired of controlling the situation. Urine gradually soaked through my mattress and onto the metal spring beneath it, rusting it. There were no innersprings back then, or Pampers, only thick layers of newspapers, which became quite soggy.

As you have learned, my incontinence was not entirely nocturnal. At age ten (by then, we were living in Bellwood, Illinois), I became probably the only altar boy in the history of the Roman Catholic Church to wet his pants while serving Mass.

That Sunday, I was serving alone; usually, there were two of us. It was the holy season in which we wore white cassocks and red surplices. During the Offertory, I felt a buildup in my bladder, but I was sure I could hold it. As the priest received his own communion, a little trickle came out. I began reciting the Confiteor, a prayer of confession. "... *omnibus Sanctis, et tibi, pater* ..." The trickle was getting stronger. What was I to do? The body and blood of Christ were present. If I left the altar during a prayer, I would be eternally damned. "... *mea culpa, mea culpa, mea maxima culpa* ..." It was a gusher! The priest then took the chalice to the communion rail; I followed with a gold paten, to hold under the chins of the communicants. A huge yellow-orange stain covered the front of my cassock. My brief career as an altar boy had ended.

Ferry with paternal grandmother and sisters Mary June (left) and Patricia, 1931

As a boy, I lived in fear of my father. His angry voice would send chills down my spine. He was a good man, but he could be cruel, especially when he was drunk. And he could be demeaning; in his eyes, I could do nothing right. As a result, I grew up with a severe inferiority complex, traces of which still endure.

Back then, child abuse wasn't even a concept. It was not generally understood that corporal punishment can be emotionally damaging and trigger such problems as enuresis. The prevailing philosophy, encouraged by the Catholic Church, was "Spare the rod and spoil the child."

A husband/father was the king of his household. He was to be deferred to in all matters, conjugal or otherwise. A wife was discouraged from holding a job; her place was in the home.

In cases of wife abuse, both the church and the civil authorities commonly regarded the wife to be at fault for not displaying proper obeisance to her spouse. (Obviously, women still had a long way to go, Baby.)

I never saw any marks or bruises on my mother, but several times she ran screaming from the house, fearing for her life. A few times, the police were called, but no charges against my father were ever filed.

From the beginning, I had an ambivalent relationship with my father. I hated his scoldings and his beatings, but I was his champion. Twenty-five years ago, in a family memoir, I wrote about that. It all happened one summer up at Birchwood. I was about six years old.

> Daddy had a great sense of humor, but sometimes he was very quiet and withdrawn, as if he were thinking of something else or wanted to be someplace else. Everyone said it was because he had been shell-shocked in the war, but I thought it was something else, something he couldn't explain to other people. And I think he knew that I knew. Maybe that's why he always took me fishing with him. He didn't talk much when we were out on the lake, except to holler at me when I did something wrong, but he hardly ever went fishing without me.
>
> Usually when Daddy got to feeling that funny way, he would walk over to Andy's Tavern or into town and drink beer. One time, he was gone all night and was still gone the next morning. Mom had heard that he had been drinking whiskey at Schultz's Tavern. She got very upset.

"You children hide when your father comes home," she ordered us. "Your father's a crazy man when he's been drinking whiskey."

At about four o'clock, Mom started to get supper ready. Then she went over to the Havens' cottage up the lake. Mr. Haven was with her when she came back. He had his shotgun. I could hear them over near the icehouse, talking about what to do when Daddy got home.

"If he harms anyone, Madelyn," Mr. Haven was saying, "we'll just have to shoot him down like a mad dog."

It all seemed very strange, like a movie that was actually taking place. Everything had been so nice, and now Mr. Haven was going to shoot Daddy down like a mad dog. Then I spotted Daddy, coming around the bend at Kringle's pasture. Mr. Haven saw him, too.

"Quick, Madelyn!" he said. "Get the children out of the way!"

Mom shoo'd us all inside. The girls ran upstairs, but I was afraid Mr. Haven was going to shoot Daddy. I went in the kitchen door and out the front door. I crawled around the side of the house and positioned myself so that I could spring out and grab the gun and holler to Daddy to run up to my secret hiding place while I held off Mr. Haven.

I saw Daddy as he came down the path from "The Office." He looked kind of tired, and his eyes were red, but he wasn't staggering or anything, and he didn't look like a crazy man. He was whistling under his breath, the way he always did when he had been drinking or when he was nervous.

As he came closer, I crouched low, ready to jump Mr. Haven. But nothing happened. Daddy walked right by Mr. Haven and didn't even notice the gun, or if he did, he didn't let on.

"Hello there, doctor," he said to Mr. Haven, and walked into the kitchen, still whistling.

He fell asleep with his clothes on. He slept the rest of the afternoon, all that night, and most of the next morning. I was down at the landing when he woke up.

"Hey, Sonny Boy!" he hollered out a window. "Dig us a can of worms!"

I grabbed my straw hat, got the fishing lines, and ran to the place behind the icehouse where we dug for worms. I knew everything was going to be all right. We caught two walleyes, six crappies, and a mess of perch, and Daddy was real funny at supper that night.

Three years later, in 1936, there were profound changes in our lives. First and foremost, after seven years of begging for work, my father finally found a job, as a clerk at the main U.S. Post Office in Chicago, a position from which he would eventually retire.

The house was filled with celebration. Daddy had a job! Daddy had a job! No more tattered clothes and worn-out shoes; no more day-old bread and oatmeal suppers. We had survived the worst of the Great Depression!

Then came the stunning news that Gramps had died. It was stunning because "Baba," our grandmother, had already been crippled by a stroke, while Gramps was in good health.

While we would care for Baba until her death, in effect, we inherited Gramps' estate, which included a 1934 Plymouth and a house on a hill in Waukesha, Wisconsin, which is sixteen miles west of Milwaukee.

"My First Communion Day, age six. I later left the Catholic Church and became an Episcopalian." Photo taken at 1701 N. Mayfield Ave., Chicago, 1933.

But solutions beget problems: a house in Waukesha, a job in Chicago, what was to be done? There was no easy answer. For the first year (1936), we lived in Waukesha, while my father rented a furnished room in Chicago and came home on weekends.

The second year (1937), we rented out the Waukesha house and moved to a rented house in Bellwood, a suburb of Chicago (where I was an altar boy).

But for financial reasons, that didn't work out. And so in 1938, we reverted to the first arrangement and moved back to Waukesha. My sisters and I were delighted, primarily because during the week, we would be free from the constraints of having an alcoholic in the house.

But even on weekends, we worried about Daddy's condition and hoped he wouldn't embarrass us in front of our friends, which he frequently did. The best family times were Sunday picnics at Golden Lake, where there was no drinking, just good, clean fun.

Although we lived there for less than six years, to this day, my three elder sisters and I regard Waukesha as our hometown. Waukesha was our coming-of-age town. The pretty Ferry sisters broke several hearts at Waukesha High School (a few of them never healed). Sonny Boy, meantime, was beginning to display his creative and organizational talents, and therein lies a story.

I was once on the program at a children's literature conference with Robert Cormier, the renowned author for young adults. He told the story of how a teacher had had a profound, pivotal impact on his life.

It was in the fifth grade, as I recall. Robert was writing a poem, when he was supposed to be paying attention to something else.

"Robert, what *are* you doing?" the teacher said.

She went to his desk, picked up the sheet of paper he had been writing on, read it, then handed it back to him.

"Robert," she said, "you're a writer."

Cormier said that if that teacher had not made that remark at that point in his life, he doubts if he ever would have become an author.

I have often been asked about influential teachers in my life. Frankly, I didn't have any. To the contrary, I had to rise above the negative influences of some of my teachers.

Ferry at age six with his father, Aunt Molly, and sisters Mary June (left) and Patricia at Lake Chetac in Birchwood, 1933

At St. Joseph School, for instance, it was the tradition for the seventh-graders to put on an entertainment for the graduating eighth-graders. I was put in charge of the project.

Well, I wrote a play, a corny play about the happenings in a house on a hill on a stormy night. I had a cast and a production staff, even special sound effects (a sheet of galvanized metal to simulate thunder).

One evening, we were rehearsing on the stage at the end of gym, when we were raided, literally, by Sister Aimee, the principal, who confiscated the script, declared it to be "trash," and destroyed it.

I fared no better at the public high school. One lovely spring morning—I was in the ninth grade—my mother overslept, with the result that we all overslept. It was too late to walk to school; we would just have to turn around and walk home for lunch. So we went to school after lunch.

Ferry, age twelve, with father and "beloved dog" Buster in front of home in Waukesha, Wisconsin, 1939

The first class after lunch was Homeroom. My teacher was Mrs. Palmatier, white-haired, blue serge dress, white collar and cuffs, pince-nez eyeglasses. It wasn't until she asked for my excuse that it dawned on me that my mother had neglected to write excuses for any of us.

No problem, I thought, it was a very legitimate absence; so I sat down and wrote my own excuse. It was pretty damn good writing. I wrote it in the present tense, setting the scene, telling about my mother's oversleeping, including the weather and a bit of dialogue, and ending at my handing the excuse to Mrs. Palmatier.

She read it and erupted. Instant reprimand. Then down to the principal's office for more reprimanding. Then the truant officer was summoned; my mother was summoned; and within an hour, I was in the county courthouse being reprimanded by a judge. For several months, I had to report weekly to a social worker by the name of Clara Schwandt, who didn't really understand why I was there.

All of that because of my creative writing. Fortunately, I drew no reprimands for my organizational activities. At various times during my grade-school years, I organized:

—A club, The Sportsmen's Lodge. We met in the loft of our garage, which had once been a carriage barn.
—A summer track meet, including pole vault, broad jump, and javelin, which was held in the stadium of the local college, Carroll College.
—Elaborate and exciting nighttime hide-and-seek games, played on the rooftops of downtown buildings.
—A dance "band," which consisted of one clarinet, three bazookas, a set of toy drums, and me on piano.

We had an old upright piano on the sun porch of our house in Waukesha. I had taught myself a few jazz riffs and some boogie-woogie, enough to get by with, in the absence of any competition.

(My sister Patricia, however, played beautifully, all by ear. If there had been money for lessons, she may have gone on to become a concert pianist; she was that good.)

Music was an important part of our lives in those days, big band music. In the summer of 1942, at age fourteen, I saw the legendary Glenn Miller Orchestra at the ballroom of the Wisconsin State Fairgrounds in Milwaukee. It was one of the most memorable experiences of my life, one that I would write about in my *One More Time!,* which almost got made into a movie.

Saxophones wailed, trombones throbbed, and pretty girls in organdy dresses glided mistily into the arms of their dates.

There is a very telling paradox about that era. Those were hard years, terribly hard years. We went from that horrible depression, the Great Depression, straight into that horrible war, World War II, yet through it all, our lives were filled with beauty—books, magazines, radio, stage, movies, everything. We routinely went to the show and saw films that turned out to be classics. The world had gone mad, but in this country, pretty girls in organdy dresses still glided mistily into the arms of their dates. And in that paradox, I believe, lies the strength of America.

There was a touch of melancholy in the air at the fairgrounds that night. Soon Glenn

Miller would go off to war and never come back. And soon we would be leaving our beloved Waukesha and moving to a new home in Des Plaines, a suburb of Chicago, where the family would quickly unravel.

When there is an alcoholic in the household, there is an underlying anxiety to life. What will there be today: anger, humiliation, scorn? After the idyllic years in Waukesha, our lives were devastated. We were never able to fully adjust to life in Des Plaines. First, Patricia dropped out of school, then Virginia. I was next. The precipitating factor was football shoes.

At Maine Township High School, I went out for the lightweight football team and made it. I played fullback and was a good one. The school furnished all uniforms and other equipment, but the players had to provide their own shoes. I asked my father for a pair of football shoes. He refused. I played one game, in my street shoes, with the stands filled with people. I felt mortified. The next day, I quit school and got a job as a busboy in a Chicago restaurant.

After that, I bounced around to a variety of jobs: stock boy, office boy, usher at a movie theater. I wanted desperately to get away from home. Twice, I ran away—abortively. And then something totally unexpected happened: My mother became pregnant, with my fourth sister, Pamela, who was born on January 7, 1944.

I used the excitement over her birth to screen my next getaway scheme. The Santa Fe railroad had advertised for young men, ages seventeen to twenty-five, to work at its big division point in Winslow, Arizona. With an altered birth certificate (Virginia did it for me), I had applied for a job and been accepted.

January 17, 1944, was my personal D-Day (departure). At age sixteen years, three months, I packed a suitcase, said good-bye to my mother and to my faithful dog, Buster, (they were the only ones at home) and went off to meet my Destiny.

The next three months of my life would fill a book. But inasmuch as this is just a ten-thousand-word essay, a few paragraphs will have to suffice.

In Winslow, I lived in a sidetracked Pullman sleeping car that had a kitchen. I bought my groceries at the company store and had a meal ticket at the local Fred Harvey restaurant. At night, I worked in a roundhouse alongside Native Americans (Navajos) and learned the hard, greasy work behind the glamorous ads of glistening trains racing through the countryside.

One evening, on a darkened freight platform, I watched the Super Chief, the famous Chicago–Los Angeles train of movie stars and other celebrities, roll to a stop for servicing.

And I found myself gazing into the compartment of Orson Welles, the boy wonder of Hollywood, and his wife, Rita Hayworth, the pinup queen.

Four years earlier, Welles had produced *Citizen Kane,* which would be acclaimed as the best movie ever made. Photographs of Rita Hayworth were treasured by U.S. servicemen around the world. And here I was, eavesdropping on their privacy.

I was hoping that Orson and Rita would do something licentious, but they didn't. He was in shirtsleeves, showing her card tricks (he was an amateur magician); Rita, in what appeared to be green lounging pajamas, was smiling and nodding.

"The day I was sworn into the Navy,"
Los Angeles, April 15, 1944

Then the Super Chief slowly rolled away, leaving an indelible impact on my mind. For it made me realize that my Destiny was not in a roundhouse in Winslow, Arizona, but in southern California. And so the next day, I packed my suitcase, lugged it over to Route 66, and stuck out my thumb. I had a total bankroll of three dollars and fifty cents.

The first car that stopped was driven by a traveling salesman, David Syne, who was on his way to his home in Los Angeles. I never forgot David Syne; he was very kind to me.

Near Kingman, Arizona, he picked up another hitchhiker, a soldier. The two of them decided to make a side trip to Las Vegas for some entertainment. When they checked into a hotel, I told them I thought I could get a better rate at another place (I was becoming quite a liar). I would see them in the morning, I said.

I knew it was imperative to run my thin bankroll into some real money. And so I went into a gambling casino. I played Horse Race Keno, betting on No. Six, my lucky number—and lost every cent.

So there I was in Las Vegas, Nevada, penniless, homeless—and hungry. I wandered around town most of the night. At the train station, a curious person befriended me, a short, stubby man, who had been working with a railroad gang for six weeks and had just gotten into town. He was a little drunk. I hoped I would get some money or some food from him, but all he wanted was to sodomize me. (I didn't know men did such things.)

I ended up, cold and hungry, sleeping in the backseat of David Syne's car (back then, people routinely left their cars unlocked, even in Las Vegas). The next day, David Syne dropped the soldier off in Barstow, California, and then he began to take an interest in me. He seemed to sense that I was a troubled kid. When he learned that I had lost all of my money gambling (I didn't tell him how little I'd had), he stopped and bought me a big lunch.

As we ate, I told him some—not all—of my story, that I had been working for the Santa Fe in Winslow and hoped to find a job quickly in Los Angeles. He said that finding a job should be easy, so long as I was seventeen. He explained that in Los Angeles, minors were required to have a work permit, and that permits weren't issued to anyone under age seventeen.

"At U.S. Naval Air Station, Fort Lauderdale, Florida, after completing flight training and being awarded my aircrewman's wings at age seventeen," 1945

Late that afternoon, after driving through the marvelous orange groves of the San Fernando Valley, David Syne dropped me off near the Los Angeles Union Station, shook my hand, gave me a half-dollar, and wished me luck.

I would need it.

In the 1940s, with railroads being the country's major means of transportation, train stations were the hub of activity in all cities and towns, like today's airports. Union Station in Los Angeles was special, with beautiful architecture, padded benches, even cushioned chairs. It was crowded around-the-clock, mostly with servicemen. After my first night in residence there, I went out to look for a job.

The first restaurant I applied at was a cafeteria on Pershing Square, across from the Biltmore Hotel. They said they would be glad to hire me, as soon as I got my work permit. Wonderful! But when I applied for a work permit, at the Chamber of Commerce offices, my birth certificate was spotted as a fake. I was denied a permit.

I lived in Union Station for over two weeks, cadging food scraps from the great trains from the East when they arrived (including the Super Chief) and tramping around Los Angeles, trying vainly to find someplace that would hire me without a work permit.

And then one day I spotted an ad in the *Los Angeles Times* (I read discarded newspapers daily):

> Young men, 17 to 25, free to travel; interesting work meeting people; immediate cash advance.

It was a typical come-on ad for magazine sales, I would learn later, but it was my salvation. I was hired immediately and given a five-dollar advance. I quickly moved out of Union Station and into the Vermont Hotel, where the magazine crew was staying. I ate a huge meal and soaked myself for a half hour in a bathtub, washing two weeks of crud from my body.

Ferry and his mother in front of house in Des Plaines, Illinois, 1945

But just as I had learned that a Santa Fe roundhouse wasn't for me, I soon learned that I was a poor direct salesman. Prospects would give me a sad story, and I would feel like giving them money, rather than selling them something. I had some interesting experiences. I sold a subscription to a movie star—Lou Costello of the Abbott and Costello comedy team—but I was unhappy.

And then one day, I was walking down Wilshire Boulevard and went past a Selective Service (military draft) office. An idea came to me. I went in, told them it was my eighteenth birthday, and registered for the draft. (I wrote about this in *O Zebron Falls!*)

Thirty days later, April 15, 1944, three months after my D-Day, I was sworn into the U.S. Navy. Although it wasn't exactly what I had had in mind, it turned out that my Destiny really had been awaiting me in southern California.

Five and a half years later, I would come out of the navy an alcoholic. For four and a half years, I served as a radioman–tail gunner on a carrier-based Avenger torpedo bomber. (*Raspberry One*, my most-honored title, is based on those experiences.)

My last year was spent in the public information office of a transport squadron, writing articles about navy personnel for their hometown newspapers. When one of my features appeared on the front page of the Erie, Pennsylvania, Sunday newspaper, I knew that writing would be my career.

To digress, reporters often ask about my education and the degrees that I hold. I tell them that I am the product of a good eighth-grade education. And I mean that quite seriously.

You see, I have very few high school credits and no college credits. In 1945, under the GI Bill of Rights, I became eligible for four calendar years of government-financed college education, with tuition of up to five hundred dollars per year and subsistence of seventy-five dollars per month. I immediately applied at Yale and, because of my navy training and test scores, was accepted. But because there were a lot of returning veterans ahead of me, I couldn't enroll until 1947. By that time, alcohol had taken firm control of my life, and I forgot about Yale.

After my discharge from the navy on September 30, 1949, I took the entrance exam at

Northwestern University, passed it, and was accepted for the forthcoming spring semester. But in the meantime, I got a job on a weekly newspaper, began a career in journalism, and forgot about Northwestern.

In 1952, when I finally made it to college, the University of Illinois, I drank my way out in less than one semester.

From a weekly newspaper, I went to a daily newspaper, then to a wire service, and then into radio news. I was chalking up honors, but I was living on borrowed time. Not long ago, at a children's literature conference at the University of North Texas, I talked quite openly about my disintegration:

> I stand before you today a very proud person. The last time I was in the state of Texas was the day I was about to commence a six-month drunken binge that would cover nine different states and land me in prison.
>
> I was twenty-five years old. I was a very promising journalist. I had worked in radio, first in Abilene (KWKC), then in Lubbock (KVSP). In newspapers, I had done award-winning work. In radio, one of my documentaries (narrated by Dana Andrews, a prominent Hollywood actor of that era) had been carried by the CBS radio network. I had a solid reputation for talent and ability. I also had a growing reputation for drinking.
>
> For more than twenty-five years, I fought a severe addiction to alcohol. I drank my way into seventeen different jails, three of them twice and one of them the largest walled jail in the world—the State Prison of Southern Michigan (SPSM) at Jackson.
>
> For more than three years, I lived with screams in the night and the rumbling of heavy steel doors. One week, in The Hole (solitary confinement), I lived in a darkened cell and lost track of time . . .

At that conference, a teacher asked me: "Mr. Ferry, with all the terrible things you've had to endure, what kept you going?"

I have thought long and hard about that. Obviously, I made some positive identification quite early in life, but with whom, what, when?

There were no role models in my life. At no point did any of my teachers or my parents ever inquire about my thoughts or my feelings, my hopes or my dreams. At school, my creative expressions drew reprimands; at home, my parents were too busy with survival to bother

about aesthetics. (Actually, they couldn't have defined the word.)

In a very real sense, Mary June was my surrogate mother. She saw good things in me and encouraged them.

Almost from the beginning, there was a touch of the poet in me. I had wit and imagination; I had an early skill with words and a strong sense of the beautiful. But most of all, I had *literature.*

Literature, I have come to realize, formed my character and hardened my mettle. Frank Merriwell and Horatio Alger were with me in that darkened solitary-confinement cell, as were Tom Swift, Nancy Drew, and many others. And they are still with me, they are still keeping me going.

Why was I sent to prison in the first place? Forgery, and uttering, and publishing—three-and-half to fourteen years. The sentence was handed down in Washtenaw County Circuit Court in Ann Arbor, Michigan, by the late Judge James M. Breakey. His sentence may seem rather harsh, but it wasn't. You see, Ann Arbor was merely the tip of the iceberg. Ann Arbor was the disgraceful culmination of my six-month, nine-state drunken binge. During that time, I was a mini crime wave. Two stolen cars, one abandoned, one totaled. Five break-ins, most of them senseless. Bad checks, whenever I got my hands on a blank one. Larceny, whenever there was an opportunity. Anything to keep alcohol flowing through my bloodstream.

In addition to Michigan, the states were Illinois, Wisconsin, Texas, Vermont, Massachusetts, New York, Pennsylvania, and New Jersey. It was in New Jersey that I left a young man, drunk and passed out, in a motel room, with nothing but his underwear, and made off with all of his possessions—his car, his clothes, his money and personal records. In *Binge,* the central character, Weldon Yeager, does the same thing and then assumes his victim's identity. Weldon becomes Richard C. Wessell; I became F. William Ross. And after totaling Mr. Ross's car, I came to Ann Arbor with his money and academic credentials and registered at the University of Michigan, an impostor.

I could continue recounting my masquerade in Ann Arbor. I could tell you about the apartment on William Street, above a bicycle shop, which I shared with two other students and where my chief activity was organizing parties. Or I could tell you about how I was a familiar figure at the Pretzel Bell, freely spending stolen money. But it is enough that you know that I soon ran out of money and decided to commit another crime.

Now, when an alcoholic commits a crime, he looks for familiar surroundings or circumstances, which will give him a sense of security. I chose St. Andrew's Episcopal Church. By this time, I had left the Catholic Church and become an Episcopalian. One Sunday evening, while activities were in progress downstairs, I slipped unnoticed into the parish library. No one was there. I sat down in an easy chair, with an open book in my lap, and pretended that I had fallen asleep. Soon the lights went out and everyone left. I was alone in the church.

Groping in the dark, I made my way up to the church office, searching for money. I found none, but in the desk of the rector—the rector at that time, 1955, was the Reverend Henry Lewis—and in Father Lewis's desk I found a large business-type checkbook on the church's seminarian fund. The next day, at two different branches of the old Ann Arbor Bank, I cashed two checks—each for $150, each made out to Charles Ferry (there was no Charles Ferry in town; I figured I was safe), and each signed by Henry Lewis.

I had no difficulty in cashing the checks; I never had difficulty in cashing bad checks. Why? Because of my appearance. I was a clean-cut young man. I was personable and had a nice smile. And I was a con artist. All alcoholics are con artists; they have to be to get away with their drinking. And so I would engage bank tellers in a pleasant conversation, distracting their attention. At the Ann Arbor bank, they never bothered to check my ID. Weldon Yeager does this in *Binge,* with a stolen credit card.

There was a kind of pattern to my binge. I kept returning to places where life had been good, where I had been good, as if those places would make life good again. Instead I simply replaced good memories with bad ones. I dirtied up my past.

And whenever I got my hands on some money, I would resolve, quite seriously, that this would be the end of the binge. I would use the money to pull myself together. I would get a job and start rebuilding my life. I would do that tomorrow. But tomorrow never came. For an alcoholic, one drink is too many; a thousand aren't enough.

And so the binge went on. I continued my high living. I even opened a checking account in my assumed name, which was a reckless thing to do. Give an alcoholic a checking account and he will cash bad checks; it's as certain as death and taxes. Soon, I had forged checks out in the name of Charles Ferry and bounced checks in the name of F. William Ross. I was leaving a trail forty miles wide.

And then one Monday morning, I was alone in the apartment above the bicycle shop, sleeping off a Sunday drunk. The door was unlocked. Two detectives came in and shook me awake.

"Mr. Ross?" one of them asked me. "Have you ever used the name Charles Ferry?"

The binge was over. The disgrace was about to commence. First, in the press—the *Michigan Daily,* the *Ann Arbor News,* the Detroit newspapers, the wire services, radio, television, the works. The University of Michigan impostor was quite a story. And then being led through the streets of downtown Ann Arbor, with other prisoners, from the county jail to the old courthouse on Huron Street. Friends I had made at the university stopped their car and stared in disbelief at the clean-cut impostor, in chains.

One day at the county jail, I was taken down to the room where lawyers conferred with prisoners. The court had appointed a public defender for me. But today, it wasn't my lawyer; it was the Reverend Henry Lewis, the man from whom I had stolen, the man whose church I had violated.

We had a long talk, and Father Lewis saw in me something worth saving. He was in the courtroom when I was sentenced. Without him, I'm sure I would have gone to pieces. For hearing a judge sentencing you to prison, at age twenty-six, has to be the most emotionally devastating experience there is. But Father Lewis was there; someone cared.

He said he would come visit me, and he did. Not just once, but several times. He was my only visitor in prison; my family knew nothing of my whereabouts.

In fair weather or foul, Father Lewis would drive from Ann Arbor to Jackson. Then a long walk from the parking lot to the administration building, followed by a long wait in the visitors' lobby. When his number was called, there was the indignity of being frisked by a guard. Then through an enormous steel door, twelve inches thick, which was locked behind him. Then through a second thick door, which was also locked behind him, while I came out through a third thick door and met him in the visitors' room, this distinguished, silver-haired Episcopal priest, in a blue suit and a Roman collar, a truly remarkable man, whose friends included the great American historian Samuel Eliot Morison, whose father had founded the University of Pennsylvania Law School and served as its first dean. He did all of this for a fifteen-minute visit with me, number 89750, three or four times a year. He did it because he had seen in me something worth saving.

But Father Lewis did much more than just visit; he became an important influence in our prison life. He arranged for the rector of the Episcopal church in the city of Jackson to hold monthly communion services for the Episcopalian inmates (there were only three of us). And when he learned that one of the inmates had never been confirmed in the church, Father Lewis arranged for Bishop Richard Emerich to come to the prison and confirm him.

Our services were held in the Protestant chaplain's private office. Our altar was a large window sill. The window looked out on the entrance to Fifteen Block, thirty feet away. Fifteen Block was the infamous "Hole," where I had once lost track of time. And that was the backdrop for a priest and a bishop administering the sacraments of the church to our tiny congregation. It tells you a lot about the Episcopal Church; it tells you a lot about Henry Lewis.

When I came up for parole, Father Lewis arranged a job for me, in Detroit, and referred me to a young adult fellowship group that met Sunday evenings at St. Paul's Cathedral. Three months after I was paroled, I attended a meeting of that group. I was immediately struck by a very attractive and vivacious woman who gave a report on a forthcoming St. Patrick's Day party at her duplex in Royal Oak. Six months later that woman became my wife. But before Ruth and I were married, I took her to Ann Arbor to meet Father Lewis. He was overjoyed by the news of our plans to marry. I think he felt that his work was done, that I was now in good hands. And I was, but I still had a twelve-year battle against alcohol.

It was the last time I ever saw Father Lewis. I learned just recently that he passed away two years ago at his retirement home in Brunswick, Maine. He was ninety-seven years of age. The Reverend Henry Lewis was a true man of God.

He was my salvation. As you will learn, I couldn't have made it without my loving wife. Without Henry Lewis, I never would have met her. My life, my books, everything—I owe it all to Henry Lewis.

Ruth was unaware of the bumpy road that lay ahead. She was unaware of how severe my alcohol addiction was—but she soon learned. A year after we were married, I joined Alcoholics Anonymous, but it was on and off, up and down, good years, bad years. I was dysfunctional for most of that time; I couldn't hold a job for very long, and I had a few good ones. Ruth, who was executive travel coordinator at the J. L. Hudson Company (the big downtown store), held everything together, but it wasn't easy. For example, in 1969, on Halloween actually, I had collected some money owed me for some work I had done. The money was to be applied to household bills. Instead, I stormed out of the house in a drunken rage, took our only car, and ended up five days later in the state of Wyoming. Ruth, meantime, was left stranded. A friend had to drive out from Royal Oak each day, drive her to work, and then drive her home at night.

But blessedly, her ordeal was nearly over. In 1970, I bottomed out. For me, hitting bottom was a matter of totally running out of gas, so to speak. I was completely drained of energy. I didn't have the energy to pour a drink or hold a gun to my head, which is what I felt like doing, I didn't have the energy to think. I was in a black pit of despair.

But once you hit bottom, I learned, once you decide that you're tired of the pain and anguish, tired of kicking yourself in the head, tired of the vomit and urine of drunk tanks, tired of seventeen different jails, three of them twice and one of them the largest walled jail in the world; once you decide you're tired of all that—there's no way to go but up.

Somehow, I found the strength to start clawing my way out of the pit. I wasn't at all hopeful; I had tried to lick alcohol so many times before and had always failed. But inch by inch, with the help of my loving wife, the principles of AA, and William Shakespeare I made it. I am now in my twenty-third year of recovery.

You're probably wondering how William Shakespeare figures into this story? Very importantly. From him, I learned a rule of life that I recommend to everyone, especially alcoholics:

Hamlet, Act I, Scene 3. Polonius, the father of Ophelia, is speaking:

> This above all, to thine own self be true,
> And it must follow, as the night the day,
> Thou canst not then be false to any man.

I have revised those words and added an important proviso: "This above all, be true to the best that is in you / And help other people." We all need help. Everyone reading this needs help; the only difference is in the intensity of the need.[1]

During my first few months in prison, the intensity of my need was critical. I was destined to do my time working in the shoe factory, which surely would have crushed my creative spirit. And then a very special person came into my life, Mr. Alan M. Krische, who was the principal of the State Prison of Southern Michigan Academic School. He saved me from the shoe factory and turned me into a teacher.

I began with remedial reading; some of my students were men in their fifties. Then third grade, and, finally, eighth-grade social studies. During my last year, I taught a college-level political science course.

Mr. Krische was a very special person. He wanted to know nothing about a student's "rap" or his criminal background. He felt that each man should be allowed to succeed (or fail) in the school without prejudice. I have never forgotten his precepts.

Mr. Krische allowed me to do my best and stood behind me. A very unique relationship developed between us. I did innovative things. I arranged for lectures by various members of the prison staff: a psychologist, an M.D., the business manager, who spoke on economics. I took full advantage of the free loans available from the Film Board of Canada and showed such things as the captured German films of the Holocaust. I introduced my students to classical music. One day, while Richard Strauss's *Don Juan* was playing, I noticed that one student was weeping.

"What's the matter, Mr. Carson?" I asked him (I addressed all of my students as "Mister"). "Bad news from home?"

"No, it's the music," he replied. "It's so beautiful."

Apparently, word of Mr. Krische's Academic School had spread far beyond the SPSM walls. The speech department of Western Michigan University challenged the Academic School to a debate. This was completely unprecedented, we were told: a university debating incarcerated prisoners.

It was sort of a foregone conclusion that I would be on the Academic School's debating team. My teammate would be a very engaging and articulate man, who had once been a preacher—Roy Harlan. The premise for the debate was, "Resolved: The United States should withdraw from the United Nations."

Roy and I took the affirmative side and got to work. At the Academic School, we were able to borrow, by mail, books from the best public library in the state: the three-million-volume State of Michigan Library in Lansing.

On the day of the debate, the school's all-purpose room was jammed with people; even the warden was there. The university's entourage included an impartial panel of three judges. After the debate, it took them about sixty seconds to reach a decision. The Academic School team had won!

A deafening roar went up. There was cheering and whistling and stomping. It was like winning the Rose Bowl.

Shortly after the debate, it was time to start preparing for parole. Mr. Krische's clerk let me read the report that had gone to the Parole Board. It began:

"I don't know what my school is going to do when this man leaves, but leave he must. . . ."

It was the most important compliment I have received in my entire life.

On the day I left the school, I choked up when I said good-bye to Mr. Krische; I think he did, too. Many years later, after he had retired and I had become a published author, I got in touch with him. It was with great pride that I inscribed a copy of *Raspberry One* to him, signed with my SPSM number, *89750.*

He received several of my books before his untimely death, in January 1995. And I think he understood better than anyone else what I

---

[1]See also *Children's Literature Review,* volume 34, Gale, 1995, pp. 57–58, and Ferry's essay "How 'Binge' Came to Be Written," in *Voice of Youth Advocates,* volume 16, number 4, October 1993, pp. 206–08.

The author signing books at Meadowbrook Hall, Oakland University, Rochester, Michigan, 1984

was trying to achieve in *Binge* and why writing it was so important to me.

You see, when I set out to write a young adult novel about how alcohol destroys young lives, my primary target was not young people who already have a drinking problem (although some would surely be influenced by such a book) but those who *don't*. Hopefully, the images in *Binge* would remain fixed in the minds of some of them and spare them the horrors of alcoholism in future years. I would achieve that effect, I decided, with a short novel that could be read in one sitting and have a stunning impact on the reader.

Binge covers a time span of about four hours, the length of the police interrogation of the central character, Weldon Yeager, in his hospital room. There are no chapters; breaks in the story are provided through the device of using a script of the interrogation between the various flashbacks. In the flashbacks, we learn about Weldon, his background, and his binge.

The narrative shifts back and forth from the third person to the first. There is a sprinkling of sex, beginning with the first paragraph, all suggestive, nothing explicit. There is also a sprinkling of hard language, but it is not used gratuitously.

Weldon Yeager is not a sympathetic character; alcoholism is not a sympathetic disease. Nor is Weldon a three-dimensional character.

The story is told through his alcoholic blur, through which all of life is two-dimensional. The story does not preach; it simply tells, unflinchingly, how alcohol destroys the life of one young man.

Binge is filled with truth, hard truth, painful truth, even smelly truth. It is a complete downer that leaves Weldon with no apparent hope. Tomorrow is another day, but for now—his life is destroyed.

I finished the *Binge* manuscript in January of 1987. Thus began five years of disappointment, in which sixty-one different publishers agreed that *Binge* was a powerful and important story, but not right for their lists. I was about to give up, when a long-standing friend and successful international businessman advanced me the money to publish the book myself. He prefers to remain anonymous in his good works (and he does a lot of them); my code name for him is "John Beresford Tipton," taken from the old TV series *The Millionaire.*

Binge was published on May 1, 1992. The book was produced by Proctor Publications of Ann Arbor, a firm that enjoys a solid national reputation for quality and integrity in the self-publishing business.

From the beginning, major national reviewing journals have ignored—and continue to ignore—*Binge.* But teachers and librarians have swung solidly behind the book. It has been chosen as an American Library Association Best Book for Young Adults. The National Council of Teachers of English has recommended it for all high school students, as has the New York Public Library. The Michigan Library Association nominated it as the best young adult book of the year, and the Pennsylvania Library Association included it in its "Best of the Best" list. In addition, *Binge* will be included in two forthcoming directories of best books for young adults and middle school students, and a movie option is quite likely. In response to widespread demand in certain domestic urban markets, *Binge* will soon be in translation (Spanish).

To date, *Binge* has sold 4,115 copies, but I haven't made a penny from the book. All profits have gone for additional advertising and promotion. We have just started a campaign to call the book to the attention of juvenile correctional facilities.

But I have learned that true wealth is invisible. You can't see love. You can't see joy. You can't see the warm glow that fills your heart when you learn that one of your books has touched the life of some young reader.

For instance, a boy in Petaluma, California, once wrote me, "Your book *Raspberry One* changed the way I think about war and life and death." A girl in Raleigh, North Carolina, commenting on my *One More Time!*, wrote, "Your books make me feel proud of my country." And I have a stack of letters from young people everywhere testifying that *Binge* is changing their attitudes toward alcohol.

All of which brings me to one of my favorite poets, who was also rich in true wealth. Emily Dickinson once wrote in a letter to an editor in Boston:

How can I know what I think until I read what I have written?

In writing this brief review of my convoluted life, I have learned what I truly think about many things. Lingering resentments have vanished, and I have gained new perspectives, on myself and on my loved ones. I have learned that we can all hold our heads high. We were Depression kids who, against tough odds, made a difference.

Except for Mary June, who worked her way through three years of college and was never much of a social drinker, all of us dropped out of high school; all of us had trouble with alcohol. This is not uncommon among children of an alcoholic parent (or parents). Our home life was unstable, unsupportive, and sometimes volatile.

It would be easy to point an accusing finger at my father, but that would miss the whole point of this essay. My father was the hero of our lives; we came to understand his weaknesses, his torments, and to love him dearly.

You see, the shell-shocked veteran and the girl who taught him how to talk again did remarkable, courageous things to get their children through the Great Depression. Today, as we enter the home stretch of life, a bond of love, strong as steel, binds us together—Mary June and Virginia, now widowed, building meaningful new lives for themselves; Patricia, experiencing a new dimension of love as she valiantly fights back from a crippling stroke; Pamela, who went on to earn a master's degree at Harvard, proudly stamping passports at the U.S. Embassy in Rome; and Sonny Boy, writing books to help us understand ourselves.

We all have had to overcome difficulties in life, and our father set an example for us to follow. He was a loving man, who was unable to express his love. He was a victim of war: a wounded body, a wounded mind, a tortured soul.

I came to know him better than anyone else, better, perhaps, than even his bride. He never talked about the Great War, but he gave little clues, from which I pieced together his story.

Because of his civilian experience in hotels, the army made him a cook. The utter horror of trench warfare is impossible to comprehend: the rumble of artillery fire, the constant stench of death. Through it all, my father had to feed the troops. He did it well. He was a great battlefront cook.

Then to escape the trenches, he volunteered for the fledgling Army Air Corps, where he served as a rear-seat gunner and was introduced to the horror of bombings and strafings and men going mad with fear.

After the war, the promise of a good life was destroyed by the Depression. And when employment finally came, it was at a steep price: lonely weeks separated from his wife and children.

Finally, in 1959, at age sixty-five, retirement on a beautiful, ten-acre spread in the shadow of a mountain in southern Oregon. Maybe now there would be peace in his tortured soul. But his luck ran out. In his first year of retirement, he fell dead on a sidewalk in Grants Pass.

He was given a military burial. His bride never remarried. She lived to the age of eighty-nine (1992), when she drifted away like a feather, with the handsome, shell-shocked veteran still in her heart.

My wife never got to know my father; he died shortly after we were married.[1] Ruth is now retired from her job at Hudson's. She was just about the most popular employee in the store. When she left, there was an outpouring of warm tributes, from the president on down. She has since embarked on a second career: spreading love. She makes friends wherever she

---

[1] See also *Children's Literature Review,* volume 34, Gale, 1995, pp. 55–58, and Ferry's essay "How 'Binge' Came to Be Written," in *Voice of Youth Advocates,* volume 16, number 4, October 1993, pp. 206–08.

goes and freely offers counsel and guidance to young people. She is a world-class shopper, with a dedicated following, and a seamstress who can make virtually anything—dresses, blouses, skirts, samplers, even coats.

We don't fully understand each other, but we're working at it. We live simply and quietly in a modest, ranch-style house in Rochester Hills, which is thirty miles north of Detroit. Following in my father's footsteps, I am a fairly good cook. My Christmas brownies are a legend at Houghton Mifflin and I make a first-rate turkey soup, one of my father's specialties. I have been baking our bread and rolls for over twenty years, and my pizza and cheesecake are regionally famous.

We have a rather legendary kitchen, in which many political and civic movements have been masterminded. It was once an advance outpost for the White House. One wall, paneled with cedar shingles, is known simply as "The Wall." It is covered with over a hundred photos and various memorabilia.

During my twenty years as a published author, I have tutored many young people in our kitchen, and this is what I advise them about learning how to write:

*

No one can teach you how to write; you have to learn it yourself, and it's hard work. But it can be very satisfying work, and it's not nearly as difficult as you may think, IF—and it's a big *if*—if you're willing to apply yourself. As the great American novelist Edna Ferber once said, "Writing is ninety percent applying the seat of the pants to the seat of the chair."

My eighth-grade teacher, Sister Joan Therese, put it another way. She said that the only way a person can achieve an important goal—in sports, medicine, writing, whatever—is by sticking to it. "Stick-to-it-iveness," she called it.

If you stick to it, if you really apply yourself, the rewards of writing can be very rich. Through it, you may come to understand yourself and your world. If you're really good at it, you might even make yourself some money.

Although learning how to write is a very private experience, a teacher can help to steer you in the right direction. Here are a few tips:

First, WRITE WHAT YOU KNOW. Those are the four most important words for an aspiring writer. WRITE WHAT YOU KNOW, and if you don't know it, *learn* it. That's the great beauty of writing fiction. By combining your personal experience with careful research, you can write about any subject you choose. There are no limits to an inquiring mind. When he wrote a best-selling novel about a Soviet submarine, Tom Clancy was an insurance agent who had never set foot on a submarine. He is a superb researcher.

To learn how to write, READ! There is simply no other way. There are over 650,000 words in the English language. Each one of them stands for a thought. "He went outside." Three words; three thoughts. It's only logical that the more words you know, the better you can think. And the better you can think, the better you can write. It's that simple. So read, read, READ! Then write, write, WRITE! And read good books; reading junk literature is like falling in with bad companions.

Where do you start? Start with yourself. At some point in our lives, most of us aspire to publish a book or a story, but few of us ever follow through on our aspirations. However, in order to make writing an important—and valuable—part of your life, you don't have to aspire to a literary career. And you can begin today. I call this approach "Writing for a Better You."

Any good psychiatrist will tell you the value of writing in helping patients to resolve personal problems. Try it for yourself. Write about your problems and you will come to understand them—and yourself. Has your mother been mean to you? Your father? Write about it. Problems at school? Write about them. But you must write with *complete honesty;* otherwise it won't work. Not honesty in the sense of factual truth, but honesty about your true feelings. Write about your problems regularly, and as you do so, you will actually be defining your *vision.*

Book reviewers often write about an author's vision as though it were some special literary quality. But it isn't. *You* have a vision. Your vision is the sum total of all your experience in life—your hopes and dreams, sorrows and disappointments, achievements and failures; your likes and dislikes, your favorite foods, your favorite TV programs, *everything* in your life, past and present. All of these things comprise your way of looking at life. And that is your vision—*you* and your way of looking at life.

The author and his wife, Ruth, with "The Wall" in the background, 1994

When you write creatively, your vision is the star of the show. Don't try to hide it; don't try to imitate another writer, don't try to pretend you're something you aren't. Write with your vision, your way of looking at life, shining bright and true for all to see. Why? Because you're a very important person, and your thoughts are important to other people.

You see, you are special. You are a one-of-a-kind. In all the world, there is no one else quite like you. You're not only special, you are a genius. I mean that quite seriously. We tend to apply the word "genius" to persons of exceptional intellectual ability. But there's much more to genius than just a high IQ. True genius simply means "exceptional ability." Period. There are geniuses in sports, music, art, carpentry, cooking, virtually every area of life. I once had a student who was poor in academic subjects but was a genius with insects. I know a twelve-year-old girl who is a genius at smiling; her smile brightens a room. Some people are geniuses at love and caring. What is *your* area of genius, your area of exceptional abil-

ity? You don't know yet? Well, writing may supply you with the answer. Writing can teach you a lot about yourself. If you let it, it will make you a better you.

Here are a few rules of the road:

First, *date whatever you write.* We live in a world of time and space. So if you write it, date it. Next, *save everything you write.* Your writings are a part of your personal history; in future years, you will treasure them. And *think about what you want to write,* what you want to express, think long and hard. Don't worry about disciplining yourself to sit before a typewriter or at a desk with pen and paper. The creative process of composition may occur *anywhere*—on a school bus, in the bathroom on the throne of thought, in a line at a grocery store. The important thing is simply to *think.* As you do, your story will grow in your mind.

When you tell a story, you will be making a statement. Not a statement in the sense of making a speech; but you will be expressing a point of view (your vision), which is an artistic statement. You may just have a yearning to write about a certain subject, but don't really know what you want to say. Which is good. A yearning means that your creative juices are flowing. So let them flow. Write what you know; write with your vision, write a story that will touch the hearts of your readers.

A couple of other things: As you go through life, you will learn that there is nothing new under the sun. Our technology changes every day, but people change hardly at all.

For example, we are told that the younger generation is going to pot. Don't you believe it. Older people have been saying that ever since there was a younger generation to bitch about.

And we are told that our schools are going to pot. Don't believe that, either. People have been complaining about the public schools ever since they first came into existence. If our schools are as lousy as some critics suggest, how does America continually manage to excel—economically, technologically, culturally, artistically?

Life is full of surprises. Here I am, a high school dropout, a drunken bum for twenty-five years, a mini crime wave who drank his way into seventeen different jails—here I am, writing an autobiographical essay that I hope will help young people roll with the punches in life.

And there will be a lot of them, but there will be even more sweet moments. It's a wonderful life! It truly is, a wonderful life with marvelous opportunities. Reach out and grab one! Read, read, read. Then write, write, write. Write for a better you. Write for true wealth. Write well, and material wealth may follow. That's what happened to Tom Clancy and John Grisham. This is America, remember; it could happen to *you.*

Finally, whenever young people ask me to sign a copy of *Binge,* I do it in a special way, borrowing the words from Robert Frost. I leave you with that inscription:

> To all of my young readers—
> You have promises to keep
> And miles to go before you sleep.
> GOOD LUCK IN LIFE!

Charles Ferry

P.S. I just got a phone call from Disney Educational Productions in Burbank, California. They're interested in making *Binge* into a movie. See what I mean? Life is full of surprises.

BIBLIOGRAPHY

FOR CHILDREN

Fiction:

Up in Sister Bay, illustrated by Ted Lewin, Houghton Mifflin, 1975.

O Zebron Falls!, Houghton Mifflin, 1977.

FOR YOUNG ADULTS

Fiction:

Raspberry One, Houghton Mifflin, 1983.

One More Time!, Houghton Mifflin, 1985.

Binge, Daisy Hill, 1992.

Wrote for International News Service and authored several radio broadcasts.

Paul Fleischman

1952-

Paul Fleischman and his violin, Maine, 1992

"Take care of the sense and the sounds will take care of themselves,'" the Duchess tells Lewis Carroll's Alice. It might seem reasonable advice, even if it weren't meant more as a play on the British proverb "Take care of the pence and the pounds will take care of themselves." It's not, I must say, a motto I follow. Nothing in a book, from the wording of the dedication to the choice of a main character's middle name, takes care of itself. More important, the sounds of the words on the page, I would like to argue, are as worthy of a writer's attention as their sense.

I'm sure most of us remember as children repeating a phrase over and over as quickly as possible, feeling the words shedding their sense and becoming a collection of vowels and consonants. Children, of course, don't need to be told that words have sounds as well as meanings. They love to rhyme words, to read alliterative tongue twisters, to laugh at funny-sounding names. As a child, I remember finding myself with a phrase repeating itself in my head for days—the title of a movie, a baseball player's name, an overheard phrase I might not even have understood. This still happens to me. Like an advertising jingle, the words attach themselves by virtue of their attractive sound rather than their sense. Why else would one go around murmuring "Twyla Tharp" or "Pancho's Mexican Buffet"?

My upbringing provided lots of exposure to the attractions of sound. Everyone in my family played an instrument: my mother and I the piano, my sisters the flute, my father the guitar. I had a short-wave radio from fifth grade onward and loved to listen far into the night to the exotic sounds of Arabic, Japanese, Russian, and languages unknown—all unintelligible to me, sounds without sense, verbal music. Most important, my father read to us—and not simply any old stories, but his own, chapter by chapter, as he wrote them. *Mr. Mysterious and Company, By the Great Horn Spoon, The Ghost in the Noonday Sun,* and the rest of the Sid Fleischman canon were all read aloud in installments to the family.

The scene was repeated all through my growing-up. I'd be dimly aware that my father had been typing. His study door would open and close. My mother would call my two sisters and me, the whole family gathering in the living room, my father always at the table in the corner. Everyone got comfortable. The phone was entreated not to ring. A brief recap of the story was given. Then he read aloud the chapter he'd just finished.

"The sun came up hot and clear," he might begin, "as if it had been cut out of a prairie fire with a pair of scissors."

Or, "Sometime during the night Cut-Eye Higgins left Hangtown for parts unknown."

Or, "At first light, Captain Harpe was up and shouting. 'Rise up gents! To the oars, my lazy mud turtles!'"

Or, "It was a week before we got out the next issue of *The Humbug Mountain Hoorah.* First we had to dig up the petrified man."

We were transported at once to the Old Post Road, to the decks of an Ohio River raft, to Hangtown or Matamoros. Part yarn-spinning session, vaudeville act, history lesson, and magic show, these readings transmitted, aside from their stories, so much of what I associate with my father.

First and foremost, we imbibed his love of language. We grew up knowing that words felt good in the ears and on the tongue, that they were as much fun to play with as toys. How could we help it, following the adventures of characters whose names were such fun to say: Pitch-pine Billy, Micajah Jones, Jingo, Hawg Pewitt, Billy Bombay, not to mention the McBroom

family's children, Will*jill* hester*chester* peter*polly*tim*tom* mary*larry* and little *clarinda.* Characters whose speech made you wish you'd been born a century earlier if only so that you, too, could shout, "By the eternal!" or "Hoolah-haw!" or "Hackle me bones!" or "Don't that bang all!"

His description was equally colorful. I feel safe in claiming that you won't find a single cliche in all my father's books. What you will find is lots of rich, visual imagery. A character wasn't simply thin. He was thin enough to take a bath in a shotgun barrel or to fall through a stovepipe without getting sooty. We never had trouble imagining the scene my father was reading. It takes a lot longer to write this way—especially when, after a long career, you're faced with your tenth or eleventh skinny character to describe. With more than thirty children's books behind him, he still, somehow, managed to fill *The Whipping Boy* with plenty of fresh imagery.

I said that these readings were part history lesson. Weeks before my father actually began writing, stacks of research books would be brought from the library, piling up on the piano and eventually making their way into his study. I remember as a child being fascinated flipping through the notebook in which he kept his research. There were sections on food, clothing, language, prices of things, and various other subjects, filled with his penciled notes. I was hooked and years later would find myself filling similar notebooks of my own.

Despite his books' historical accuracy, listening to them read aloud was not at all like attending a classroom lecture. Here was history brought to life, the history that rarely gets into textbooks: gold miners sending their clothes all the way to China to be laundered, sailors' fear of ghostlike "dredgies," Gypsy signs and lingo, goose pulls. The dusty corners and vivid details of history have always attracted my father. Walking into his study when he was out, I would find myself wanting to read all those strange-sounding books on his shelves: *33 Years Among Our Wild Indians, Hawkers and Walkers in Early America, Extraordinary Popular Delusions and the Madness of Crowds.* A few years back we gleefully joined in combing the used bookstores in search of all four volumes of Henry Mayhew's *London Labour and the London Poor,* a book he eventually drew on for *The Whipping Boy.*

In grammar school my father became interested in magic, learned the tricks of the trade—inventing quite a few along the way, the subject of his first published book—and after high school, during vaudeville's last days, toured the country with Mr. Arthur Bull's Francisco Spook Show. This experience came out in his books, several of which involve magic or adventuresome journeys or both. I suspect that his stage experience influenced his writing methods as well. He's an improviser and likes to keep himself as interested and in the dark about what's going to happen next as his readers. When he sits down at the typewriter in his silent study, he might as well be a comic stepping on stage in a noisy nightclub, trying to get a read on his audience, always thinking on his feet.

His reading aloud, likewise, partook of the stage. We four were his New Haven. He could tell from our reactions if a scene had worked or if it needed work. Our opinions were asked for. I remember being proud when my suggestion that Mr. Mysterious and his family get lost turned up in the following chapter. My younger sister, a little jealous, had less success with her proposal that their family piano ought to burn down.

These readings were live literature. Live like an old-time radio show, with the attendant tingle of excitement and the necessity of imagining the action. It's perhaps not surprising that we're all fans of "A Prairie Home Companion" and of the British radio game show "My Word." Or that I went on to write two books of poems designed to be performed aloud by two readers.

My father's specialty in magic is sleight of hand. No birthday party was complete without a few tricks; likewise, these days, no school visit, when my father, reenacting his past, takes his act on the road each spring and fall. This style of magic is reflected in his writing. When he gave up being a professional magician, he became instead a prestidigitator of words, palming plot elements, making villains vanish, producing solutions out of thin air. He knows how to keep an audience guessing, how to create suspense, how to keep readers reading. A sleight-of-hand artist must be skilled at misdirection, keeping his audience's eyes away from the real action. My father is a master at doing the same with words, stealthily slipping in a clue, unnoticed by the reader, that will reappear in the book's climax, just as he used to miraculously pull nickels and dimes out of our ears. His

"Listening to my shortwave radio," about 1962

adult characters are also sleight-of-hand men of a sort. Mr. Mysterious, Uncle Will, Praiseworthy, Mr. Peacock-Hemlock-Jones are all tall, strong men. They rely, however, on their cleverness. They're quick with their wits, magicians at manipulating a villain through his vices. Though Praiseworthy throws a notable punch at one point, these figures are advertisements for the superiority of brains to brawn.

As much as his use of language and history and clever plotting, it's those irresistibly appealing adult characters, I suspect, that explain why his books are nearly all still in print and that the letters from children continue to pour in. How wonderful to imagine yourself out adventuring—but with an Uncle Will to watch over you. Someone who respects you yet protects you as well. Someone brave, big-hearted, never discouraged, whose mere presence reassures you that everything will work out. With so many children growing up away from their fathers these days, it's no wonder that the warmth and security offered by these figures has a strong appeal. My sisters and I were lucky. Sitting in the living room, ruminating on the chapter just read, we knew we had exactly such a figure—for a father.

It's hardly surprising that the authors, after him, who influenced me most were Mark Twain, with his ear for dialect, and Dylan Thomas, with his supremely ear-entrancing prose. Though it may have struck my publisher and readers as a departure, *I Am Phoenix* and *Joyful Noise,* books of poems to be read aloud by two voices as in a musical duet, were just an extension of my interest in the music inherent in language. We expect, of course, that poetry will appeal to our ears through rhythm, alliteration, rhyme. My endeavor, aside from telling my stories, has been to bring this aural element into prose.

Of *Joyful Noise*'s many tributaries, music was the widest. I began taking piano lessons from Miss Dixon when I was seven years old. Ironically, my mind never mastered eighth notes and quarter notes and the rest of the code for conveying rhythm. My heart, however, lusted after the small plaster busts of the great composers that she presented to worthy students, and so I listened to how she played a piece and duplicated it. I often played duets with her and with a close family friend who had two pianos.

Upon graduating from elementary school, I determined to put away childish things, specifically piano lessons. In eleventh grade, however, I rediscovered classical music. It began with *Scheherazade.* Then Brahms's Fourth Symphony. Then *The Firebird.* Then one day my father brought home from the library the score of Tchaikovsky's *Romeo and Juliet,* which we followed with our fingers while the music flew by. I was entranced by the visual beauty of a score and by all that simultaneous activity, so carefully worked out by the composer. Writing books held no exotic appeal for me. But writing music, filling those twenty-five staves with all manner of intricate goings-on, precisely timing entrances and exits, whispering secrets with the double bass while the listener's ear was fixed on the woodwinds—there was a notion that kept me awake nights. At a time when future writers are usually devouring books, I was racing through the newly appeared record collection in the Santa Monica, California, Public Library. Schubert! Chopin! Beethoven! Brahms! I felt like the first miner to hit the gold fields.

Like writing, Los Angeles held little lure. Following the laws of the physics of adolescence, having grown up in the southwestern corner of the country, I desired to move as far as possible in a northeasterly direction. After two years of college I rode a bicycle up the coast to Vancouver, took the train across Canada, and settled down in the woods of New Hampshire. One town away, in Henniker, was

Young Paul, "sitting at my father's desk, with one of his pipes in my mouth," 1963

a college that sponsored a recorder consort. Though I'd brought along no winter coat, no gloves, no scarf, and no long underwear, I had prudently packed my alto recorder, an instrument I'd taken up a few years before. I sat down and learned my quarter notes and eighth notes. I joined the group, the first I'd ever played in—and found myself back in the gold fields.

Purcell! Morley! Loeillet! Telemann! This time, however, I was *making* the music. This new role effected a revelation. Playing a piece of music, I discovered, gave far more pleasure than merely listening to it. And playing music with other people was infinitely more enjoyable than playing alone. It was glorious fun and at its best gave a rapture I've never found elsewhere. In the 1930s an Austrian composer, Ernst Toch, had written a work entitled "Geographical Fugue." It was composed in the strict style of a fugue but was meant not to be played but rather spoken by a chorus. "Trinidad," begin the tenors, "and the big Mississippi and the town Honolulu and the Lake Titicaca"— followed by the altos, then the sopranos, then the basses. It was a brilliant idea. Back in high school, a friend of mine had heard the piece. As a project for a class on the Bible as literature, he'd written his own "Biblical Fugue," scored for four solo voices and making use of the Bible's rich store of proper names. I was one of the speakers who performed it.

That was in the twelfth grade, when I was writing what seemed to me to be poetry. By coincidence—an uncanny one, since I only recently heard "Geographical Fugue" for the first time—I had in my notebook an Ernst Toch-like line, a line I didn't know what to do with. It was "Cyprus, Sicily, Corsica, Crete." Next year, for a college music class, I composed my own multivoiced piece. It was written for three voices and called "Fruit Mélange." The title was all too apt. It began with "Cyprus, Sicily, Corsica, Crete," then wandered on through "Merrill Lynch, Pierce, Fenner, and Smith," Asian geography, heavenly bodies, bicycles, berries, and sundry other matters.

After some exposure to real musicians I realized that I belonged to a different flock. I also decided that I wasn't meant to teach history, my main subject in college. Writing, however, seemed a possibility, and as I was on the brink of graduation, needing to earn a living, it was time to reach for the possible.

It turned out to be the perfect choice. I could continue to scavenge among American history—I was an inveterate trash can searcher as a child, combing the alleys of Santa Monica. I could still loiter in libraries and used bookstores, hunting information on silhouette cutting, binnacle boys, yellow fever, wig-making or serendipitously stumbling on something I wasn't looking for, something that might lead to a future book.

Similarly, I found that I could make use of my musical interests. Writing prose had much in common with writing music. From Berlioz and Britten and company, as much from Twain and Gogol and Dylan Thomas, I learned to seek a form with a pleasing shape, to build in both unity and contrast, to love both entrances and the cadence of closings. Every chapter, every paragraph, every sentence, I discovered, has an arc to it, like a musical phrase. Every word has both a meaning and a music.

Writing, for me, is in fact very close to play. A childhood demonstration of how to string flowers in a chain came as an epiphany. I moved on to building with driftwood at the beach. At Berkeley I made pine needle houses. In New Hampshire, waiting to catch a ride at the bottom of my road, I used sticks, weeds, cans, whatever was at hand, searching for a way to connect them. Play is usually viewed as among those childish things one does well to put away. I've always remembered flipping through my mother's copy of *Minute Sketches of Great Composers.* Each page featured a grim-faced portrait, a brief text, and a motto, such as "The Chopin of the North." It was the entry on the Scarlattis, Alessandro and Domenico, that fascinated me. Seeming to point out the terrible wages of play, their motto read "Serious Father, Frivolous Son."

Here was my shameful destiny prefigured! A leather-skinned beach bum building driftwood sculptures, peddling painted rocks for drinks in bars, telling all who would listen that my father was the famous author of children's books! In actuality, frivolity, improvisation, experimentation—play—led me to becoming a writer. What can you make out of a handful of sticks? How can you connect a half-dozen characters? It's much the same problem and the same joy: the joy involved in joining both post to lintel and hero to villain, in rummaging for supplies at the beach or among books, in watching a wall go up or a paragraph. The joy found in making has begotten all my books.

After six of those books had been written, I took another look at "Fruit Mélange" and wondered if it might be possible to do a multivoiced book for children. Birds attracted me as a subject. They'd been my clock hands and calendar in New Hampshire. I would write a suite, beginning with the finches' exultation at dawn and ending with the calling of the owls at night. Here was a chance to cast aside sense—or at least plot and character development—and devote myself almost solely to sound. "Berries everywhere, there's berries everywhere" from "Fruit Mélange" became "Sparrows everywhere / there's sparrows / everywhere." The pieces came quickly and easily. I was in paradise, as close to writing music as I'll ever get. I didn't know whether such a book would be published—all I knew was that I'd never had so much fun writing one. The book *was* published as *I Am Phoenix.* I'd no idea what response it would get. One of the first reviews to come in could be summarized with the three words "Shred this book." When I visited schools, however, I found that a reading of a single poem removed the book's arcane aura and that even the poorest readers wanted to step up and perform. Performing poetry, of course, is old, not new, as old as Homer, the revered father of rap music. Meter, rhyme, alliteration—they're all forms of repetition, something children don't need to be taught to love, having

Paul Fleischman

by Sid Fleischman

Our kids didn't get hand-me-down clothes. They got hand-me-down typewriters. My old Olympia, resettled on Paul's bedroom desk, sat largely silent while Paul was away at college. When he returned for the Christmas holidays in 1977, I could hear the machine rattling away again.

Late one afternoon, he ambled downstairs and casually tossed a few typewritten pages on the couch. "I've written a story," he said, "if you'd like to read it."

Here was a situation of some delicacy. Amateur scripts generally remind you of someone trying to play on an untuned piano. Would he feel I'd be disappointed in him if the story was no good?

Not to worry.

I read the pages with growing amazement. This was not a story written with the telltale creaks and groans of the beginner. It was a skilled handling of a difficult subject, the uncanny relationship between a boy and an apple tree planted in celebration of his birth. It was a bravura performance.

I looked up with a rush of paternal pride. "It's wonderful!" And then, "Paul, have you been writing stories in secret?"

No. He hadn't.

Paul's gift for writing surfaced in early childhood. But sculpting a story demands an additional set of skills. Long after *The Birthday Tree* was accepted by the first editor to whom it was submitted, Charlotte Zolotow, I remained somewhat mystified. Without the usual apprenticeship, how had Paul learned to stage manage his scenes, to fine tune the story tensions, to bring his characters to life?

It slowly dawned on me that he'd had an apprenticeship after all, I simply hadn't noticed it. There have always been writers and editors in and out of the house, talking story. We forget that kids are listening. Paul was a lightning-quick study. I believe he could have defined *dénouement* before he was nine—and spelled it, too. At the dinner table I'd often ask the kids for help with some balky story problem, and ideas would bubble up.

You can tell what was turning over in his mind from the whimsical little booklets he'd hand-craft for my birthdays. Almost all focus on the theme of the working writer. From *Misery and Happiness* (copy-right, it says, 1964), illustrated by his sisters Jane and Anne:

"Happiness is having a good illustrator."

"Misery is not knowing if you should trust I before E except after C."

"Happiness is capturing the villain on the last page."

"Misery is having to autograph books with a blister on your finger."

"Happiness is a phone that unplugs."

When *The Birthday Tree* was published to extraordinary reviews, those who didn't know Paul very well, or at all, assumed that I was tutoring him through his pages. Far from it. Only once did I take him aside to show the power of cutting a word to sharpen a sentence, a sentence to sharpen a paragraph. For the rest I have been a happy spectator. He has a sense of privacy about his writing, and when his forthcoming novel, *Saturnalia,* was a work in progress, he would reveal nothing but the title.

Our middle child, Paul was born in Monterey, California, and grew up here in Santa Monica. He was a whiz at school who was almost never seen doing any homework. We later discovered that he was tossing it off on the school bus. Music has been a constant in his life. When he'd cut school, it was to sequester himself at the public library and listen to Brahms or baroque or chamber music. Returning home these days, he heads for the piano in the living room. He celebrated the Newbery Medal by buying a piano for his Pacific Grove home.

He's an autodidact, who taught himself to play the recorder and had a brief fling with a rented saxophone. With characteristic consideration, he'd practice in the basement to spare us the foghorn blarings and bleatings.

Paul has a sharp-shooting sense of humor. You have to listen closely, for he is soft-spoken, and his wit is apt to come out in muttered asides. Over the telephone he was reporting on his son Seth. "He's beginning to talk a lot." And then the aside: "I think it's early Serbo-Croatian."

The moment of truth for a writer is his second book. Paul picked up a mechanical pencil, his writing instrument of choice, and forged ahead on a novel about a boy, born mute, who becomes separated from his mother during a storm and must fend for himself.

In *The Half-a-Moon Inn*, the earlier foreshadowings are confirmed—the freshness of imagination, the gift for imagery ("the stars . . . sleepwalking across the sky"), and the haunting sense of fantasy in the midst of life. Miss Grackle, the villainous proprietor of a country inn, peels back the eyelids of her sleeping guests to read their dreams.

Mr. Cyrus Snype in *Coming-and-Going Men* is an itinerant cutter of silhouettes in vengeful and cunning pursuit of a human form who casts no shadow—the Devil. In his Newbery Honor Book, *Graven Images*, Paul wrote of New England villagers whispering their secrets into the ear of a binnacle boy, the carved and lacquered figure off a death ship, unaware that they are being watched by a girl who can read lips.

In a television interview Isaac Bashevis Singer said that an author needs an address. It may seem unlikely that a writer who grew up on the sunny beaches of southern California should find a literary address in New England, where Paul has set so many of his tales. I choose to think that there's more to this than the two years he lived in Bradford, New Hampshire. I regard it as a prodigal's return after more than three centuries; on his mother's side Paul has ancestors who debarked about twenty minutes after the Mayflower. The family scandal is that the kids are descendants of Mary Parsons of Northampton, Massachusetts, who was ahead of her times—she was tried as a witch years before Salem. She got off on a technicality. She wasn't a witch; but she was uppity.

Paul plans his books in detail and writes in a small hand in spiral-bound notebooks. He doesn't cross out; he erases as he goes along, so that his early drafts are swept away like bread crumbs.

Some years ago Paul and his wife, Becky, a registered nurse, bought their own home among the pines in Pacific Grove on Monterey Bay. The increase in their family can be followed in Paul's book dedications. The picture book *Rondo in C* says "For Dana, con amore." Dana was two. *Joyful Noise*, ablaze with the gold seal of the Newbery Medal, was for then four-year-old Seth, "our porch light." *Multum in parvo.*

"My father, Sid Fleischman, and sister, Anne (both standing), at the Newbery banquet, 1989.
I'm seated at the table behind them, next to Chairperson, Phyllis Van Orden."

been tutored in the womb by their mothers' heartbeats, followed by graduate work in the rocking chair. Performing poetry brings out those repetitions more forcefully than silent reading. As Donald Hall has said, "Poems happen mostly in the mouth."

Shortly before *I Am Phoenix* came out, I thought of doing another such collection but quickly dismissed the idea. Sequels were for Nancy Drew and Rocky. Instead of moving backward, I would move ahead. I would write a different sort of multi-voiced book, one with not just two voices, but twelve. This became the picture book *Rondo in C*, a book with a roomful of narrators, each of whom gives his or her associations evoked by a single piece of music played at a piano recital. Miss Dixon, I hope, would approve.

The idea of more two-voiced poems, however, wouldn't leave my head. Though I'd spent many hours watching birds, I was led to insects as a subject through books and serendipity. When I'd taken the train across Canada, I'd run out of reading material in Manitoba— it's a big country. In the Winnipeg train station I'd bought a book called *Beyond Your Doorstep* by Hal Borland. In it he mentioned his marvelous fellow nature writer Edwin Way Teale. I read several of his books, and many years later, when I happened to notice Teale on the spine of a volume in a used bookstore, it jumped out at me. The book was *The Strange Lives of Familiar Insects.* Others are touched by destiny at birth or in battle or on mountain tops; with me the scene always takes place in used bookstores.

At the time I was at work on a novel. As a dessertlike reward for finishing it, I promised myself a try at another two-voiced book, on insects. Unfortunately, that novel struck a rock and sank in Chapter 4. I certainly wasn't raised to eat dessert before finishing a meal— but what else was I to do? Trying to drive from my mind my broken pact, I started on the poem I'd been itching to write, a requiem for the insects slain by the first frost of fall. But when I put pencil to paper, nothing worked out. Perhaps this was due to the fact that I was using the first lines of the requiem mass in Latin, not their English translation. Or perhaps it was a sign from above. I tried the moth's fevered serenade to the porch light. Again, unlike with *I Am Phoenix,* the words wouldn't come, wouldn't fit, wouldn't rhyme. If this account

were rendered as a gothic novel, a storm would be bearing down at this point, the wind shrieking, "Finish your novel," the rain striking the windows with a sound remarkably like "No sequels."

I took the hint. I abandoned the book. I'd never failed to finish one book before, much less two in a row. I'm grateful I didn't know at the time how many abandoned books I would shortly claim to my credit. After snatching up the nuggets in my own gold field, I found the pickings suddenly scarcer. To avoid repeating myself, I had to tiptoe around all my previous books as well as those on the horizon. Perhaps after eight years of writing it was time to lie fallow, to soak up the rain.

Unaware that I was supposed to be lying fallow, I kept myself frantically busy. Various chimerical projects dazzled me, then disappeared. I tinkered with the requiem and the serenade over a period of months. Eventually I got them right but only after such toil that it seemed clear to me I wasn't meant to continue. I labored to salvage my novel, without success. More months passed. I kept opening my file, taking out "Requiem" and "The Moth's Serenade," reading them, and putting them back. But like a cricket in the house, they kept chirping to me. They were polished now. I forgot their difficult deliveries and grew fond of them. I couldn't let them go to waste—it would be like throwing good food away. Fall came, a time when I often start a book. Desperate to prove to myself that I could finish one, I set to work and, with much less struggle, wrote the other twelve poems. It was like building a house because you happened to have a nice pair of doors on hand.

Insects might seem an unpromising choice of subject to some. The creed "Nothing human is alien to me" would seem to exclude the doings of arthropods. I've never found them impossibly foreign, dating from the day, years ago, when I went to retrieve an open gallon of paint and found a wasp, completely enveloped in white, laboring to swim to the side of the can. I don't believe I'll be guilty of anthropomorphism if I allege that the wasp was struggling to live. I happened to be in a deep depression at the time. I found no barrier to identifying with the wasp.

Or with any of the other creatures in the book. Though some were chosen purely for their musical possibilities, most struck me as metaphors for myself. Like A. E. Housman, who could tell a line of true poetry by the bristling of his skin, I search for something—an object, a character, a historical happening, an insect— that produces a similar effect because it embodies my current circumstances. Like the self-absorbed shoemaker's apprentice in *Graven Images,* I see signs and symbols everywhere. But I write fiction, not autobiography. Just as a snowflake forms around a speck of dust, I build a story for children around that metaphorical center, a story in which my own situation is transformed past recognition. For my loyalty, once I've found my idea, is fixed entirely on the snowflake—on the facts of a digger wasp's life, not my own. Sometimes, as with a dream, even I don't understand how the book is related to me, the knowledge often arriving years later, like light traveling from the stars.

If insects seemed a strange choice of subject, two voices must seem an even stranger method. This method itself attracted me as a metaphor as much as a form. We all have more than one voice within us. A writer lives off these multiple voices. I recall an interview with John Nichols, who said there were close to two hundred characters in his novel *The Milagro Beanfield War*—and that every one of them was him. The composer Robert Schumann gave names to his three dominant voices: stormy Florestan, sweet-voiced Eusebius, and the introspective Raro. I think of my own as Eros and Thanatos, characters who inhabit us all. The former writes my comedies of courtship, my fast movements; the latter loves sculptures and silhouettes, lifeless images of the living, and writes all my darker pieces. Both are always present. Both demand their due. I feel that my best books are those they've both had a hand in, the books that embrace both spring and fall. In *Joyful Noise,* which makes a circuit of the seasons, their authorship is clear. As it is, I notice in retrospect, in that first impelling pair of poems, a love song and a requiem.

A book for two voices requires two readers. Reading it is a social, not a solitary pastime. All through my years at home it was my

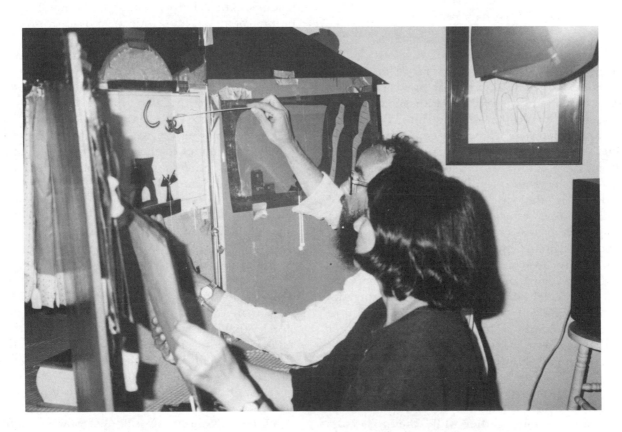

"Performing with my wife, Becky, in our annual shadow theater performance, given for friends and family"

Paul Fleischman

parents' habit after dinner to retire to the living room to play a game or two, games my sisters and I often joined. As with geologic eras, those years could be divided into Concentration and Rummy, Early Cribbage, Chess, Double Solitaire, Late Cribbage, and so on. For a time, my mother copied out the cryptogram from the *Saturday Review* and raced my father in decoding it. I'm sure that those thousands of evenings, that education in the pleasures of being with others, in the joys to be found in joint amusements impossible alone, led in large part to my two-voiced books. One hand can't produce a clap, or play a game of checkers. Two can. Synergy! The television, I might add, was in a different room and seldom seemed to be on. A family watching television together isn't engaged in a cooperative activity; they're each playing solitaire.

When I speak of this, people tell me about the entertainments of their own youth. One friend described a small cigar factory in which the workers sang together while they rolled the tobacco leaves, entertaining themselves and the people in the neighborhood, who would gather around the open doorway to listen. The sight of anyone doing something, producing something, seems to fascinate us. Think of people watching sports or construction projects. The doer acts, putting his stamp, large or small, on the world. To be the doer oneself, to sing instead of merely listening from the doorway, is an empowering experience, one that performing a poem also provides. For me, to do one's doing with others, to be one of several hands producing a clap, multiplies the magic. I grew up without brothers, in a neighborhood full of girls. Perhaps this explains the lure that groups— usually small and nondenominational—have had for me. Like many children, I also grew up apart from extended family and without a strong sense of membership in a religion, ethnic group, or community. I wanted to be a part of something larger than myself—the very thing that previous generations, builders of the suburbs and the nuclear family, had struggled to be free of. In college I discovered the Greek myths. Like a newborn duck imprinting on its mother, I decided that the Greeks were my group. I would learn by heart their history and their legends. Their heroes would be mine. I would be one of them, and, indeed, motifs from those myths appear in many of my books.

There were, however, very few ancient Greeks around to associate with. I needed a more tangible group, the sort that met on Wednesday nights. I found it, at last, in the recorder consort. Here were the pleasures of doing, of making, of playing, engaged in with six or eight others. The joys of joining voices, from sopranino to bass, of connecting people, of building music—that monument to synergy.

I've tried to put those same joys, that same excitement, interplay, spontaneity, partnership into my books of verbal duets.

I grew up acquainted with my father neither by sight nor by scent, but solely by report." This is the opening of *Rear-View Mirrors*. If you read that sentence with rhythm in mind, you'll notice that the accents fall on *up, acquainted, father, neither, sight, scent, solely,* and *report,* that the accents fall into groups of four, and that the sentence could be said to scan. The same goes for the entire book and for the nine books before it.

I never consciously set out to write metrical prose. It didn't even dawn on me that that's what I was doing until I'd finished five or six books. It was simply instinctive, and although I have no trouble reading books that don't scan, I find it impossible to write one—much as I've sometimes wished I could. For while this type of prose does have the advantage, ideally, of gracefully unfolding, never jarring the reader's sense of rhythm, it makes the writer's life miserable. If I need to say that a character is tall, I can't pick out any adjective I want: it might have to be a three-syllable word, for instance, with the accent on the first syllable. What's worse, the accents in a sentence might fall here for one reader and there for another, and they often fall in different places when I read a sentence and then reread it a moment later. Occasionally I've run into the problem of the beats in a sentence falling too obviously so that the sentence sounds like it came from "The Song of Hiawatha." In that case I have to re-phrase what I'm saying, since I don't want the reader to be conscious of the meter but only of the sense that the prose flows smoothly.

Rhythm can do more, though, than set the sense of the story to a beat; it can convey sense on its own. Like a speaker's gestures, rhythm can express and underline what a writer is saying. A striking example is the opening of an Emily Dickinson poem: "The Soul selects her own Society—/Then—shuts the Door." The four beats in the first line create the expectation of four more in the second. But instead of four beats, or even three, the line ends abruptly after only two—an aural shock power fully reinforcing the sense of the words. You really feel a door slam in your face.

In prose, the length and construction of sentences can be used to create a similar effect. Though I'd no burning desire as a child to learn to write, hearing my father's books read aloud taught me what sort of sentences to use where, an education I'd no idea I was getting. Here is the first paragraph of his *Chancy and the Grand Rascal*:

> Pushing his belongings in a squealing wheelbarrow, Chancy set out for the Ohio River fifty miles away. He clicked his heels once or twice and began to whistle through his teeth. His travels had begun.

What is there about these types of sentences that suggests, strongly to me, the sense of opening contained in their sense? Perhaps it's their gradually shrinking size, giving emphasis to the final sentence and its message—or the fact that the three beats in the last sentence, rather than the four there are room for, allows it to hang in the air an extra second, its meaning reso-nating. Writers' tastes in sentences vary. I natu-rally grew up absorbing my father's, and though I might not be able to pinpoint the reason, I can feel that those lines are just right for an opening.

Even more effectively, rhythm and sentence structure can be used to create a sense of closing at the end of a chapter or book. Here is the ending of *Path of the Pale Horse* in which the apprentice Lep and his master, Dr. Peale, are leaving yellow-fever ravaged Philadelphia:

> "We did what we could," Dr. Peale spoke up, viewing the streets in which they'd battled the fever. He turned toward Lep.
> "And Mrs. Uffington was correct."
> He cast a glance at Lep's Latin book.
> "*Discipulus bonus habeo,*" he stated, indi-cating that he had an excellent pupil. Lep looked up into his master's eyes.
> "*Magister bonus habeo,*" he replied.

Parallelism is a powerful tool, as debaters and speech writers know well. The two linked Latin phrases serve to snap the book shut with an almost audible click, reinforced by the near rhyme of *eyes* and *replied*.

Sentences not only have rhythm and struc-ture; they have sound. Every word is a con-glomeration of vowels and consonants. And though this aspect of words can't often be used to convey sense on its own, exploiting it can add a strong aural element to prose that pro-vides pleasure to the ears over and above the pleasure given by the sense of the story.

Consider alliteration. In the course of a writing workshop I once gave, a woman wrote a paragraph dealing with a character's traumatic first day in a nursing home. Her last line was "All those rooms in a row." If you doubt the power of alliteration, compare that sentence to "All those rooms in a line." Same sense, but what a difference in sound. And what a differ-ence in the strength of the line—all because of the repetition of r. For this reason you'll notice alliteration's use, and overuse, everywhere—in the titles of books and movies, in advertis-ing, in the names of breakfast cereals. Part of its power, I think, derives from the fact that when we read "Frosted Flakes" on a box, the repetition of *f* is both aural and visual. This is also the problem with alliteration: it draws too much attention to itself. Used judiciously, it's fine. But I don't want "Peter Piper picked a peck of pickled peppers" cropping up in my writing. I prefer to be a bit less obvious, alliterating the second syllables of words or using words with the same sound but different spellings (i.e. *cruel kindness*) or words with the same letters but different sounds (i.e. *thin tendrils*) to avoid bombarding the reader with both visual and aural repetitions.

Vowels, of course, can be repeated as well. Indeed, I've found repeating vowels and using rhymes and near-rhymes much more effective than alliteration: the sounds of *I* and *eye* are identical, much closer than those of Peter and Piper but not overly attention-attracting since they begin with different letters. The vagaries of English spelling come to the writer's aid here, allowing the writer to put *sign* nearby *wine* and *stein* without drawing unwanted notice.

At first, I only picked a word for its vowels and consonants in the case, say, of a place name that might appear only once in a book. Since I could choose any name I wanted, I realized that I might as well do so with an eye and ear to the other sounds in the sentence. Gradually it dawned on me that every word could be subjected to this test. Which explains why I only write one page a day. Of course, it's simply not possible to make every sentence a garden of aural delights. Here is the first paragraph from the first story in *Coming-and-Going Men*:

> Fresh snow had fallen that morning on the road leading to New Canaan, Vermont. A fresh catalogue of tracks had accumulated since: weasel, wolverine, chipmunk, mink, plus the trail of an apparently three-legged creature whose prints, two very large and one small, stretched miles away to the south. At their head, spruce staff in hand, trudged Mr. Cyrus Snype, cutter of silhouettes.

I spent a long time writing that paragraph and managed to get in lots of repetitions: the short *a*'s and hard *c*'s in catalogue, *tracks,* and *accumulated,* the near-rhyme of *chipmunk* and *mink,* the many *s*'s in the final sentence. If my tongue gets twisted reading the paragraph aloud, I know that I've done a good job. I don't want the repetitions too rife, however. "I caught this

morning morning's minion, kingdom of daylight's dauphin" belongs in poetry, not prose. For better or worse, most paragraphs don't offer one the opportunity to sound like Gerard Manley Hopkins. People "walk downstairs" and "sit down to eat" and "have seconds of pie" in my books, without any aural fireworks, just as they do in other writers'.

But, if I can please my readers' ears while telling my tale, such that a listener who knew no English would enjoy it read aloud purely for its music, so much the better. Since I think the sense of my stories out in some detail before I put them into words, the spontaneous, joyful, serendipitous, and most satisfying side of writing for me is trying to do exactly that: moving this clause to take advantage of that rhyme, finding a four-syllable word for slender, playing with the length of the sentences. Giving the sense a sound.

> My father was in the shower when his Newbery call came. I was in a dentist's chair. Apparently genes do indeed rule our lives. The receptionist told me to call home before leaving. When I did, my two-year-old, Dana, answered, then his older brother Seth took the phone and spoke the words "New baby." I paused. I was not aware that my wife and I were planning to have a third child. "You're kidding," I said. Then Becky got on and made a minor adjustment in pronunciation. "You're kidding," I said, and said again, and again. And occasionally still say.

At the author's request, this essay is comprised of articles originally appearing in *Horn Book Magazine;* written by Paul Fleischman, except as noted: "Sid Fleischman," July/August 1987; "Sound and Sense," September/October, 1986; "Newbery Medal Acceptance" and "Paul Fleischman," by Sid Fleischman, July/August 1989.

BIBLIOGRAPHY

FOR CHILDREN

Fiction:

The Birthday Tree, illustrated by Marcia Sewall, Harper, 1979.

The Half-a-Moon Inn, illustrated by Kathy Jacobi, Harper, 1980.

Graven Images: Three Stories, illustrated by Andrew Glass, Harper, 1982.

The Animal Hedge (picture book), illustrated by Lydia Dabcovich, Dutton, 1983.

Finzel the Farsighted, illustrated by Marcia Sewall, Dutton, 1983.

Path of the Pale Horse, Harper, 1983.

Phoebe Danger, Detective, in the Case of the Two-Minute Cough, illustrated by Margot Apple, Houghton, 1983.

Coming-and-Going Men: Four Tales, illustrated by Randy Gaul, Harper, 1985.

I Am Phoenix: Poems for Two Voices, illustrated by Ken Nutt, Harper, 1985.

Rear-View Mirrors, Harper, 1986.

Joyful Noise: Poems for Two Voices, illustrated by Eric Beddows, Harper, 1988.

Rondo in C, illustrated by Janet Wentworth, Harper, 1988.

Saturnalia, Harper, 1990.

Shadow Play (picture book), illustrated by Eric Beddows, Harper, 1990.

The Borning Room, HarperCollins, 1991.

Time Train, illustrated by Claire Ewart, Harper-Collins, 1991.

Bull Run, illustrated by David Frampton, Harper-Collins, 1993.

Nonfiction:

Townsend's Warbler, HarperCollins, 1992.

Copier Creations, illustrated by David Cain, HarperCollins, 1993.

Contributor to various journals and magazines, including *Horn Book.*

Belinda Hurmence

1921-

WHERE I COME FROM

Belinda Hurmence, with her husband, Howard, at home with two of their dachshunds, 1981

I won an essay contest when I was a sixteen-year-old senior in high school and that cinched it—I would be a writer.

The year was 1938. The U.S. Post Office Department had invited high school students across the nation to mark the twenty-fifth anniversary of airmail in America by participating in an essay contest. Winners from the forty-eight states would fly to Washington, D.C., for a week of sight-seeing that included a tour of the White House and an audience with the first lady, Eleanor Roosevelt.

My entry won for the state of Texas. I had just six days to get ready for the big trip and six dollars in savings to spend on a new wardrobe. (The Great Depression of the 1930s gripped the country, remember.)

For five dollars my talented seamstress neighbor cut down and sewed an old dress suit of her husband's to fit me. My mother, with equal talent, stitched a one-dollar length of crepe de chine into a blouse. My workman father, who ordinarily left all family clothing purchases to my mother, went downtown on his own initiative and bought the hat he thought I should wear to Washington. It was a white, felt, Texas cowgirl hat that tied under the chin.

"I just hope it fits," I lied.

"It'll fit," Dad said confidently. "I tried it on myself."

"But it's loose on my head. It'll fall off."

"That's why you've got one with strings on it, daughter—so it won't fall off."

"I guess it's the brim that bothers me. Don't you think it's too big?"

"Girl, you *want* it big. You want all Washington to know where you come from."

At the Wichita Falls airport, the local Sears, Roebuck presented me with an orchid. The chamber of commerce presented me with an envelope of welcome spending money. A newspaper photographer arrived.

"Wear your hat for the picture," my father said. He retrieved it from behind my back where it dangled out of sight (I hoped) and set it rakishly on my head.

"Say cheese," said the photographer.

I gave a sickly smile and a limp, white-gloved hand to the town postmaster. I climbed the two-step ladder into Braniff's finest passenger airplane, its egg-beater engine roared, and off we flew to Washington.

The essay contest winner and her white felt hat, on her way to Washington, D.C., 1938

We flew from Wichita Falls to Washington by way of New York City, if that makes sense. The airplane made stops at nine intermediate airports. I ate three airline meals aloft. The trip took all day long. A representative from the postmaster general's office met me at the Washington airport and drove me to the Mayflower Hotel where I was to stay, along with the other state winners. I arrived there after dark but still in time for the winners' mixer in one of the hotel's social rooms.

At age sixteen, I already knew there were pleasures I enjoyed far more than plunging into a roomful of strangers. I had devised a system, however, that worked pretty well for one of my limited experience: I browsed the refreshment table. For one thing, I got a crack at the nut bowl before all the cashews disappeared; and for another, one of those strangers, also checking out the refreshments, might remark, "What's in that delicious chicken spread, do you suppose?"

Then I could say, "Mm-m-m . . . chicken?" and an acquaintance might begin.

At the Mayflower mixer, a dainty girl wearing a New Hampshire badge poured me a cup of punch. "I don't have to look at your badge," she said. "I knew you were a Texan when you came in the room, the minute I saw your hat."

The delegate from North Carolina saluted me with her cup. "Hey, Tex," she said.

My father was right. I had been in the town less than an hour, and already all Washington knew where I'd come from.

But I was not born in Texas, and I have moved other places since; I have lived in North Carolina for many years now. So where's my home? Where does anybody in this transitory world come from? Is home, in a sense, more a philosophical location than geographical?

I had occasion to ponder those questions while I was writing *Dixie in the Big Pasture,* set in the Oklahoma Territory, in the land the nomadic Kiowas called the Big Pasture. All four of my grandparents homesteaded there in 1907, and I was born in Oklahoma, in the tiny town of Grandfield, only fourteen years after the territory became the forty-sixth state in our nation.

My aunt Dixie, who is the heroine of *Dixie* (and my heroine in real life too), says the Big Pasture pioneers, when first they met, always asked one another, "Where do you come from?" because everybody there had come from somewhere else. Aunt Dixie had traveled by the Rock Island Railway from Tennessee with her parents (my grandparents) and her brothers. Her youngest brother, fourteen-year-old Warren Watson, was to become my father. If the Watsons hadn't homesteaded in Oklahoma, they would never have met the Bonnells. Ah, history!

In the Big Pasture, Warren admired a trio of pretty girls, the Bonnell sisters, and over a ten-year period he escorted all three, together or singly, to the play parties and picnics and schoolhouse socials that the pioneers organized for their leisure time. The Bonnell family had come to the Big Pasture from Kansas, over the Old Chisholm Trail, in two covered wagons.

By 1919 Warren's squiring of the Bonnell sisters had narrowed down to Eula, the middle girl, and the couple married. They began their long life together (seventy-two years!) in Oklahoma, where their two daughters were born— first, my dear sister Faun, and then Billie (that is, me; I changed my name to Belinda because I thought Billie sounded frivolous for a serious writer).

I have been a serious writer for as long as I can remember, so perhaps this is the generic "place" I come from—a state called Writing. When I was four years old, I composed a poem, which I recited at a Sunday school program. The applause that rewarded my performance gave me immense satisfaction and set me on the path to poethood. Read these immortal lines:

> I like the dog, but the dog runs away.
> Come back, dog, come here and play.

Even better than applause, a poem I wrote for a contest in first grade won the prize: a copy of Beatrix Potter's *Peter Rabbit*. This poem has not survived in my memory, but I haven't forgotten what my teacher wrote on the flyleaf of my prize book:

Dear Billie,
I am very proud of you. *You are a good writer!* [Italics mine.] Always remember your first teacher,

Mrs. E. T. Quinlan

My first critical acclaim, at age six! No question of my vocation after a review like that. My published books, by and large, have all been well received over the years, but only Mrs. E. T. Quinlan's flattering words remain with me verbatim. Mrs. E. T. Quinlan, wherever you are, I do, I do remember you!

When I was thirteen, my English teacher, Shumake Baber, gave two of my poems to a journalist friend of his who printed them in his column in the local newspaper. After our father died in 1993, my sister Faun and I sat down together and sorted through his papers. We came across a brown and crumbling newspaper clipping that he had pasted in an album. There they were again, the two poems of my adolescence.

"These are *good*," said Faun, my loyal sister.

In the intervening years, I had forgotten those verses. I had forgotten that they had appeared in print.

My first published work—*forgotten?*

Well, Faun was wrong. The poems weren't good; in fact, they were truly forgettable. What in the world possessed Mr. Baber to give those callow rhymes to his friend for publication? Perhaps he did it out of astonishment over a student who was willing to rewrite. Because in seventh grade, I loved rewriting more than I did the writing. I still do.

On a first draft, I dread that my work is tiresome and will bore a reader; I worry that I

Father, Warren Watson, at the age of fourteen in 1907, the year the Watson family homesteaded the Oklahoma Territory

will grow tired of it myself, and that I will abandon it. A few times that has happened. But no more than a very few times. Usually I am a pretty good finisher—and what a relief it is to write that final word. Done at last! Now the fun of rewriting can begin.

Did I say *fun?* Yes. I agonize so over the first draft that to me the work of rewriting becomes play, a refreshing pastime, like puzzling out a cryptogram (which I also delight in doing). I enjoy making the changes that help the puzzle of my writing come slowly clearer, that bring it into focus so that it makes sense to the reader.

Back in the seventh grade, Mr. Baber said to me, "Why don't you try writing a story?"

I must have looked blank. "What about?"

It was his turn to look blank, but he quickly rallied. "The best stories come from authors who are familiar with their material. Write about something you know well."

In Mr. Baber's class, we had studied Longfellow's poem *Hiawatha,* and I had memorized many passages from it. I had also begun reading the sentimental novels Faun devoured by the dozens; the two of us thrilled to almost any tale of romance. So, since I knew *Hiawatha* well, I essentially rewrote Longfellow's poem into sentimental prose (the part where Hiawatha marries Minnehaha).

I described the countryside where the newlyweds traveled on their honeymoon; in fact, I wrote more about the forest they journeyed through than I did about the bride and groom. A book about tropical plants from the library supplied me with names for the flowers that Minnehaha exclaimed over in my story. I saw to it that she exclaimed a lot over the local vegetation.

The exotic blossoms bougainvillea and frangipani sounded exactly right for such an exotic couple, I believed, so I put them in. I filled the forest of my story with loquat and papaya trees, never asking myself if tropical plants had grown by the shores of Lake Superior, where the young brave Hiawatha was supposed to have lived.

I've since become more careful about getting the shrubbery I write about appropriate to the climate and setting. To my credit, though, appropriate or not, I did go to the library for that book of tropical plants, and I used it. Writing a story for Mr. Baber taught me what poetry hadn't—that *all* stories require research.

And Mr. Baber's class taught me that I was not a poet. My tactful teacher knew what he was about in hinting that I might try moving on to fiction. Never, I realized, would my leaden verses approach the lilting ballads we memorized in his class. And the research I had done for my story pleased me in some obscure way I had yet to analyze. I renounced my career in poetry and took up short stories.

In my college years I worked on the literary magazine of Hardin Junior College (now Midwestern State University) in Wichita Falls. I worked on the literary magazine of the University of Texas at Austin. I joined the Writers' Club. I took all the creative writing courses I could and studied journalism—but not for long. I quickly learned that I was no better a journalist than I was a poet. I wrote stories that I felt sure the *Saturday Evening Post* would want to publish. I wrote stories in the style of *Atlantic Monthly, Cosmopolitan, Harper's* magazine.

The three Bonnell sisters, with the author's mother, Eula (left), about 1911

Belinda (right) at age thirteen, with her mother and sister, Faun

J. Frank Dobie, the great folklorist of the southwest, and my teacher at UT, encouraged me to try out one of my *Harper's* style stories on the magazine. He showed me what a professional manuscript ought to look like, and assured me that my writing merited publication. He told me the name of the editor I should write to, and gave me the address.

"Feel free to say you're writing at my suggestion," he said. "My name will get you a reading, although it won't get your story published."

I knew better. If Mr. Dobie said my writing was good enough to publish, any magazine would be honored to publish it. I typed the story nicely, wrote the cover letter, and sent the manuscript off to *Harper's* to await their acceptance and enclosed check.

I had not long to wait. Within a week the *Harper's* envelope showed up in the mail, with a rejection slip inside. At the bottom of the bland, printed message, someone had scribbled in pencil, "Send self-addressed stamped envelope for return of manuscript."

What had gone wrong? Nothing. I had merely been introduced to one of publishing's standards: always enclose SASE for return of manuscript. Today a publisher would simply pitch any manuscript lacking the SASE into the wastebasket. Standard.

Rejection is also standard for writers. Most beginning writers take a long time, as I did, to understand that the best teacher in the world cannot get a student's story published on his or her say-so. Some would-be writers never learn this. They believe that if they only pull the right string, publication will follow.

But the story has to make its way on its own merits, and on the author's persistence. I sometimes think persistence counts for more than merit. It has never been an editor's job to go out looking for some discouraged writer who has given up on trying to market his or her talent.

The Japanese bombed Pearl Harbor the December before I graduated from the university in June. Young men who enlisted in the armed forces began leaving the campus less than a month after Pearl Harbor. I, too, wished to join the war effort. I applied for admission to the Officer's Training Corps for women on the recruiter's promise that I would be allowed to graduate before reporting for training.

The wheels of government turned nearly as slowly in 1942 as they do now. By the time the corps got around to accepting my application, I had finished college and taken a job in another branch of military service. I rented a room in a decaying mansion on West Sixth Street in Austin and went to work as a secretary-typist at Camp Swift's Station Hospital, not far from the capital city.

I had learned my shorthand and typing in high school. I figured that these skills would help me get a job after college, and they did, but even then I knew I was preparing myself for the mechanical work that goes with being a writer.

My old high school shorthand and typing have served me well in that respect. And I've always loved the tools associated with writing. Even today I'd rather nose around an office supply store than look at clothes in a dress shop.

How I wish I'd kept a journal of the two years I worked at Camp Swift! I remember that the highway from Austin trapped us commuters in one convoy of army trucks after another.

At the post itself, miles of chain-link fence enclosed raw, new wooden structures that sprawled over the dusty Texas plain. Inside, Jeeps shot like waterbugs from one building to another. At the hospital complex, where I reported for work, long ramps led to the various wards for medical, surgical, and dental services.

On my first day there, the personnel officer rushed me by Jeep to a separate outpatient building where innoculations were being given and physical exams performed on an entire company of soldiers due to ship out that night. I was to help process their records until the task was completed and was instructed to work through the night, if necessary.

The overwhelmed corporal struggling to register a bewildered bunch of soldiers milling around his desk did not even ask my name. "Check everybody's dogtags against this file— name, rank, and serial number," he said. "Send the matches to EENT. All others wait outside until I can get to them. Route them from GU to EENT, *then* to cardio, *then* for shots, in that order, understand?"

I didn't understand, but no matter. I'd heard the words dogtags and file and thought I'd catch on to the rest as it cropped up. "Let me see your dogtags," I said, reaching for the metal identity tags chained about the neck of the first soldier.

Pandemonium cropped up right away. I was bending over the card files when a great shout rang out. The building shook from stampeding feet. I looked up to see a crowd of naked soldiers all fighting to retreat through the single narrow door they had just entered. They had been sent by the lone corporal to the examining rooms, required to strip, and in returning to the registration desk certainly had not expected to find a female intruder at the corporal's side.

"Just turn your back," the laconic corporal told me. That seemed the best, indeed the only, solution. There was no unoccupied room or office in the building where I could closet myself to work. Some kind of screen might have helped, but the outpatient building was new and still short on everything—space, personnel, equipment; besides, modesty screens would probably have rated way down on anybody's order list.

The stampede repeated itself twice more before my first dispatches caught up to the corporal's. The soldiers I registered improvised their own modesty screens with their shed cloth-

ing, and the rest of the day proceeded with no further shocks.

The corporal and I jeeped to the mess hall for a ten-minute lunch at noon and again at five for a ten-minute supper. My Austin car pool returned to the city without me. The corporal and I finished our work at eleven that night. I never saw him again after that.

Another Jeep took me to the civilian barracks where I showered and fell onto a bare mattress in a vacant cubicle. Here there were plenty of empty cubicles and beds to choose from: at that time the hospital was staffed at perhaps no more than one-quarter capacity. Later the camp would have to build more barracks to accommodate the civilian workers required to live on post.

When I reported for my second day of work, the personnel officer assigned me to the X-ray service. Its chief, Major Guy A. Finney, was a gangling, fatherly roentgenologist from Topeka. I liked him at once, and the job fascinated me. When Major Finney saw how interested I was in the work he did, he took it upon himself to extend my education.

He read films every morning and, after he dictated his reports on them, showed me what to look for in the films. He described treatments he predicted the attending doctors would follow in each case. He invited me to observe patients under fluoroscopy in the X-ray department, and many times arranged for me to observe interesting or unusual surgical cases in the operating room.

I know that Major Finney liked that I could spell, and that I pored over the *Gray's Anatomy* that he kept on his desk. He told me that he had hoped his son, who was my age, would go to medical school, but the boy had been drafted into the army. Major Finney had then enlisted in the Army Medical Corps.

"I bet you'd make a good doctor," he told me. "With the war siphoning off their graduates, the medical schools are more receptive to women students now than they have ever been."

I didn't know what a doctor's education cost, but I knew it was a lot. I had worked all through college to pay my tuition fees, but there had been plenty of other expenses for my parents to meet. I knew I didn't want to ask them for any more financial support.

"I could never afford medical school," I told the major.

"Depends on which medical school," he said. "I've got some fair connections that might help."

I pointed out to him that my liberal arts degree lacked almost all the science courses required for pre-med students. "Besides," I said, "what I really want to do is write."

The major stared in disbelief at the stack of film reports I had just typed. "You *want* to write stuff like that?"

"That's not writing, it's typing," I said. "I'm going to write the Great American Novel." I meant it as a joke. I didn't want to admit that I couldn't yet write a publishable short story.

Major Finney responded in perfect seriousness. "Well, I don't know what it takes to write a novel," he said, "but whatever it takes, good luck to you."

My feeble joke had served its purpose. I didn't have to admit anything.

A great many writers feel insecure about their writing, as I did, and do. I imagine those naked soldiers felt the same, that first day at Camp Swift—exposed, their privacy violated. That's how I feel when someone looks over my shoulder at what I'm writing. It's how I feel when people ask what I'm writing. We are all vulnerable about something. My friend George Davis used to say that only embezzlers were as secretive about their craft as writers. I tend to evade questioning, to say frankly but vaguely, "I'm working on a novel for middle-grade readers."

Camp Swift gave me more than a job; it also brought me a lively, if fleeting, social life. All the young soldiers on the post were on their way to somewhere else. For their brief sojourn there, the hierarchy arranged structured diversion for these soldiers. Often the nurses, female technicians, and workers at the hospital would be asked to the recreation hall for an evening's entertainment—a variety show, for example, or a dance.

I went to many dances at Camp Swift. On one occasion, for an event something like a high school homecoming, I attended as the Sweetheart of X ray, with a raffish bunch of hospital workers for my escorts.

Whenever I worked overtime, or went to a dance at Camp Swift, I usually spent the night in the civilian barracks. I enjoyed "sleeping over" there, because I had become friends with a lot of the nurses; we often sat up talking until very late, the way girls sometimes do in dormitories.

Hazel Gray, a lab technician friend, dropped in on one of these sessions one night. She had just discovered that a course in petroleum testing was being offered at the university, in the evenings, and she wanted me to sign up for it with her.

I said, "What makes you think I'm interested in petroleum testing?"

"It's a new job skill," she said.

"I have a job," I pointed out.

"Yes, but you might not have it long if the war ended tomorrow."

I can't remember why I let her persuade me. Everybody knew the war wasn't going to end tomorrow. Maybe I'd grown tired of dancing.

Our course taught us how to perform a few standard tests on oil samples. Instruction lasted only a few weeks. In the Engineering Building where it was given, a studious-looking fellow, Howard Hurmence, kept coming into the lab to confer with our teacher. One night he introduced himself to Hazel and me and offered us a ride home after class.

In the car, he told us a little about himself. He had recently completed his course work for his Ph.D. in chemical engineering and was presently engaged in writing.

"Writing . . . ?" I said, intrigued.

Howard smiled. "Sort of. It's my dissertation. It's called 'The Separation of Olefins from Diolefins by Extractive Fractional Distillation.'"

Hazel and I burst out laughing.

Howard pretended to take offense. "I think you're rude," he said. "I think I'll make you walk the rest of the way home." By then, of course, we had arrived.

Hazel and I went out with Howard and his roommate, Bill Randall, several times after that evening. We went together on picnics; we canoed on Lake Austin. I liked Howard. I liked his intelligence and his subtle sense of humor. He was unlike any of the boys I was used to, perhaps because he was older—in his thirties already. I'd just turned twenty-two, that second year at Camp Swift.

Hazel liked Bill, too, but both of these young men soon left Austin to work for a government agency called Rubber Reserve. The nation had lost its access to natural rubber when the Japanese took over the great plantations in the South Pacific. All of those lumbering convoy trucks and, in a sense, the whole army, ran on rubber. The search was on for a pro-

At Camp Swift Station Hospital as the "Sweetheart of X ray," 1943

cess to make a viable synthetic rubber. Howard's timely doctoral work (culminating in the dissertation with the title Hazel and I had thought so funny) had coincided with Rubber Reserve's search.

Shortly after our course ended at the university, the Phillips Petroleum Company offered Hazel and me jobs in its laboratory in Dallas. My parents had by then moved to Dallas, and I decided to take the job. Ironically, Hazel was the one who decided to continue working at Camp Swift.

After being out in the world on my own for two years, I found living in a Dallas suburb confining. True, by moving there I had gained more time for writing, but I missed my friends in Austin and Camp Swift. My conventional parents cramped my style. I knew I should be grateful to these good and decent people for providing me with a peaceful, well-kept home—but I wasn't. I wished I had never gone there.

Looking back on that time, I can't say the way I felt was wrong. I believe that grown children need to be out from under the parental roof, if at all possible, and they deserve the goad of misery to drive them forth, if that's what it takes.

To make matters worse, my writing was going nowhere. No editors took any interest in the stories I sent them, and I couldn't blame them. My stories seemed empty and shallow, even to me. I blamed my wretched writing on Dallas. As soon as the war ended, I vowed, I would head for Manhattan and the literary life.

I felt at home in New York City from the day I arrived there. Its grid plan made it an easy place for me to learn my way around. Its subways were swift and cheap. I could go anywhere in the five boroughs for a nickel.

Living quarters were almost impossible to come by in 1945, though, and horribly expensive. The real estate department of my Wall Street employer, the Mutual Life Insurance Company, finally located a large studio apartment for me on East Seventy-second Street at a rental I could afford. It had been frozen at fifty dollars a month by wartime regulation and remained at that figure for the three years that I lived there.

I bought a studio couch, one chair, and a card table from a furniture store on Second Avenue. I moved in, ecstatic—a New Yorker on her own!

The job in Wall Street was a perfect one for me. I never had to work overtime. The firm allowed generous breaks, morning and afternoon, and I could use those breaks (and the Mutual's typewriter) to type up my stories.

My job in the firm's securities investment department called for me to transcribe reports on various prospectuses and to type endless spreadsheets. I wish I could say I tried to learn about investments and the workings of Wall Street, the way I had worked at learning about X-ray and medical practice at Camp Swift. But in New York I was bent on pursuing a career in writing.

After a day's work, I subwayed from Wall Street to Columbia University. Columbia offered night classes that seemed designed for my schedule. There, once or twice a week, various professional writers taught classes in the novel, the short story, playwriting, etc. In between, students produced the work that would be critiqued in class. I wrote obsessively on weekends in my apartment.

I found I could write other places as well as at home, and I did. I wrote on the subway going to work, often standing up in rush hour. I wrote on buses, in the luncheonette, between acts at the theater.

I went a lot to the theater, once I'd got settled in my apartment. Broadway was a lively place in the 1940s. Dozens of new plays opened in a season, and seats in the peanut gallery cost only $1.25. A play or a musical had to close mighty fast for me to miss seeing it!

And the theater brought me a perspective that went far beyond the scene before me on the stage. I wondered if the structure of plays might be applied to short stories. I weeded a lot of description out of my stories and tried different ways of transitions. Brief notes of encouragement began replacing rejection forms on the stories magazines sent back to me.

In 1946 Columbia hired George Davis to teach a night course in the short story, and I hastened to register. By day, Mr. Davis was associate managing and fiction editor at *Mademoiselle* magazine. He was a witty, quirky man, who had come to *Mademoiselle* from the old

Vanity Fair. He lived in a comfortable New York brownstone house which constantly sheltered writers, painters, actors, and musicians in the various times of their need. He was unfailingly generous to those struggling to make their way in the arts. At Columbia, our class fell under his spell.

Mr. Davis taught us details about writing that most of us had never thought of—about writing in scenes and using dialog, about how crucial accuracy was (research!), and how important the names of characters were. He talked about simple visual things, like using short paragraphs to make a typed page look clean and readable.

I'd never heard such talk from any of my teachers. In those days that sort of information simply wasn't readily available to the novice. Today there are scores of books about characters, setting, dialog, plotting, submitting manuscripts. My writers' group keeps a reference shelf of these books handy. But in my apprenticeship I'd had to write from instinct, making the same mistakes over and over again.

A year went by. I registered for another Davis class. I couldn't tell whether he liked my stories or not. Work was never graded in his class. He simply read everybody's stories aloud and asked what we thought of them, then he commented on our comments. He made us careful of what we said, for we hated to sound foolish to this sophisticated editor.

Just before Christmas, a week after I had turned in a story to him called "Big Guy," I arrived at class and he handed me an envelope with my name on the outside. I still have the letter. Typed on *Mademoiselle's* prim white, gray-lettered stationery, it read, without preamble:

> *Mademoiselle* would like to buy your story. I gave it to the editors without comment, and the reactions were unanimously for buying it. Naturally I am most pleased, with a qualm or two about the class. It seems best that we keep it a secret at the moment; do you mind? It leads to a confusion of issues at this stage, or could; and I even hesitated about telling you until the end of the term. However, with Christmas and all, I didn't have the heart to hold back. May the magazine pay you three hundred for First North American and Canadian Serial Rights?
>
> *George Davis*

Mentor George Davis at Mademoiselle

"*Oh,*" I said. I must have sounded as though I had been punched; I felt that way. I gripped my desk. My heart thudded; I drew deep breaths. What if I did something idiotic, like collapse?

At his desk Mr. Davis organized the week's stories in the order in which he meant to read them. He did not meet my eyes but he smiled faintly.

I thought the class would never end. I couldn't trust myself to comment on the evening's stories. I could only think of the incredible letter and how I longed to rush home with it so I could reread it as many times as I chose. I was dying to look in a mirror, to see how different I appeared, for I was no longer a secretary, or a typist, or an ordinary student. That night I had become an AUTHOR!

"Miss Watson," said Mr. Davis when the class ended, "may I consult with you for a moment?"

He shuffled papers until the last student had departed. Then he said to me, "Perhaps you'd like to think my letter over. Sleep on it."

"Not at all!" I said quickly. "No indeed. Three hundred is fine."

"Then we're in business," he said. "And since we'll be working together on the story, may I call you Billie?" (In the 1940s, students and teachers were fairly formal in the way they addressed one another.) Needless to say, I gave Mr. Davis permission to stop calling me Miss Watson.

We walked downstairs and out of the building together. George hailed a taxi heading downtown and said he would drop me off wherever I liked. In the taxi, I tried to tell him how much selling the story meant to me.

"I'm a writer myself," he said. "I haven't forgotten my own first sale. I know there's nothing like it. Nothing. And it only happens once."

Mademoiselle bought a second of my stories not long after that first sale, and what I felt was delight, of course, but George was right. The second time I wasn't about to faint. I felt confident. I was sure that this second success meant that I had made my start in literature, that fame and fortune lay ahead for me. What it really meant was that my life was soon to take an unexpected turn. Two, in fact.

That spring I had a telephone call from my Austin friend Howard Hurmence. He had left Rubber Reserve and was coming to work for Allied Chemical in Manhattan. Since I was by now an old hand at living in the city, he hoped I would show him the ropes.

Gladly, I told him. I hadn't forgotten what a clever fellow Howard was and how I'd liked his sense of humor.

He called me again the first day he arrived, from the St. George Hotel in Brooklyn where he planned to stay while he hunted for an apartment. Could I possibly meet him for dinner? The St. George had recommended Keen's Chop House for its thick mutton chops.

So I met him at Keen's, which I had heard about, but where, because of my limited budget, I had certainly never dined. Hundreds, if not thousands, of numbered clay pipes covered the low ceiling of the venerable restaurant. A steward brought Howard, who was then a pipe smoker, a new clay pipe to be numbered and stored for him with the others on the ceiling. (Is it still there today, I wonder? With that enormous collection of pipes as its signature, does Keen's dare have a nonsmoking section?)

The next night I met Howard for drinks at Fraunces Tavern, which was near the Mutual's offices, and we dined *italiano* afterwards in the Village. With so many wonderful eating places to choose from, Howard pledged he would take me out to dinner to a different restaurant every night. That was fine with me! But then he discovered the Queen of the Ocean, just around the corner from my apartment. There the waiter draped us in huge cotton bibs and served us beautiful broiled lobsters dripping with hot tarragon butter sauce. Howard modified his pledge. Queen of the Ocean was our favorite restaurant, he said, and we would eat there at least once a week. That was fine with me, too.

Meanwhile, the term at Columbia neared its close. My short-story class was about to end, and George told us that it would be his last, for he had grown weary of teaching. I said good-bye to him almost tearfully.

But this needn't be the end, George protested; he offered me a job at *Mademoiselle.*

"Our assistant fiction editor has resigned, for reasons of health," he said. "The work involves a lot of reading and correspondence. It's demanding, more complex than you'd think, but I know you could handle it. Would you be interested?"

When I hesitated, he suggested that I think it over before deciding. Sleep on it, he said.

I did want to think carefully about the job, tempting as it was. I liked working in the ma-

"Howard, pipe smoker, the year he came to New York," 1947

jestic canyons of Wall Street. The Mutual provided me with many benefits—it had even found me an apartment—and although the work paid modestly, it suited my needs perfectly. I was able to leave the office without a care. At night, I still had the time and energy to go to the theater, to meet Howard for dinner, write on weekends, study at Columbia. Should I give up this ideal situation for a job that George had called demanding? I shared my misgivings with Howard.

He said, "Try thinking of either job as your lifetime work. Will you be happy living under constant pressure, as George warns you will? Or would you rather type spreadsheets the rest of your life?"

"Say no more," I said. "You just made up my mind."

I've mentioned George's generosity. Three hundred dollars is not generous compensation for a story in today's market, but at the time of my first sale, it represented the magazine's highest payment for a short work of fiction; after I went to work for *Mademoiselle,* I learned that George had fought to get it for me. Management had been reluctant to pay their top rate to an unknown like me, but George had insisted.

He took my part in other ways, too. He assigned me tasks that taught me about the magazine's operations, tasks that surely were not in any job description for an assistant fiction editor. He gave me nonfiction articles to rewrite ("run it through the typewriter," he'd say), and introduced me to literary agents. He sent me on "shoots" of people in the news, fashion, and in the arts; to movie screenings and play openings that the magazine wanted covered. In short, George looked after my interests at *Mademoiselle,* and later at another magazine; we became close personal friends.

Howard and I married in the spring of 1948, at city hall, on our lunch hour (in those days, people in the arts in New York considered it chic to get married at city hall). Our only child, daughter Leslie, was born in 1949 in New York at the old Gotham Hospital. New York is filled with people who come from somewhere else; Leslie is one of the few true Manhattanites I know, and she came to us in true literary Manhattan style—between magazines.

By then George had left *Mademoiselle* to start up the new magazine *Flair,* financed by the Cowles family, publishers of a chain of midwestern newspapers. As soon as I'd found a nurse for Leslie, I too went to work at *Flair,* first as fiction editor, later as executive editor.

The new venture was a luxury periodical, in appearance and content something like *Vogue.* Fleur Cowles headed up the editorial staff. She was a petite blonde, talented, charming and soft-spoken, but also a steely businesswoman with a cruel streak. *Publishers Weekly* titled a profile about our chief "The Hand That Cradles the Rock."

Mrs. Cowles's interest in *Flair* waned when advertising revenues failed to meet her expectations, and she allowed management to end the periodical's short life—prematurely, most of her staffers thought.

The pressures of magazine work grew as I struggled to balance my job with marriage, a home life, and the care of an infant after hours and on weekends. I felt overworked. I had long ago put my own writing on hold. Early in my term at *Mademoiselle* the concentration on other

Baby daughter, Leslie, at a picnic in Central Park, 1950

writers' stories and articles had dried up my own "juices."

Women of the 1940s juggled their careers with marriage and children just as today's women continue to do. Our baby took up more and more of our lives—and this little six-pound girl used more than her share of our already crowded apartment. I complained that I had no place to write, even if I had the time.

Howard sympathized. He had never felt thoroughly at home in Manhattan, as I did. "Besides, the city is no place for a baby," he said. "I want Leslie to have her roots where grass grows outside her door."

So we moved to a New Jersey suburb, but once there the added stress of commuting hit us both. We forgot about the grass and moved back to the city, then back again to New Jersey when Howard was made chief engineer for Allied. We zigzagged up and down the state a couple of times until we settled in Morristown, the company's corporate headquarters, where Howard became director of research.

It was toward the beginning of all this shuffling about that *Flair* suspended publication. I, too, suspended my editing career, with plenty of good memories but little regret: it was time for me to get back to writing.

After *Flair* folded, George Davis married the actress and singer Lotte Lenya, widow of the composer Kurt Weill, and the couple lived mainly at Lenya's country place on the Hudson River, north of Manhattan. George and I still talked often on the telephone. We met for lunch occasionally in the city. He read and talked over with me the novel I had begun writing; he told me why he thought my short stories were bringing me only rejections.

This loyal friend, never a very robust man, died of a heart ailment in 1966. I still think nostalgically of him.

In Morristown, New Jersey, I began writing for young people, almost by accident. I had sold one short story to *Redbook,* but the market for adult fiction had shrunk dramatically since the 1940s. Many magazines folded as once-avid readers turned more and more to TV. I had finished my novel and begun another, but I had doubts about its future. The first one had collected only rejections in its tour of the New York publishers.

At Neighborhood House, Morristown's community center where I took on an assignment

"With Howard and Leslie at a party for her,"
Morristown, New Jersey, 1967

as volunteer librarian, I noticed, to my dismay, that there were no black picture books on the shelves. Most of the children using the library at "The Nabe" came from African American families, and I felt they ought to have at least a few literary models that reflected their culture.

When I went to buy the books, however, I made a discovery that shocked me. Virtually no books were being published about and for black children. Furthermore, picture books had *never* been published for black children.

In the newly integrated schools of the 1960s, educators all over the U.S. lamented that the African American children they taught were not very good readers. I thought it a mystery that the children were inclined to read at all when the books available to them featured only white heroines and heroes. Clearly the need existed for black books, and I resolved to write them.

I began by retelling *Cinderella* in a black picture-book format. Publishers ignored it. I thought perhaps that was because they consid-

ered the classic tale overworked, so I started writing stories about the youngsters I knew at Neighborhood House. The publishers were still indifferent.

Years went by, dry years. Writing for young people demands special skills; it took me a long time to realize that, and an even longer time to acquire some of those skills.

In 1968 Howard retired and we talked about moving somewhere below the snow line, perhaps to North Carolina, where we had enjoyed a few winter vacations. We'd wait, though, we said, until Leslie graduated from college (she was then a sophomore at Skidmore).

"Don't wait! Move now," said our daughter. "I'd like to live in North Carolina myself. I can transfer to Chapel Hill. That way we'd still be close."

Close for two years, anyway. Upon graduation from UNC, Leslie promptly headed back to Manhattan. There she opened a graphics design studio and began building her business.

"I love living in New York!" she wrote. "It's such a friendly town, you get to know the people in your apartment building and the shop owners in your neighborhood. Makes you feel right at home."

"Oh yes," I wrote back. "Yes, I remember. . . ."

Leslie's young business flourished. In 1985 she married Peter Abrams, a computer systems manager and a dedicated New Yorker. "We just love New York, we'll never live anywhere else," said Leslie. "Apartment living suits us to a T. We never want to live in a house, where something's always breaking down, and you have to mow all that grass."

Leslie and Peter now live in Raleigh, in a house, and the move there is permanent, they declare. (More about that later.)

In the small North Carolina town where Howard and I settled, mothers of the African American community had started up a day-care center so they could get jobs and perhaps improve the lives of their children. Among themselves, they scraped together just two dollars to offer as down payment on the four-room shack they proposed to use for their project. The owner accepted the offer and a mortgage was drawn up for the balance of two thousand dollars.

To pay off their debt, the mothers held fund-raising fish dinners. They collected and sold tons of discarded newspapers. They called the place Ruthie's Day-Care Center, in honor of the senior woman of their group.

As a newcomer hunting a meaningful volunteer job, I undertook to read to the youngsters at Ruthie's on a daily basis. For want of black picture books, I photographed the children re-enacting the plot of *Cinderella,* and I put the snapshots together with my old, spurned text in a small loose-leaf notebook. The toddlers loved it; so did the preschoolers who enrolled in the center during the next twenty years. My writing had at last reached the readers I intended it for.

The town rallied behind those remarkable women at Ruthie's. My own church contributed a yearly sum toward a library of picture books at the center. A talented artist friend taught me how to use brown and black inks like watercolors to make the characters in these books more nearly match Ruthie's children. I got pretty good at blackening blonde curls and shading pale faces. Before long, the library owned a solid collection of classic and contemporary black picture books.

The toddlers loved these books, too. They wore to tatters their copy of *Where the Wild Things Are.* Teachers in the town began remarking to me on the reading readiness of Ruthie's graduates. Well, no wonder! Our youngsters entered kindergarten as familiar with good literature as the most privileged children in town.

Also in North Carolina, with the speed of a tortoise, my own literature finally began finding a market in children's magazines! *Humpty Dumpty's Magazine* published my story "Everything We Ever Want" in 1975. Other stories modeled on the children I knew at Ruthie's appeared in subsequent issues. *Humpty* even published the words and music I wrote to a tune called "Soul Food Song," which was surely my very last attempt at writing verse!

The life of a magazine story is lamentably short. When a reader finishes with a periodical, that periodical usually goes into the trash can. A book, on the other hand, becomes a part of our history. Libraries may circulate a book for many years after the title has gone

Ruthie's Day-Care Center

out of print. Although I rejoiced to see my byline in *Humpty Dumpty's Magazine,* I wished I could somehow get my stories into a more permanent form.

"Why don't you write a book," Howard said—as if such an idea could not possibly have occurred to me. Still, his suggestion made me think more intensely about what I'd gained from Ruthie's. I knew the children there intimately, and often their families. Some of the first youngsters I'd read to were now in high school.

Most of Ruthie's enrollees came from poor families. Their lives were often heartbreaking; but they had triumphs, too, and in a curious way, their triumphs moved me more than the heartbreak.

I'll write about their triumphs, I thought; and I did. *Tough Tiffany,* my first book for young people, came out in 1980. I modeled the characters on the children of Ruthie's and their community. In the book, Tiffany's granny and a friend reminisce over a story about how slavery time affected their families. The scene itself is brief; I wrote it almost exactly the way it happened. I had been present at the telling of the story, and the power of it had stuck with me after I'd finished *Tiffany* and was wondering what to write next.

Why not write about children in slavery time? I asked myself. If Granny's story had touched me so deeply, I felt sure there must be other equally strong stories about slave children around somewhere. The idea for a plot came to me easily, in a flash. My second novel, *A Girl Called Boy,* is built around that flash. The research for it was the hard part.

I spent two years looking for stories about slave children and finally found exactly what I needed in the archives of the Library of Congress—*Slave Narratives: A Folk History of Slavery in the U.S. from Interviews with Former Slaves.* After I found the *Slave Narratives,* I spent another two years reading them and taking notes. These narratives are the oral histories of more than two thousand former slaves collected in the 1930s under a government project, the Works Progress Administration. The records run to over ten thousand manuscript pages. The pages themselves were often poorly typed and I had to read everything from microfilm.

Yet, from my first look at the *Slave Narratives,* I knew that I had come upon a national treasure. I thrilled at the discovery, not only because of the novel I was writing, but also

Grandson Ross Henry Abrams, the subject of new picture book

because the ex-slaves' stories changed my view of history.

History had plagued my school years; I'd loathed memorizing dates of wars and treaties. I'd yawned over history books that made slavery sound like nothing more than a political or economic issue.

But the *Slave Narratives* were different—here was *good* history, the story of what happened to real people, as all good history ought to be. I went back to the narratives again and again, after *A Girl Called Boy* was published, after I'd written another novel, *Tancy,* based on those amazing stories.

I wished that everybody in the U.S. could read how the people who had actually lived through it felt about their bondage. I dreamed of putting the *Narratives* into book form, so that young people who felt indifferent to history, as I had, might be given a new insight into this critical part of our nation's past.

But the ten thousand pages of *Slave Narratives* is too much to ask of most young readers. So, instead, I made a careful selection of twenty-one narratives from the 176 recorded in my own state of North Carolina. The publishing firm John Blair, brought out this selection in 1984. The same firm later published my selections from the South Carolina and Virginia narratives. The three volumes are sold as adult books, but in recent years a number of teachers have taken to using them as textbooks in their high school and junior high history classes.

My dream come true!

*

My youthful dreams of being a writer took a long time to come true. I never expected to serve such a lengthy apprenticeship. Nor did I realize that writing would require such hard work—that instead of getting easier, it would just get harder.

The kind of writing I chose to do made it harder, I'm aware, but it enriched me in ways that no amount of money or early success could have done. When a schoolboy like Antonio Drummond writes to me from PS 208 in New York City, "I love all of your books because I am black and most of your books are about African Americans," his letter amply repays me for the roadblocks I've encountered.

But what about the books that didn't get published? What about all those picture books I wrote with such high hopes? Well, I'm still serving my apprenticeship, after all, and I still have dreams of publishing a picture book. I have more incentive than ever, now that I am a grandmother. Ross Henry Abrams was born in Manhattan in 1992. His parents moved to Raleigh on his account just after his first birthday.

"It's too hard, trying to raise a baby in the city," says Peter.

"And we've always loved North Carolina," says Leslie. "It's so beautiful here, and we just felt he should grow up with trees and grass and flowers outside his front door."

Yes, I thought. Oh, yes, I remember that feeling. . . .

Lately, I've been writing a picture book about my young grandson, Ross, and his day-care center. Maybe I'll write another after that, as he grows, and another after that, as his world opens to him. Because I believe that books—more than TV, or movies, or anything else—tell us our history. And even the very youngest readers need to know where they come from.

BIBLIOGRAPHY

FOR YOUNG PEOPLE

Fiction, except as noted:

Tough Tiffany, Doubleday, 1980.

A Girl Called Boy, Clarion, 1982.

My Folks Don't Want Me to Talk about Slavery: Twenty-one Oral Histories of Former North Carolina Slaves (slave narratives; also see below), John Blair, 1984.

Tancy, Clarion, 1984.

The Nightwalker, Clarion, 1988.

Before Freedom, When I Just Can Remember: Twenty-seven Oral Histories of Former South Carolina Slaves (slave narratives; also see below), John Blair, 1989.

Before Freedom: Forty-eight Oral Histories of Former North and South Carolina Slaves (combined edition of *Before Freedom, When I Just Can Remember* and *My Folks Don't Want Me to Talk about Slavery*), New American Library–Dutton, 1990.

Dixie in the Big Pasture, Clarion, 1994.

We Lived in a Little Cabin in the Yard: Twenty-one Oral Histories of Former Virginia Slaves (Virginia slave narratives), John Blair, 1994.

Nancy Winslow Parker

1930-

Nancy Winslow Parker with her cat, Clyde, her great-nephew John Parker, and her great-niece Elaine Parker, New York, 1993

It seems meet and right, in this highly technical age of genetics and DNA, that instead of beginning with the arrival of the stork on October 16, 1930, in Maplewood, New Jersey, I should commence my story in 1620, when the Pilgrims landed at Plymouth Rock with Edward Winslow, the leader of the Mayflower Compact, who would become the first governor of the Plymouth Colony. Alas, my Winslow forebear, Kenelm, missed the boat. He was the younger brother of Edward Winslow, too young to come to America on the original Mayflower, but he did come before 1633 and lived in the Plymouth Plantation. My branch of the Winslows included a yeoman, doctor, deacon, and clockmaker; lived in Massachusetts until the early 1800s, when they moved to New York and settled in Greenpoint, Long Island, now Brooklyn, across the East River from New York City. My grandmother Anna Winslow was born there, attended the First Baptist Sabbath Church, and rests in peace in Mt. Olivet Cemetery with her family and her brother, George Washington Winslow, who served as a private in Company E, seventy-first New York Volunteer, in the Civil War.

The Parkers' roots in America begin with a Captain James Parker who came from England in the 1600s, settled in Groton, Connecticut, and served in King Philip's War. (To confuse future generations, these Parkers named five generations of sons "James.") It was this branch that moved to Poland, Maine, in the 1700s, Belfast, Maine, in the 1800s, and from there settled the fishing villages and towns along the rugged Maine coast, the "Country of the Pointed Fir." Here, among the farmers and sailors and fisherman, James Parker, M.D., raised nine children—four boys and five girls. Of the four boys, at least two served in the Civil War, answering the call of their country when the Maine towns and villages were literally emptied of men. Many men did not return from the war, and many villages never recovered from that loss. Marcellus and Aurelius Parker were both volunteers in Company B, First Maine Cavalry, and served in Virginia. A few days prior to Chancellorsville, Marcellus was patrolling in the woods on a black horse when he was taken prisoner by rebel cavalry at Louisa Court House on May 2, 1863. He was transported by boxcar to Richmond and the infamous Libby Prison. In his memoirs Marcellus wrote, "We had a fine view from the window of our prison—The James River ran near its walls and a canal full of busy boats plied between us and the river. Beyond the river green fields, noble trees and some fine residences appeared. It made us think of our own New England homes." A few weeks later the prisoners were paroled and were marched from Richmond to City Point, where the steamer *James Spaulding* took them to Annapolis and the Union camp in Washington, D.C.

Aurelius Parker was wounded at Deep Bottom, and also at Auburn and White Oak Swamp. He fought at Culpepper and Brandy Station, and was cited for bravery at Antietam (Sharpsburg). He was recommended to the War Department for a captain's commission, which was approved by General Burnside, but nothing ever came of it.

Another son, my grandfather Linden James Parker, claimed to have been in the Civil War, and earned the headline on his obituary in the newspaper, but no record can be found of his service.

The daughters stayed in Maine. One married a sea captain and one a fisherman, one was the local postmistress and another a schoolteacher. Aurelius did not return to Maine after the war but settled in New Orleans, where he was employed at the U.S. Mint. His veteran's pension papers were filed from Greenville, Mississippi. Aurelius is buried in the National Cemetery in Chalmette, Louisiana, just across from New Orleans on the battlefield where General Andrew Jackson won his victory over the British in the War of 1812.

Marcellus returned to Rockland, Maine, to live with his wife, Jessie Acker, whom he had met in Fernandina, Florida, and married in 1855.

Linden James, my grandfather, left Maine and settled in Greenpoint, Brooklyn, New York, where he met his future bride, Anna Winslow. They were married in 1870 and had four children—George, Anna, Flora, and Winslow Aurelius, my father. I can find no trace of anything creative, artistic, or musical in the Parker side of my family. They were hardworking, silent, kind Yankees, who perhaps passed on to me the spirit of tenacity, "never give up and never give in," as Hubert H. Humphrey was wont to say when he lost an election. It is a saying I repeat from time to time at the appropriate crises.

Great-grandfather Jefferson Gauntt,
a portrait painter in the early
to mid 1800s

My mother's paternal forebears are extremely well-documented—one would think they created work for generations of records clerks. Peter Gauntt and his wife arrived in Massachusetts from Lincolnshire, England, in 1630. They settled in Lynn and Sandwich. However, they were Quakers and not welcome in Massachusetts. Their son Hananiah moved to Jobstown, West Jersey, not far from the Delaware River and Philadelphia, Pennsylvania. Hananiah bought 500 acres of land from the local Indian chief Annanikeon, and there the family lived on the same property for over 200 years.

Uz Gauntt, my great-great-grandfather, was a farmer and surveyor. He was an eccentric character who never ate his meals with anyone. He wore undyed clothing of mixed black and white wool, and the buttons on his coat were solid silver with the initials U.G. engraved on each button. He married Sarah Jones and had seven children—Samuel, Benjamin, Israel, Hannah, Elisha, Lewis, and Jefferson (my great-grandfather.) The most extraordinary thing about this Quaker farmer is that he recognized in his youngest son Jefferson an unusual talent for art and sent him to Philadelphia to study painting at the Pennsylvania Academy of Art. While there, Jefferson lived with cousins across the street from the old Custom House on South Second Street. When his studies were over and he had painted portraits in Rochester, New York, Philadelphia, Pennsylvania, and New Bern, North Carolina, he settled in Brooklyn, New York, rented a painting room on Pineapple Street, and painted portraits of eminent New Yorkers. He married Mary Ann Harrison from England. They had eight children—Theodore, Edward, Josephine, Willis, Louis Frederick, Ella, and E. Pluribus and Unia (twins), the latter born in 1861 at the outbreak of the Civil War. E. Pluribus died as an infant, but Unia, my great-aunt, lived to be ninety-two years old and was the closest thing to a grandmother I ever had. She is buried in the family plot in Greenwood Cemetery, Brooklyn, a magnificent Victorian burial ground for New Yorkers since 1838.

I grew up with Jefferson Gauntt portraits in the house—a Byronesque self-portrait in cape with fur collar, a full-length portrait of Cousin Emma in party dress next to a stone urn filled with flowers, and a portrait of his wife in her wedding dress. I knew that he was a very good painter, and I knew that I wanted to be a painter, too. A Gauntt historian wrote, "Jefferson

A Gauntt family portrait, Coney Island, New York, about 1892: (front row, from left) Uncle Wilmer, Aunt Lucille, mother, Beatrice; (back row, right) grandfather Louis Frederick. The two women could not be identified.

Gauntt was a eminent artist in New York, and was at one time negotiating with the St. George's Society of New Jersey to go to England to paint a portrait of the Queen (Victoria) but declined the honor."

His daughter Unia told me he was too busy at home nursing the family through scarlet fever. He died in 1864 at the age of fifty-eight from scarlet fever and exhaustion. Of Jefferson's eight children, three died early in life, one went to Chicago and another to Utica, New York, and three remained in Brooklyn—Theodore, Unia, and Louis Frederick, my grandfather.

The Goodes from Virginia, my mother's maternal ancestors, did not keep accurate records and tended to ever-exaggerate their past with wild claims to English aristocracy and stately homes in Scotland. It has been even more difficult to trace this family because, during the War of 1812, the British burned the building in Washington where the Virginia records were kept.

The Goode roots in this country seem to begin in the mid 1700s, when John Jacob Goode, a doctor, was sent by the crown to take care of the colonists. He settled in Winchester, Virginia. His descendants moved to Pittsburgh, Pennsylvania, but were back in Virginia by 1870, this time in Danville, Virginia, where they had a farm. My great-uncle Harvey Davis Goode describes his boyhood on the farm in a letter to his daughter, Estelle, many years later:

> We were on a 380 acre farm, later reduced to 280 acres then to less than 50 acres due to poor topsoil. We had four colored families living and working on the farm, later we had only one colored family. My mother gave and deeded free of all encumbrances six acres of land to the school, church and playgrounds; she also deeded off six acres of roadside property to the last colored family, in reality not a family—it was a sister and a brother. The brother was blind and had both legs off at the hips. My mother was the farm boss. She rode over the saddle paths every day. Later I also rode alongside on a blind horse. We raised pigs—about 50 a year, calves, heifers, veal, chickens, etc. and plenty of fruit. We raised and cured tobacco, watermelons, peaches galore, cherries, quinces, mulberries, plums, blue, red, yellow and Damson plums, apples—great Variety of all choice stock.
>
> During the three years between nine and twelve, my brother Loton and I shot game for the market and did well at that. In 1884 mother sold out everything, except what we could move on to Brooklyn, New York.

My great-grandfather David Taylor Goode was buried on the farm in the middle of a field. His widow, the woman who ran the farm for so many years, brought her children to Brooklyn. Her daughter, Dora Theresa, met and married my grandfather Louis Frederick Gauntt after a three-week courtship, and had a honeymoon at Lake George, New York. They had three children—Wilmer, Lucille, and my mother, Beatrice.

And there in Brooklyn, New York, in 1911, Winslow Aurelius Parker, descendant of Maine Yankees and New England Pilgrims, wed Beatrice Gauntt, the descendant of New Jersey Quakers and Virginia farmers. They had three children—Alfred Gaunt, Muriel Beatrice, and me. The family had lived in Brooklyn, Cedarhurst, Long Island, and Maplewood, New Jersey.

"Line upon line, precept upon precept, here a little and there a little," as Ann Ridgeway often preached to her flock in the Society of Friends, brings me to the point where the stork delivered me to 76 Maplewood Avenue, Maplewood, New Jersey, on October 18, 1930, in the height of the Great Depression and the last years of the Hoover Administration.

At the time of my birth, the Parker family consisted of my father, age fifty-three, my mother, age forty-four, my brother, age seventeen and away at college, and my sister, age fourteen. There was a Russian Blue cat, Beauty; a fluffy white dog, Mickey; a maid, Marie, from an Iowa farm; and a laundress, Anna, who lived in Newark with her husband. This well-established family was stunned at my arrival and hardly knew what to do with me. My brother was asked to give me a name, and he picked "Nancy," the name of one of his girlfriends.

Maplewood is a leafy tree-lined town about twenty miles from New York City. The Morris and Essex Branch of the Delaware, Lackawanna, and Western Railroad runs through the town, collecting commuters and shoppers on their way to the city. The tracks go by at the foot of the hill where our house was, and we lived with the sounds of the local train clattering by, or the express whizzing by, or—best of all—"The Chicago Train!" as my mother would shout when it roared by at night, dining car lights visible through the leaves of the trees that separated us from the train tracks.

The house, a white frame colonial built in 1925, was furnished in a mélange of styles and periods—Oriental rugs and bric-a-brac from Grandfather Gauntt, tables and Victorian chairs from Great-aunt Unia, portraits by Jefferson Gauntt, wicker furniture from the previous residence in Cedarhurst, and a new veneered bedroom set in my sister's room from Grand Rapids, Michigan. The dining room was furnished in Hepplewhite. A sideboard held the Chinese bronze candlesticks and urns, later stolen by an antique dealer appraising the contents of the house. Above the white wainscoting was a continuous-scene wallpaper of gardens, weeping willow trees, Chinese pagoda, and duck ponds, a scene I looked at a lot as children were seen and not heard at the dinner table. Between the dining room and the kitchen was a butler's pantry with glass-doored shelves bursting with china and crystal, bronze statuettes,

"The only picture of the entire Parker family together, 1931": (front row) father, Winslow, mother, Beatrice, and Nancy; (back row) brother, Alfred, and sister, Muriel

and assorted 1911 wedding presents. The plates and dishes were of all sizes and embellished with gold rims and flowers. This was the best china. The everyday dishes were kept in the kitchen.

My room was on the southeast corner of the second floor. There was a door connecting it to the master bedroom, and I occupied this room, sleeping in a cradle, then a crib, and finally a real maple bed, from infancy to the day the house was sold in 1948. There was a window on the south which looked over the porch roof onto a magnolia tree and a quince tree, until my mother backed the car into the trunk of the quince tree and gouged the bark so deeply that the tree died, and we no longer had homemade quince jelly.

My room was not, however, exclusively my own, as the sewing machine was against one of the walls. It was a Singer sewing machine with a foot pedal and a wheel that drove the needle. It had been used before 1930 to make costumes for my sister's dancing recitals. I was required to wear these costumes, such as Rag-

gedy Ann, to Halloween parties because they were well-made and saved the expense of buying new costumes. Now this ugly machine of varnished oak and black iron was utilized once a month when Mrs. Thomas, the sewing lady, came to the house. She and my mother would camp out in my room all day long while hems were shortened or lengthened, buttons sewed on, and the other drudgeries of sewing executed. Fittings were torture.

I resented the takeover of my room, never liked sewing, and wanted a dressing table with fluffy skirt and perfume bottles in place of the sewing machine. After much pleading, a wooden top was made to fit over the machine, and a straight flowered skirt was tacked around. It was a poor substitute for the real thing, especially since the drawers still contained spools of thread, attachments for sewing rickrack and pleating, cards of needles, and other sewing accessories. No mirror, no vanity chair, no swing-out arms revealing drawers filled with lipstick, cotton balls, Chen Yu nail polishes, and mysterious cosmetics yet to be discovered.

The east window of my room looked out over the driveway, the lawn and gardens, a wooded area, and the train tracks at the bottom of the hill. It was in this room that I battled mumps, chicken pox, measles, colds, stomachaches, tonsillitis, and appendicitis. Sometimes I would wake in the middle of the night, and if the weather were fair and the windows open I could hear train whistles from far away. It was a lonely, frightening sound, evocative of dark, deserted streets in warehouse districts, run-down riverfront dead ends where out-of-work men huddled over oil drum fires, the kind of places Dos Passos would write about in his novels. I was glad I was home in bed, safe, with my mother and father in the next room.

The third floor contained two large storage rooms filled with round-top trunks, themselves bursting with three generations of family treasures. A maid's room and bath looked out over the front and side lawns and contained an iron bed and Mission-style dresser.

Muriel, Alfred, Nancy (on her brother's shoulders), and Beatrice Parker at the Breakers, Mantoloking, New Jersey, 1936

At the age of five, along with thirty other children from Maplewood, I entered kindergarten at Jefferson School, a fifteen-minute walk from my house. The kindergarten room had a cloakroom for our coats, hats, boots, scarves, gloves, rubbers, and umbrellas. Shelves held our sneakers, which we changed into every day to play. (The floors were brown linoleum, and our regular shoes made one slip and fall down during games.) It was in front of these shelves, as I sat tying the laces on my sneakers for the morning games, that I decided to be an artist when I grew up.

Every summer, during those early years, we would go to the Jersey shore. For the first years, when I was still an infant, we stayed at the Breakers Hotel in Mantoloking, a turn-of-the-century firetrap on the beach front. My mother, father, and I stayed at the hotel for a month, and my sister and brother (who had jobs in the city) came down on weekends. Later, in 1937, our beach house was built not far from this hotel.

The preparations for the annual trip to the shore were exciting in the extreme. The boxy, black Buick with the battery under the front seat, running boards, and mouse-gray cloth upholstery was loaded up in the driveway by the back door; hampers of food packed in ice, suitcases of clothes, an old lamp downgraded to the beach house. We drove during the week, as my father was at work in New York and would come down by train on the weekend. In the driver's seat was my mother, fussing that the car would boil over, run out of gas, or have a blowout. My sister, a bundle of anxiety and indecision, sat up front with my mother and read the road map, never quite sure which road to take. I sat in the back with the maid, the dog and the cat. I also had, every year, a brand-new metal beach pail and shovel with seashore scenes painted on its sides. It was shiny and smelled like the five-and-ten-cent store from whence it came. I also had a roll of peppermint-flavor Life Savers and a towel, as I would get carsick at about Perth Amboy, yell "I feel sick," and throw up in the beach pail. To this day, I do not carry any negative associations with beach pails, peppermint Life Savers, or towels, but I do associate cloth upholstery in cars with agonizing auto trips, gas fumes, and impending nausea.

By the time our car reached Colts Neck, the road was running through pine woods and the shoulders were sandy gravel. This was a sure sign that we were leaving behind the elms, maples, and oaks, and the bustle of the suburbs and the beach was getting nearer. When finally we drove to the top of the Brielle Bridge, we could see the ocean off to the east and my mother would always shout, "Oh, smell the sea breeze." And indeed, you could. It was a sort of fishy, wet, ocean smell. It was heaven on Earth.

The grades one through six were also taught at Jefferson School, which was an English Gothic-style, three-story stone building set on a hill with lots of lawns and playgrounds. The classrooms were bright and airy since one wall was entirely windows that the teachers spent an inordinate amount of time raising and lowering with a hooked pole. (The pole was needed to catch on the lock, which was many feet over their heads.) The shade arrangement was also unique: the top shade went up from the middle sash, and the bottom shade went down from the middle sash. The desk arrangement was rigid, to say the least. In each classroom desks were placed in five rows of six and screwed to the floor. A cloakroom that ran the length of the back wall was a wonderful place to horse around in when the teacher left the room. I have a scar on my inner right leg, just above the knee, where the skin was pinched HARD when two chairs crashed together while we were playing "train wreck."

We began classes every day with opening exercises—a joint pledge of allegiance to the American flag hanging in the corner of the room, and then reading aloud by turns from the Bible. We could read anything we wanted, but for no longer than three or four minutes. Most children chose the 100th, 117th, or 134th Psalm. The Bible was the King James Version, with its beautiful Elizabethan English. The Bible the class used was about one-quarter as big as the suitcase-size Bible the Quaker Gauntts had had in Jobstown, from which they read by candlelight every night, and whose kings and prophets gave names to several generations of children.

A favorite candy among my classmates was a bubble gum that came in a flat wrapper with a trading card backing. Often the cards carried pictures in lurid detail of the Sino-Japanese War of 1936. The pictures were gory in the extreme; Japanese soldiers sticking bayonets into the bellies of Chinese peasants, burning barns and huts, tearful families fleeing their burning villages along country roads with chairs and mattresses on their backs, farm wagons loaded to the sky with tables, children, and old people, drawn by starving horses. We traded these cards with relish, acquiring two-inch-thick collections. In quiet moments at home, looking out the window at the tree-lined street in front of the house, I wondered how our family would escape the Japanese soldiers if they came to Maplewood. Where would we get a wagon, a horse, or a truck to carry us and our furniture? Surely all our furniture would not fit on one truck. Would my father get home from work in time to get on the truck with us?

In the seven years I spent at Jefferson School, there were two tragedies of regional significance well known to anyone who lived in New Jersey at that time. On September 9, 1934, the steamship *Morro Castle* of the Ward Line en route from Havana to New York caught fire and burned, off the coast of New Jersey. It was so close to land that many of the passengers jumped overboard and swam to shore, some of them actually ending on the beaches of Manasquan, Spring Lake, and Sea Girt. Others were not so lucky, and their bodies washed up on the beaches for days, many of them wearing cruise clothes, and diamond rings and bracelets. Eighty-six passengers and forty-nine crew lost their lives. The burning ship was finally beached a few days later at Asbury Park. People flocked from all over to see the wreck. My mother, Aunt Maude, and I drove the forty miles from Maplewood to Asbury Park. We went to an ocean-view restaurant on the boardwalk, and from a table upstairs, we could see the *Morro Castle* on the beach. It was completely burned with not a flake of paint on it, the previous gleaming black and white bulkhead now a rusty reddish black. The ship was listing heavily, with water running out of some of the portholes, and smoke out of others. A black cook in a chef's hat leaned out of a forward porthole. Lines had been stretched from the ship to the shore with breeches buoys running along them, as the ship was too high off the ground for people to get to the ship by ladder or gangplank. It was later proven in court that the fire had been started by the radio operator and he was convicted and sent to jail.

In 1937, my mother decided to build a beach house at Mantoloking, the barrier island off the coast of New Jersey where we had been

"With Muriel, visiting the airship Hindenburg *at Lakehurst, New Jersey,"* 1934

spending summers. My mother built the house at the beach because my father liked the mountains. Contractors were hired, and work began on the summer house. From time to time, the great airship *Hindenburg* would fly overhead, on its way from Berlin, Germany, to Lakehurst, New Jersey, to the Naval Air Station where it could land. On May 6, 1937, the workmen decided to drive to Lakehurst after work and watch the *Hindenburg* land. They thereby witnessed the tragedy when the airship exploded and burned. Thirty-six people lost their lives. After that, airships never again were used to cross the Atlantic.

One Sunday in December, the family had been invited to visit old friends in Cedarhurst, Long Island. It would be a two- or three-hour drive from Maplewood. I refused to go, as I suffered from car sickness if the journey were more than five miles. The visit could not be cancelled, so my father volunteered to take me on the train, while my mother and sister drove in the car. My journey would be via Lackawanna train from Maplewood to Hoboken, the end of the line; subway to Pennsylvania Station at 42nd Street; and then the Long Island Railroad to Cedarhurst. The trip went smoothly, the visit in Cedarhurst was boring but a success, and at the end of the visit my father and I headed back home on the train. When we got off the train at Penn Station and walked through the waiting rooms, we saw that the newspaper stands were mobbed with people. The huge headlines read, "Pearl Harbor Attacked by Japanese. War Declared." My father bought a paper and read it for the rest of the trip, looking very grim and saying less than usual.

The war came quickly to Maplewood as to thousands of other American towns. My brother, a chemical engineer working in the oil refineries in Linden, New Jersey, was not allowed to leave his job and enlist as he was in essential war work. If an enemy bomb had ever found its way to New Jersey, the first place it would have hit would have been Linden and the refineries. My father, now sixty-four years old, was too old for active duty, so he was made an air raid warden and issued a white helmet and nightstick. He and other wardens patrolled the streets during the air raid drills and blackouts, checking to be sure people stayed indoors and that no lights were visible to guide enemy planes. My father's company, a textile manufacturer with offices in downtown New York, was swamped with orders from the government for vast quantities of khaki material for military uniforms. Three months later, on March 19, 1942, on the train to New York, my father was stricken with a coronary thrombosis and died. He was taken off the train at Newark.

My sister was also on the train going to her job as a legal secretary on Wall Street. She was several cars back when the express train stopped, she knew something terrible had happened, raced forward, and saw her father being taken off the train on a stretcher. It was her birthday.

As the war years went on, my sister grew restless staying home and seeing all her boyfriends drafted—one was sent to Siam, another to Alaska. She joined the Red Cross Military Welfare Service, was trained in Kentucky, and shipped out of Seattle for the South Pacific. She arrived at her hospital assignment on the day the war ended. But she wasn't sent home right away, and served on the islands of Guam, Tinian and Saipan, and Iwo Jima. She met her future husband at the officer's club on Iwo Jima.

The influences on my life, other than family, environment, and formal education, were the magazines, books, radio programs, and movies I enjoyed as a child. When I was in my crib, my mother used to give me copies of the *National Geographic* magazine. I would turn the pages carefully, looking at the pictures. One day, a friend of the family saw me with a *National Geographic* in the crib and told my mother that I would ruin the magazine. No, my mother said, she loves them. She will look at them for hours. To this day, I cannot let go of the *National Geographic*. It still comes to my mailbox every month, although the features of the 1930s—Arabs on camels in the desert, or first photographs of remote African tribes—have been supplanted by pictures of butchered elephants, polluted rivers and streams, noxious air, a dying planet.

The very first books were *Five Little Kittens,* a book of photographs of kittens dressed in clothes, propped up with invisible stands and doing the wash, ironing, fishing, etc; *Little Brown Bear; The Night before Christmas;* and *Little Black Sambo. Little Black Sambo* was a favorite because of the small trim size, and the happy ending when the mean tiger is turned into butter and Sambo gets his clothes back.

The next reading stage was comic books (banned at home by my father, so read at other people's houses) and Big Little Books, which I bought at the local five-and-ten-cent store. I read all the Bobbsey Twins books, and all the Nancy Drew books. *The Victor Book of the Opera* was the only book with pictures on our book-shelf at home, so I read that too; glorious photos of all the opera houses of the world and Metropolitan's Diamond Horseshoe, and the great artists—Bampton, Caruso, Gigli, Galli-Curci—and all the stories of the operas that had been recorded by RCA with pictures of the sets and costumed artists. These pictures became a reality at the age of ten when my mother started taking me to the opera in New York. My first performance was *Der Rosenkavalier.* I do not recall the great artists I heard on that marvelous Saturday matinee, but I recall many more operas with Milanov, Traubel, Pinza, and Melchior, the greatest heldentenor of all time. I read lots of books in the summers of 1940 and 1941, finishing off with *Gone with the Wind* just before entering junior high school. It never occurred to me that I would ever become a writer of books. I thought I would be an artist and paint pictures that would hang in museums.

Radio programs took a big chunk of time out of my early years. We all listened to "Jack Armstrong" and "Tom Mix" in the afternoon;

Nancy Winslow Parker, eight years old, at a neighbor's garden wedding, Maplewood, New Jersey

"The Shadow," "Green Hornet," and "Lone Ranger" in the evening; and when sick in bed, the soaps—"Stella Dallas," "Our Gal Sal," "Mary Noble, Backstage Wife," "Road of Life," and "Portia Faces Life." A psychoanalyst, the Freudian kind, told me she became a medical doctor because she listened to the radio soap opera "Joyce Jordan, M.D." when she was a child. The entire family listened to "Amos 'n' Andy" at dinner. A waste of time? Not at all, it was another form of storytelling, learning about life, forming opinions, becoming aware of plots, character, good and evil, visualizing the scene—an unconscious absorption of the writer's trade.

I wonder if Shirley Temple Black, former actress and former ambassador, realizes the influence her early movies had on young children in the 1930s. When I look at them today with sixty-five-year-old eyes, I am astonished at the immense talent she possessed—she was perfect. She was also my age, and I was supposed to look like her! So my hair was permed into curls, and I was given tap-dance lessons. I had a Shirley Temple doll and milk pitcher, and a songbook with piano music from all the songs in her movies. I was taken to every one—*Little Miss Marker, The Little Colonel, Curley Top, Captain January, Baby Take a Bow* to name a few. One day, my friend Betty and I were playing at my house. My mother was not at home. I suggested we play "Shirley Temple": Betty would play songs from the songbook and I would tap dance on the top of the piano, a baby grand. Betty was a little hesitant, but I talked her into it. So while Betty played, I danced on the piano lid and sang "On the Good Ship Lollypop," my favorite. Days later, my mother noticed the scratches on the piano lid. She was mystified and asked how they got there. I explained cheerfully that I had danced on the piano lid just like Shirley Temple did in the movies. My mother never said a word. The top was quietly refinished, and I was told not to dance on the piano again.

The next school I attended was Maplewood Junior High School, about half a mile away. I walked there every day, as I would do for high school too. Only in very cold weather or pouring rain were we ever driven to school—it was considered a luxury no healthy child need enjoy, especially in gas-rationed wartime. The school consisted of the seventh and eighth grades, combining students from several elementary schools in the district and providing us with a whole new cast of characters to meet. It is a blur of memories—trying to decide whether to take Latin or French, struggling through math, feeling amazed that I did not flunk algebra or geometry (which I actually enjoyed, as it was a

"Two Mantoloking Houses with Flying Boat," an oil painting by Parker, dated 1984

lot like drawing pictures). I had an inspiring music appreciation teacher who played "Ride of the Valkyries" on the phonograph, and the art classes, which were the most fun of all.

The next step in the education of Maplewood children was Columbia High School. Here all the teenagers from South Orange and Maplewood were crowded into an English Gothic building and went to class to the sound of bells. Crowded lockers, crowded gym classes, crowded cafeteria. It was a place where the social structure was more complicated and treacherous than eighteenth-century France at the time of the revolution. It was a time of studying for college and having a set of braces complete with rubber bands on my teeth. The braces were tightened every week at the orthodontist's office. My mother would drive me the ten miles to East Orange, where the doctor's office was, in a building right next to the funeral home where my father's funeral service had been held. From the dentist's chair I could look down on the roof, the terraces, and the parking lot filled with hearses and long black limousines. After the dentist, we always stopped at a Chinese restaurant and took out chow mein, rice, and fried noodles. I could hardly wait until we got home and I could eat that wonderful runny mixture—the only thing that kept my mind off my aching teeth and bleeding gums.

In high school, I took all the classes required for college entrance. It is a miracle I passed chemistry, a subject I could hardly understand then and certainly don't now. But the seemingly wasted year of sitting in a chemistry class bore strange fruit, for three years later, in a pottery class in college, a knowledge of chemistry was essential in mixing glazes. I was one of the few students in the class who actually understood the complex chemical mixtures used in compounding glazes, and passed the exam.

In the fall of 1948, I boarded a TWA four-engine transcontinental plane headed for California to begin my freshman year at Mills College in Oakland. Mills was founded in 1852 to educate the daughters of the gold miners and settlers moving to California in the 1850s. It had a charming campus of Spanish-style buildings, and was a forty-five-minute drive to Danville, where my sister and her husband, Sandy, lived, the former army engineer she had met in the South Pacific and who was now a nurseryman in the Bay Area. Before my first day as a fresh-

man, he made me aware that one of Mills's most famous faculty members was Howard E. McMinn, professor of botany and chairman of the department.

My first impression of the Mills campus was that of a showcase of West Coast flora, a warm, sunny, and inviting environment. The original campus of bare rangeland had been transformed by the founder, Cyrus Mills, who planted hundreds of trees, mainly eucalyptus and acacia imported from Australia. When Howard McMinn arrived, he used the campus as a testing ground to grow some of the native California plants— ceonothus, redwoods (Sequoia sempervirons), and huckleberry (arctostapylos), a Howard McMinn variety. On the campus there were also a Magnolia grandiflori planted by Cyrus Mills from a Mt. Vernon seedling, elms from New England, and a Lagunaria pattersonii from Australia. This jungle-like atmosphere was a welcome sight to one used to sleet, snow, cold, bare trees, or no trees at all on the barrier beaches of New Jersey. I knew immediately that this was where I belonged.

Mills was then and is still a liberal arts college for women, devoted to maximizing a woman's potential. I announced right away that I would be an art major and took drawing classes the first year. I also had to take the other requirements for a Bachelor of Arts degree, some of which almost proved to be my undoing, as humanities and philosophy did not penetrate a mind bent on painting pictures. On the other hand, my semesters in biology, studying phylum charts and the evolution of species and memorizing insect bodies, enabled me decades later to research, write, and illustrate one of my most comprehensive and successful books, *Bugs,* and other science books for children. (The chicken or the egg problem for artists has always been: should one go to a liberal arts college and study art part-time, or go to an art school and study art all the time.)

The first week at Mills was devoted to choosing classes, taking placement tests, and finding one's way around the campus. One test, whose purpose was not fully explained, took place in Lisser Hall, a large lecture hall which could accommodate the entire freshman class. We were told to write our impressions about some slides projected on the screen, slides which turned out to be Rorschach inkblots. I knew they were inkblots used in psychological testing. I knew that if you saw butterflies in the blots, that

Illustration from Poofy Loves Company, *written and illustrated by Nancy Winslow Parker*

was healthier than if you saw devils, hatchets, or bloody knives. I felt it was a sneaky trick to give freshmen a mass psychology test in the guise of essay writing, so I responded in kind; I wrote about the inkblots in the style of e. e. cummings. The test, it turns out, was an English placement test, and my essay in free verse sans punctuation landed me in bonehead English! One session and one paper later, the instructor took me aside and said she was transferring me to an advanced English class. The new class was hardly an improvement for me, for it was conducted by a wildly popular English professor who taught by the Socratic method of argument and animated discussion, rather like CNN's *Crossfire*. I remained a silent listener in this class, preferring a lecture-like atmosphere, it was living proof of someone ill-prepared in

public school for what was to come in higher education.

My favorite moments were connected with the art department; back-breaking afternoons hunched over a drawing tablet sketching a figure in charcoal over and over and over again in circular motion, drilled into us by our Russian instructor; three-hour sessions in the painting room brushing oil paint on cotton canvas with scratchy pig-bristle brushes; evening classes in the pottery sheds calculating and mixing glazes, wedging clay and throwing pots; waiting patiently by cooling kilns to see the pots emerge that we had thrown; molding pieces of clay in the sculpture shack that would later be cast in Portland cement and marble chips into real sculptures (mine were a duck the first semester and an anteater the second semester). And hunched over a table in the jewelry room soldering a blob of silver onto another and trying not to burn up the window shade. (Unfortunately someone did, and the building burned to the ground.)

Being at Mills also meant tennis all year round, and endless fun and laughing among my friends in Mary Morse Hall. I graduated in 1952 with a B.A. degree in fine arts.

It had always been a dream of mine to work in New York City, mainly because of the influence of Hollywood movies. Who can forget the films about young ladies like Ginger Rogers going to New York with their portfolios of sketches and showing them to just the right person, like Adolph Monjou. Their breaks come,

and soon they are heads of fashion houses or magazines, pursued by handsome men like Fred Astaire in pinstripe suits and snap brim hats, and living in penthouse apartments with Art Deco furniture and white telephones.

And so, in the fall of 1952 I boarded the train in Summit, New Jersey, where my mother had settled after selling the house in Maplewood, and headed for New York City to become rich and famous. I wore the uniform of the day for college graduate job seekers; suit, trench coat, and Grace Kelly white cotton gloves. Shoulder bags were for riveters. I descended on Madison Avenue and found my first job with the Hearst Corporation's fashion magazine *Harper's Bazaar* at probably the lowest wage in the city of New York. The office was on the

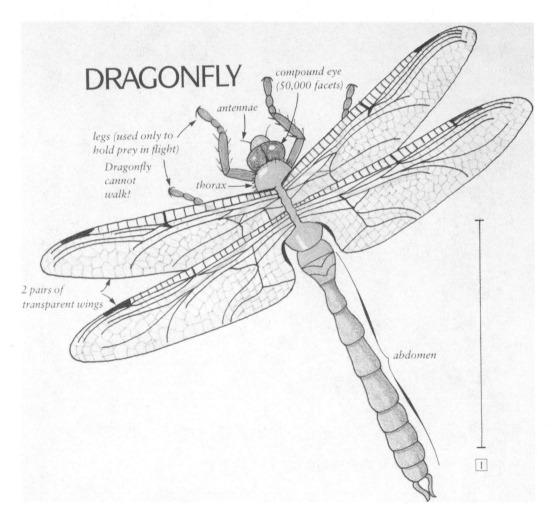

Illustration from Bugs, *written by Nancy Winslow Parker and Joan R. Wright, illustrated by Parker*

corner of 56th Street and Madison Avenue in a sixteen-story, narrow, Renaissance Revival building. It also housed Hearst's other publications, *Yachting* and *House Beautiful*. The editor-in-chief of *Bazaar* was Carmel Snow, a legendary figure in the fashion world of whom I stood in awe, and the fashion editor was Diana Vreeland. Her closet-size office was decorated in faux leopard skin—sofa, cushions, chairs, walls. My desk was on the fourteenth floor in a room with the five other people who made up the Sales Promotion and Production Department. Mr. Cham-

"Shoot, if you must, this old gray head,
But spare your country's flag," she said.

Illustration from Barbara Frietchie, *a poem by John Greenleaf Whittier adapted and illustrated by Nancy Winslow Parker*

berlin, Muriel, Marcy, Ginny, Bob, and I serviced the advertisers in the magazine with tear sheets and counter cards of their ads, and logged in the ads for the magazine. The actual ads arrived on the fourteenth floor on a dolly. They were made of metal plates, nailed onto inch-thick wooden boards, and they weighed a ton. It was Bob's job to lift the plates off the dolly, check them in, and reship them out to the printer. My desk was by the windows facing south, overlooking Madison Avenue and the buildings downtown. In summer the sun beat in; during the winter the drafts took over. We took turns going downstairs to Henry Halper Pharmacy to fetch Cokes with lemon, or coffee—black, lite, dark, sugar on the side, served in glass jars with paper tops. At the end of a week, bags of empty glass jars would be returned to the pharmacy. We had one hour for lunch, which was usually a BLT on toasted cheese bread and a glass of milk. It was a wonderful first job, and first year, working in the city at a salary only an heiress could afford, but it was clearly not the future for me and was far away from the artist I wanted to be. And so, after one year, I quit my job and looked for greener pastures.

For the next twenty years, I worked in many places in New York City. I continued to commute to New York from Summit but found the travel time-consuming and exhausting. I moved into the city and found an apartment in a brownstone that was built in 1912, complete with tiny elevator, high ceilings, huge windows, and clanging steampipe. It oozed turn-of-the-century charm. For me, living in New York was and still is like being a chocoholic in a candy store.

One of the glamorous corporations I worked for was the National Broadcasting Company in Rockefeller Center. I was in the TV Network Sales Promotion Department, where our job was to convince advertisers to buy time on NBC-TV programs. We designed and printed elaborate sales promotion brochures for major clients like automobile manufacturers. I later moved to the Press Department, where we tried to get publicity photos and articles of the shows and stars in the New York newspapers. I saw everyone who was anyone in the corridors of NBC. But this too was far removed from my original dream of being an artist, so I went back to school—the School of Visual Arts on East 23rd Street—for commercial art courses

and meat-and-potatoes subjects such as type specification and paste-up and mechanicals.

Then I started all over again, this time working in the art departments of various textbook publishers. After a few years of sizing pictures, designing books and jackets, and being an art director, I gave up the security of the corporate paycheck to start over again for the third time as a freelance writer and illustrator of children's books.

After eighty-eight rejection slips covering a multitude of stories, my first book, *The Man with the Take-Apart Head*, was published by Dodd Mead and Company in 1974. It was cataloged by the publisher as being for ages seven to ten and is my parting shot at the workaday world of time clocks, lunch hours, boring work, and paycheck bondage. The story is about a Magritte-type man who works in a factory on the other side of a woods, but who is always late for work, a man who has to take his head apart every night before he goes to bed. I am very proud of this little book: forty-eight pages with black-and-white line drawings and a crisp, sales-brochure-like design on the jacket showing the protagonist, Mr. Goozpah, and his three friends of the woods—a ferret, a rabbit, and an eagle. It is a modern fairy tale, and when read aloud sounds a lot like Carl Sandburg.

Poofy Loves Company was my sixteenth book, coming right after a book about a tranquillized and tagged American black bear and before a book about a marmalade cat's ailments. *Poofy* is the true story of my own dog, a bichon frise, who shared my life for eleven years. He was also a dog of my very own breeding as his mother, Mimi-Gladys, had two litters of puppies right in the living room of my New York apartment. Poofy was the firstborn of the first litter, and when born was the size of a baked potato, fitting warmly in my hand. Poofy's littermate was unfortunately undeveloped, and died six agonizing days later after mornings and evenings of bottle feeding. The dead puppy was wrapped in tissue paper, boxed, and in the darkness of night driven down to the Hudson River for a burial at sea. I tossed the box off the pier into the water, where it bobbed along and finally was swept down the river and out to sea. Poofy grew into a happy, healthy dog.

One day, a neighbor came visiting with her granddaughter. The child was a toddler, well-mannered and shy. Cookies and puppy biscuits

Checking proofs with Ava Weiss,
art director for Greenwillow Books, 1989

were passed around. While the grandmother and I talked, the child never let out a peep when Poofy stole her cookie, and it wasn't until minutes later that I noticed Poofy was zeroing in on another cookie from the passive child. I shouted, "Give Poofy the puppy biscuit and you eat the cookie," but it was too late. The cookie was gone and the child, having been knocked to the ground by the excited dog, was left holding a puppy biscuit. I raced for pencil and paper, as I knew this would be a good story, letting the grandmother sort out the situation while I wrote the nineteen-line story in another room. The illustrations raced through my mind— the entire book was visualized in minutes. Then came the months of creating the sketches, dummy, and final art. How difficult to preserve that first moment of inspiration in order to produce a clear, fresh story six months later!

Poofy and his mother, Mimi-Gladys, were with me a total of thirteen years. Mimi-Gladys was the dominant one of the pair, as is usual with an older dog. She did all the barking for the two of them—at visitors, birds, rabbits, and at any dog of any size from the safety of the car.

Bugs was book #27. It was born one day when a friend came to the house at the beach after a tennis game and said that her daughter, then two years old, loved to follow her in

the vegetable garden and pick up bugs and ask what they were. She seemed so captivated by pill bugs and crickets that a book about them was surely needed. I knew that there were lots of books about insects for children, but I was extremely tired after the United Nations book (#26) and did not want to begin another project of exhausting political import, so a book about one of my childhood interests seemed viable. I too loved bugs and used to turn over rocks and watch them run for cover as I hovered over them with a magnifying glass in hand. I said, yes, I would do a book about bugs if the friend would help me write it.

So Joan Richards Wright and I dove into the project, making several false starts as to trim size, pages, rhymes, and what kind of bugs to select. The project was submitted to my publisher, Greenwillow Books, and its hands-on team of editors and art director—Susan Hirschman, Elizabeth Shub, and Ava Weiss. After much hair pulling by us and agonizing fact checking by scientists, we came up with the final sixteen bugs, the couplets, and the neat labels for the giant-size specimens. I had nightmares months before publication, as we had combined age levels, mixed silly rhymes with cold scientific data, tossed in the unfamiliar Latin names of the specimens, and simplified the art. What a mixture! Who would want our book? It turned out that everyone, especially children, did. Who could resist the fat, disgustingly engorged dog tick (Rhipicephalus sanguineus), the kind I used to remove from my dog Peggy at the beach, or the lightning bugs (Photuris pennsylvanicus) like the ones I used to capture after dinner at dusk on summer evenings around the Maplewood lilac bushes? Doesn't everyone marvel at the fact that a black carpenter ant has between the thorax and abdomen a tiny pedicel (waist) so small that you wonder why the two ends of the ant don't break off? And that this marvel of God's creatures is walking under our very feet, through the grass, over the stones, in our very houses?

I had forgotten how much children like poetry. From Mother Goose to Dr. Seuss, the range is endless. In the fourth or fifth grade I was required to memorize Henry Wadsworth Longfellow's "Paul Revere's Ride" for a Saturday acting group. I accomplished the task with much agony, as memorizing has never been easy for me, and spouted out the lines without knowing exactly what the words meant—i.e., "Charles Town shore." Now I knew at the age of ten that Charleston was in the South, so why did Paul Revere "silently rowed to the Charles Town shore just as the moon rose over the bay" when he was in Boston? The two places sounded alike, but I never looked it up.

Forty-five years later, while standing on the tennis court waiting for a serve, I watched the fluffy October clouds move silently overhead. I asked, "What's that poem about 'lonely as a cloud that drifts on high'?" No one knew. So that night I ransacked the bookshelf and finally found William Wordsworth's "Daffodils."

> I wandered lonely as a cloud
> That floats on high o'er vale and hills,
> When all at once I saw a crowd,
> A host, of golden daffodils;
> Beside the lake, beneath the trees,
> Fluttering and dancing in the breeze.

I also found, in the long search for "Daffodils," "The Midnight Ride of Paul Revere," and read it again after so many years. How wonderful it sounded now that I knew where Charles Town was, what alders were, and why grenadiers wore tall hats. I decided on the spot to illustrate this classic, line by line, and explain to my readers what each word meant. It needed a map too, and military notes, and a description of the setting to explain things that modern readers wouldn't know or understand. Thus *Paul Revere's Ride,* book #25, was launched. It was to be the first of several books I did based on historical poems that I felt could be revived happily for today's poetry fans.

Barbara Frietchie by John Greenleaf Whittier became my thirty-seventh book, a poem my mother used to recite from time to time. The poem is made to order for a twentieth-century reappraisal: a story of wild-eyed ninety-two-year-old feminist who confronts famous general, Civil War theme, unforgettable lines. The poem tells about Stonewall Jackson's march through Frederick, Maryland, his confrontation there with an old lady over the American flag, and his march out of town. What it doesn't tell the twentieth-century reader, but which was well known to readers in 1863, was that General Jackson was leading his troops to the Battle of Sharpsburg (Antietam), where 26,134 men would be killed, making it the bloodiest single day in the Civil War. I love Barbara Frietchie, who

represents all civilians in all wars. A relic from the days of the Revolution, she holds up the hard-won stars and stripes of the Union, confronting the forces that would destroy that Union. The reaction of the South's second most beloved general to this old woman's bravery was:

> "Who touches a hair of yon gray head
> Dies like a dog! March on," he said.

I liked the idea of distilling that one event in the Civil War into a thirty-two-page book with maps of Maryland and the battlefield, clarification of obscure references, and biographies of the Abolitionist Quaker poet-author and the Southern general hero.

It wasn't until I had finished working on *Barbara Frietchie* that the military records of my great-uncle came from the National Archives in Washington, D.C., and I discovered that Aurelius Parker had been at the Battle of Sharpsburg! All the time that I had felt compelled to write about and illustrate this event, invisible forces must have been pushing me forward until they finally surfaced with the official War Department documents about Sergeant Aurelius Parker of First Maine Cavalry, Army of the Potomac.

My most recent book, #41, is *Money, Money, Money, the Meaning of the Art and Symbols on United States Paper Currency,* published by Harper-Collins, spring 1995. The title tells just what it is about; no boring stuff on rates of exchange, what money buys, or the life of a dollar bill, but a presentation of what is actually engraved on the front and back of our currency and why. The book was years in preparation and covers a range of subjects, including American portrait painters and engravers, ancient Greek and Colonial architecture and design, and the history of the United States from George Washington to Woodrow Wilson. Researching the book took me to some of America's most popular historical places—Washington, D.C., to watch money being printed at the Bureau of Engraving and Printing; Philadelphia; the gold vaults at the Federal Reserve in New York—and to all kinds of libraries. It was a wonderful experience to unearth all the information and tie it into a neat thirty-two-page package.

If the Secretary of the Treasury were to call me tomorrow and say, "The Bureau of Engraving and Printing is going to issue a commemorative $10.00 bill of 1,000,000 notes. What American woman would you like to be on the bill?" I think I would be at a loss for words. But I would not hesitate to suggest my favorite male president, Theodore Roosevelt, with a vignette of the Panama Canal on the reverse of the bill.

This brings me to my current work in progress about the Panama Canal, which was inspired by a trip through the canal several years ago, and by the unbelievable Treaty of 1977 between Panama and the United States, which provides for the United States to turn over the Panama Canal to the Panamanians in the year 2000. My book is about the history of the isthmus from the Spanish conquistadors through the failed French effort to build a canal; about the horrors of the jungle, the mosquitoes, the diseases and death suffered on the isthmus; and about the American success in completing this engineering wonder. It also has a completely illustrated poem by the poet of "The Isthmus," James Stanley Gilbert. The book will be published by Greenwillow Books, who for many years have published a big chunk of my work that covers insects, frogs, history, and numerous picture books written by others and gleefully embellished by me.

Now that I have just about finished book #41 (a clerical notation I attribute to the record-keeping Gauntts and Mozart's numbered works) I find that I am bringing my major lifelong interests—genealogy, art, and American history—and weaving them together in my books. I will therefore sit quietly as a receptive vessel and wait while heredity and environment battle it out for my attention in the next work, whatever that may be.

BIBLIOGRAPHY

FOR CHILDREN

Books written and illustrated:

The Man with the Take-Apart Head, Dodd, 1974.

The Party at the Old Farm, Atheneum, 1975.

Mrs. Wilson Wanders Off, Dodd, 1976.

Love from Uncle Clyde, Dodd, 1977.

The Crocodile under Louis Finneberg's Bed, Dodd, 1978.

The President's Cabinet and How It Grew, (nonfiction), Parents Magazine Press, 1978, revised edition, introduction by Dean Rusk, HarperCollins, 1991.

The Ordeal of Byron B. Blackbear, Dodd, 1979.

Poofy Loves Company, Dodd, 1980.

Puddums, the Cathcarts' Orange Cat, Atheneum, 1980.

The Spotted Dog, Dodd, 1980.

Cooper, the McNallys' Big Black Dog, Dodd, 1981.

The President's Car (nonfiction), introduction by Betty Ford, Crowell, 1981.

The Christmas Camel, Dodd, 1983.

Love from Aunt Betty, Dodd, 1983.

The United Nations from A to Z, Dodd, 1985.

(With Joan R. Wright) *Bugs,* Greenwillow, 1987.

(With Joan R. Wright) *Frogs, Toads, Lizards, and Salamanders,* Greenwillow, 1990.

Working Frog, Greenwillow, 1992.

Money, Money, Money, the Meaning of the Art and Symbols on United States Paper Currency, HarperCollins, 1995.

Locks, Crocks, and Skeeters: The Story of the Panama Canal, Greenwillow, 1996.

Books illustrated:

John Langstaff, *Oh, A-Hunting We Will Go!* (songbook), Atheneum, 1974.

Carter Hauck, *Warm as Wool, Cool as Cotton: The Story of Natural Fibers,* Seabury, 1975.

Charles L. Blood and Martin Link, *The Goat in the Rug,* Parents Magazine Press, 1976.

John Langstaff, *Sweetly Sings the Donkey* (songbook), Atheneum, 1976.

Mildred Kantrowitz, *Willy Bear,* Parents Magazine Press, 1976.

Ann Lawler, *The Substitute*, Parents Magazine Press, 1977.

John Langstaff, *Hot Cross Buns and Other Old Street Cries* (songbook), Atheneum, 1978.

Jane Yolen, *No Bath Tonight*, Crowell, 1978.

Caroline Feller Bauer, *My Mom Travels a Lot*, Warne, 1981.

Henry Wadsworth Longfellow, *Paul Revere's Ride*, Greenwillow, 1985.

Eve Rice, *Aren't You Coming Too?*, Greenwillow, 1988.

Rachel Field, *General Store*, Greenwillow, 1988.

Shirley Neitzel, *The Jacket I Wear in the Snow*, Greenwillow, 1989.

Eve Rice, *Peter's Pockets*, Greenwillow, 1989.

Ginger Foglesong Guy, *Black Crow, Black Crow*, Greenwillow, 1990.

Eve Rice, *At Grammy's House*, Greenwillow, 1990.

John Greenleaf Whittier, *Barbara Frietchie*, Greenwillow, 1991.

Patricia Lillie, *When the Rooster Crowed*, Greenwillow, 1991.

Shirley Neitzel, *The Dress I'll Wear to the Party*, Greenwillow, 1992.

Thomas Buchanan Reed, *Sheridan's Ride*, Greenwillow, 1993.

Shirley Neitzel, *The Bag I'm Taking to Grandma's*, Greenwillow, 1994.

Charlotte Pomerantz, *Here Comes Henry*, Greenwillow, 1994.

The following books have been adapted for motion picture: *Bugs,* "Reading Rainbow"; *My Mom Travels a Lot* (filmstrip), Live Oak; and *The Ordeal of Byron B. Blackbear.*

Joan Tate

1922-

When you have lived as long as I have, when you have been reading since you were four, when you have been brought up English, been to school through the pre-war period with refugees from the horrors of Franco's Spain and Hitler's Germany, when you have lived in another country and learnt another language almost as well as your own, when you have returned to wartime Britain, married and had children and written books and translated other people's books for nearly forty years—and then someone says please write about yourself so that what you write can be included in a series "at junior high school level, with extension into high school as well as the upper elementary grades," so that those who read it can meet the author "in person"—then you at once know that that is not only impossible, but particularly impossible in ten thousand words. A lifetime would fill many books, and an autobiography fill at least one whole volume, at worst two.

What do they want to know? That is the first question you ask yourself and you ask them. Your life. Written by you. That is what autobiography is. Easy. Born 1922 in England, schooling coeducational together with students of various nationalities, university education in Sweden, return to England, mixture of jobs once children (three) went to school, beginning to write for broadcasting on the BBC radio, moving into journalism, book reviewing, newspaper articles, books for young adults, reading and reporting on books for publishers, both Scandinavian books and English language manuscripts, including American, gradually only writing books and translating from Swedish and Finland-Swedish at first, later also from Norwegian and Danish, adult books, children's books, books for young adults, nonfiction for all ages, television scripts, film scripts. Still doing the same, full time, as before. That has been most of my life and still is, and says nothing about me whatsoever, except that I am mostly rather busy.

What else? How did I come to live in a foreign country and learn another language? That question is often asked. The answer is simple—the second world war broke out and I was stuck in Sweden, with no communications with home at all. When survival is at the top of your agenda, you learn a language very well and it becomes part of you. When you are stuck, while young, in a foreign country, you learn to be independent very quickly, as there is no one else to help you. Swedes are kindly, civilised people and they helped as best they could, but in the end you are out there on your own.

When you have two languages, in a strange way you are almost two people, one with your own language, the language which is in your very bones and which is, of course, at the root of all your writing, and the other person with the foreign language, which when you speak it in that country, or read it in that country's books, you are not quite the same person as you are when you are speaking your own language in your own country. Language is not just words. It is also absorbing everything, small and great, major and minor, about that language, whether your own or another country's. It is absorbing, not learning in the school book sense, but learning in the proper sense. So in a way, I absorbed a whole country. And there are always books to read in whatever language you can read.

What made you start writing? That is another question often asked, in fact always asked. I don't know. But I have always written letters since I could write. Letters are talking on paper, not usually works of great literature. We always had to write thank-you letters when we were children. If you are away at school, in my day you had to write home every Sunday, a boring chore, so I used to jot down every day what I had done that day and then filled pages and pages every Sunday with what I had done, and occasionally what I thought about what I had done. My parents endured the letters without comment or complaint. Presumably they were content that I had something to write about. I never asked them what they thought of them. Writing for radio broadcasting—television was in its infancy then and anyhow ceased altogether during the 1939–1946 war— is also talking on paper, but you have to talk succinctly, and it is no use launching into long and beautiful descriptions of glorious landscapes which your audience can't see. So broadcasting—and in those days you had to speak anything you wrote for radio yourself—taught me to write simply and clearly, not to waffle, and preferably to write so that the listener could see in his or her own mind the picture of what I was saying—in other words, each incident broadcast had to be a kind of story.

Transferring that into journalism, book reviewing and article-writing were a natural follow-on. There is a beginning and end to any article or any book review, just as there is a beginning and an end to any story. The only difference is that you have to *invent* the story, whereas in journalism and broadcasting and articles, you are usually dealing in facts, the truth as you see it, if you can get anywhere near it. Story-writing is another kind of truth. If it isn't "true" and if the reader senses that, he or she will not go on reading it.

What inspires you? That is impossible to answer in simple terms, but I suppose it could be said that everything about life inspires a writer, anyhow this one. I used to jot down notes onto handy pieces of paper and shove them into a file euphemistically called the Ideas File, then leave them there for sometimes months or even years, then forget all about them. When asked for another "story," or the time had come to write one, I would riffle through this scruffy collection of bits of paper, torn-off newspaper, backs of menus, old cards, etc., and read some of them. I had always completely forgotten what was written on them, but the moment I read them again, I remembered with crystal clarity what they had been about, and that became the core of a story, the initial idea.

"Girl imprisoned for stealing a baby," said one. I remembered the sense of outrage at any young girl being sent to prison (which

actually happened many years ago) and wondered first what made her steal a child, and secondly what kind of system did we, a civilised country, have that didn't find out what made her do it and try to help her? So I invented a story about a girl who stole a baby, which was eventually called *Sam and Me.* It was short, succinct, in relatively simple language and was one of the first books to be published in paperback and then later in the more conventional hardback. It floated away all over the world, in other languages, too. I have been a paperback fanatic since the very first Penguin books were published when I was twelve, and I bought the first six (sixpence each then, a sum that today would not buy half an ice cream). I still have four of them.

"Boy who grows roses" said another scrap of paper. I can't remember where that came from, but it grew into a kind of allegory, a kind of Christ story, called *Luke's Garden,* a story about a boy who was different and everyone was either rather scared of him or disliked him just *because* he was different. The story also brought in a form of crucified death, that is, death brought about not by shooting, or knifing, or illness, but by others' total lack of understanding of what was not only different, but also utterly harmless and beneficial.

Then I have always been fascinated by and liked camels, by which I mean they have the most extraordinary and riveting faces, with those great rubbery lips, huge mouths, enormous eyes and absurd knobbly legs and huge feet, though most of all, the haughty disdainful looks they bestow on human beings. They also eat almost anything. Combined with a family scene of constant but good-humoured bantering between two children and two parents, all with slightly different views of each other, many, many years ago, I invented a story called *Dad's Camel,* about the day Dad brought a camel back from the pub, saying it was a result of a bet he had made. This threw the whole family into paroxysms of upsets and disorder and some recriminations, largely because the average urban family in this country is not really terribly good at coping with camels. Naturally, it had to be a young camel to fit in with the scale of a family and an ordinary house and garden, but the results were fairly exasperating for both parents and neighbours, the police and the milkman, though the children gained considerable experience from it all. A silly story, far from reality, but fun, and the book is still in print today. My grandchildren think, and persist in thinking to this day, that I wrote it about *them,* because the two children in the book are the same age as they were when they read the book, and the parents in the story seem to them to be much like their own parents, despite the fact that the story was written long before the parents had even met and in fact when their father was still at school.

Another grubby piece of paper I remember said "Living on the moor." I had been walking on the Yorkshire moors in the north of England one holiday, and their mysterious shadowy distances and wide open spaces were lonely, and the sudden mists that descended even in summer were quite frightening. I combined that with a "north-south" story about two older boys, one from the small Yorkshire town who knew the moors and had known them since childhood like the back of his hand, the other the smart guy, the sharp-witted, runaway, street-wise London boy, who tried living alone on the moor with disastrous results, as you have to be street-wise about moors, too, if you want to survive on them. That story was combined with the fact that the slow country boy finds that this clever, silver-tongued, angry London boy, so different from him, can't read at all, so, somewhat hilariously, the country boy sets about trying to teach him. *Wild Boy,* it is called in most countries, *The Boy on the Moor* in German.

Another story is about a girl with a highly organised and busily competent mother, but, although the girl herself has a very independent mind, she doesn't seem to fit in anywhere, nor is she any good at anything much, or so it seems to her. It is a kind of love story. It is called *Whizz Kid* in English, the scribbled note originally "anything *but* a whizz kid." In America it is called *Not the Usual Kind of Girl,* in Danish and Norwegian *Three Long Days,* and in French *A Cornet of Chips* (French fries), and in the latest Penguin edition *Clee and Nibs,* all titles of the same story. That tells you more about publishing minds in different countries than it does about the story. Or me. Actually, the story is about what she does when her boyfriend gets out of the car for a moment on the way back from a football match and completely disappears. The story is told in two halves, first her view or what happened, and then, secondly, his.

Then there were more stories for young people who were no longer children, who hadn't started reading when they were four, who had never read a whole book, who had no books at home and whose parents never or rarely went into a library or a bookshop. They wanted books about the real life they actually lived themselves, not stories about bunny rabbits or squirrels going shopping or improbable "adventure" stories. So I wrote a whole lot of long short stories about human beings between about sixteen and twenty-five, who had ordinary boyfriends and girlfriends, ordinary jobs and parents, perhaps only one parent, or awful aunts or even more awful uncles, or lovely or horrible grandparents, young people who had ordinary "adventures," went dancing, drove cars, got into trouble, got out of trouble, wept or laughed or hurt themselves, stories with a beginning, middle, but very rarely a conclusive end, for when you are that age there is no end in sight, you are just beginning adult life. I avoided school, moral lectures, thrillers and detective stories, and let the characters, good or bad, speak for themselves. The publisher published them in the form of a thin paperback book, much like a Penguin book, and they were often the very first "proper book" the readers had read. The first hurdle was over and they could move on to longer books. Once started, readers go on.

Then I was asked to do the same for young readers in other countries, countries such as Sweden, Norway, Denmark and later Germany, where they learn English in school and after a while need something to read that is not too difficult in language, certainly not childish tales about rabbits going shopping or adventures, but real stories which bear some relation to their own lives, to their own ages, at a time when they still couldn't really manage to read adult books in another language even if they could in their own. That took me back to Scandinavia again, then later on to Germany, and some of those stories were published in this country for exactly the same kind of readership, but in that case for those who even in their own language could not yet tackle a whole adult book.

All this time in between writing stories in book form, I was translating other people's books, the narrative within them invented by someone else, books mostly from Swedish, but some from Danish and Norwegian. All three languages have the same stem, but are different languages, and many words which look the same have different meanings in the different languages, so there are plenty of death traps to fall straight into. All this time, too, I was reading as usual, not only English and American and Australian and South African books for my own pleasure, but also books from the Scandinavian countries. You could say that for me having nothing to read is as bad as having nothing to eat, though I have little experience of either. When the family were all still at home, I kept a book on the go in most rooms, one in the kitchen to read while the dratted potatoes were boiling, another in the bathroom, several by my bed, and one or two in the living room and my work room. I read on trains and in cars when not driving, and I always read at airports and in planes to relieve the tedium of both waiting and flying. All I need today—in this world overflowing with books, far too many for any one person even to keep track of, not to mention actually read—is a brand new pair of eyes.

Letters. I have had letters from people of all ages from everywhere English is spoken, from the far northern wastes of Canada and Alaska, and the hot deserts of Western Australia, and various countries of English-speaking Africa. I have had letters from Scandinavia, also from all over the United Kingdom (which is seldom really united but has the same language and is what we label England, Scotland, Wales and Northern Ireland), and also from other parts of the United States of America. Most letters ask the same questions. Some letters from young writers are moving, for the writer has perhaps identified with a character in a book and wants to know how I knew. Some are amusing and ask a large number of difficult questions. Some are very chatty and tell me about the letter-writer and his or her family—it is nearly always her, though occasionally a boy or a man takes up a pen and writes. Some letters are a result of some enterprising teacher who has set her students some project or other. Sometimes they have been letters from parents who have borrowed the book from their children and "read a book for the first time." Sometimes they have been from stern librarians who tell me they don't want to see books containing such inappropriate subjects in their libraries. The inappropriate subject tells me more about the librarian than anything else. I always answer all letters by return post. Writers seldom meet their readers, and anyone who has taken the trouble to write a letter is owed an equivalent effort in return.

Ben and Annie is a story about two young people who live on different floors in the same multi-occupied house, one in a wheelchair, so the other invents a means of their talking to each other through the two floors, at first with two tin cans linked together with string (try it—it works like a crude telephone), then later on one of the fathers rigs up a secondhand cast-off intercom. They talk in riddles and silly, chitterchattery, gobbledygook verses and other nonsense which they make up, all the time saying something to each other. It has been a favourite story with many readers, written in the present tense, not entirely happy, but actually happening *now*. When that came out, I eventually had two similar letters, one from abroad, from people studying for post-graduate degrees on subjects such as "The Place of Disability in Children's Literature," and please could I answer the following questions, a great number, all of which I found unanswerable as the writers of the letters seemed to think that story-telling was a solemnly thought-out academic process, which it isn't. Story-telling is story-telling and nothing much else.

It is sometimes difficult to explain that stories written in the first person singular, in the I, are not about *me*. If they were, I would be the most peculiar personality in the universe, whereas actually in reality I am quite an ordinary person, who spends almost every day in working hours banging away on a machine in a small room in a small house in a small market town in an agricultural area of England, quite near Wales, and the post office does quite well out of me. Once upon a time, I worked on a manual typewriter, then graduated to an electric typewriter, then an electronic typewriter, and now I have a magical, computerised word processor, which is really nothing but a very sophisticated typewriter, and a laser printer, which means I no longer *bang* or *thump* on keys but delicately tap out the letters and words. They come up on the screen and I can read whatever has been seething round in my head. The printer does the rest, provided I remember to press the right keys. Word processors have made life fifty times easier for this writer, even more so for this translator, as a translator is always altering the order of words in any given sentence, as word order is very often different in different languages.

You make a spelling or punctuation mistake, or wish to change a word. You look at the screen and put the mistake right, or change the word—so the mistake and the first word have never been there. They have gone. Not scratched out and messy, but vanished forever. If that's not magic, I don't know what is. I have always believed in various kinds of magic, all of which are perfectly explicable, but which I prefer not to know, and to regard them as magic, like rainbows. I have never been able to copy-type, but type with two fingers at tremendous speed, always trying to catch up with what I am thinking, or dreaming, or trying to get down on paper. Therefore another great advantage of the new machinery is not only that it is easy to use (and *quiet*, I hear my long-suffering family saying), so that the sheer hard work of transferring a story you are trying to keep going in your mind down onto paper is made that much simpler, physically less strenuous, but it also *frees* your mind, like a great boulder being lifted off your back. Not that I know what that is like, but I can imagine it, just as I imagine stories. However, despite the convenience and storage facilities of the hard disc, I still have to print out a story before I can really believe it exists. I think I have worked with the printed word for so long, that is my reality, and it doesn't exist unless it is actually there on paper in front of me. The next generation, or indeed the present generation of writers, perhaps already has a "screen-reality" and trusts that hidden disc, while I am still surrounded by stacks of printed texts, paper and files, books and print, proofs and more proofs, all accumulating dust.

All my stories have been concerned with real life. The stories and characters are all invented, but not fantasies. A publisher once asked me to write some "crime" stories for young readers. When I was a "young reader," I read a lot of crime books, writers such as Agatha Christie, and I very soon realised that they *cheated*—the author left out all sorts of clues all through the book to keep you, the reader, in the dark, and then had her brilliantly clever little detective explain everything in one fell swoop at the very end. Annoyed, I started reading the first chapter to find out who had been murdered, etc., then the second to scrutinise the suspects, not him because it's too early in the story, not her because that's too obvious, not him because he's too nasty, not him because policemen are never the murderer, then I skipped the rest of the book and read the last chapter which explained all. That was the end of my detective story reading period. I wanted stories that made me work it out for myself. So I said no, there were plenty of crime books of that kind, the Agatha kind, around.

But then I thought again and wrote three books with nursery rhyme titles: *See How They Run* ("They all run after the farmer's wife, who cut off their tails with a carving knife, did you ever see such a thing in your life, as three blind mice"), *Turn Again Whittington* (Lord Mayor of London, an American girl, and her father in the village of Whittington in Shropshire, England, looking for their ancestors), and *The House That Jack Built.* They were the exact opposite of Our Lady of Agatha of such fame, because the *only* person who knew what was going on was the *reader*—all the characters in the books had to find out by being in the story and following the case, in other words, crime solving as it is in reality, solved by a long, often tedious series of painstaking putting together of small facts, which you could tell the reader, then the reader knew them from reading, but the characters didn't. The books did rather well, so I started on another called *London's Burning* ("London's burning, London's burning, Fetch water, Fetch water, Fire! Fire!, Pour on water, Pour on water"), but the publisher ceased publishing that year so it was never finished, and London, fortunately for us all, is still there.

Translating for television, particularly translating the works of Ingmar Bergman the filmmaker, is, as our American friends say, quite a different ball game. Translating film scripts is another, as is drama. Translating picture books for very small children from Scandinavian countries is yet another—children there start compulsory school very much later than in the UK (mostly for climatic reasons) so the stories in their picture books for their seven- and eight-year-olds are far more sophisticated than our three-, four- and five-year-olds can take in, i.e., the *concepts* within the stories are often beyond them, so the story has somehow to be simplified, not necessarily the words, without ruining the story. Picture books in the UK are usually for two kinds of readers, children who are being read *to* by parents and kind friends, and children who are just beginning to learn to read by themselves.

Translating nonfiction is another field, particularly if the book has a specialist subject such as archaeology (digging up the past), medicine (diseases and their history), natural sciences (plants and animals), ethology (animal behaviour), anthropology, and psychology (human behaviour—much worse) or architecture (buildings and houses). As a result of this, I have come across some very interesting people with languages of their own, as I have to find an archaeologist, a psychologist, an ethologist, or an architect, etc., then ask him or her to read through the manuscript for me, so that the terminology I have used matches the terminology they use in their own particular subjects. It is often called jargon. Every trade, profession or occupation has a language of its own, so in one way the translator becomes multilingual over the years, learning half a dozen different jargons as the work continues. Translating from a translation.

Poetry. I read a great deal, have written some, and the poems have been published or broadcast. I have translated two volumes of Swedish poetry and numerous poems in books. The first poem of my own I ever had broadcast pleased me so much I crazily went into town and bought a set of tall slender ceramic "glasses" with a tall slender jug to go with them. They were intended for ice-cold drinks when lolling about on the terrace by the sea or on a veranda. As we did not drink many ice cold drinks, nor had we a terrace or a veranda, nor much time for lolling about anywhere, we used them for coffee, very impractical as they were, but beautiful. I still have two left and they always remind me of that first poem.

I also wrote a whole slim volume of pomes for young readers. Yes, pomes. Every typewriter I have ever had has always spelt the word poem pome, whether my battered old manuals, electric, electronic, or the present wizard computerised machine, just as they have himslef, siad, yes, so help me dog, untied instead of united, as well as pome. So I have reluctantly come to believe it has something to do with me. I wrote simple pomes about anything and everything, a beholder of life.

I am me,
I like the soft folds of my skin,
my own smells,
my secret tears
and rules and regulations.
I like my secret conversations
unspoken
with myself.
I am me.
What you see
Is the squared polished shell
glittering
in the light.

I wrote some in different rhythms, the rhythms matching the subject matter of the pome, like the skating song.

The skates sing
on the black ice of the lake,
for linked Columbine and Harlequin,
on the willow pool,
in the frosty bright air,
to the tune of the merry widow.
And for Sue and Jim
at the rink
in West Hartlepool,
the song is the same.

or waltzed about—

The waltz is for ladies
and nice polite young gentlemen
who can circle the ballroom
with a decorous air,
romantic and charming,
approved in all circles,
you can waltz with a princess
or a twice millionaire.
It's a riot too
on the barn's bare boards
when the lads and lasses
stamp and whirl
and wheel
in the sweat and dust
to the fiddler's squeal
and nobody cares
a tuppeny
damn
for decorous airs.

There were pomes about supermarkets, freedom, loneliness, war, and stealing apples, about a clown, a road-sweeper, and a tramp, about a dog, and puns on nursery rhymes about runaway girls.

Pussy-cat, pussy-cat,
where have you been?
I've been to London
to see
the bright lights,
the bad boys,
the tall towers,
the green parks,
The trains and the buses,
the shops
and the palaces,
the thundering rumbling
roar that is there.
Pussy-cat, pussy-cat,
why are you back?
Well, you see,
Here I am Queen.

Even an epitaph got into the book, at the end, to round it off, to show that pomes could be about anything or everything.

Here lie I
beneath this earth,
not famous
nor great, but I lived life
on my earth stage
without mask
or costume.
I was me
straight.

The book was slipped in with the others, in the hopes that it would counter antagonisms the very word poetry sometimes, no, often gives rise to, the view that it is difficult, that poets are always famous or dead, that poetry is for others, not for you. A positive hurricane of poems came back, some much better than those in the book.

The epitaph will serve just as well today, for the writer about whom you now know everything or nothing, the publisher, the editor, the illustrator, the printer, the binder, even the librarian and the bookseller, all those people who go into producing a book, they are unimportant. What matters is what is inside.

BIBLIOGRAPHY

FOR CHILDREN

Fiction:

Coal Hoppy, illustrated by J. Yunge-Bateman, Heinemann, 1964.

The Crane, illustrated by Richard Wilson, Heinemann, 1964.

Jenny, illustrated by Charles Keeping, Heinemann, 1964.

Lucy, illustrated by Richard Willson, Heinemann, 1964.

The Next-Doors, illustrated by Charles Keeping, Heinemann (London), 1964, Scholastic (New York), 1976.

Picture Charlie, illustrated by Laszlo Acs, Heinemann, 1964.

The Rabbit Boy, illustrated by Hugh Marshall, Heinemann, 1964.

The Silver Grill, illustrated by Hugh Marshall, Heinemann, 1964, Scholastic, 1976.

Bill, illustrated by George Tuckwell, Heinemann, 1966.

The Holiday, illustrated by Leo Walmsley, Heinemann, 1966.

Mrs. Jenny, illustrated by Charles Keeping, Heinemann, 1966.

Tad, illustrated by Leo Walmsley, Heinemann, 1966.

The Tree, illustrated by George Tuckwell, Heinemann, 1966, as *Tina and David,* Nelson (Nashville), 1973.

Bits and Pieces, illustrated by Quentin Blake, Heinemann, 1967.

The Circus and Other Stories, illustrated by Timothy Jacques, Heinemann, 1967.

The Great Birds, Almqvist & Wiksell, 1967, Blackie (London), 1976.

Letters to Chris, illustrated by Mary Russon, Heinemann, 1967.

Luke's Garden, illustrated by Quentin Blake, Heinemann, 1967, Longman (London), 1976.

The New House, Almqvist & Wiksell (Stockholm), 1967, Pelham (London), 1976.

The Old Car, Almqvist & Wiksell, 1967.

Polly, Almqvist & Wiksell, 1967, Cassell (London), 1976.

The Soap Box Car, Almqvist & Wiksell, 1967.

The Train, Almqvist & Wiksell, 1967.

Wild Martin, and the Crow, illustrated by Richard Kennedy, Heinemann, 1967.

Sam and Me, Macmillan (London), 1968, Coward McCann (New York), 1969.

The Ball, illustrated by Mary Dinsdale, John Dyke, and Prudence Seward, Macmillan, 1969.

The Caravan, Almqvist & Wiksell, 1969.

The Cheapjack Man, illustrated by Richard Rose, Jenny Williams, and Mary Dinsdale, Macmillan, 1969.

Clipper, Macmillan, 1969, as *Ring on My Finger,* 1971, Scholastic, 1976.

Edward and the Uncles, Almqvist & Wiksell, 1969.

The Gobblydock, illustrated by Richard Rose, Jenny Williams, and Mary Dinsdale, Macmillan, 1969.

The Letter, Almqvist & Wiksell, 1969.

The Lollipop Man, illustrated by Mary Dinsdale, John Dyke, and Prudence Seward, Macmillan, 1969.

The Nest, illustrated by Prudence Seward, Macmillan, 1969.

Out of the Sun, Heinemann, 1969.

Puddle's Tiger, Almqvist & Wiksell, 1969.

The Secret, Almqvist & Wiksell, 1969.

The Treehouse, illustrated by Mary Dinsdale, Macmillan, 1969.

Whizz Kid, Macmillan, 1969, as *Not the Usual Kind of Girl,* Scholastic, 1974, as *Clee and Nibs,* Penguin, 1990.

Gramp, illustrated by Robert Geary, Chatto Boyd and Oliver (London), 1971, revised edition, Pelham, 1979.

The Long Road Home, Heinemann, 1971.

Wild Boy, illustrated by Trevor Stubley, Chatto Boyd and Oliver, 1972, Harper (New York), 1973.

Wump Day, illustrated by John Storey, Heinemann, 1972.

Ben and Annie, illustrated by Mary Dinsdale, Brockhampton Press (Leicester), 1973, Doubleday (New York), 1974.

Dad's Camel, illustrated by Margaret Power, Heinemann, 1973, new edition, Red Fox/Anderson Press, 1991.

Dinah, Almqvist & Wiksell, 1973.

Grandpa and My Sister Bee, illustrated by Leslie Wood, Brockhampton Press, 1973, Children's Press (Chicago), 1976.

Jock and the Rock Cakes, illustrated by Carolyn Dinan, Brockhampton Press, 1973, Children's Press, 1976.

Journal for One, Almqvist & Wiksell, 1973.

The Man Who Rang the Bell, Almqvist & Wiksell, 1973.

The Match, Almqvist & Wiksell, 1973.

Night Out, Almqvist & Wiksell, 1973.

Taxi!, Schöningh, 1973.

Dirty Dan, Almqvist & Wiksell, 1974.

Ginger Mick, Heinemann, 1974, revised edition, Longman, 1975.

The Runners, illustrated by Douglas Phillips, David and Charles (Newton Abbot, Devon), 1974, revised edition, Longman, 1977.

Sandy's Trumpet, Almqvist & Wiksell, 1974.

The Thinking Box, Almqvist & Wiksell, 1974.

Zena, Almqvist & Wiksell, 1974.

Your Dog, Pelham, 1975.

Billoggs, illustrated by Trevor Stubley, Pelham, 1976.

Crow and the Brown Boy, illustrated by Gay Galsworthy, Cassell, 1976.

The House That Jack Built, Pelham, 1976.

Polly and the Barrow Boy, illustrated by Gay Galsworthy, Cassell, 1976.

Turn Again Whittington, Pelham, 1976.

You Can't Explain Everything, Longman, 1976.

See You and Other Stories, Longman, 1977.

See How They Run, Pelham, 1978.

Cat Country, Ram, 1979.

Luke's Garden, and Gramp: Two Short Novels, Harper, 1981.

Jumping Jo the Joker, illustrated by Maggie Dawson, Macmillan, 1984.

Other:

Going Up, Almqvist & Wiksell, 3 volumes, 1969–74.

Your Town, illustrated by Virginia Smith, David and Charles, 1972.

How Do You Do?, Schöningh, 3 volumes, 1973–76.

The Living River, illustrated by David Harris, Dent, 1974.

Disco Books (Big Fish, Tom's Trip, The Day I Got the Sack, Girl in the Window, Supermarket, Gren, Day Off, Moped), illustrated by Gay Galsworthy, Jill Cox, and George Craig, Cassell, 8 volumes, 1975.

Your Dog, illustrated by Babette Cole, Pelham, 1975.

On Your Own 1-2, Wheaton, 2 volumes, 1977–78.

Frankie Flies, Macmillan, 1980.

Club Books (The Jimjob, The Totter Man, Trip to Liverpool, New Shoes), illustrated by George Craig and Jill Cox, Cassell, 4 volumes, 1981.

The Fox and the Stork and Other Fables (retellings from Aesop), illustrated by Svend Otto S., Pelham, 1985.

Avalanche!, illustrated by Svend Otto S., Pelham, 1987.

The Donkey and the Dog (retelling from Aesop), illustrated by Svend Otto S., Pelham, 1987.

Twenty Tales of Aesop, illustrated by Svend Otto S., Pelham, 1987.

Translator of more than 70 books for children by Gunnel Beckman, Astrid Lindgren, Svend Otto S., Gun and Ingvar Björk, Irmelin Sandman Lilius, and others. Also translator of over 60 books for adults, including works by Maj Sjöwall and Per Wahlöö, Maria Lang, Elisabeth Söderström, Carl Nylander, Ingmar Bergman, P. C. Jersild, Britt Ekland, and Thomas Dinesen.

Cumulative Index

CUMULATIVE INDEX

The names of essayists who appear in the series are in boldface type. Subject references are followed by volume and page number(s). When a subject reference appears in more than one essay, names of the essayists are also provided.